BOYS TOGETHER

John Chandos

BOYS TOGETHER

English Public Schools 1800–1864

OXFORD UNIVERSITY PRESS

1985

Oxford University Press, Walton Street, Oxford OX2 6DP

London New York Toronto
Delhi Bombay Calcutta Madras Karachi
Kuala Lumpur Singapore Hong Kong Tokyo
Nairobi Dar es Salaam Cape Town
Melbourne Auckland

and associated companies in
Beirut Berlin Ibadan Mexico City Nicosia

Oxford is a trade mark of Oxford University Press

First published 1984 by Hutchinson & Co.
First issued as an Oxford University Press paperback 1985

British Library Cataloguing in Publication Data
Chandos, John
Boys together: English public schools, 1800–1864.
1. Public schools, Endowed (Great Britain)—History—19th century
Rn: John Lithgow Chandos McConnell   I. Title
373.2'22'0942   LA634
ISBN 0-19-281882-1

Printed in Great Britain by
Richard Clay (The Chaucer Press) Ltd.
Bungay, Suffolk

To John and
Gay Chichester-Constable

Contents

Illustrations

Preface

Since the passage of time promoted the nineteenth century from the status of a quaint, satirizable yesterday to the more eminent remove of 'History', the English public schools have received a respectable share of the attention bestowed upon the institutions of the period.

There are two main reasons why I have ventured to add this modest contribution to the literature of nineteenth-century public schools. The first reason is that the treatment of the subject has been, on the whole, panoramic and general, rather than intimate and particular (even in the histories of individual schools), producing better or worse views of the wood, but without imparting any distinct impression of individual trees. I have tried to take the reader on a ramble into the wood itself, to inspect at close range the nature and behaviour of particular growths and, as far as means allowed, to enter into the actual events and daily life of identifiable inmates, juvenile and adult, from the beginning of the century to the third decade of the reign of Victoria. The second reason is that modern attention has hitherto been directed chiefly to the 'reformed' schools of the period which followed the report of the Clarendon Commission, that is, approximately, from the Public Schools Act of 1867 to the end of the Second World War in 1945, the period during which the public schools acquired the image, by which they are known to modern public opinion, of authoritarian, uniformed communities, governed by close and strict adult surveillance and control, where not merely courses of academic study, but patterns of morals and manners are imposed by coercion from above. It was natural that the reformed public schools should have been chosen to typify the system for, as the shadows closed over the recent past in a fast-changing age, it seemed to the later Victorians and their successors as if only one kind of public school had ever existed. The image of a drilled and lustrous régime, standardized by adult warrant, already prevailed in the public eye by 1867, when the Rev. W. L. Collins expressed the hope that the contents of his second book might 'help to preserve some record of earlier phases of Public School Life, the very traditions of which are growing fainter year by year'.[1] It is these earlier forgotten 'phases' which are the subject of this book, tribes of self-governing boys that waged irregular warfare, generation after generation, against titular adult overlords endeavouring to trench upon their independence.

At the end of our story the old order is seen to be passing away into the groves of asphodel, beyond recall, as it seemed to the well-pleased apostles of the new reign of adult-regulated proprieties. But the new order, mortal also, has become in its turn the old; the wheel continues to revolve, and much of what would until recently have seemed improbable and bizarre to those of us bred in the reformed public schools, will now strike a note, neither alien nor unfamiliar, to boys of the late twentieth century.

If it appears that Eton has been awarded a disproportionate share of attention this should be ascribed not to partiality but to provision. No other school has collected and preserved its records with such perseverance and continuity. Unfortunately, in some historic schools much of value has been stolen or destroyed, or merely lost and dispersed. It should be noted that the status of a school today does not necessarily correspond with its circumstances in the times I engage. Harrow was rescued from near extinction by Charles Vaughan. Westminster, once the most fashionable and scholastically eminent of all the schools, had fallen on evil days during the period we cover. Happily, its decline was later reversed, and today Westminster is again in the high position of repute it enjoyed from the sixteenth to the end of the eighteenth century.

Some revelations in the following pages may surprise, and even shock, a reader unprepared for them. After the broadcast of a BBC programme which I wrote in 1972 I received a chilly rebuke from J. C. Royds, then headmaster of Uppingham, advising me, in reply to a routine inquiry, that 'Uppingham boys long dead' could not help me 'in my entertainments', because they seemed to have been 'so decent and happy'. But, for the most part, headmasters, and others concerned with the management of public schools, have shown no disposition to perpetuate delusions of a precedent Eden, inhabited by boyish Adams uncorrupted by the wiles of girlish Eves, where virtue flourished inviolate in a paradise of juvenile innocence. Almost without exception I have met everywhere with generous and thoughtful help. One casual, but perceptive comment comes to mind on the contradictions that co-existed in the unreformed public schools to puzzle their friends and baffle their enemies. John Thorn, headmaster of Winchester College, remarked to me, 'The surprising thing is that one or two accounts of the nineteenth century nevertheless give the impression that amid all the horrors quite a lot of people rather enjoyed themselves.' It is my hope that in what follows something of the enjoyment as well as the horrors will be transmitted.

Acknowledgements

My thanks are gratefully tendered to the Provost and Fellows of Eton College for the liberal hospitality of the college library and the access to its resources with which they favoured me, and for permission to read and use the manuscript journal of Dr Keate's sister-in-law, Miss Margaretta Brown. I would have liked to thank my friend, the late John Carter, a Fellow of Eton College, for the encouragement and counsel I received from him before his untimely death in 1975. Most of all my thanks are due to the Eton College Archivist, Patrick Strong, upon whose erudition and familiarity with Etonian memorabilia I called with shameless frequency, and never in vain; to P. R. Quarrie, College Librarian, and to P. B. Devlin, Assistant Keeper of the Pictures. I wish to acknowledge gratefully my indebtedness to Peter Gwynn, former College Archivist at Winchester, for his help in finding relevant manuscripts, and to thank the Warden and Fellows of Winchester College for permitting me to read and quote from them. Mr Gwynn's successor, R. D. H. Custance, has patiently answered supplementary questions of biography and dating. I am obliged to the headmaster of Rugby School, James Woodhouse, for permitting me to spend several days of research into the books and manuscripts of the Temple Reading Room, where the librarian, the late N. C. Kittermaster, simplified my labours by making copies of some of the more obscure documents I wished to use. I am grateful also to Mr Kittermaster's successor, Jennifer McRory, for investigating pedigrees and assembling a selection of illustrations for a later visit I made to the school. L. C. Spaull, former Librarian and assistant master of Westminster School, kindly guided me to, and discussed with me, relevant manuscripts in the school's archives, and I am grateful to him for his help, to his successors, Charles Keeley and John Field, for discovery of further information, and to the headmaster, John Rae, for allowing me to study and use these sources. C. H. Shaw, assistant master at Harrow School, made me welcome to the Vaughan Library, when he was librarian, and I thank him and the headmaster, B. M. S. Hoban, for the facilities provided. J. B. Lawson, the librarian of Shrewsbury School, kindly furnished me with biographical notes on several prominent delinquents in the 1818 rebellion, and provided a copy of the manuscript of a prize elegy by the rebel leader, Thomas Coltman. I am indebted to him and to the headmaster, W. E. J. Anderson (now headmaster of Eton), for their helpful cooperation.

The former librarian of the London Library, Stanley Gillam, kindly granted me access to the manuscript of the unpublished autobiography of J. A. Symonds which is in the Library's custody, and I am grateful to the present librarian, Douglas Matthews, for consenting to my quoting from the text of this record, unique in its detailed candour, of a clandestine facet of public-school culture.

The original version of *Boys Together* was considerably larger than the present one. To my regret, economic conditions prevailing internationally necessitated a reduction of the text for publication by more than a third. In the performance of this severe surgery I benefited from the aid of three editors, Susan Hogg, Christopher Chippindale and, in the latter stages, my old friend Harold Harris, formerly editorial director of Hutchinson. That the mutilated survivor remains capable of coherent discourse is due in a large measure to their skill and judgement.

Tom Brown's Universe, by John Honey, was published in 1977, after the longer version of *Boys Together* was already written; but in the course of reduction I was able to utilize several revealing illustrations of the author's which reinforced my own arguments. For these I am grateful and I hope my debt is adequately acknowledged. I have also enjoyed the benefit of Professor Honey's kindness and patience in casting a corrective eye over my proofs.

A school shows as undisguisedly as any place the corruption of human nature, and the monstrous advantage with which evil starts . . . in its contest with good.

THOMAS ARNOLD to Rev. C. Blackstone, 26 February 1834

We were all boys together in a genuine and honest English way.

WILLIAM ROGERS, *Reminiscences* (1888), p. 19

Ah, happy years: once more who would not be a boy.

BYRON, *Childe Harold* CII, xxiii

I cannot say that I look back upon my life at a public school with any sensation of pleasure, or that any earthly consideration would induce me to go through my three years again.

C. L. DODGSON, *The Diaries of Lewis Carroll*, edited by Roger Lancelyn Green, 2 vols (1953), vol. I, p. 106

Boys under private tuition are preparing to live, at public schools they live.

WILLIAM JOHNSON, *Eton Reform* (1861), p. 30

Forsan et haec olim meminisse iuvabit

VIRGIL, *Aeneid*, i, 203

ONE

The Birth of the Mystic

Conferring with his two sons on the eve of the younger one's first half at Eton, midway through the nineteenth century, an old Etonian remarked upon his memory of the school, 'For my part I am sure the happiest days of my life were spent there; and there is no reason to expect that Charley will find it otherwise if only he keeps out of scrapes, avoids debts and is sufficiently industrious to keep in favour with his tutor.'[1]

With his father's judgement Charley in due course heartily concurred, and it is to his record of school life that we owe our knowledge of his father's opinion as well as his own. These judgements were in no way exceptional and, warmly expressed as they were, their tone was mild compared with the intensity of the tributes offered up by some later Victorian gentlemen to the memory of their schooldays. To illustrate his feelings for his school, one 'Old Boy' invokes the notion of a schoolboy in his first term told he may go home directly for an unexpected holiday: '. . . the riot, the Bacchanalian tumult in his breast, the bubbles of joy which made his heart too big for his ribs, the dreamland haze in which all things swam . . .' The nearest thing to that 'mystic rapture' of childhood was, he avowed, 'the feeling of an Old Boy going back to school'.[2]

Less exhilarated in tone but no less positive in conclusion, another reluctant adult prescribes return visits to the school as the best help to 'an honest man's endeavours to keep himself sweet in the close atmosphere of artificial grown up life',[3] while another declares that 'when we look back upon our schooldays . . . we . . . come to the conclusion that leaving school was the greatest mistake we ever committed'.[4]

Such judgements were not only made in sentimental retrospect. Asked what he wanted to be, W. C. Clayton, at the age of sixteen in 1858, declared that he would like to spend the rest of his life in the 'upper fifth' at Harrow.[5] The fourth Lord Lyttelton was haunted by the poignancy of his loss at leaving school. Seated in the carriage he took one last look 'and – it was over: I had left Eton. It was one of the heaviest and deadliest feelings I ever knew, to find that I was no longer a boy.'[6] The entry of another boy's diary dated 13 December 1865 reads: 'My last day at Eton . . . I can hardly believe it. . . .' December 14: 'I watched the old place from the train till I couldn't see it any more; and so now I have done with the happiness of school life. I don't at all comprehend it and I think it's a good thing I don't.'[7]

These sentiments are characteristic of a considerable body of writing, published and unpublished, throughout the nineteenth century. The constituents are not literary exercises upon a universally shared experience of boyhood; they are celebrations of a tribal mystic peculiar to a caste in England which flourished from the eighteenth and reached its meridian in the second half of the nineteenth century. Loyalty to the mystic was capable of co-existing in one person together with painful and contradictory memories. The Rev. R. W. Essington, who had been a noted athlete at Eton, composed a wistful and tender fantasy in verse on the theme of revisiting Long Chamber, '. . . where I for years had dwelt the gayest of the gay'.[8] He also recalled, 'From 1828 to 1830 after I was in College I knew nothing of what went on, except that I was starved and flogged, beaten and dirty.'[9]

The tribal character of the mystic is what distinguishes its expression from other European and from American records of juvenile society. Most writers of Western culture have at some time explored the vivid wonders of childhood memory. The French, in particular, have been attentive to the eye and ear and nose of childhood. There is the famous school scene in *Madame Bovary*; there are others in Maurice Barrès's *Les Déracinés*, in Chateaubriand's *Mémoires*, and in Proust's *Jean Santeuil*; but in these instances (as in English literature prior to the mid-eighteenth century), school is merely the environment in which the young individual struggles and is examined; the events never shape as the celebration of a valuable *corporate* experience, nor is there anything to correspond to the mystic as expressed by an old Shrewsbury housemaster to a departing prefect: 'I want your school to be a kind of minor religion with you, ranked by the side of patriotism. Make it a sort of bond, a freemasonry between you and all those who have been here.'[10]

There are instances of the early blossoming, in boys still at school, of the mystic, which in many cases would continue to flower, growing in potency rather than declining with the passing of years. When he was over eighty Colonel Henry Clavering, the Old Westminster, once a sportsman and man of action, now blind, crippled and near to death, used to arrive early at the Abbey for Sunday service, and before the door opened he would walk round and round the Westminster School Cloisters, every corner of which 'brought up some old recollection', reviving by touch experiences of long ago. He remembers the dark beginning. 'It was on the first Sunday after Bartholomew holiday, about four in the afternoon when I was conveyed to Mother Clapham's. I shall never forget were I to live a thousand years, the melancholy which came over me when arriving in Dean's Yard, a solitary silence prevailing on every side, disturbed only by the rustling of decayed leaves falling from the old Elms, succeeded when ushered into the Hall by the necessary question "I say, you, Sir, what's your name." I believe few boys ever joined a public school without feeling that indescribable sensation as to what may be their future lot.' Between the age of fifteen and sixteen the alchemy works; he enters into his inheritance, and more than seventy years later the voice of the sublimated boy speaks out of the body of the old man. 'Could the blessing of sight be restored to me it would be with indescribable pleasure I should revisit the scenes of my former days lamentation.'[11]

Such a sentiment would have struck no response from the mind of an Elizabethan or Jacobean. Shakespeare's urchin going 'unwillingly to school' might not have been idle but merely apprehensive. School was too often a place to be dreaded, and Sir Richard Sackville, first cousin to Queen Elizabeth, was reporting experience confirmed by many contemporaries when he expressed regret that 'a schoolmaster before he was fullie fourteen years old, drove him with fear of beating from love of learning'.[12] Yet, at least by Sackville's time, learning and the arts were in the ascendant, and the nobility were vying to give their sons (and even occasionally their daughters)* the best available in the new concept of virtue, a 'liberal education'.

It had not always been so. The standards prevailing among the nobility up to the middle of the sixteenth century are reflected in the words reported by Richard Pace of a gentleman who said he should rather his son 'should hang than be learned', and in the corollary of Sir Thomas Elyot's complaint, 'Some . . . without shame dare affirm

---

* Notable examples of late Tudor women of learning include (besides the much-cited Lady Jane Grey) the daughters of Sir Anthony Cooke, tutor to Edward VI, one of whom, Ann, became the mother of Francis Bacon.

that to a gentleman it is a notable reproach to be well learned and to be called a great clerk.'[13]

But even as they complained, the educationalists of the mid-sixteenth century were beginning to win a sweeping victory. A liberal education became fashionable; literary graces a social asset; the whole situation was so changed in a short time that William Harrison could complain that the sons of the rich were not only filling up Oxford and Cambridge, but the great grammar schools too and pushing the poor out of the scholarships.[14] The importance of higher education to the ruling classes, if they were to continue to rule in a rapidly changing world, weighed so heavily with William Cecil that he proposed to compel education on the nobility by Act of Parliament, binding them to school their children in learning at a university from the age of twelve to nineteen.

In this exploratory period of changing values there was no fixed pattern for the education of the upper-class male to follow before he went – if he did go – to university. There was still a residual inclination – it was nothing more definite or measurable – for the great to keep their sons at home with tutors; but there was nothing socially daring or remarkable in young noblemen going to school, especially to a good local grammar school, as Philip Sidney and Fulke Greville did, to Shrewsbury in 1564. As the second half of the seventeenth century progressed the tendency became gradually more marked for the upper classes to send their sons to boarding schools and to narrow their choice to a few schools which had by degrees gained an ascendancy over the rest in fashion and scholastic repute. Prominent in this company were the endowed collegiate schools of Winchester, Eton and St Peter's, Westminster, but there were up to and beyond the end of the seventeenth century strong rival private schools in and around London.* However, many of the nobility continued to educate their sons privately at home, before sending them either to university, or to travel in Europe or, if they were younger sons, to read in the Inns of Court. It was not until the second half of the eighteenth century that the practice by the nobility and gentry of sending their sons to one of the 'great public schools' set into a prevailing fashion.

To the question how many 'public schools' there were, and what constituted a public school, there was no authoritative ruling, but in practice by this time not less than five, or more than seven, were

---

* 'Dr Thomas Farnaby who taught 300 noblemen and gentlemen during the reign of Charles I. . . .'[15]

recognized by public opinion as lying within this category. The inner five were Winchester, Eton, Westminster, Harrow and Rugby.*

Winchester lays claim to being the oldest of the public schools, although its precedence may be challenged by Westminster if the continuity of the latter is traced back beyond the refoundation of the school by Queen Elizabeth. Winchester College, in its setting perhaps the most aesthetically memorable of all schools, was founded in 1382 by William of Wykeham, 'a priest,' said Froissart, '. . . so much in favour with the king of England that everything was done by him and nothing was done without him'. Before Wykeham's foundation there had been a school in the same place since time immemorial; it had been known as the school of kings. There Egbert had placed his son Ethelwulf under the tutelage of Bishop Helmstan; tradition says that before the monks built their cloister on the spot it had been the site of the Temple of Apollo. William of Wykeham established two sister collegiate foundations, Winchester College and New College, Oxford, each with a governing body composed of a warden and fellows as well as chaplains, clerks in orders and deacons as executive officers and servants. Winchester College contained a school ruled by a headmaster (Informator) and an undermaster (Hostarius), the object of which was to prepare talented boys for reception by New College to restock with learned men the higher ranks of a clerical body depleted by the Black Death. The boys, commands the statute, were to grow up 'Christian scholars and gentlemen' and they must be 'careful to maintain amongst themselves kindness, concord and brotherly love . . . to esteem no man's person and hold all distinction of birth or wealth amongst themselves to be merged in the grand fraternity of letters'. Reverence was to be paid only to masters and praefects of their own body. In addition to seventy foundation scholars, who were distinguished by a black gown, provision was made for the reception of an unspecified number of other paying pupils who were known as 'commoners', some day boys, some boarders, the latter to be housed separately from the 'scholars'.

In 1440 a charter was issued by Henry VI to found Eton College 'in the parochial church of Windsor, not far from our birthplace'.[18] The prime purpose of the foundation was that the provost and fellows might constantly say masses for the repose of the founder's soul. The founder was eighteen years old at the time. As at Winchester, on

* Sydney Smith himself was in difficulty when he tried to define a public school for his opening broadside in 1810.[16] The question remained without an answer thirty years later.[17]

which the new college was modelled, a school was attached to the college, where the twenty-five, later seventy, foundation scholars should be instructed free of all expense by two schoolmasters to supply Eton's sister foundation, King's College, Cambridge, with a succession of competent scholars who might adorn the university. After visiting Winchester and inspecting the College chapel, almost a hundred feet long, the king approved a plan to build a church at Eton almost twice as long, intended as a place of pilgrimage. There is no evidence even of a school in operation at Eton before 1443 when Waynflete was installed as provost, but there are earlier references to Etonians.[19] The first schoolroom at Eton was not Lower School, but a building, '*nova constructio*', erected at one end of the church.[20] Disaster came in 1461 with the deposition of Henry, followed by affrays in the struggle for power which developed into civil war. The establishment was threatened with extinction. In 1466 the number of scholars had sunk to twenty-one. The school may even have ceased to exist for a time.

Despite the overt association with King's College, in practice Eton's early connections turned out to be closer with Oxford. The first Cambridge provost, Roger Lupton, was not elected until 1504, and only one other provost had come from Eton and King's before 1724. But in the eighteenth century the formula, Eton College to King's, Cambridge, became established as a rule, and thereafter a place on the foundation carried with it a chance of substantial material benefits. The traffic was reciprocal and mutually advantageous. The headmaster, lower master and all the assistant masters at Eton were former Eton Collegers and Kingsmen. Eton was a 'closed shop' providing 'jobs for the Old Boys'.

The origins of a school at Westminster are, as at Winchester, of great antiquity; but the school in its present form, adjacent to, almost, it seems, part of, the precincts of Westminster Abbey, dates from its restoration by Queen Elizabeth, in 1560, after the dissolution of the monastic house which had contained the previous school. Besides forty foundation scholars, *pensionari*, eighty more pupils were to be taught in the school as *oppidini* and *perigreni*.

From its inception Westminster dominated in intellectual performance the great schools of England and continued to do so until the end of the eighteenth century. Unrehearsed disputation was used as an exercise for teaching boys to analyse an argument, order their thoughts rapidly and express them fluently. Boys from the London grammar schools would 'repair to the churchyard of St Bartholomew where upon a bank bordered under a tree some one scholar hath stepped up and there opposed and answered till he were of some better scholar put down ... and in the end the best opposer and answerer had rewards'.[21] John Evelyn, attending the election of scholars at Westminster in 1661, marvelled at the accomplishment and wit of little boys of twelve and thirteen years of age.[22] In those heroic days before the contraction of the curriculum in the eighteenth century, Westminster boys could be heard capping one another's sallies in Chaldee and Arabic, as well as Hebrew, Latin and Greek.*

Harrow School, founded by John Lyon in 1571, and Rugby School, founded by Laurence Sheriff in 1567 as a local charity, were no different in their early history from the many other endowed grammar schools throughout the country, except that their endowments were rather bigger than most. By the second half of the eighteenth century, through exploiting the clause admitting paying pupils, the character of both Harrow and Rugby had changed. From being local schools serving the needs of local inhabitants, and especially the children of the poor, which had been the founders' intention, they had become schools designed to provide a classical education for the sons of the higher ranks of society drawn from all parts of the British Isles.

To this nucleus was often added the Charterhouse, but with reservations, for it had been founded in 1611 by Thomas Sutton, a gentleman commoner and captain in Elizabeth's service, expressly for the education of the sons of poor gentlemen.[23] In the early years of the nineteenth century Shrewsbury, a school much decayed and almost extinct, was revived to such spectacular effect under the direction of Samuel Butler, that its claim to inclusion was irresistible.

Like all grammar schools, the public schools taught the learned languages, classical Greek and Latin, grammatically. The factors which they had in common and set them apart from the rest were, first, that they admitted not merely children of the local inhabitants, but paying pupils from any part of the country, being thus in character 'boarding schools', and second, that the government of the school was conducted on principles of delegation of authority to selected senior boys and of performance of approved services by junior boys, a system known as 'fagging'. Fagging, with the administration of discipline by senior boys, had its origin, in part at least, in the numerical disproportion of a fixed number of assistant masters

* The boys probably spoke only a very little Chaldee, Arabic and Hebrew, but it was enough to make a lasting impression on someone who, like Evelyn, knew nothing of all three.

to a variable number of boys which increased if a school grew fashionable. It also provided the school with a useful unpaid supplement to hired servants. The prime purpose of the fagging system was, by giving legal authority to an élite of senior boys, to maintain good order and just discipline, and protect the smaller and younger boys from bullies and oversized juvenile delinquents to be found in all large schools.

It was this pragmatic schooling of boys in self-government to which parents, sometimes confidently, sometimes with nervous hesitance, chose to commit their sons.* Caroline Fox, who had had her reservations, came to feel, she said, 'more and more every day that if health permits it school is the best place for boys'.[24]

The view of a man who, having been bred at a public school himself, harboured no illusions yet preferred the system to any other, is expressed by Lord William Russell, in a letter written from Rome on Christmas Day, to his kinsman, Lord Tavistock, in which he alludes to the latter's plans for the education of his only son:

> I cannot tell you how happy it has made me to hear that Russell is to go to a public school – be it Eton or Westminster or elsewhere a public school is what is necessary & is that which will add to his happiness hereafter & be a source of great satisfaction to yourself. I grant the system of education is bad – that a boy learns little and there are many objections to a public school – but it fits a boy to be a man – to know his fellow creatures – to love them – to be able to contend with the difficulties of life – to attach friends to him – to take part in public affairs – to get rid of his humours and caprices & to form his temper and manners – to make himself loved and respected in the world – in short it is an essential part of our constitution and makes our patricians so superior to those of the continent. . . . I wish you could see how a young Roman nobleman is brought up – you would not wonder at his turning out the being he is.[25]

The boy's being an only child, destined to inherit estates and power, made 'public education more necessary', to give him the test of making his way, unaided by privilege, in a society of his equals and superiors, where in

> The daily intercourse of boy with boy
> Appear the true realities.[26]

---

* Thomas Arnold was himself subject to such mixed feelings: see below, p. 253.

The public schools also offered a potentially tangible advantage to which friends and enemies were both alive, and that was the benefit of the allegiance which a school generated. Sir Robert Walpole's partiality to fellow Old Etonians was made conspicuous by the scale of his power of patronage and occasioned some resentment in those who felt, rightly or wrongly, that they had been passed over in favour of men who had gone to the prime minister's school. 'Cole says he had a letter from Bishop Tanner to a friend saying he does not hope to be preferred till all the Eton and Kings men have been provided for.'[27] Walpole's son Horace would have done no less had it lain in his power and, indeed, did much by enlisting his father's influence to advance his own schoolfriends, including members of his Etonian 'Quadruple Alliance', Thomas Gray, Horace Walpole, Richard West and Thomas Ashton.*

But in Horace Walpole and Thomas Gray the presence of a new element is felt – something more than ordinary and practical allegiance to schoolmates – the stirring of a mystical tenderness and romantic nostalgia; sentimental revisitations exquisitely savoured. To Richard West, a member of the Quadruple Alliance, Walpole writes, 'Gray is at Burnham, and what is surprising has not been to Eton. Could you live so near it without seeing it?' But Eton was never long out of Gray's mind, and if he could not say masses for the royal founder, he could write verses:

> Ye distant spiers ye antique towers
> That crown the watery glade
> Where grateful science still adores
> Her Henry's holy shade.[28]

Richard West writes to Thomas Gray as 'one who has walked hand in hand with you, like children in the wood',

> Through many a flowry path and shell grot
> Where learning lulled us in her private maze

'The very thought of you see tips my pen with poetry and brings Eton to my view,' writes Walpole to his con.[29]

With these spellbound celebrations we enter an enchanted private world, sacred to its initiates, of boyhood preserved.

---

* 'Cole' was William Cole, the Cambridge antiquary. 'Bishop Tanner' was Thomas Tanner, who could not be said to have missed preferment: Archdeacon of Norwich, 1700; Canon of Christ Church, Oxford, 1723; Bishop of St Asaph, 1732.

In the absence of earlier discernible breathings, the Quadruple Alliance may be treated as the first stirrings of the infant mystic, which, fragile and ephemeral curiosity as it seemed, took root in the soil of the public schools and acted upon the impressible nature of adolescent boys in ways which in many cases proved permanent. 'My whole fame,' wrote one eminent man to another, 'My whole character, whatever success has attended my life . . . whatever I can hope to be hereafter are drawn from that (to me sacred and hallowed) spring.'[30] There is a certain piquancy in the circumstance that the writer, the Marquess Wellesley, was enabled to enjoy the benefits of the public school he so revered (Eton) only after having been expelled from another (Harrow) for riotous behaviour. The cynicism of the young Lord Byron was not proof against the mystic, despite 'the harsh custom of our youthful band'. In his last term at Harrow he 'counted the days before leaving in sorrow'.[31]

Thus, partly due to habit and fashion and despite criticism and divided feelings, and a severe contraction of the liberal seventeenth-century range of studies, a public school came to be widely accepted in the course of the eighteenth century as the place where boys destined to be bred as gentlemen might most conveniently be initiated into the life of a community of their peers and contemporaries. The experience was one of lasting consequence for its subjects, leaving an indelible impress of social identity even upon those who might have preferred to have lost the stamp. Few forgot those vivid years of collective puberty. Many ascribed in adult life an enhanced moral confidence, whether justified or misplaced, to the process, some stressing the social adaptability acquired in learning 'to endure and live with equals',[32] others the lesson of self-reliance. Lord Sherbrooke thanked Winchester for the 'invaluable discovery that a man can count on nothing in this world except what lies between his hat and his boots'. Fitzjames Stephen affirmed that Eton taught him 'for life' the lesson that 'to be weak was to be wretched and that the state of nature is a state of war'.[33] There were those, too, like J. A. Froude and Anthony Trollope, who cherished no feeling of gratitude for their schools and held the ordeals they had suffered responsible for permanent injury to their personalities. Whatever their feelings and afterthoughts as men, the boys whose transactions at school we are able to examine at close range, through their own, or their companions' eyes, were all born between the end of the eighteenth century and the fourth decade of the nineteenth century, being by translation or by birth 'early Victorians'. They were separated from their sons, and even, perhaps, from their own younger brothers, by the unrepeatable distinction of having passed through an English public school, before English public schools were reformed.

Life and society were themselves changing. But the concept and memories of a 'free' society of boys were cherished by most of those Englishmen whose own boyhood had been rooted in the experience; they formed a potent body of defenders and they helped to defer an inevitable modification to closer conformity with the changed outside world for as long as possible.

One of the most important components of post Napoleonic-war society was an assertive claim to the right of interference by government and (if government faltered) by tutelary public opinion, in the personal lives of *all* men and women. Such interference was canvassed as a benevolent, improving, and morally irresistible duty laid upon authority; and official and quasi official investigators began to extend their tentacles into areas which had lately been, for a minority, a private domain. If corrective regulation of the pastimes and entertainment of adults was deemed legitimate, how much more strictly did the principle appertain to the nature of juveniles.

The young were to be formed by the surveillance and diligent indoctrination of reliably patterned adult teachers. Such was, in broad terms, the educational philosophy of the new order. The notion of boys left, in practice, in a state of collective self-government appeared to neoteric theorists of what would later be called 'social engineering', as malign, almost blasphemous. But the self-government of boys was, in effect, what the old public-school system meant.

So the new order denounced the old and called for reform, while the old order scorned the new and stood contemptuously aloof. The two were already, when the curtain rose upon the nineteenth century, worlds apart.

TWO
'Nurseries of All Vice'

The public schools have never been without critics and detractors. Some objections raised were thoughtful and honest; others were venal and disingenuous. 'Sir,' says a wayfarer in *The Adventures of Joseph Andrews*, by way of opening an account of his misfortunes, 'I am descended of a good family and was born a gentleman. My education was liberal and at a public school.' Henry Fielding, himself an Etonian, makes another character remark of the previous speaker, 'A public school, Joseph, was the cause of all the calamities which befell him. Public schools are the nurseries of all vice and immorality.'*[1]

The objections to the public schools' régime which were most frequently raised were the subjects taught and the so-called 'fagging system' with its alleged consequence of the elder boys corrupting the younger.

In principle, the responsibility for the regulation of a public school was the headmaster's, except in as far as he might be controlled by a provost, or warden, and collegiate fellows, or other governors. But in the course of time, what had begun in the seventeenth century as a convenient and pragmatic delegation of power to senior boys had come to be regarded as a formal *separation* of authority, and treated by the boys as theirs of right, sanctified by tradition. Any attempt to abridge this independence was resented and resisted. In 1776, Huntingford, the future Warden of Winchester, observed, 'They [the boys] have been taught to think that it was the duty of an assistant master by no means to interfere with the discipline of the founda-

---

* The expression was borrowed and used (usually without attribution) by a succession of partisans (including Thomas Bowdler and Sydney Smith); and some modern writers, having traced the origin to Fielding, have taken it to be the assertion of his own opinion (see, for example, E. C. Mack, *Public Schools and British Opinion 1780–1860*, p. 63). But Fielding had put the words into the mouth of a disgruntled tutor who felt that Eton had robbed him of an affluent pupil.

tion.'* Dr Goddard, not an unpopular headmaster, suffered a rebellion in 1808 because he had attempted to convert a saint's day, normally a holiday, into a school day, without first having obtained the consent of the praefects.[2]

The reliance of a headmaster upon his boy officers, under whatever title they acted, and the strength of their union, was such that, in an early open collision between the two forces at Eton, in 1768, the sixth form's most potent weapon was a *strike*, a cessation of their normal administrative disciplinary office.[3] Boys' self-government in the public schools persisted because men who had experienced it as boys emerged with a predominantly favourable impression of the system, and sent their own sons to get similar experience. The force of precedent and tradition in public schools might indulge vicious or reckless, or disreputable propensities of temperament. 'Nobody could have guessed,' said Leslie Stephen in a sarcastic sally, 'that an ideal education would be provided by bringing together a few hundred lads and requesting them to govern themselves.'[4] But if 'nobody could have guessed', there were those who could, and did, observe and remember, and draw the conclusion that an identifiable process of evolution took place in boys who remained at a public school long enough to gain seniority and carry its burdens. *The Times* remarked in 1858 that it remained an unsolved problem how 'those fierce passions are tamed, how the licence of unbridled speech is softened into courtesy, how lawlessness becomes discipline . . . and all this within two or three years and with little external assistance', and suggested that 'parents may well abstain from looking too closely at the process and content themselves with the results'.[5]

The objections to the subjects taught were that they were ancient Greek and Latin and nothing else, and that they were taught by application to the works of pagan, often licentious, writers. The attitude of the Church towards the learned languages had always been ambivalent, for the choicest literary expression of these languages was not Christian and was frequently contrary to the spirit of prevailing Christian doctrine and morals. But in the eighteenth century churchmen of the higher and middle range of Anglicanism felt little, if any, difficulty in accommodating themselves to the dichotomy. Indeed the majority of those bred up to a taste for classical literature seem scarcely to have been conscious of the contradiction.

* There were rebellions at Winchester in 1770, 1774, 1778 and 1793, and again in 1808, 1818 and 1828.

Theologians could weave patterns of interconnection between the thought of the fathers of the primitive church and their borrowings from Gnostic teaching, pseudo Sibylline Oracles, Orphic prophecies and neo-Pythagorean religious systems; but true classicists, in or out of holy orders, cared for no such shifts and did not hide their preference for their beloved pagan poets with whom they had been on terms of loving familiarity since childhood. It was the custom at Winchester in Holy Week to take as a subject of study Grotius's *De Veritate*. When the class conducted by Dr Gabell, proceeding through this pious work, came to a quotation from Ovid, the master sighed, paused, and said, 'Ah! this is like some fresh oasis in a great desert; let us rest in it and not get again into that barbarous stuff.'[6]

Such concentration could produce from superior talents dazzling results within fixed boundaries, often accompanied by contempt for all that lay outside them.* A clever boy who did nothing but read and construe and learn by heart the works of classical antiquity, and himself write Latin and Greek verse, cultivated a powerful memory, a quick and orderly mind, an elegant and correct mode of expression, and built up a reservoir of quotable passages from the literature which was believed to be the sum of all that was wise and valuable in the history of human experience. George Osborne Morgan at the age of eleven was reading the eleventh book of the *Aeneid*, Xenophon's *Anabasis* and making original Latin verse. J. Conington, at the age of eight, could already repeat a thousand lines of Virgil to his father and amused himself by comparing different editions of the poet.[8] Charles Merivale, at the age of twelve, was writing an epic poem in Latin and had completed a hundred lines.[9] Eighteenth-century boys with a bent for scholarship grew up into men who daily read Greek for pleasure, like Thomas Apperley, a modest country squire,[10] and who conversed comfortably in Latin, like Robert Walpole, who used the language to 'govern' a king of England who could not speak English.[11]

What a classical education was designed to do was to forge a bond of shared thought, sensibility and manners between gentlemen of all ranks, uniting in one caste – the caste of a gentleman – nobility,

---

* William Johnson describes a notable such product, Dr H. A. Woodham, Hon. Fellow of Jesus College, encountered at King's College dinner table at Cambridge, 7 September 1864: 'He has a strong stomach, capacious of beer and wine, a very strong voice, a good, manly, shrewd face, a flat, fine hand, a great memory, a rare plainness of speech. . . . He is an enthusiastic Latinist, talks of Horace, Lucan, Catullus with more force and warmth than anybody I ever met: a first class Historian and Archaeologist. Boasts of never having read a play of Shakespeare.'[7]

gentry, and their kin, the professional classes, requisite to the ordering of society. But what classical education did in practice was to deny the designation 'gentleman' to increasing numbers of Englishmen who aspired impatiently to acquire it. Once a barbarous aristocracy had despised the classics. Now their standard had been stood on its head and prejudice reversed.

> Kings may make titles, heralds scutcheons plan
> But education makes the gentleman

and by education was meant that 'every gentleman must understand Greek and Latin'.[12]

The discontent of subordinates with their station in life was violently stirred by the French Revolution, as a generation of Englishmen began to change their expectations and question the limits of horizon and code of deference prescribed by the past. Men whose fathers might not have contemplated an immediate translation in rank, developed an itch for instant gentility.

The higher in society one went the more men might be found living in private as their grandfathers had lived, but the more private their lives became. They knew that while they were envied and travestied, their immunity from the moral inhibitions of the expanding middle classes, alternately obsequious and pert, but of increasing political strength, was resented. Reticence became a virtue in 'this portentous age of reticence',[13] for whatever became known was ventilated and, if possible, made cause of scandal, even the fact that 'a lord or a gentleman of £10,000 a year may admire Voltaire, Diderot or Spinoza without being expelled out of the pale of social communion'.[14]

At the centre and base of the old order stood the public schools, of all the traditional institutions which lingered by preference in the past, the most tenacious and powerfully supported. The men who administered them, and the parents who sent their sons to be governed, and then in turn to govern others, in them, while prepared to make, if necessary, certain conspicuous alterations in their public image, viewed with repugnance and alarm the lineaments of 'a total revolution of political thought'[15] and united to defend above all the education of their sons against contamination by the Age of Vulgarity. 'No Innovation!' was the watchword of Winchester's Warden Huntingford,[16] and one might say (with acknowledgement to Bagehot) that within the schools an old world survived which was not as the new – nor was it meant to be – dedicated to perpetuating a caste different and separate from the rest of society, until the needs of the caste itself and its own nature were modified.

Reticence was, perhaps, the only change worth remark in the style of conduct the public schools displayed at the start of the new century. This was especially true of Eton. Old Etonians who wished to send their bastards as well as their legitimate sons to Eton as Oppidans continued to do so. In 1842 two of the Marquess of Wellesley's five children by one mistress* were helping to edit the *Eton Bureau*; but a measure of discretion was now observed. Fathers would no longer make rather more than private jokes of the business, as Lord Pembroke had done when he allowed Lady Pembroke to dispatch one of his natural sons to Eton at the earliest possible age with the playful anagram, Reebkomp, for a surname.†

It was because of what the public schools were and did that they became the focus of hostile criticism by men who wished to change society in one way or another, and who might have no common interest other than the shared view of the public schools as the main obstacle to the achievement of their respective ends. 'Fifty years ago,' said Sir Walter Besant in 1888, 'we were in the eighteenth century.'[19] It was true that, at least until the development of the railways, England remained closer to the past than to the future, and even after the railways and the Industrial Revolution, there remained great pockets of rural seclusion where life had changed little since the seventeenth century and 'even the passing of a cart was of great interest to the children'.[20] There were country gentlemen who gave visible expression to their dislike of the changes they saw by continuing to wear the style of clothes fashionable in their youth. As late as 1870, survivors of the world which had resisted the Reform Bill of 1832 attracted the attention of the curious when they visited London and displayed themselves in the bay window of Boodles 'dressed in the style of fifty years ago'.‡ At the public schools a similar

---

* Hyacinth Gabrielle Roland, who later married Wellesley's brother, Lord Mornington. According to the diary of Lord Hatherton, the Marquess Wellesley's son-in-law, the Duke of Wellington was also illegitimate, and only half-brother to Lord Wellesley. The entry for Monday, 26 September 1832, reads: 'Lord W. speaking of the different qualities of his brothers said to me significantly, "But you know only Lady Anne and I are Wellesleys, Arthur's father was Mr Gardiner." ' Mr Gardiner was their mother's Irish land steward.[17]

† Augustus Retnuh Reebkomp (or Repcomb), natural son of Henry Herbert, tenth Earl of Pembroke, by Catherine Elizabeth Hunter (Retnuh being Hunter reversed). The child was brought up by Lady Pembroke, who sent him to Eton at the age of four, the youngest Etonian ever.[18]

‡ Boodles Club in St James's Street is transparently disguised as 'Noodles' in a waggish report, *The Gentleman's Art of Dressing with Economy by A Lounger at the Clubs*, '. . . there is old Lord X—in tightly buttoned blue coat and brass buttons; coat collar about a fathom deep, cravat knotted in a manner that Beau Brummel might have approved.'[21]

collective cultural protest of dressing 'in the past' was performed all the year round. Kinglake's description of Dr Keate, headmaster of Eton 1809–34, acquired immortality. 'He wore a fancy dress partly resembling the costume of Napoleon and partly that of a widow woman.'[22] In fact John Keate was comparatively responsive to change;* but other pedagogues and college dignitaries appeared daily, arrayed in a fashion which the outside world would have deemed 'fancy dress': 'knee breeches and buckled shoes at Eton in the eighteen forties, with very high collars and voluminous folds of neckcloth',[23] when modern wear was trousers, frockcoats and neckties.

The public schools, despite their name, were not then 'open places'; little of what went on in them was intentionally revealed, and inquisitive strangers were not encouraged to pry. Rumour abounded, but only the initiates knew for certain what was truth and what was fancy in reports on these sequestered worlds; and they had long tended to be silent other than in private. But in 1802 a solemn rebuke was delivered to the public schools from an unlikely source. It came from a well-known cleric and preacher in the Church of England, Dr Thomas Rennell, Master of the Temple. The charge brought was the historic (and once more fashionable) one of Sin. Those old, seasoned companions, pagan literature and Christian doctrine, which generations of English clergy had learned to live at peace with, were set up like puppets in formal confrontation as symbols of evil and good.

Dr Rennell's position, however piously reached, was compromised. He was himself an Etonian, and his son was at Eton. His declared aim was religious revival not class conflict, but the kind of followers his public attack upon the education of his own class was likely to attract might have interests different from his own. Dr William Vincent, headmaster of Westminster, inferred as much in the icy reply he published in an open letter to the Bishop of Meath. He was not authorized, even if he were willing, to substitute Prudentius for Virgil or Gregory of Nazienzen for Homer. 'Our authors are not intended to teach paganism,' he said with the disdain of a high priest for a wretch guilty of *trahison de clerc*, 'but to set before our youth the best examples of writing that the world affords.' By his failure to make this distinction Dr Rennell was appealing 'from the learned to the ignorant'.[24]

---

* Keate incurred the censure of Etonian traditionalists like Canning and Lord Clanricarde when he modernized Montem wear from knee breeches to trousers in 1825. See Brown, vol. 60, 19 April 1826; Gaskell, 11 May, *Eton Schoolboy*, p. 72.

The point was immediately confirmed by the quality of the support for Dr Rennell which appeared in print. A Mr David Morrice, uniting the claims of righteousness and utilitarianism, followed in the wake of Dr Rennell to demand – in the name of religion, of course – the outlawing of the 'corrupt influence' of 'Latin and Greek authors, call them either Pagan or Classical' (which he himself could not read) as 'injurious to the youthful imagination and religious principle' in a class of society with which he manifestly had no familiar intercourse. Then, to beat the English upper class with their own rod, he proceeded to suggest that their 'pagan education' might be an incentive to revolution; for the principles of the constitution which had rendered France 'the scourge and terror to all its neighbours' had derived from the records of 'that ambitious nation which would never be satisfied with conquest till she became mistress of the world and destroyed the inoffending, peaceable, commercial Carthage'.[25]

Morrice, and others like him, protested against the performance by schoolboys of Terence's *Eunuchus*, 'the *most indecorous* of all his comedies'. Once their voices would have gone unnoticed, or merely raised more laughter. For generations the acting of the play had been a favourite annual event at Westminster School, enjoyed by the boys and their parents. It would continue to be performed, but the old order was on the defensive in the 1830s when it pleaded in justification of the continuance of the play that 'acting copies had been judiciously castigated'. In 1846 the performance was actually suspended 'out of deference to what was supposed to be popular sentiment'.[26] But the recoil was so strong in the form of a petition presented by Old Westminsters, led by the Archbishop of York, that *Eunuchus* was reinstated.

A more dangerous threat than the pulpit rhetoric of an earnest Evangelical was to be trained on the citadel. In 1810 a notice in the *Edinburgh Review* of an unimportant little book called *Remarks on the System of Education in Public Schools* was made the occasion for an attack, not merely on one aspect of the schools, but upon the whole system from top to bottom. The author was the periodical's editor, Sydney Smith, and although he was a clergyman, he was so far from being a religious 'enthusiast' that some people questioned the propriety of his being in holy orders at all. What nobody questioned was his wit as a controversialist or his ability as an expositor. 'The greatest master of ridicule,' his friend and admirer, Macaulay, called him, 'that has appeared amongst us since Swift.'[27]

Smith's hostility to the public schools, although outwardly rational, was fuelled by hidden emotions that sprang from his own experience as a boy at Winchester. What happened to him there is something of a mystery, for he left an impression on his Wykehamist contemporaries of a bright, even mischievous and successful boy* – he became captain of the school – but we have it on the authority of his daughter that the recollection of his school life was hateful and agonizing to him, and even the occasion of bad dreams. Concerning his own experiences he was reticent, but he left the world in no doubt of his opinion of the effects of the public schools, 'premature debauchery that only prevents men from being corrupted by the world by corrupting them before they enter the world . . .', a system of 'abuse, neglect and vice' in which a boy who began as a slave was likely to end himself as a tyrant.[28]

Sydney Smith's articles in the *Edinburgh Review* provoked a stir. They are not, in fact, high in intrinsic merit among his efforts in journalism, but the response which anything he wrote attracted served to ignite a chain reaction amongst the adversaries of the public schools who had been waiting for such a signal to level a concerted attack on the enemy. The hostility expressed had changed its character and dimensions from the moral protest of individual tender consciences to the political warfare of organized parties bent on social reform, which rightly regarded the public schools as nourishers of resistance. Adversaries of a new breed were appearing in high positions in public life, no longer polite critics like Chatham and Chesterfield, who had aired their reservations inconspicuously, in private, but new men, 'outsiders', who had not arrived by way of a public school and, having breached the social barriers erected by the system, used their eminence to challenge and denounce all the components – fagging, boy-government, corporal punishment, unsupervised social liberty, the monopoly of the classics – which the great schools venerated as essential elements in the sacred ordeal formative of 'that noblest work of God, an English Gentleman'.[29]†

Appropriately, the most active enemy of the public schools was not an Englishman, nor a result of English education, but a Scotchman, Henry Brougham, co-founder with his friend Sydney Smith of the *Edinburgh Review*. Himself the product of a Scotch day-school, Brougham could not have been by temperament and training more

---

* Some of his contemporaries described him and his brother less favourably: 'overbearing and intolerable boys' (Adams, *Wykehamica*, p. 159).
† Not the writer's own opinion; he was quoting with irony a popular notion.

alien to the English gentleman's tradition of pragmatic, almost unsu-pervised, trial-and-error, sink-or-swim test for survival in a self-gover-ning community of male juveniles. In 1816, having at last obtained a seat in the House of Commons as a member for Winchelsea, Brougham succeeded in having appointed a select committee to inquire into the education of the lower orders and the 'abuses of charities connected with the education of the poor'. That had been the intention of the House, but under its term of reference the commis-sion's warrant could be taken to include even the public schools, for these were, technically, endowed grammar schools, expressly estab-lished by the will of the founder in some cases to serve what were called '*pauperes et indigentes*'.

The committee making a general appreciation in 1818 reported that 'considerable unauthorised deviations have been made, both in Eton and Winchester, from the original plans of the founders', and that 'these deviations have been dictated more by a regard of the interests of the Fellows than of the scholars who were the main objects of the foundation and the founder's bounty'.[30]

Many years later, a letter of Richard Okes (dated 25 March 1864) revealed that, on this occasion, Eton had been betrayed from within by Peter Hind, a fellow of King's, in requittal for the offence he had taken at an indiscreet pleasantry from the Provost of Eton, Joseph Goodall. Making fun a little of the tranquillity of a fellow's life at King's, Goodall had remarked in company, 'Well, Mr Hind, I suppose you have nothing to do but read the statutes and the senior scholar's book.' Hind later made an ominous rejoinder: 'He shall see I shall read the statutes to some purpose.'[31] Having read them with a careful and malicious eye he bore the results to Henry Brougham, who used them to frame his indictment. As he had proposed from the beginning, Brougham had drafted a bill aimed at bringing the schools under government control. The reaction was violent and immediate; and the counterattack upon Brougham charged him, rather than the venerable schools, with plotting the betrayal of the founders' intentions and subverting those studies – the classics – and their teachers, to whom, according to Samuel Butler, headmaster of Shrewsbury, 'the country owes all that is tasteful and elegant in literature'.[32] The terms used 'in disparaging the most revered institu-tions of this country . . . by those who themselves do not happen to have enjoyed its advantages' could not be read 'without a feeling of something like disgust'.[33]

The cleverer of Brougham's opponents in both houses took care not to present a face of resistance to change, in principle, but rather appeared as eminently reasonable, moderate English gentlemen, constrained to protect their just rights against the sweeping and destructive innovations of this barbarous Scotchman who seemed to 'wish to expell the ancient masters and reduce all teaching to Hume, Adam Smith and Dugald Stewart' and to fill the schools with Scotch lecturers on the human mind and essayists upon the errors of Bacon, Newton and Locke. Brougham was learning that the two most potent weapons of debate in the armoury of the English upper classes were ridicule and a modest deportment. They were 'as zealous as the Honourable gentleman himself for the due education of the lower classes', said one correspondent, reflecting upon his pursuit of that alluring chimera, a system of education which was at once national, practical and choice, but 'they think Winchester, Westminster and Eton should be destined to the education of another class than the Philanthropic and Borough Schools. They think the education of the middle classes from which the learned professions are supplied to be no less useful to the public than the education of the poor; and they will not sanction the breaking into funds which the will of the donor has set apart for assisting gentlemen of large families and small fortunes to keep their children within the same rank of life as themselves.'[34]

The issue was the continuity of caste, and the force turned upon them by the exalted friends of the public schools was stronger than Brougham's sponsors felt capable of resisting. To get the Bill passed they insisted that Brougham agree to the exemption of charities with visitors, governors and overseers from the power of his commissioners. His manoeuvre to entrap the wicked public schools had failed. Writing with bitterness unpurged nearly half a century later he recalled 'reluctantly being forced to insert the exemption because Rosslyn, Holland and others . . . were apprehensive on our being beaten on a further stage if we held out. . . .'[35] He had been baulked by, he jeered in his frustration, 'the romantic attachment which English gentlemen feel towards the academic scenes of their early life'.[36] Brougham, brilliant and contentious, some thought slightly mad, could not begin to comprehend the mystic of the public schools. But his defeat was not the end, only an early engagement in a war which was to continue for half a century more in its present form (and for indefinitely longer in modified forms). Although Brougham had failed to penetrate into the public schools as he had plotted to do, he spotlit them with a beam of critical inquiry which was never to be extinguished. His followers patrolled the perimeters of the schools, sometimes insinuating themselves, cultivating the disaffected, gleaning every piece of intelligence and every reverberation of a whisper which might be of future use in the conflict.

The boys themselves were aware of being under observation. 'It seems that everything done at public schools is soon known all about,'[37] William Churton wrote to his father from Rugby in the same year that Brougham opened his campaign. An Eton boy, writing to his father, on Sunday 1 July 1834, requesting money to contribute to a fund to make good damage to property which he had not himself caused, justified the appeal by saying, 'there are many who are trying to get anything they can to ruin Eton'.[38] A decade later, George Moberly, headmaster of Winchester, declared, 'Now . . . there is the utmost disposition to publish everything that takes place . . . the outcry out of doors is raging louder and louder and day by day something occurs.'[39]

During the period spanned by these quotations the reformist critics and adversaries of the public schools maintained their moral siege, and predictions of early doom were broadcast. 'With a blindness which baffles explanation because it leads directly to their own downfall,' 'A Parent' exclaimed, nearly a decade after Brougham's miscarriage, 'they hate reform as if it were revolution, being apparently ignorant that they are proceeding the right way to ensure a revolution which will be no reform.' Singling out for particular censure Eton, in the constitution of which he alleged there was 'an inherent principle directly repulsive to reform', he charged the establishment with 'a contemptuous and scornful rejection of the demands of a reasonable and enlightened age' and of disregarding the 'spirit of uncompromising enquiry and reformation which was developing its full energies throughout the country'. It was not Eton's adherence to 'antiquated errors' alone which provoked the ire of this militant moralist, but her tranquil indisposition to subscribe to the brand of new uniformity which he canvassed. 'Surely the idea of conducting a great public school on principles that have no harmony with the opinion and ideas of the public is an egregious folly. . . . But they are wrestling with a power that will laugh to scorn their puny endeavours. Their brazen gates will be but as touchwood before the strong arm of the giant.'[40]

The identity of 'A Parent' is not known for certain. In style and aim the writer bears a resemblance to the author of two censorious articles on the public schools published in the *Edinburgh Review* in

1830 and 1831 which received much public attention. We know that George Cornewall Lewis was the author of the articles in the *Edinburgh Review*[41] and that he was an Old Etonian.* He may also have been 'A Parent'. Apart from similarities of tone between the two pieces, the contents of each are an alternative display of the evidence and arguments of the other: criticism of teaching Latin by writing verse; 'private business' as the only means of learning anything useful; adverse reviews of the curriculum.[43]

The identity of Sydney Smith's successor in the war upon the public schools as an Etonian revealed another crack in the integrity of the caste from which he came. If Horace Walpole's Quadruple Alliance had been the first recorded manifestation in public life of the mystic, Sydney Smith and George Cornewall Lewis (a future Chancellor of the Exchequer, Home Secretary and Secretary for War) may be said to have been the first undisguised public exhibitors of the anti-mystic, an unquenchable hostility posing as a spirit of moderate reform, but driven by a missionary passion to destroy.

The 'giant' on whose strong arm 'A Parent' relied to batter down the 'brazen gates' was for Lewis the benevolent servant of 'progress'. To the champions of the public schools it appeared as the embodiment of shallow, vulgar materialism, a symbol of the envy and malice of the vandal mob, lusting to desecrate and deform the graces of a civilization which, being unable to understand, it hated. The public schools, albeit imperfect, were custodians and protectors of that noble heritage, 'of all our great institutions perhaps ... the most characteristic'.[44]

There appeared to be no reconciliation between the two parties. Their eyes on different objectives, they were separated not merely by principles and aims, but by emotions of well-nigh religious antipathy. Lewis (like 'A Parent') manifestly saw himself as a humanist of pure benevolence. Something of the character of his 'humanism' is revealed in his wish to replace 'indecorous' corporal punishment as a form of discipline for boys with the 'decorous' punishment of 'solitary confinement'. 'It – enough of it –' he remarked with relish, 'would drive most people to distraction.'[45] He was correct in his estimate of its effects, at least.

Of all the belligerent political crusaders, the one which kept up its

* George Cornewall Lewis was at the same prep school as Francis Doyle, under M. Clement who, observed his brother innocently, 'contrived by some means to make his pupils speak French'.[42] Sir Francis Doyle could have told him how it was done. See below, p. 53.

attacks longest and most acrimoniously upon the public schools was the *Westminster Review*. Its writers were radical social idealists with some good and positive suggestions to make, but they forfeited sympathy and credit which they might otherwise have gained, by the puerile intemperance of their language, which sauced, without improving, the borrowed aphorisms of Sydney Smith. Eton was designated the home of 'aristocratic dunces' who 'snubbed an aristocracy of talent' in a 'slave tyrant relationship'. More formidable and better informed was the *Quarterly Journal of Education* which, in the years 1834 and 1835, bombarded the schools with charges drawn from evidence biased and selective, but not imaginary. The stern quality of their intent was signalled by the pronouncement that 'those who believe that manliness consists in premature vice may here find opportunities for the indulgence of every sensual inclination . . . a taste for gluttony and drunkenness, an aptitude for brutal sports and a passion for female society of the most degrading kind'. The domain of vice alluded to was Eton, and the opportunities for indulgence were posited as compensation for suffering an environment such that 'in 1834 the inmates of a workhouse or gaol are better lodged than the scholars of Eton'.[46]

Ostensibly the objections were to 'a system of education' which 'does not belong to the present age', permitting Etonians to work or not as they pleased; but the writers' real concern was seen to be less for the improvement of the present order of Etonians than for the admission of other classes of the community to share the disadvantages of Eton. 'We are of the opinion to build and uphold such an anomaly as Eton upon a liberal endowment for poor and indigent boys is not fit work for these times and belongs to a past age when Exclusiveness had a stronger garrison and more faithful soldiers than now belong to her.' The inner motive of the attack was one of political philosophy firing a resentment that Eton (with other public schools) had succeeded in surviving a recent measure which should have swept her away 'with the rest of a system of jobbing and corruption' of a time 'when patronage was the all in all of our aristocratic institutions'. Eton, the writer asserted, was the main instrument of working this patronage. 'Eton belongs to that old political system; it was part and parcel of it. The system is gone but Eton remains unchanged.'[47]

Yet, despite the reverence ritually paid to tradition and antiquity, change did occur in the schools in correspondence with events in the outer world beyond their walls. Change, though never welcomed and usually opposed, was, if established, more rapidly absorbed and accepted in a public school than in the outside world. In a school, an innovation, once successfully imposed, quickly itself graduated into a tradition, for in a very few years after its appearance there would be no member of the 'republic' who had known life without it.

Thus to consider the most spectacular of all social changes to occur in our time, the railways – 'oh! those detestable railways'[48] – were execrated by a generation of boys at school bred to worship equestrian and coaching skills, and bitterly resisted by school authorities as an agent of social and moral pollution. The proposal in 1833 by the Great Western Railway for a line between Paddington and Slough occasioned a rare collector's piece, a letter from the headmaster, Dr Keate, to his former pupil, W. E. Gladstone MP, soliciting his support in opposing a project which 'must be to the greatest degree injurious to Eton, as interfering with the discipline of the School, the studies and amusement of the Boys affecting the healthiness of the place, from the increase of floods, and endangering even the lives of the boys from their thoughtlessness and spirit of adventure'.[49] Eton College did succeed in delaying the inevitable, and when the line from Paddington to Slough was opened in 1838, the service was hedged with protective conditions required by the college. But once a railway existed, its effects could not be kept away. Soon the railway had grown its own tradition and attracted its devoted followers, many of them juvenile. The vanishing stagecoaches were mourned not by boys who had never known them, but by ageing men who did not forget. Thackeray was one of those who remembered, for whom 'it was only yesterday; but what a gulf between then and now!'[50]

The more intemperate and rancorous the attacks on the public schools, the less favourable the impression they made upon those capable of influencing the course of the schools. It was when loyal friends began to show signs of uneasiness and qualify their approval that danger signals were manifest. An early example of reluctant discord is revealed in a pamphlet entitled *The Eton System Vindicated*, produced in 1834 in refutation of 'A Parent'. After rebutting 'A Parent's' complaints, 'Vindicator' himself feels constrained to introduce certain other criticisms of the holy place, two of which are of particular note. One applies to the congested environment of Long Chamber, where most of the Eton Collegers slept and lived together in one room without adult supervision, and where, he says, by 'the constant intercourse of such large numbers in a public room not only are the private pursuits of the scholar effectively interrupted but there is an entire want of that individual existence and inviolate retirement which, *according to the present habits of this country*,* are essentially necessary even among boys for the production of pure and exalted feelings'.

Here was a loyal traditionalist and supporter of the old system petitioning for a change at Eton on the ground of change *outside* Eton. No one had hitherto openly proposed amendments in the name of a *right* to changed expectations. 'I am no advocate of unnecessary innovation,' says Vindicator, 'especially in these times when the spirit of desecration is spreading like a plague over England.' But his second criticism goes straight to the heart of the character of the public schools: 'There is an entire lack of effective control over boys while they are in their chambers.' He does not mean lack of control of the senior boys over the junior: 'The elder scholars . . . themselves require the most constant and watchful superintendence.' This directly challenged the central tradition and unwritten law of boys' autonomy in their own social government. The result of this system was, he asserts, 'unnatural freedom', and adds, greatly daring, a phrase to be remembered. 'The name of Long Chamber has become a proverb and a reproach wherever the name of Eton has been spread.'[51] These were straws in a wind that was growing in force.

The political attention focused upon the public schools had made them in a short time objects of popular interest. But the accounts offered and the arguments adduced in the national periodicals, wherever their sympathies might lie, were too general in their terms and abstract in their language to impart any graphic impression of the life lived – what was said and what was done – in the schools to readers who had never been inside one. Coy innuendo – 'It is not for us to depict the traditionary iniquities'[52] – merely added to the 'utter bewilderment' of those who, seeking enlightenment, suffered 'hopeless confusion'[53] by receiving contradictions so extreme that they might have been descriptions of different worlds. A public school produced an 'honourable character',[54] making boys 'gentlemen in manners and mind, liberal and generous'.[55] It made boys 'rough and rude, but life is rough and rude',[56] yet it taught them 'manners and courtesy and the ability to move in the best society',[57] though at times they were reported 'Now flushed with drunkeness now with whoredom pale'.[58] A public school 'teaches a boy his place in the world and in practical

---

* My italics – author.

fashion his duty towards other boys, and to his superiors as well as his inferiors';[59] yet 'we hear of cruelties that would disgrace the most barbarous savages that ever destroyed one another by torture'.[60] Fagging, said one critic, 'caused want of independence'.[61] Fagging, said a former fag, 'was just what was wanting to brace one up to face the realities of life'.[62] Said one Etonian, 'The happiest years of my life.'[63] Said another, 'The only unhappy years of my life.'[64] One Harrovian declared, 'My boyhood was, I believe, as unhappy as any young gentleman's could well be.'[65] Another, 'If a boy's not happy at Harrow . . . it's his own fault.'[66]

In 1857 an illusion of enlightenment, at least, was vouchsafed by the appearance of *Tom Brown's Schooldays*. In that compound of romantic fiction and expurgated fact, the popular taste was given what it wished to receive; not the truth, which would have been too strange, ambiguous, savage and, sometimes, shocking, to be readily assimilated by the general public, but a 'good yarn' which modified into acceptable terms of simplicity and propriety a remote and foreign other world, and persuaded a legion of readers who had not been to a public school that here at last was a faithful likeness of the genuine article. 'Everybody is reading it,' Charles Kingsley told Thomas Hughes, 'from the fine lady on her throne to the redcoat on his cock horse . . .' and 'I have heard but one word, and that is, that it is the jolliest book they ever read.'[67] The whole truth, 'good' and 'bad', of the unreformed public schools could not be told openly in an age which was, on certain subjects, as has been observed, an age of reticence.

Parts of the hidden reality could be flashed in cabbalistic allusions between initiates. Thackeray was a master of this kind of fleeting, almost subliminal, private signal within a public utterance, so that many readers did not always apprehend on the surface of their consciousness how much he had told them;* and those who did apprehend and, like Bagehot, disapproved, found it impossible to nail him.† More candour could, of course, be used in confidential exchanges between men, but these were seldom recorded, only sometimes alluded to obliquely, or in private journals. These fugitive

* E.g., '. . . a prodigious thing that theory of life as orally learnt at a great public school. Why, if you could hear those boys of fourteen who blush before mothers and sneak off in silence in the presence of their daughters, talking among each other – it would be the woman's turn to blush then.'[68]
† 'He never violates a single rule, but at the same time the shadow of the immorality that is not seen is scarcely ever wanting to his delineation of the society that is seen. Everyone may perceive what is passing in his fancy.'[69]

intimations, uncollated, and dispersed among many letters, memoirs, autobiographies, diaries, some published, some secreted and suppressed, made no popular impact. But as the century advanced and the scale of change ensuing in the world was felt – and felt most keenly by those who had known life before the railways, and school life before the Clarendon Commission – men of the 'two worlds' evinced as never before a need to write about their boyhood at a public school on the receding side of the great dividing line, to repel fallacies, correct misunderstandings and recall to mind and 'help to preserve some record' (albeit censored) of earlier times of public school life, 'the very traditions of which are growing fainter every year'.[70]

It was natural that professional writers like Thackeray and Brace-bridge Hemyng, who had been to public schools, should store up and make use of the distinctive qualities of their early environment and transmute them by alchemy into literature. It was less natural, or at least less obviously so, that men who were not professional writers, and were to publish little or nothing else, should feel constrained to record in detail and publish anecdotes of their school life. This phenomenon, wrought by the force of the debate upon the public schools, enables us to reconstruct and enter in greater intimacy into the life of the schools than we might otherwise have done. Some of these books, long forgotten and unread, not only have merit as entertainment, but are much more accurate and authentic records of reality than *Tom Brown's Schooldays*. The authors' education admirably qualified them to perform their appointed tasks of piety; for, whatever else was neglected, the practice of learning by heart and construing large quantities of Latin and Attic and Homeric Greek literature developed the memory. Some of our witnesses (among them George Keppel, Roundell Palmer, William Tucker, William Tuckwell, Charles Allix Wilkinson) commanded a prodigious although, again, censored, recall. George Melly, geographer, shipowner and member of Parliament, wrote only two books: the first, *The Source of the White and Blue Nile*, appeared in 1851. In 1854 followed his *chef d'oeuvre*, *The Experiences of a Fag*. Sir Alexander Abercrombie, writing his memoirs after a long career as an imperial pro-consul in India, called them not 'England and India' but *Rugby and India*. Professor Gilbert Bourne was remembered for his *Introduction to the Study of the Comparative Anatomy of Animals*, but the book which gave him most pleasure to write was *Memoirs of an Eton Wet Bob*, where he let his pen 'run riot in reminiscence'.

In the company of the boys these old men had once been, we can leave our external observation posts and enter into the schools on visits of inspection for as long and to see as much as our guides allow. Where there is a gap we must use intuition and experience to fill it, without forgetting that what we offer to complete or clarify an imperfect picture is conjecture and not certainty.

It was generally considered desirable that boys should receive some educational introduction, appropriate to their prospects, before entering their public school. This might be provided at home by tutors, or it might be dispensed at a day-school, or at a boarding school designed for younger boys, which undertook to 'prepare' its charges for the conditions to be anticipated at their public school. The purported benefit of what later came to be known as a 'preparatory' (commonly abbreviated to 'prep') school was that, as well as teaching them the rudiments of their formal education, it would initiate small boys, gently, it was hoped by loving parents, into the realities of communal living.

THREE
Preparation

Roundell Palmer was the son of a country clergyman. Born in 1812, he grew up with his two brothers in his father's vicarage at Mixbury in Oxfordshire, and in many respects he was very fortunate. The boys received a strict schooling, Latin at five and Greek at six. Work began early in the morning under the tuition of their father, who was an accomplished classic, not an 'exact' scholar in the sense that two of his sons would become, but in a practical sense 'a good one'. They could not, as they appreciated later, have been better prepared for a public school by any teacher then living in England. They learnt Latin accidence from Dr Russell's Charterhouse grammar and then passed to Phaedrus' fables; by the time Roundell was nine years old he was fairly well grounded in Virgil and Horace, practised in verse and prose translation, and had begun the Greek testament. The works of Pope and Dryden were familiar to them. By the time they were approaching the age for dispatch to a public school, they had made some progress in Homer and had read the *Prometheus* of Aeschylus. They were also acquainted with Shakespeare, Milton and some other English classics. It may sound a rather oppressive régime for little boys but, having aptitude, they did enjoy their work, and it was only one side of the régime.

Out of the schoolroom they ran wild, Arcadian infants in a pastoral paradise. And, as they played and grew up, the faculty of their imagination, nourished by the springs of Hellenic mythology, grew in potence, colouring all their childish pleasures, mixing animistic dreams of the pagan supernatural with the most ordinary everyday things. They carved out of cleft sticks what passed with them for images of humanity and stuck them into the damp wood at night hoping, even praying to them, that they might find the effigies endowed with life when they returned to them in the morning. Moving through time by magic, as they slid over frozen pools, their resting places were the islands discovered by Columbus or Cook.

Their pious father, unsuspecting the appeal of the old gods in his reverence for the literature which immortalized them, instructed his sons in the elements of religious knowledge on Sunday afternoons with the children of his parishioners.

Shortly before Roundell and William were due to go to school, their idyllic existence was broken by an event which plunged them for the first time into the presence of the dreadfulness of life and death. The three boys were playing their usual cheerful and energetic games in the grounds when the youngest, Tom, received an accidental blow on the head. He collapsed and, after three days of horrible distress, died. The grief of bereavement almost crushed both parents. The sight of his little brother, so lately full of life and love, lying 'in all the beauty and awfulness of death, surrounded by snowdrops and hepatica flowers' made an impression on Roundell which never faded.

The dead child had been making 'good progress' in Latin, and on the day of the fatal accident had essayed his first translation of Latin verse into English. Although by ordinary standards Tom would have been considered a boy of high ability, he was judged by his father, who loved him dearly, as less accomplished than his brothers at the same age. In the light of this opinion Tom's performance gives some indication of the standards which were expected and attained in the vicarage at Mixbury, and of the literary precocity which rigorous cultivation could produce in a clever child of nine. The verse which he translated was Horace's *Ode to Leuconoe*:[1]

> *To Leuconoe*
> Seek not ('tis wrong) to know Leuconoe
> What fate the Gods shall give to me and thee
> Nor to attempt the Babilonian strains
> To bear the times how better would it be
> Whether our age more circling years shall see
> Or this the last which now th' Etruscan sea
> Dashes against the foamy rock. Be wise
> Pour thou out wine nor think of what will come
> While we yet speak, perhaps we'll speak no more
> Injoy what is, not caring what will come.
> (HORACE, *Odes* I. 12)

Thomas Adolphus Trollope and Albert Pell were contemporaries of Roundell Palmer; like him they were prepared for their public school mainly at home, but unlike Roundell, 'home' for them was more often London than the country because both their fathers were practising barristers. Trollope senior, a member of the Middle Temple, with chambers in Old Square, Lincoln's Inn, was a Wykehamist and had been a Fellow of New College and held the Vinerian Fellowship. He was therefore a learned, but he was not a successful, lawyer. If he could have exchanged some of his learning for a little tact his practice might have greatly improved. But a compulsion of temperament to rub everyone else's noses in his own rectitude made him neither loved nor as favoured on or off the bench as his intellectual abilities would otherwise have merited.

Every morning at seven found little Thomas at work in the drawing room of 16 Keppel Street (which was used as a breakfast room to save lighting another fire in the dining room), kneeling on the carpet before the sofa on which he rested his Eton Latin Grammar. The tea urn had not yet been brought up by the footman. Mr Trollope was a poor man by the standards of his class, and kept a modest establishment, but it would never have occurred to him or to his wife that they could get on without a footman in livery. Later Thomas and his brother Henry (the youngest and more famous-to-be brother, Anthony, was still too small to join the party) used to walk to Lincoln's Inn in time to trot back with their long-striding father, while he tested them on their prepared Latin verse.

At home Thomas received individual tuition from his father in his study. Mr Trollope did not thrash his children and would have rejected with indignation any suggestion that he might be unkind. Pupil and teacher sat side by side on a comfortable settee, the parental arm resting in what seemed an attitude of benign protectiveness along the back. But a glance at the child, tense and taut, on the edge of his seat, suggested that the tableau might have a less comfortable sequel. Questions were asked and answers given; and between the delivery of the one and the other the beringed hand was languidly raised; then, if the answer was short of satisfactory, the hand flicked forward to deliver a rap on the back of the respondent's head. Anticipation of the blow paralysed thought; as a means of stimulating attentiveness it was not a success, and one gains the impression from Thomas's picture of his father that Mr Trollope would have liked to use the same method in his cross-examinations of hostile witnesses, even in his examination-in-chief of his own witnesses.

Between these uncomfortable sessions of home tuition the Trollope boys were allowed to run as wild in a metropolitan environment as the Palmer boys were doing in a rural one. By day the brothers roamed London from Tyburn pike to the East India Docks. Their favourite haunt was the White Horse Cellar in Piccadilly where the most reputable of the fast coaches started and arrived. The boys would spend hours enraptured, watching the changing scene, and looking with contempt at the White Bear on the opposite side of the road, for that hostelry served the 'slow coaches'. The highest flight of ambition they could conceive was to be booked passenger on board one of the crack fast coaches, *Telegraph*, *High-Flyer*, *Magnet*, *Independent*, *Wonder*, or its rival, *No Wonder*, setting forth with a delicious sense of belonging to 'some select and adventurous section of humanity' which clattered through the streets of quiet little country towns at midnight or even three or four in the morning, 'the only souls awake in all the place'.[2] Then came the glorious day when they did in reality travel as passengers on a coach – perhaps even the *Quicksilver Mail* – to distant Devonshire to visit their kinswoman Mrs Fanny Best. Devonshire was another world from London, and in the country Mrs Best changed her mode of speech as easily and with as little affectation as she changed her clothes. In London she spoke with the accents of the Georgian court society which were still fashionable speech. Rome was pronounced Room; gold, gould; James, Jeames; beef steak, beef steek; oblige, obleege; and the 'a' in danger and stranger was sounded as in man. In Devonshire her voice took on the accents and syntax of the county, which is not capricious; 'a complete grammar of it could be compiled,' said a Devonian mid-Victorian. The classic phrase was 'her told she'. A pious person of Calvinist persuasion might say, 'Us didn't love He, 'twas Him loved we.' They never said 'we are' but 'us be', or else 'we am' contracted into 'we'm'. They said 'I be' as well as 'I'm', but never 'me'm' or 'Me be', though invariably 'me and George be', or of 'me and Urn', or whatever the name was, and never 'Earnest and I', or 'George and I'. They said 'to' for 'at', 'Her liveth to Moreton', and 'at' for 'to', 'I be goin at Bovey'.[3]

For the boys, no part of the holiday expedition could have been more exciting than the journey itself, as they surveyed, from their perch on the roof of the great coach that swayed along the country roads at twelve miles an hour, the fairyland beauty – still unblemished by the 'ostentatious nightmare of railway arches and viaducts' – of the western shires in the second decade of the nineteenth century. The changing of the horses was an important operation, performed with expert celerity and precision. The fresh team would be waiting ready, two on the off side, two on the near side, and the coach would pull up 'with the utmost exactitude' between them. Four ostlers jumped to the splinter bars and loosed the traces, the reins having been already thrown down. The driver usually retained his seat or, if he jumped down to inspect any particular, swarmed up again instantly like a monkey. Within the minute, sometimes within fifty seconds (timed by Thomas from his watch), the coach was off again.

The romance of coaching continued to fascinate English schoolboys for two generations to come. Albert Pell, a decade younger than Thomas, whose father's town house was Tow House in Harley Street, carried on the tradition of 'coach watching' with even greater enthusiasm. As the Pells' nearest country house was close to London, between Watford and Pinner, Albert enjoyed something of the best of both worlds. Beyond his London front door was a world of hurly-burly and unceasing interest. The beggar in Cavendish Square who feigned epileptic fits, the dancing bear, the orange sellers and hawkers with their jargon and peculiar street cries, the pickpockets with their light fingers and, when not light enough, the hue and cry of a chase after them down Wigmore Street and in and out of the warren of lanes off Marylebone High Street. In contrast, only an hour's ride distant, the country house surrounded by lawns and gardens ran down to five acres of wood and plantations and gave Albert something of the rural pastimes, if not the companionship, enjoyed in more distant Oxfordshire by the Palmer boys.

Being destined for Rugby, Albert Pell had to be prepared in Latin and Greek but, being also the son of a liberal and radical lawyer who was a friend of Brougham, his attention was directed to contemporary social problems along lines which Mr Trollope Senior, Tory and highchurchman, would have disapproved. The Trollopes' moral and religious education amounted to two precepts, 'obey', and 'tell no lies'. Anything further, even in the way of religious teaching (before confirmation), would have been disdained as savouring of 'evangelical tendencies'. Evangelism and low churchism were equated with the kind of vulgarity of mind which might be expected to be met with in tradesmen's back parlours and 'academies' where youths who came from such places were instructed in English grammar and arithmetic, but not to be met with and 'utterly out of place among gentleman and in gentlemanlike places of education where nothing of the kind was taught'. But out of place or otherwise, there were gentlemen sympathetically connected with the evangelical movements, and their alliance with the religious activities of their social inferiors was particularly resented by the Tory highchurchmen because it was judged, often rightly, to be associated with political doctrines of a radical character. When the family was at Pinner, Mr

Pell took Albert to see the village idiot shackled to the wall by a chain attached to a metal ring on a fixed iron rod and at the other to his ankle. Passing from left to right and right to left to the limit of his chain, 'in the blazing sun and bitter wind' the imbecile 'took his exercise and wore away his life'. Albert remembered his father saying to him, 'This sort of thing must be altered. If it is not done in my lifetime, mind you help to do it in yours.'[4]

Not all boys resident in London who were being prepared for public schools enjoyed the relative indulgence of home life. Frank Doyle was a contemporary of Roundell Palmer. They did not meet as children and there were some notable differences in the preparations they received for their public schools. In contrast to Roundell's old world and private régime of a home tutor, who happened to be his father, Frank went to an establishment in Chelsea, fashionable in the more sophisticated and cosmopolitan court circles, but far from ordinary or orthodox, for it was kept by a Frenchman, M. Clement. In later life Sir Francis Doyle appreciated the advantages he had received from the experience, for he became one of a select few English men and women who could speak French accurately and fluently, but, at the time, the little boy Frank Doyle felt that the knowledge was dearly bought.

During their entire sojourn in the school the pupils were not allowed to breathe a word of English from morning till night, and twice a day the bearers of a stigma called '*la marque*' were summoned before the master to be 'kept in' while others amused themselves in play. That in itself is an ordinary enough process of any school; the factor which gave *la marque* its sinister distinction was the condition on which alone it could be discharged. *La marque* was never quiescent; it had to be passed on by the holder, and this could only be done by detecting and denouncing some other unfortunate comrade in a lapse, however trivial or private. A brief involuntary exclamation at play – 'Up with the ball, there, quick!' in the midst of a game of cricket – was enough to draw upon you betrayal by a lurking carrier who pounced with the cry '*Prenez la marque!*' If a holder of the mark neglected or was unable to pass it on, he had his ears boxed at the first summons, and if he had nothing more acceptable to report the next time he was called up, the cane came into play, and thereafter 'an infinite vista of punishments loomed large in the distance'. Naturally such a system poisoned the air and produced an atmosphere of suspicion and mistrust even in the midst of games and fun. The senior boys in the school, who were the most accomplished at French, took counsel together how they might liberate the community from a system which they found morally odious and disgracing. It was decided to create a roster for the receipt of *la marque* which boys would accept in turn as a duty of honour. The scheme was planned with care. Cases of disputed grammar were got up in order that the French master might solemnly determine whether the mark had been lawfully passed on.

Even though they beat the *la marque* system, Sir Francis Doyle said that he felt later in life 'as if some of the original bloom had been rubbed off my natural frankness and sincerity in the process of living under the screw of "*prenez la marque!*" '[5]

What is historically interesting is that the *la marque* machinery, and the kind of morality it presupposed, and sought to cultivate in the relations between the boys and masters and between the boys themselves, of spying and surveillance and denunciation, was common in continental countries,* and not uncommon in private schools in England. It was the antithesis of the public-school constitution, and every attempt to penetrate and oversee the recreational freedom and self-government of the boys by the surveillance of masters or ushers was fiercely resisted by the boys themselves, and viewed with suspicion as contrary to the spirit of the public schools by almost every headmaster before Liddell and Thring.

M. Clement's preparatory school was not a happy place. Unlike the Palmer boys, cherished in their snug vicarage, with the run of pleasure grounds all around, the boys at the expensive Chelsea school were, as Doyle recollects, 'ill fed, ill warmed and ill play-grounded'. As he wrote his memoirs in old age Doyle could still see the scar on his finger caused by a chilblain suffered at school. In some respects it was an effective school. Boys not only learnt to speak French perfectly, they learnt Latin and Greek adequately. There was also good teaching in Italian and mathematics by M. Hall, a teacher of merit with a weakness for snuff and gin. But Monsieur Clement had favourites and was capricious. To joke was a hazardous practice. M. Clement would stand over the little culprit brandishing the cane, with vigorous passes of which he reinforced his words. '*Je pardonne l'indolence souvent,*' menacing swish, '*la desobéissance, quelquefois,*' swish, swish, '*mais l'insolence, JAMAIS!*' crack, crack, crack over back and shoulders.

---

* *La marque* was used in French schools to discourage children from speaking their ancient regional language, whether Langue d'Oc, Breton, or any other.

Meals could be an ordeal. Distressful pudding was habitually served as a first course to smother hunger before the service of meat. One small boy called Codrington* so abhorred the particular vile mess which was served on Tuesday before the roast mutton that he once allowed a grimace of disgust to be seen briefly, but not briefly enough, for thunders of accusation and justification followed.

'*Codrington, que faites vous là? Si le Prince Regent venait diner ici*' – 'An event,' observed Sir Francis in retrospect, 'more unlikely than Bishop Butler's typical improbability that the sun should fail to rise at his appointed hour' – '*Je ne le donnerai pas le meilleur pouding que cela. Mettez vous à genou, M. Codrington, et mangez cela tout de suite.*'

Monsieur Codrington was, as the Reverend William Barrow would have put it, 'without option', and had to obey, while his enemy watched every move in the process of deglutition 'as the spoon tired in its stride like a beaten racehorse' with 'a look of cruel glee'.

As soon as the last morsel had disappeared and Codrington's sigh of relief, silently delivered, was nevertheless registered, a bellow was heard. '*Donnez encore du pouding à Monsieur Codrington.*' The persecution served two purposes: it gratified the persecutor and it disabled Monsieur Codrington from attacking the mutton which was to follow.

Far from Chelsea, Monsieur Clement and the régime of *la marque* – two days' journey by coach – another small boy, a contemporary of Roundell's and Frank's, who was destined to meet the latter at their public school, was receiving his preparatory education. He too, like Frank, was being sent to a boarding school, but a more conventionally English one, and he was taught the same subjects from approximately the same books which Roundell had studied, though less ambitiously than those cultivated in the academic greenhouse of Mixbury Vicarage. The boy's name was James Milnes Gaskell. He came from the richest family of the boys considered up to now, being the son and heir of Benjamin Gaskell MP. At the age of eleven, Milnes left the protection of his parents' seat at Thorne House above the river Calder at Wakefield, to attend the school kept by the Rev. Dr Roberts at Mitcham, and there he had his first experience of a sudden change, as remarkable as any other he would ever suffer in after life, 'the removal of a child', as Gibbon put it, 'from the luxury and freedom of a wealthy house, to the frugal diet and strict subordination of a school; from the tenderness of parents and the obsequiousness of servants, to the rude familiarity of his

* Admiral Sir Henry Codrington KCB (1808–77).

equals, and the insolent tyranny of his seniors, and the rod, perhaps, of a cruel and capricious pedagogue'.[6]

Mr Roberts was severe but not capricious, and the food seems to have been good rather than bad; but transference at the age of eight or less may itself be a cruel ordeal, even an unendurable one, except under compulsion, for some boys. Mrs Gaskell had an ardently devoted son in Milnes who gave his feelings at separation from his mother uninhibited expression on his arrival at school:

Wednesday, September, 1821

My dearest Mamma,
   I am heartily sorry that I am obliged to leave you, you whose sole care has been in endeavouring to improve my understanding and to give me those advantages for which every day I perceive that to you and you alone I am indebted. Oh, dearest light of my eyes, may I again crave of you that you take very, very great care of yourself, for if I lose you I shall not be able to lift up my head or live for a day.[7]

The boys rose at 6.30 and translated Ovid until eight, when there was breakfast of boiled milk and bread. Until eleven they learnt twelve lines of Ovid; from eleven to one there was 'play'. Dinner was at one, and in the afternoon they read English and did sums. At 5.45 supper was served and after prayers there was play until bedtime at eight.

Milnes, in his letters to his mother, seems to have adapted himself to his new condition fairly smoothly; not so another new arrival, a 'very military looking little boy', who had been got up by an adoring mamma to cut a dash, 'with a long handsome tassel hanging by the side of his hat, and olive greatcoat and large tremendous looking cane which he carried'. The sartorial swagger was pathetically misplaced. The child was, Milnes says, 'brokenhearted', suffering such miseries of homesickness that he was allowed to have his dinner by himself in the drawing room 'so that he might compose himself'. However, 'he did not, poor fellow'. Milnes's naturally kind impulses had to give way in the next sentence to the demands of his lively interest in food, which was never far from his thoughts. The unhappy new boy, he told his mother, 'had his choice of hashed hare, roast veal, roast mutton or venison (which we all had), but preferred cold beef . . .' and 'he gobbled it up as fast as a half starved mongrel'. But the heartbroken boy refused to be comforted and presently ran away. He was followed and discovered asleep in an ale-house.

Brought back to school under escort, he was locked in a room reserved for such occasions, before being returned home, a delivery he must fervently have welcomed. 'What alas,' Milnes wrote to his mother 'can such a boy do in the world? I am fond of hashed hare. Tell cook to practise making it. . . .'

Milnes Gaskell's early letters home are useful contributions to a broad picture of boarding-school life at the beginning of the century. He expresses himself with more freedom and informality than was usual at this period in written communication between upper-class children and their parents. At eight he was already rather a prig, writing to his mother of his distaste for the literary 'indelicacies' of Ovid and Tibullus with the precocity of a child accustomed to spending much of its time in the company of attentive and indulgent adults. Of the school's scholastic prodigy, Henry Burton, 'He can make sensible verses and is only six years old,' he advises his mother. 'There's forwardness for you!' He knew how to respond appropriately to adult misconduct. Upon the notorious murder of a Mr Thurthell, 'Two clergymen are engaged in this scandalous affair,' he gasps. 'Two clergymen of the Church of England!'

On the whole Mr Roberts's establishment seems to have been quite a good school by the standards of the day. Milnes had no complaints about the food (the boarding schoolboy's immortal grievance), except at the lack of fruit, for a supply of which he makes urgent application home. Some of the boys had brought their own ponies to school. Milnes's was, he says on 13 December 1823, 'going beautifully', and emulation in this pastime was as feline as any girl's could be. 'Eglinton,' he adds, 'has his pony here, a frightful dun animal which he calls a pretty light bay. Mounted on his pony he scours the country and his groom accompanies him.' In pupil room Milnes managed to do better than average, which was just as well for him. 'My dear Mamma,' he writes, 'Mr Roberts is quite well and scarcely had been in the pupil room half an hour when poor Bonar was flogged for idleness. Kemp at the same time met with the same fate.' Later he reports with natural pride the profitable commendation he was rewarded for his Latin verse by the headmaster. 'Such a composition deserves a reward; ergo I ask you to sit up for supper.' Dr Roberts (a brother of the Eton Fellows, 'Peely' and 'Hog' Roberts)* might have mellowed a little by the time Milnes Gaskell arrived at his school at Mitcham, in 1821. A more forbidding portrait of him is

* See below, p. 121.

painted by the sixth Lord Monson, who had entered the same school more than a decade and a half earlier, in 1804. 'Roberts,' says Monson, 'was the most inflexible disciplinarian I ever met. He seemed not to have a grain of pity in his constitution.' Roberts liked (at least in Monson's time) to teach peripatetically, and he used to wander about the house from room to room, discoursing, or asking questions of the little boys who trotted anxiously after him. For his convenience canes were placed within easy reach along the route, so that at any stage in his progress, he could stretch out a hand to the wainscoting of a wall or a bookshelf, grasp a ready instrument of chastisement and perform 'furiously' summary execution, with scarcely an interruption of the parade.

When to his joy Monson at last left Mitcham and the grim Roberts's ménage, in March 1809, after 'a very melancholy five years', the prevailing convention occasioned him to write a departing verse, *Valete et Plaudite*, in tribute to the virtues of the headmaster, the last six lines of which read:

> Adieu, Ye Groves, my tribute is my tears
> Adieu, thou Shepherd of my early years,
> You cherish in my mind sweet Wisdom's ray
> Ah! Gratitude alone can thee repay.
> Adieu then thrice Adieu, for now I see
> A friend, instructor, Parent, all in thee.

Such was the force of fashion that neither the dedicator (at the time) nor the dedicatee seem to have felt any twinge of incongruity or even irony in the transaction. Dr Roberts received the offering with 'cordiality'.[8]

Altogether Milnes Gaskell seems to have been happy at his preparatory school, but although it aimed to prepare boys for Eton, it did not give him any notion of what to expect at Eton in 1824, or make him better able to ride the kind of turbulence to which he would be exposed. For both Roundell Palmer at Rugby and Milnes Gaskell at Eton ordeals of painful and unexpected initiation lay ahead.

No examination of the 'preparatory school' (the expression was not in contemporary use but is convenient) would be complete without some regard to the letters home of another boy, called Thomas Arnold, writing from his school at Warminster,[9] just over a decade earlier than Milnes Gaskell. The writer's subsequent career gives them an irresistible claim to our attention.

Thomas was a distinctly wilful little boy, ribald when he felt inclined, and given to proffering, in the name of jocularity, unflattering observations on his elder relations, at least the female ones, but quick to wax indignant when he was in a different mood and anyone did not treat him or any judgement he had espoused as seriously as he wished. It was a characteristic which time did not erase.

Both Thomas Arnold and Milnes Gaskell record in sharp focus the unending contest in school life over letters, waged, without essential change, generation after generation, between the boy at boarding school and his relations and friends in the outside world. In part the demands for letters and more letters were genuine *cris de coeur* from exiles who wished to be assured that they were remembered and cherished in thought; in part it became a game played to enhance status, the object being to obtain as many letters as possible in exchange for as few as practicable. Sometimes when duty was done, a writer seemed to be almost overwhelmed by the generosity of his condescension. William Grant to his mother from Rugby, 6 March 1795: 'You see I have filled my paper but without much chit chat or news, tho it cannot be expected for a sixth form Rugby boy to write letters like a lower boy. However, whether upper or lower boy I am your dutiful and affectionate son.'[10]

Not all letters bore good tidings, and there was even letter-writing which was an involuntary act performed under duress:

My Dear Parents,
    We have committed a great sin. For William Denison spat on the usher's back as we went to bed.
    I remain,
    Your affectionate son,

My Dear Parents,
    We have committed a great sin. For we have bought apple tarts without the leave of the Master, when we have plenty to eat and that of the best quality.
    I remain, etc.[11]

Milnes Gaskell, in his precocious way, appealed to reason. 'Tell pappa he shall and must write to me. There are two people to write to one and one to write to two.' Thomas Arnold is cheeky and pert and demands lavish returns for a letter which, after a few lines on having a little garden, goes, 'This is such a stupid place that I can tell you no more news and therefore must conclude.... P.S. Pray tell someone to answer this soon.' Then on 20 August 1804, 'As Frances Arnold has so much leisure I hope she will write to me.... P.S. Please tell one of my sisters to answer this.' Again on 8 September 1804, 'What is the reason Matt never writes to anyone here?'

In fact, almost without exception Thomas's letters contain appeals for more letters. His acknowledgement of letters received is perfunctory. To his sister Frances, in reply to a letter written 'during sermon time', 'if you had disappointed me I should have sent you a *rowing* instead of a thoughtful one'. His own letter, however, must be short because local conditions are not favourable to literary composition.

It is not surprising that some of his letters caused domestic friction. 'I suppose, Aunt,' he wrote in one sally, in March 1807, '. . . that you expect a few compliments to be passed to you; but really, until you can shorten your nose, I must shorten all panegyric on your beauty.' The only criticisms of himself which Thomas seemed to treat with respect, were his occasional excursions into self-criticism with the pleasing opportunities for a display of quotation and rhetoric which they provided. To his former master the Reverend T. Lownes he wrote shortly after leaving Warminster, '. . . my name is frequently on the list of those who *matutinis precibus abfuere*; you see my old fault of laziness still hangs on me.'

We shall follow Thomas Arnold later to Winchester. The letters he wrote from that school would be of value as evidence of the quality of life at an English public school in the early years of the century, even if the writer had not become the most controversial headmaster of the century.

Not all boys were as fortunate as Frank Doyle, Milnes Gaskell and Tom Arnold in the private schools where they were prepared to enter the public schools which had been chosen for them.

The number of private schools greatly increased in the early years of the century, and the majority were operated by cynical or careless or dishonest or incompetent educational quacks, out to turn a quick penny on an expanding market. Without any kind of supervision or visitation from a licensing or governing body, public or private, appalling neglect and ill treatment could be perpetrated against little children whose parents, if they gave the subject any consideration, must have supposed, from the measure of fees paid, that they were doing well for their young. 'An existence among devils,' said Lord Salisbury of his experience at his preparatory school.[12] 'An aristocratic version of Dotheboys' was the description of his preparatory school by Gilbert Bourne.[13]

George Melly made it his business to collect the reports of others as well as recording his own experience at 'Elm-House School'. The headmaster was a kind, weak man who disapproved of corporal punishment, and so parents who shared his views innocently consigned their children to Weston School under the delusion that it must be a kindly place where their little ones' bodies would not be punished. But what the headmaster did not do was more than made up for by the bigger boys who, immune themselves to physical retribution, beat, kicked, pinched, pricked and, in a variety of other ways, oppressed and ill treated their chosen victims in a juvenile jungle community. There was no fagging – officially – so the excesses of despotic unofficial fagging were entirely unrestrained by any law or discipline, and led to scenes which Melly remembered as 'too gross and revolting to be even hinted at'. Sometimes, in extremity, a desperate victim would resort to a knife in his defence. 'On the two or three occasions when such a sight was seen,' says Melly, 'I sat wondering how the elder ones could sit still and see such things. . . . I am unable to understand,' he declares, 'why they did not hold themselves responsible . . . to protect the weak.' But demoralization is a highly infectious condition and there was no remedy from above. The hideous truths could not be uttered nakedly to the headmaster, and when hinted at only drew the bland disengagement of 'boys will be boys and must not mind a little teasing'. One must read between the lines to interpret his hints at 'the existence of much more terrible crimes' which he cannot describe.

Soon afterwards, 'harrassed past endurance and disgusted' by much that he had to see, feeling that he 'was not among gentlemen – scarcely among beings with human sympathies', George Melly took the plunge and ran away from Weston. Fortunately for him he had a sympathetic father who did not return him to the place, and even more fortunately, at his public school, Rugby, he was as happy and grateful as he had been miserable and resentful at his first. Looking back on Weston about twenty years later, he remarked, 'Many of us try and most of us succeed in blotting out such recollections in after life,' and sometimes he could scarcely believe in the reality of the unhappiness he had suffered at that time. But a glance at a child's letters, in a shaky round hand, revive the experience 'that such things really were; and each word strikes some chord which vibrates to an angry feeling'. His motive for publishing his experiences at Weston is not to denounce the private school – 'Nothing induces me,' he said, 'to think it was worse than any other under a similar system'[14] – but by contrast to justify and glorify the public school, upon which we shall hear him, as a votary of the mystic, call down every blessing.

FOUR
Trial by Ordeal

'What's your name? Who's your tutor? Who's your Dame?'* These three questions, with the alternative to the latter of 'Where do you board?', were the inevitable introduction of a new boy to life at Eton; variants were in use according to tradition at Winchester, Harrow, Rugby and Westminster. The examination was the beginning of a course of tests which might be rough or smooth according to many variable circumstances.

William Tucker was brought to Eton by his father in the spring of 1811, at the age of eight and a half. After landing from Thumwood's coach at the Christopher Inn and being entered in Keate's chamber as an Oppidan, he was introduced to his Dame, Mr Hawtrey, in Western's Yard.† William suddenly found himself surrounded by strange boys, large and small, who, after he had answered the three primary questions, bombarded him with detailed inquiries concerning his family and background and kept up 'far from complimentary running commentaries on each'.

Or it might begin, as it does for 'Jim Oxley'‡ on the pavement of Piccadilly, outside the White Horse Cellar and Hatchetts, where Eton boys congregated on the day appointed to return to school, to board in parties the *Quicksilver Mail*, or the *Berkeley Hunt*, or the Bristol

* Everyone, male or female, except classics tutors, who kept a boarding house to accommodate Eton boys, was a 'Dame'. At an earlier date a male Dame had been called a 'Domine'.
† The spelling of this name was later changed to Weston.
‡ 'Jim Oxley' is an invented, probably composite, name given to the story-teller in *Eton Memories*, by an Old Etonian.
  This book is a curiosity. The copy in Eton College Library is inscribed with the interpretative legend, Captain Pelham Bullock. But there is no record of a 'Pelham Bullock' at Eton. There were Pelhams and there were Bullocks. In particular, at the time covered by the narrative, there were Dudley Pelham (a younger brother of Lord Yarborough) and James Turner Bullock ('brother of the late Common Sergeant' says Stapylton) who were contemporaries and together in the Upper Fourth in 1823. Captain the Hon. Dudley Worsley Pelham RN died on active service in 1851. It may be that many years afterwards, James Bullock, then an ancient, arthritic solicitor at Debenham in Suffolk, put together these wistful recollections of happy boyhood at Eton, combining, in a gesture of affection to his long dead 'con', the initial letters of their

Emerald or the *Light Oxford*, driven by the renowned Black Will Bowes. On this occasion the coach is Lillywhite and Moodey's *Original*. It has started from the Bolt and Tun in Fleet Street and its only occupant when it arrives at Hatchetts is a fourteen-year-old boy in deep mourning. Six urchins between the ages of nine and fourteen climb inside with their baggage and, seeing a new face amongst them, turn the usual greeting on him. 'You a new boy? What's your name? Who's your tutor? Who's your Dame?' At first they are inclined to resent the quiet and serious air of the first occupant as a disagreeable dampener upon their own gaiety. Mr Neville, a kindly parent of one of the boys, thinks the sad-faced child is simply homesick and tries to raise his spirits:

> 'Cheer up!' ejaculated Mr Neville; 'here's my son; you'll find him a chip off the old block, once well known at Eton. You must be friends, and if he suffers you to be bullied unjustly, he's none of mine; nor will my friend Fluke there, nor any of your sons of old "Etonians and gentlemen", stand it.'
>
> 'Bravo!' roared Fluke Wilding.
>
> 'Three cheers!' cried Jack Horner.
>
> 'Give us your hand!' vociferated the united voice, led by Hunt maj., who was big enough to '*lick*' the whole 'inside' together with one or two out added.
>
> 'Floreat Etona,' exclaimed Neville, and the oil which he had timely thrown on troubled waters had its full effect.
>
> Quiet being somewhat restored, Mr Neville asked the new boy his name.
>
> 'Fuller,' he replied.
>
> 'Son of John Fuller?' asked Mr Neville, 'once in the 56th and in the West Indies with that regiment?'
>
> The new boy's eyes filled.
>
> 'The same,' he said.
>
> 'A brother officer of mine', continued Neville, 'and an old con.* We were at Eton together. In the same remove! At Dame Durden's too!

continued from page 63

respective surnames, P and B, to represent the identity of the author, or 'editor', the mask much favoured by coy Victorian adventurers into print. Bullock may even have incorporated diaries or other written records of Pelham's in the early part of the text. There are allusions to contemporary naval issues in the midst of juvenile escapades, and the writing is erratic enough in tone and character to suggest an unhomogeneous mixture of source materials. That is one conjecture. Another is that the book may have been published posthumously by a friend or relative who knew enough of the background to unite the dead friends' testaments of youth under the initials PB. Haklyt and Lang, in *English Psendonymous Literature*, ascribe authorship to William Tucker, a quaintly inappropriate and certainly erroneous guess.

* 'con' – probably confidant.

Good fellow! Tell your father Bob Neville saw you off today, and was right glad to make your acquaintance.'

Young Fuller was speechless.

Neville jun. pressed his father's hand as he leaned against the window; and a few hushed words passed between them.

Young Fuller then said, 'My father will never hear your kind message, sir.'

The chain of anecdotes of which this Etonian story consists are of value for the ingenuous candour with which the author displays the Hyde as well as the Jekyll of early nineteenth-century schoolboy cordiality. 'The wheels of the "Original",' says the loving story-teller, 'now gave notice of a move, bearing as plucky and merry six "insides" as could be found in a long day's march, and, as the sequel will prove, as well up to fun as any that could be selected from all the public schools of the United Kingdom.'

The first instance of 'fun' in the sequel is the beating up of a single and helpless and corpulent commercial traveller who at the last minute is pushed into the coach by Harry Bowman the porter, with the words 'only a small parcel, young gentlemen':

'At him!' was the cry, and at the word forty eight fingers and twelve thumbs assailed the covering of the parcel.

'Hard all!' shouted Hunt maj.

'Again and again!' cried Sharp mi.

Fuller forgot his grief, and the ability which he displayed on this occasion secured for him a very high place among his school fellows at the commencement of his Eton career.

'If you are gentlemen, behave as such,' said the assailed, in an imploring tone. 'My name is Settle.'

'We'll settle you,' exclaimed Fluke Wilding. . . .

The beating of the wretched man by the six in concert goes on without pause from Piccadilly to Hyde Park Corner and thence to Kensington Gate, and past the Marquis of Granby (celebrated for its Early Purl*). Battered and frantic, in an attempt to escape, he smashes his head on the roof 'bonneting his face with his damaged

* 'Early Purl' was a beer, sometimes spiced, conventionally drunk by Londoners in the morning as the first drink of the day, and much favoured by porters who, as a class, rose early and drank early. One receipt for Purl prescribes Roman wormwood, gentian root, calamus aromaticus, snake root, horse radish, dried orange peel, juniper berries, seeds or kernels of Seville oranges, all placed in the beer and allowed to stand for some months. A simpler version, hot beer with a dash of gin, became better known as 'dog's nose'. See J. Bickerdyke, *Curiosities of Ale and Beer* (1886), pp. 389, 387.

beaver'. 'Nothing could have been more pitiable than his state'; but pity is not what he receives. When he slips down between the seats his assailants kick and tread on him, while their common ground of classical education enables them to enjoy the jocular simile of Aesop's fable of the 'Bear and the Bees'.

At Hammersmith the desperate man manages, or probably is allowed, to open the door and 'gathering his torn tails of his coat about him and shielding his bruised form as well as he could', he swings himself out just as they are passing Hammersmith Turnpike gate. 'It was a fearful fall,' writes Oxley, but the toll-bar keeper receives the 'parcel' full in front, thereby breaking the force of the shock. 'A victorious cheer bursting from the window increased the speed of the horses. . . .'

Arrived at Eton, the contents of this particular coach divide themselves between the houses kept by Dames Atkins and Middleton, and settle down cheerfully to vocational warfare, waged as conventionally as a medieval campaign. The weapons consist chiefly of large garden squirts, with mouthpieces of extra length to increase their power and accuracy. These are charged with water, ink and various compounds. Peas dried as hard as pebbles, reinforced with coals and chestnuts, provide a formidable armoury.

Oxley himself was not a particularly violent boy, but it was still an age in which there was an abundance of open violence on the surface of life, and a violence not only tolerated, but sanctioned as a necessary evil, if not approved. The exposure of a small boy to the bottom of a public-school hierarchy was itself a hazard charged with violence, often taken with uneasy reluctance by dutiful parents in what were believed to be the ultimate interests of the child. Some boys came to satisfactory terms with the régime more quickly than others; some almost immediately, some never. But it was at this time undoubtedly wilder, rougher and more riotous than anything suggested by Jim Oxley.

'You have no idea how savage the boys are,' Milnes Gaskell wrote to his mother. He had arrived at Eton on 7 May 1824, and after being greeted at his Dame's house with the inevitable questions, the same day he wrote his first letter home. It contains an ominous entry. 'A fellow by the name of Murrell sleeps in the room next to mine and makes furious noises whether he wants the maid or not. "Betsy", balls he, "Betsy, hoi, Betsy", stamping and kicking etc.' Milnes is not favourably impressed by his room, which is 'buggy and gnatty' and (8 May) 'the boys in general swear excessively', especially this same Murrell. 'I do not understand the scandalous words which they alone know the meaning of,' he writes on 9 May, and two days later he alludes to 'the vulgarest, coarsest . . . the most brutal species of swearing in existence'. But by 11 May he has more violent injury than swearing and obscenities to complain of. A boy called Trench who 'is very strong and blustering and rough . . . came into my room yesterday and tore my verses on "Magic" to pieces'. On 13 May he reports:

> I have done derivations yesterday for three or four subsequent lessons of Potia; so Trench said he would break my head if I refused to give them to him and he brought two or three others who compelled me to yield these up and if Mr Knapp asks you for your derivations in school which he often does and you cannot produce them you are flogged. There does not appear to be any use in doing these if you are not allowed by boys stronger than yourself to reap the fruits of your industry.[1]

The anguish in the panting rush of words from her little boy in his cruel new world must have harrowed Mrs Gaskell, who we know was a most loving and solicitous mother. But there is no suggestion anywhere in the letters that she responded, or that Milnes expected her to respond, by either removing him from the school, or by applying to the headmaster for redress or mitigation of his grievances. She had probably learned enough from her own brothers and her husband to know that the latter was beyond the power of the headmaster, while as for the former, it would have been a betrayal of the faith to which he subscribed that the experience of public-school education would prove *in the end* the best training for what was expected of him in life that an English gentleman could receive.

Her conduct is consistent with the attitude of other mothers of her class and her time to the sufferings at school of their sons, even when what might have been considered an excess of hard usage was not unofficial, but magisterial. In a letter to the headmaster of Westminster School, a mother accounting for the lateness of her son's return to school at the end of the holidays explains that the boy's hands were so blistered that he had been obliged to wear kid gloves throughout the holidays, and on the day when he was due to return to school the physician had not judged him yet fit to travel. The cause of the boy's condition was the frequency and severity of the 'handings' he had received. A 'handing', technically a minor punishment at Westminster, was the switching of the back of the hands with a birch by the headmaster at the instance of an assistant master for, it might be, not more than a fault in construing. But the mother was not writing to complain; she was apologizing for the boy's absence.*

Meanwhile, Milnes Gaskell's ordeal continued. His windows were broken, his desk smashed; 'My poor hat,' he reports dolefully, 'has suffered in the wars for Halifax and Murrell have made it their football this morning and tossed it about most cruelly.' The tragic nature of the events deserved, he felt, to be celebrated in classical rhetoric. 'I defy the godess Nemisis [sic] herself,' he declaimed, 'to find out any means of "teazation" which she has not already but too effectively tried.' As far as propriety permits he even indicates the sexual nature of some of his persecutors' interests. 19 May: 'Yesterday evening Trench obliged me to come to his room, where he, Tucker, Brophy and the two Bullocks agreed . . . to break my head if I was not able to answer to their satisfaction all the questions which were to be put to me . . .', questions 'of a sort and nature which it is indeed difficult to conceive'.

His best friend was a victim too: 'Wellesley minor who is quite a little boy and whom I am sorry to say I have seen carried perfectly senseless to his room for the same cause that I was a short time ago.' His only sanctuary was the room of a boy called Hoseason, who was so large and so strong that no one dared interfere with him. Hoseason was a 'queer, easy, goodnatured boy' who 'never learns or writes anything', and confesses that he has not come to Eton to learn but to 'play the fool' and cultivate his interests which he says are 'sporting coves, horses, dogs, ladies, etc.'

Gaskell seems to have been fortunate in his relations with Hoseason, who was himself 'inclined to bully little boys'. The first stages of Tom Hoseason's rake's progress were pathetically charted by Margaretta Brown, the headmaster's sister-in-law, in her diary. Miss Brown felt tenderly protective to this strong, handsome boy (the son of a Suffolk friend) who reminded her of her own beloved dead brother, 'poor William'. William had been a rogue too. Tom Hoseason's career of delinquency at Eton began by his having obtained, as a small boy, tea and sugar in another boy's name and having run away with a tart. He soon graduated to serious mischief. Only a year later he stabbed a boy with a knife in Chapel and when he was fully grown he split open the head of a guard who would not admit him

---

* I have not read the letter, which has been mislaid, but Mr Leslie Spaull, former assistant master and librarian of Westminster School, to whom I am indebted for this information, assured me that he had himself read it.

to a private party. In modern terms Hoseason would be designated a 'criminal psychopath', dangerous to himself and to others in his alternations between apathetic despond and intense excitement. A plausible and uninhibited liar, he did not deceive everyone as he long deceived his hopeful benefactress. The tutor, Dupuis, warned the sisters, Fanny and Margaretta, against 'that vile boy who you all think such a fine fellow – all except for Dr Keate – he is not blind to him. . . .' In those days one was not expelled from Eton for mere 'grievous bodily harm'.* Serious outrages were hushed up (including the stoning unconscious and cerebral injury by Hoseason of a child of four) and, for the rest, Tom was ritually flogged and forgiven almost weekly, while Miss Brown's allusions to him changed from 'dear, sweet boy' to 'dear volatile boy', to 'sad, giddy boy', until Hoseason, in debt far beyond his – or his father's – means, was detected in a serious theft (almost certainly not the first he had committed); as he left Eton for ever, the despairing entry in Miss Brown's diary was just 'Tom Hoseason!' Predictable degeneration followed. A fugitive debtor, he got to India with the help of Lord William Bentinck, whence came news of him there, running off with his dead sister's jewels and selling them, a folly for which he paid with the forfeit of £200 a year his uncle had been paying him. Thirty years after his departure in disgrace from Eton, he was writing begging letters to Miss Brown in, she said, 'the most dreadful state of destitution', soliciting £10 to help save him from 'the work house'.[2] According to Stapylton, Thomas Hoseason died serving in the Bengal Native Infantry.

When Gaskell was in Hoseason's company, his sanctuary was inviolable, but the moment Gaskell was unprotected the persecutors returned to the attack. 'I do not remember having ever been bullied more than I have today,' he wrote home on 15 March 1825, 'and it shows that at Eton it is useless to attempt to get on well. The whole system is one which puts one in a fever.'

Rowles, the harshest of the bullies, was drilling the smaller boys in his house to a point of exhaustion, after the manner of certain kinds of 'killer' sergeant majors. Somehow that was stopped. Rowles next took to riding his victims with spurs and driving them to a 'leap' said Milnes, 'positively impossible to be leapt over with a person on your back'.

---

* It may be recorded to the credit of Dr Wool, Thomas Arnold's predecessor at Rugby, that he was said to have expelled some Rugbeians for rape. See Meriol Trevor, *The Arnolds: Thomas Arnold and His Family* (1973), p. 23.

In addition to his person, his belongings and even his clothes were the targets of his persecutors, who seized one of his new coats and, 'after pulling at it for a long time', succeeded in splitting it all the way up. Milnes wrote on 9 February, 'It is torn so badly that I fear the tailor, Mr Polehampton, will not be able to mend it.'

About this time Mrs Gaskell seems to have been unable to continue to maintain her stoical posture, for Milnes was kept at home for one 'half'. Perhaps she felt that his physical health or his 'nerves' might suffer permanent injury. But he returned later in 1825 to Eton, where we shall hear from him again.

Even allowing for a possible element of dramatic exaggeration, the letters reflect a fairly wild régime; but it would be misleading to suppose that these conditions were peculiarly Etonian. On the contrary, life at Eton, for reasons which will be examined, was on the whole more chivalrous, if not more civilized, than life at its principal rivals. James Lee Warner writes to his mother from Rugby: 'My dear Mamma, The Sunday I am sorry to say is spent if anything worse than other days being spent in talking the vilest indecencies and they try to catch me. . . .' James having been pursued into his study says 'they bully me most dreadfully so that I am not very sorrowful when I have to go into lessons'. They destroy his books, prevent him from studying and make him repeat 'the most horrid words by pretending to know such things as boys ought not to know'.[3]

This letter is chosen from many youthful cries *de profundis* because it occurred *after* the myth of an Arnoldian transforming purification at Rugby, exalted in their hagiographical cults by Stanley and Thomas Hughes.

Like Mrs Gaskell, Mrs Warner could do nothing practical to relieve her son in his misery; and the force of the conventions to which both women felt obliged to submit is, if anything, more impressive in the case of Mrs Warner, because she was a devoutly religious and puritan evangelical. Her only recourse can have been to prayer. At the bottom of her son's tear-stained letter she has written the words 'May the word of God ever be thy safeguard my precious boy.'

What today would be accounted grievous bodily harm, or worse, abounded. Little short of death seems to have been taken much notice of, and not always that.* Hawtrey, the future headmaster of Eton, very nearly died from the effects of injuries inflicted on him by other boys who set upon him at Datchet where he had been visiting rela-

---

* See below, p. 137.

tives. George Keppel's eldest brother, William, did die, it was said, as a result of ill treatment received at Harrow.[4] At Winchester William Tuckwell came within an inch of death at the hands of an oversized psychopath who alternated between friendliness and paroxysms of uncontrolled fury.

> I was sitting up in bed one night doing my Latin verse while he was at his washing stool. Something that I said angered him; he grasped the heavy iron shovel in the fireplace and flung it with all his force. I ducked behind the mahogany writing desk which stood beside me. The missile took off a corner of it as clean as by the stroke of a hatchet. Had my head been there I should not now be recounting the adventure.[5]

'My first experience of roughness and badness at Rugby,' says Joseph Lloyd Brereton, who was at the school in 1839, under Arnold, 'was without mitigation and intensely painful. Within the first few hours I was brutally struck, and might have been almost fatally injured by one of the biggest boys in the school, who was in a state of maddened intoxication.'

Brereton provides one of the very few instances of a boy who went for redress from bullying to the headmaster, and he went direct, by-passing his housemaster Bonamy Prince, a classical scholar of considerable eminence and the future Professor of Political Economy at Oxford, whom he did not like and was unwilling to confide in. 'Prince will not do it in half so straightforward or gentlemanly manner as the Doctor.'[6]

Brereton was a boy of moral courage. He followed an unusual course. But his was an unusual circumstance; he did not go to Rugby until he was eighteen and he was in the sixth form at the time, and some of those harassing him were below the sixth. He obtained his protection at the price of an unpopularity which endured until the end of his schooldays.

Most men bearing scars tended to recall their occasion in the relatively harmless form of gratitude to former protectors. One old man, G. M. Berford, wrote from San Remo to another, William Cotton Oswell, older and famous as a daring explorer:

> I can perfectly remember what a sickly, puny, timid, insignificant lad I was in those long past days; I had never before been to any school and I gratefully remember that you sometimes stood between me and the oppressor. In those days 'all the current of my being set to thee'. It was a case of uncouth Orson and splendid young Valentine. I

believed you to be the handsomest, bravest, most generous of created boys (perhaps I was not much mistaken). Be that as it may, you were my superb young hero, and I have never forgotten you.[7]

Up to now the picture has been harsh and sombre, and all the reports presented are from authentic, once living, voices. Another cross-section of genuine contemporary letters and memoirs of school life in this period would reflect similar experiences. They are true as far as they go, and they go much too far for peace of mind; many anguished letters have been lost or destroyed, and we must allow for the boys who remained silent from pride or lack of sufficient intimacy with their parents, or some other reason, or who sweated the ordeal out stoically. But such letters do not represent a complete picture of the lives of even the unhappiest boys, providing they were allowed to complete a normal cycle of time at school. There would be a sequel to these black days and, usually, the evidence suggests, a happy one. Some school tyrants had themselves at first been bullied; but others who had suffered did not perpetuate the oppressions practised upon them;[8] and again, others were never bullied and enjoyed their school life from the start. A letter written from Winchester on 13 February 1808, by a boy in his first year, reports himself to be 'very well and happy' and even praises the most commonly dispraised element of communal school life. 'Our dinner of mutton [was] some of the best I have ever tasted, which I relish exceedingly.'[9] The writer was Thomas Arnold, whom we have already heard from at his preparatory school at Warminster. Just over three decades later a boy, William Adams, writing home from his first term at Rugby which had become famous under the headmastership of Thomas Arnold, declared, 'We have pretty good studies and I have with me a very nice fellow. They do not see our letters and we may write as often as we like. I am as happy as a king.'[10]

Such ecstatic delight is rare *early* in school life. A letter probably written by Walter Congreve, who entered School House at Rugby in 1839, hits a more common note from a boy in his first term. It is addressed to 'Dearest Papa and Mamma' and, after some gentlemanly compliments, desires his 'thanks conveyed to Cookie . . . for the *capital* plum cake'. He continues: 'I and Proctor had a topping spread in our den last night when we both opened our hampers and he had some murphies from the tuck shop.' There is a further piece of cheerful intelligence. 'This week I did much better at arithmetic and didn't have the birch once.' At the bottom of the page is an observation frequently recurrent in boys' letters: 'It's very cold here.'[11]

The woe suffered by Anthony Trollope at Harrow and Winchester has passed into literature by way of his autobiography. His elder brother Thomas, more robust in body and spirit than his better-known junior, also had an enduring hatred of his days at Harrow, where he was sent until the vacancy secured in college at Winchester should ripen. But part of the reason for the Trollope brothers' unhappiness at Harrow was that they were day boys – the kind of pupils whom John Lyon's bequest was designed to serve; but, with the social metamorphosis of Harrow from another grammar school into a rival of Eton's, the reigning grandees, the paying boarders, insulted and persecuted the day boys on principle, viewing their presence among their betters as an insulting reminder of the school's humble origins which might otherwise be forgotten. There was no such 'snobbery' at Winchester, Thomas tells us. On the contrary, the 'scholastic dignity' of the college boys made *them* an élite, and the physical conditions of their environment were better than the commoners.'

The distinction of classes, or class sub-divisions composing the school, varied in practice by tradition. Collegers (foundation scholars, or king's scholars) and Oppidans (boys not on the foundation) existed at Eton as separate societies, the latter being treated not only by tradesmen,* but by the assistant masters[16] (themselves former Collegers) as superior in social rank. At Winchester Foundation Scholars and Commoners lived separate lives with little feeling of shared allegiance, but there was no social subordination of one to the other.[17] At Rugby a not impassable gulf divided boarders and day boys;[18] at Harrow a wider one separated the two tribes and class hostility was peculiarly virulent.[19]

The translation from Harrow to Winchester was a happy one for Thomas. But this does not mean that Winchester, in distinction from Rugby and Harrow, was a community of sweetness and light. It means that Thomas was lucky in the conjunction of circumstances governing his situation; not Winchester alone, but the time of his admission, his particular contemporaries and the master to whom he was subject, suited his temperament. Also his wretched father

---

* '. . . the Gentlemen (as the tradespeople had the impertinence to call the Oppidans)';[12] 'The system of fagging in College is such as no gentleman's son ought to undergo.'[13] 'The evidence of a feeling of class distinction between Oppidans and Collegers at Eton is strong, and sometimes partisan.'[14] But one witness at least, with long personal experience of Eton, denies that there was any distinction whatever.[15]

managed somehow to pay his bills. To do the same for his younger
son was beyond his power, and Anthony's experience of Winchester
was, accordingly, radically different from his brother's:

> My college bills had not been paid, and the school tradesmen who
> adminstered to the wants of the boys were told not to extend their
> credit to me. Boots, waistcoats and pocket handkerchiefs, which with
> some slight surveillance were at the command of other scholars, were
> closed luxuries to me. My schoolfellows of course knew that it was so,
> and I became a Pariah. It is the nature of boys to be cruel. I have
> sometimes doubted whether among each other they do usually suffer
> much, one from the other's cruelty; but I suffered horribly! I could
> make no stand against it. I had no friend to whom I could pour out
> my sorrows. I was big, and awkward, and ugly, and, I have no doubt,
> skulked about in a most unattractive manner. Of course I was ill-
> dressed and dirty. But, ah! how well I remember all the agonies of my
> young heart; how I considered whether I should always be alone;
> whether I could not find my way up to the top of that college tower,
> and from thence put an end to everything?[20]

The great public schools prided themselves on their classlessness of
social intercourse and indifference to rank. Charles Wilkinson cites
with piety the case of 'a noble Lord, who,' he says, 'lived and died
beloved and respected by all who knew him, old and young, high
and low, rich and poor, who always thanked Eton for its democratic
system of taking the shine out of him, and making him pocket his
pride and dignity, which had been instilled into him by an over-
loving mother and over-obsequious dependants, but which he himself
said was literally kicked out of him'.[21] Wilkinson had in mind the
Marquess of Londonderry as the kicked, and the Reverend William
Rogers* as the kicker. The kicker's version of this *acta sacra* deserves
consideration:

> When we came back at the beginning of one half there appeared at
> my dame's a smart boy dressed in a light blue jacket, faced with velvet,
> white trousers and waistcoat, with a turned down collar and frills. I
> spotted him and at once put the question – 'What's your name,' and
> 'Who's your father?' He replied, 'I am Charles Stuart Vane, Viscount
> Seaham, and my father is the Marquis of Londonderry.' Upon receipt
> of this information I kicked him three times, once for Vane, once for
> Seaham and once for Londonderry. I do not vouch for this story. It is

---

* 'Hang theology Rogers': a vigorous and influential proponent of popular secular education.

a very old story. As a matter of fact I do not believe it. But I heard
the late Lord Londonderry tell it so often that I am afraid he did.

Whether the anecdote was apocryphal or authentic, Rogers himself
affirmed that it was not uncharacteristic of real life and 'illustrative
of the absence of any false standard of worth' at Eton at that time.
'Of tuft hunting in the modern sense there was none. . . . We were
all boys together in a genuine and honest English way. . . . The power
of the purse was an unknown factor amongst us, and the boy who
came from home with two or three pounds to last him as pocket
money all through the half could be and was happy as one who
commanded large sums.'[22]

Any big school is a mixed deal of human nature and of course not
every boy acquired the grace and modesty which the kicker and the
kicked appear to have done. Some were as odious as their fathers
must have been, but at Eton they did tend to be nailed quickly by
public opinion, like the arrogant and dissipated boy, 'proud without
property, sarcastic without being witty, ill temper he mistakes for
superior carriage, and haughtiness for dignity'.[23] There is no evidence
of class animosity at Eton at this time, except in the factional rivalry
between Oppidans and Collegers. An individual was not derided as
'Buttons' as he was at Rugby, because his father was a button
merchant.[24] Nor, if your father was a grocer, were you 'beaten for his
sake'[25] as at Charterhouse.

But while a liberal order of social equality prevailed, subject to
certain qualifications, at Eton, and in varying degrees at the other
public schools, its spirit did not extend beyond this fellowship to those
who were, and were described as, 'outsiders', and most especially to
'outsiders' who aspired to become 'insiders'. In a cosy and affectionate letter from one Old Westminster to another – both being
clergymen – the writer reminds his former schoolmate how their
friendship, 'firm, sincere and discriminating as it is – is but one
among thousands of like kind – begun, cemented and consolidated
at a great Public School'. A few lines later he adverts to how judicious
discrimination was exercised in the event of an unsuitable entry into
the school:

> You cannot but remember the sturdy flaxenhaired pot boy whom an
> ambitious and aspiring publican sent to Westminster in our times, as
> a qualification, doubtless for the *bar*. He was neither bullied nor beaten.
> But he was taught, by unequivocal lessons from those he wished to

make his playmates, that he had been missorted, and the blunder was rectified in little more than three months after its commission.[26]

The account is given without sign of regret or uneasiness, but with an undisguised approval and satisfaction: 'And so it should ever be with such as intrusively flock. . . .' There was nothing of value to be lost from crops 'produced from unnaturally transplanted slips'. Nor advantage to be gained by having 'any gifted (such I believe is the present technical word) chimney sweep . . . dragged by a sickly philanthropist from his sootbags to literature'. Once in a century, perhaps, 'prodigies might in truth occur'* but 'the Mechanics institutes and the London University' were 'now sufficient safety valves'. Only mischief could ensue from 'bringing into undue contact and unnecessary collision those between whom an almost impassable gulph is to be fixed as soon as they cease to be schoolboys'. There was no impropriety in the mixing of boys destined for the 'liberal professions' with boys 'from our highest nobility' for all were of the same *caste* and could continue to consort together in afterlife; indeed, the former, 'by the successful execution of their talents may, and often do, become enrolled among that privileged order'.

We have here the osmotic process by which a group protects the value of its identity from 'debasement' and the solidarity of its character from dissolution. In most cases the boys, as a commonality, were not rejecting another on principle, but reacting self-protectively by instinct to the alien signals which he emanated. Given the social constitution prevailing, the action was natural. One of the purposes of a public school was to guard its charges against 'those habits of faulty pronunciation, against those vulgar and offensive tones in reading and speaking which it is afterwards so contemptible to retain and so difficult to correct'.[27]

Old men kept in touch and visited each other to relive in detail the contests and adventures of school life. Physical courage in the mêlée – the Rugby scrum – whatever Dr Arnold may have taught in the sixth form – was the virtue most highly regarded by Rugbeians as a tribe, and culpable defaulters were neither forgotten nor excused after an interval of seventy years. In long talks at Newington between Tom Hughes and his contemporary, Sir Alexander Arbuthnot, they recalled and denounced the pusillanimity of another boy, notwith-

---

* The example of Porson, the great eighteenth-century scholar, was too gigantic to be disregarded.

standing the headmaster had thought fit to exalt him to the morally rarefied air of the sixth form. 'Even then I thought him rather unscrupulous and cruel,' reflected Arbuthnot, 'but what had always struck me was his want of physical endurance in the scrimmage at football; he would always get out of it if he could manage to do so. Tom Hughes' recollections agreed with mine. He well remembered his brother Charles (who was small for his age) extracting the football from the densest of scrimmages and running with it until overhauled by some bigger boy.' Worship of field games, even of one particular game, which began to be cultivated in the time of Hughes and Arbuthnot, tended to narrow the recognition of honourable merit to prowess at the favoured game, and votaries were puzzled when they found that a contemporary who had shown little zest for their sacred sport afterwards distinguished himself in a way which could not be ignored. Arbuthnot and Hughes in their nostalgic reminiscences agreed that they were both surprised by the reputation which their contemporary, Hodson, had achieved as a bold and dashing soldier. 'The opinion which both of us had formed of him as a schoolboy had not at all prepared us for the feats which he accomplished in afterlife. We could neither of us call to mind having seen him in the thick of a scrimmage at school. He was generally hovering outside, looking out probably for the chance of running with the ball.'[28] There is even a touch of censure in their concession to achievement.

On the whole, old late-Victorians' memories of early or pre-Victorian school life remained vivid, and the pulse of feeling strong and sometimes passionate, a long lifetime later; but sometimes inevitably there were, after long intervals, errors of identification. The Rev. W. G. Rowstorne writes to Arbuthnot: 'My cousin Archdeacon Rowstorne had just sent me your letter of May 21 from which I can see that your recollection of him and me are rather mixed, but most of those contained in your letter refer to me. He is four years younger than me, and when I left Rugby in October 1838, he was a boy of fourteen at Lee's house, and a good way below the Sixth. William Rea (Billy whom you mention) was an exact contemporary and a great friend of mine. We went to Oxford together straight from Rugby, in 1838, on the Rugby coach (the 'Pig') – do you remember that old name? – and were upset together, and one man, a stranger, killed, and one of our party, Whateley, whom perhaps you remember, a nephew of the Archbishop got a bad knock on the head, which however he survived, and I believe he is now living as a clergyman in Yorkshire. . . .'

Thereafter the right Rowstorne and Arbuthnot not only kept up their correspondence but visited each other's houses, and in July 1900, discovering that one of their old form mates, Fred Gell, was still alive and Bishop of Madras, residing in retirement in the Neilgherry Hills, they concocted a letter of greeting for old times' sake:

> Dear Lord Bishop
> We two old Rugbeans who were your school fellows and form fellows long ago, being this today together in the same house, desire to bring ourselves to your remembrance and to send you our kindest regards and best wishes that by God's mercy your remaining days, like the rest of your life, may be passed in happiness and peace.
> We are, dear Gell,
> Yours most sincerely,
> Alexander J. Arbuthnot
> W. E. Rowstorne.

The partners received the following reply:

> My Dear Old Friends,
> I was immensely pleased with your kind remembrance of me expressed in your joint letter, and return my thanks and best wishes to you both in Browning's beautiful lines, which Robert Clark, Punjab missionary, sent me last February, three months before his death.
>
> > 'Grow old along with me
> > The best is yet to be,
> > The last of life for which the first was made
> > Our times are in his hand
> > Who saith, A whole I planned
> > Youth shows but half, trust GOD, see all, nor be afraid.'
>
> and in faithful promise 'Even to old age I am He, and even to hoar hairs will I carry you. . . . I am his the same yesterday and today and for ever.'
> I have not the strength to make another voyage to England, and expect to end my few remaining days in this charming station, looking for the better home where I hope we shall all meet in glory.
> Your affectionate friend,
> F. Gell, Bishop

The reply, although 'a very nice one', was not in all respects found satisfactory by the recipients. Rowstorne remarked, 'from the absence of Rugby allusions, I guess that his recollections of the old place are not so keen as those of the other two *boys*'. When Gell died in 1902, and three years later the *Memorials of Bishop Gell* were published, Sir Alexander Arbuthnot 'did not allow a few inaccuracies in his references to Rugby to go uncorrected'.

The pleasures of this kind of correspondence for the livelier members were inevitably clouded, as they had been for Clavering, by the tendency of letters to become obituaries. In August of the same year, W. L. Bevan, Archdeacon of Brecon, wrote to Arbuthnot. 'There is nothing I so much regret as having lost sight of old school-fellows, very much in consequence of the remoteness of my abode and my addiction to my parochial duties. Bradley I have seen pretty regularly: he has always been a creaking hinge, and it is wonderful that he has held on so long; but now he looks somewhat decrepit. Lushington, whom you remember, succumbed to the dense fog which occurred last October, and which also proved fatal to my brother-in-law, Dew (of Anstey's) about a couple of years your senior, who happened to be staying in London at that time.'[29]

At its strongest, the mystic could still enforce ties as strong as the bonds of blood. When Colonel Clavering, feeling himself to be approaching death, made a supreme effort and dictated a last letter, it was to say farewell to his former classmate John Benn.[30] In these magnetic fields a breach of allegiance was the unforgivable; and defection, especially if it was due to pride in worldly advancement, drew upon the offender enduring odium.

In practice at a public school, or, at least, at Eton and Winchester, a boy would have a fair chance of being accepted, whatever his father's rank, provided he showed no blatant blemishes in manners or address, and was prudent, modest, tactful and a quick learner; in short if he did not attract displeasure by making himself prematurely conspicuous. As the historian, Charles Pearson, recalled, looking back at his own days at Rugby, 'Much . . . depended upon the boy whether he was a victim or not. I remember in the first form I was in there was a boy of rare promise. He came out head of the class though he was by far the youngest in it, and might have seemed especially liable for bullying, as he was a "swat" – that is a conscientious worker – and a town lout – that is, living with his widowed mother in the town, and not – as a gentleman was supposed to do – in a boarding house. I believe the boy was never touched or spoken to except in kindness thanks to a certain quiet charm of manner which he possessed.'[31]

But if a boy's personality found disfavour with his seniors, or worse, with his contemporaries, neither rank nor intelligence could protect him from reprisals; and independence of mind and spirit in a junior was regarded and punished, perhaps at Winchester more keenly than elsewhere, as an aberration of peculiar depravity. There is, indeed, an arguable case for calling Winchester, at its *worst*, the most sinister of the schools. Rugby and Harrow were both brutal, with their initiation ceremonies of boys running the gauntlet between rows of executioners armed with knotted handkerchiefs, or having to endure being stoned with rolls baked as hard as pebbles; and Westminster was perhaps the most savage of all, because of the challenge the boys had to learn to meet on their doorstep from notoriously the roughest element in London. But at Winchester (and Westminster) the cruelties were more formal, carefully thought out, ritualistic as became a collegiate foundation with ancient sacerdotal associations. There was the venerable institution of 'tin gloves'. 'It was conveniently supposed,' says the Rev. William Tuckwell, looking back to the 1840s:

> that a junior's hand doomed 'ferre inimicus ignem', to grasp hot handles of coffee pots, broilers, frying pans, would be hardened by a process of searing with a 'hot end' or burning brand of wood and to this ordeal every junior was submitted. I kicked and struggled I remember when I saw Hubert preparing his implement:
>
> > Heat we these irons hot
> > And bind the boy which you shall find with me
> > Fast to the chair.
>
> But I was captured and my hand held fast and I can still recall the grinding thrill of pain as the glowing wood was pressed upon it by the ministering fiend. It was the prologue to the continuous barbarity which was to walk up and down with me . . . a year at least of college.[32]

James Warner was subject to a peculiarly vile practice associated with an otherwise harmless initiation ritual called 'Lamb Singing', then in vogue at Rugby. New boys were required to stand on a table in turn and sing a song of their own choice. If the performance was approved that was the end of the business; but if a majority of judges gave thumbs down, the singer was penalized by having to drink 'a brimmer of muddy water crammed with salt'. In effect the song and the singing were irrelevant to the outcome, which was no more than an expression of favour or disfavour for the subject on trial. Boys forced to swallow the noxious potion could be ill for days. One does not know how serious some of its effects in fact have been, for in the event of graver complications evidence of the origin would have been religiously suppressed. After swallowing the foul draught James Warner collapsed and 'speech was gone for an hour'. His throat was 'as if it had been skinned and eight cups of tea, four mugs of milk and as many of water' were consumed, but his comrades were afraid to let him drink any more.[33] Another boy was so ill that he was off work and prostrate for days, but the cause of his condition does not seem to have been seriously inquired into and adult authority did nothing then or later to put down the evil. It is in a sense encouraging that the enforced drinking was brought to an end by the boys themselves when a public opinion formed that not only was the practice depraved, but its victims were commonly boys who turned out to be voted later especially 'decent fellows'.

Fire was used to roast boys, as described in *Tom Brown's Schooldays*. What does not appear in that book is the use at Rugby of the opposite element, water, to provide sport. Anstey's Hole, notorious for its depth and mud, was the place of execution. Albert Pell, whose acquaintance we have already made, took part at Rugby in the sport, and remembers 'a most exciting seizure of a Liverpool boy whose aversion to water was constitutional'. He was 'of palish green complexion, much marked with small-pox and stood on unusually large feet'. Having been surrounded and captured he made 'a most resolute resistance to our proposal to take him down town and across the meadows'. Shop windows at Rugby were protected by shutters on hinges opening back against the outer wall where they were held by iron catches. The boy, forcing himself and the 'press gang' against these walls, made desperate efforts to stop progress by clutching at the shutters as he was dragged along, and as they slammed to one after the other against the windows they brought the inhabitants to the door with indignant cries of 'shame' and exclamations of pity. 'All these,' says Pell, 'added to the enterprise and excited us to quicker and more remorseless action.' The town was cleared, the meadows and stile hurried over till the stream was reached. At the sight of the clear water 'a paralytic submission succeeded resistance and clothes were stripped off with very little loss of buttons'.

Physically passive, the boy continued to plead with his captors for mercy, but their excitement only increased as they approached the climax of the sport; and 'the terrified and now naked creature' was seized by the arms, legs and neck and with practised skill was thrown clear of the bank and the bordering hedges. As the child flew through the air 'between the swing and the splash' he had one moment to utter the cry, 'Lord receive my soul.' Recalling the occasion many years later as an old man, Pell asked himself, 'What must have been the agony to cause such a cry?' and he does not seem sure of the answer even then.[34] He was not an imaginative man and *he* enjoyed swimming.

At Harrow, tossing in a blanket was a favoured ordeal, as there was no suitable water conveniently near. This need not, but could, be hurtful. An Etonian witness, the Rev. Charles Allix Wilkinson, remembers that a small Oppidan, Sir John Bligh,* used to go into Long Chamber and ask the bigger Collegers to toss him for fun.[35] But there was always an element of risk. Rowland Williams was dropped through the clumsiness of one of the tossers and was scalped when his head brushed the edge of an iron bedstead.[36] Tucker, a contemporary of Wilkinson's in Long Chamber, gives a contradictory account of tossing. He says that it was then used at Eton to terrorize, and that it was employed to accelerate the interrogation of suspects after a disgraceful trick had been played on a boy called Pratt. Both accounts could be true; tossing might be agreeable in one set of circumstances but not in another.

At Harrow it was, whatever else, an initiatory ordeal when a boy was moved from one form to another in the lower school, and a certain number of bumps on the ceiling were required to validate the ceremony. It was succeeded by a barbarous custom of 'pinching in'; the new boy had to subject himself to the fraternity pinching the new member, a right 'limited only by the tenderness of their dispositions' and the strength of their fingers, and 'adepts who had studied and taught others tenderest places and the most artistic mode of taking hold carried this evil knowledge with them from form to form. By the time the tossing stage was reached the more vulnerable subjects might be frantic with pain and fear. A small boy sought refuge in the chimney and was dragged out choking with soot and almost insane with terror.'[37]

Traditions of suicide committed in intolerable anguish of spirit are sombre threads winding through the weave of school history and mythology. The words of the Winton song 'Dulce Domum' were said to have been carved on the bark of the old Domus tree by a boy before he took his life. Anthony Trollope says that he contemplated suicide at Winchester,[38] and Rich says that there were two attempts

---

* Sir John Duncan Bligh, KCB, Minister at Hanover, Fellow of All Souls. At Eton he was Captain of Oppidans and of the Boats, and in the XI.

at suicide in his time.[39] Such evidence may indicate little more than the stress of adolescence; but sinister reports did leak from the confines of Winchester. They were known to Jane Austen who wrote with whimsical relief, on Monday, 16 December 1816, to her favourite nephew Edward (J. E. Austen Leigh) after she knew that he was safely translated out of Winchester into young adulthood:[40]

> One reason for my writing to you now is that I may have the pleasure of directing you Esqre. I give you joy of having left Winchester. Now you may own how miserable you were there; now it will gradually all come out, your crimes and your miseries – how often you went up by the Mail to London and threw away fifty guineas at a tavern, and how often you were on the point of hanging yourself, restrained only, as some illnatured aspersions on poor old Winton has it, by the want of a tree within some miles of the city.*

One observation must be made in favour of Eton. Although unlawful bullying could occur there as elsewhere, there is no sign of the quasi official atrocity, like 'tin gloves' at Winchester, or 'Lamb Singing' at Rugby, or the stylized kicking ordeals at Westminster. There are the cruel outrages as elsewhere, like the branding of the future Lord Denman with a hot poker when he refused to make a speech for the amusement of some older boys. But that was an isolated atrocity, not part of a pattern.

In their efforts to prevent change, the beneficed incumbents enjoyed the support of two widely separated parties, the very young, the present boys, who were fiercely conservative, and the very old, the 'Old Boys', who clung with nostalgic passion to sacred memories, reinforced, wherever possible, by boyhood friendships.

In an historically interesting and significant unpublished letter, a parent and Old Westminster gives his opinion that it is useless to expect the rank and file of schoolboys to acquaint authority with their wrongs and the crimes of bullies. Fear and the force of taboos and of prevailing codes of supposed honour are too strong. The letter's significance is an early, clear expression of certain changes of attitude which were beginning to occur as the century approached

---

* Jane Austen shows an ambiguous bias against public schools and their products. In *Sense and Sensibility* her hero's coxcomb of a brother has been to school at Westminster, and he ascribes his elder brother's lack of initiative (as he sees it), social and professional, to his not having followed the same course, but instead having been educated privately by a tutor. The basis of Jane Austen's never explicit preference may be wholly rational, but it should be noted that her father, as the tutor of boys who might otherwise have gone to a public school, had a competitor's interest in the appraisal.

the halfway mark. Positive concepts of reform were being asserted with a new confidence; among them the arguments for closer protection and supervision of the young at school, even if this meant interfering with venerable patterns of precedent, when these showed signs of failure or abuse, and for the parents' right to expect school authorities to intervene in traditional practice when abuses were discernible. Expression of the ensuing change of standards would be likely to be directed first at the weakest link in the chain, and the weakest link had become what had once been the strongest, Westminster; while the weakest link in the internal constitution of Westminster was now what had also once been the strongest, the Foundation. The precipitous decline of Westminster from its seventeenth-century pre-eminence began at the end of the eighteenth century and reached its nadir about 1840. It was due to a conjunction of causes. One was the expansion of London, the increase of factories and building development around the school which invaded the once open Tothill and Battersea fields without improving the social quality of an area which had been for centuries an infamous criminal quarter, and would later be called by Dickens 'Hell's Kitchen'. The new and primmer concepts of gentility were sensitive to such environmental considerations. In addition the cult, or 'prejudice', in favour of country air over 'unwholesome' London air, was in circulation. Eton had flourished as never before in the favour of George III. Westminster had grown unfashionable. Morale declined correspondingly and a symptom of deterioration was the weakening of lawful authority and a freer rein than ever for the bully.

It was in this state of affairs that the Rev. Allen Cooper, himself an Old Westminster, addressed his letter on bullying in college to the headmaster, Dr Williamson.[41] Cooper is throughout courteous; his anger is under control. He is not going to make specific complaints or mention names, but simply, he says, 'to assure you that what is feared by the world . . . and what deters so many parents from sending their sons to Westminster with the view of entering College is founded on just grounds'. A good deal of what occurs might be prevented, he suggests, if form masters and the Dames of the boarding houses 'were to look at the countenances of the boys a little more minutely than they do'. A parent, he suggests, 'has some little ground of complaint when he sees the face of his son disfigured, or his hand mutilated, or it may be his legs lamed and that no notice of the circumstances has been taken by the master of the form or the dame of the house'. Such cases as these had happened during the last year.

In seeking the perpetrators of such savagery it would be worse than useless asking the boy himself the cause of his appearance. The captains and monitors should be required, as a point of honour, to investigate a case of ill treatment and 'to give up the name of the offender'; it might 'deter many a hasty spirit from the too hasty application of his feet', while it would also 'operate as a check upon the captains and monitors themselves who are often as much at fault as others'. The crux of the innovation is in the last phrase. It was not only unlawful bullying which was to be investigated, but the system in general of government through the top boys of the school.

The appeal had no immediate effect. Soon afterwards Dr Williamson was himself blamed for much that had gone wrong with the school when an investigation was held by official visitors, and Williamson departed. His successor had a mind closer to Cooper's, and one of his hardest battles was to be not against ordinary lawbreakers, but against officers and monitors of the sixth form who believed that they were bound by no law but their own. The letter is an historic signpost pointing to an issue which, although distant, was already discernible enough to be controversial. At Eton the little Colleger Hawtrey, who had nearly died under ill treatment, grew up to become headmaster, and tried to improve the conditions of life of the younger boys, especially those little Collegers in the Long Chamber. He declared that wanton ill treatment could cause 'lasting sensations of bitterness'; and there were two cases he remembered with particular vividness. He does not mention the victims by name, but one was Sidney Walker and the other was the poet Shelley, and their suffering occurred 'when I was too young to feel and understand what I do understand now'. The talents of one, 'however abused, earned for him a reputation which will probably not perish while our language is spoken'. But the boyhood of the poet was made miserable, his mind was 'tortured' with a 'wantonness of persecution' which Hawtrey believed had contributed to 'pervert' its 'noble qualities'.[42] Yet, despite this strong feeling, when the time came, Hawtrey found it very difficult in practice to amend a system over which the headmaster's powers were limited. The headmaster of Eton was himself answerable to a provost and fellows who were unqualifiedly conservative in all things, apprehending that any change would be to their disadvantage. 'No innovation' remained the watchword.

FIVE

Fags and their Masters

The fag and his master were interdependent members of a traditional system which had evolved, unplanned, out of antiquity. They were meant to serve each other for the discipline of the community. The fag performed duties required by the master; and the master protected and watched over the fag. That was the principle. For an explanation of the origin of the system, one does not have to look further than the shortage of servants,* and, in the civil wars, to the shortage of masters. In Keate's time of succession at Eton in 1809 the headmaster had seven, rising to nine, assistants for the instruction and control of 515 boys. If the society of a public school in the eighteenth century were not to dissolve into boiling anarchy, some power had to be allowed to the older and more responsible boys. Etonians would contend, then and later, that there were no prefects nor prefectorial government at Eton. This is true only inasmuch as the word 'prefects' was not in use. The sixth form at Eton, captains of houses and grades of sport (paramount being the Captain of Boats), held similar powers to those conferred on senior boys called prefects and monitors at other schools. Addressing a rather frisky remove (including Gaskell) in June 1824 on the subject of 'insubordination', Dr Keate reminded them that the sixth form was authorized to punish them, a practice which was already in daily and continuous use. Later in the century the orthodox view of the prefectorial system was that it was the 'system alone' to which 'we can look for an adequate counterpoise of the physical strength of the bullies'.[1] Dean Farrar approved along the same lines. 'Supposing there were no monitors about what would be the state of the school? Above all what would be the condition of

---

* The Commissioners, in their Report on the Public Schools (1864), invited the attention of the Dean and Chapter of the Collegiate Church of St Peter to the manifest need of additional servants to relieve the junior boys of some of the menial offices which almost of necessity fell to their share.

the younger and weaker boys? They would be the absolutely defence-less prey of the most odious tyranny.'[2]

Oppidan fags' duties at Eton varied in weight according to the house and the master. At Atkins, his Dame's, Milnes Gaskell had to set the table, run down to 'Crips' for ham, bacon, bread and chocolate and such delicacies, and then receive several blows on his return from the frightful 'Morrell' because he had not been quick enough. He had to boil eggs for Taunton, fetch up the rolls, butter, etc., and then was generally employed in the servile offices of brushing Halifax's clothes and cleaning his shoes. When he moved to Okes's house, fagging was comparatively light. All he had to do was in the morning and evening to 'fetch up Egerton Major's kettle and make tea'. Egerton Major had three fags, one got the milk, another the kettle, and another the rolls and butter, and unless the master gave them any further orders their duties were done. 'Egerton Major,' James Milnes remarked, 'certainly has an authoritative manner of speaking, but he's very kind.'

In the collegiate institutions of Winchester, Eton and Westminster, the regimen in college among the foundation scholars, whatever they were called, was distinct and apart from the rest of the school in many respects and, in general, living conditions and discipline were more severe and consistent.

Men who had passed through the experience often differed in assessing the benefits and injuries it might cause, but on the point of its hardship nobody disagreed. 'Inexpressibly hard,' said Tucker,[3] without a trace of self-pity. 'As hard, and as barbarous as the treatment of the negroes in Virginia,' said a Westminster.

In one long dormitory forty boys at Westminster and fifty boys at Eton in Long Chamber between the ages of nine and nineteen would be locked up at night and left without supervision till morning, a 'free', self-contained, self-governing community, with its own class system, moral standards, public opinion and legal code. The physical condition of the environment was not so much primitive as decayed. Nothing changed generation after generation except as it broke or wore away. Rough beds were covered (at Eton) with a thin flock mattress which was expected to last eleven years; the rest of the bedding was three thin blankets, a sheet, bolster (no pillow) and a woollen horse rug, woven in long worsted string, for counterpane. Beside each bed was a 'universal desk', with folding leaves disclosing a shelf and pigeon holes; below, doors opened into a side cupboard. It was a 'stand-up' desk. No chairs were provided. Collegers were not supposed to sit down. But a few senior boys obtained and were allowed chairs. Through cracks in the walls and unrepaired windows swept the winter draughts of icy wind, and at Westminster, when the weather approached freezing point, juniors were roused in the middle of the night to pitch buckets of water down the length of the dormitory for a slide in the morning. This was preferable to having a bucket of water poured down one's back, not for any wrong done, but merely, on the whim of a senior, to toughen up a junior. The Prince Regent, attending a performance of one of the plays in Latin for which Westminster was famous, passed through the dormitory and, looking about him, exclaimed in disbelief to the master escorting him, 'You don't mean to tell me, sir, that Arthur Paget* ever slept in one of those beds.'[4]

Partisans of the ordeal of College extolled the hardships as 'that preparation for the roughening of actual life' which was one of the 'advantages of public school training'; 'the best preparation for the hardships and disappointments of life was the life of a great public school'. Diehards went further and claimed that only the ordeal of College stood between England and decadence. 'Were it not for the dormitory at Westminster and the quarter deck of a man of war, we should be a nation of macaronis,' said Dr Barrow,[5] quoting an admiral.

Okes recalls that when he went up to Cambridge he had no difficulty in obtaining a favourable policy when he applied to the University Life Insurance officers. Anyone who had passed eight years of his youth in Long Chamber and was alive at the age of twenty-nine was deemed a fairly safe life.

Even loyal Etonians were uneasy about the survival of the institution. 'There is no exaggeration in saying that some of the best men I have ever known ran a considerable risk of becoming the worst from the ordeal of Long Chamber as I remember that famous dormitory.'[6]

If any one of the three had to be distinguished as the 'hardest' life for fags it would probably have been Westminster, though Collegers at Eton would never have conceded it priority. At a slightly later date the old dormitory at Westminster was described by a former occupant as 'not much better for juniors than the Casuals in a "union" workhouse'.[7] A fag in college had to begin to call his master at three or four a.m. and thereafter at intervals till early breakfast. He wore a college waistcoat of peculiar pattern, designed to contain

---

* Sir Arthur Paget (1771–1840), diplomatist and courtier.

the objects he must be able to produce at all times on demand: two penknives, two pieces of india rubber, two pencils, two pieces of sealing wax; two pieces of pen string, two 'dips' (little globular ink bottles), two dip corks, two wedges, two pieces of gutta-percha (for the points of foils) and any number of pens, plus a portfolio containing quatrens of paper. Much of a fag's leisure hours were spent running errands for his masters or on 'station', that is, attending games in the Green in Great Dean's Yard, or on a rainy day in College. He might be fagged to fight one of the 'barbarians' or 'Skis' (derived from Volsci) from 'thieving lane' beyond the pale, against whom Westminster boys waged continuous warfare. Any Ski who ventured into Dean's Yard was engaged in medieval fashion in single combat. If the intruder was a heavyweight, one of the bigger boys attacked him; if he was smaller game a junior about his match was ordered to do battle. One junior, called the 'watch', had to remain in college during play hours, to answer inquiries and take messages; and another, *monitor osti*, remained on duty to guard the door as sentinel, to exclude suspicious characters. The latter assignment carried with it exemption from lessons for the day. In the evening the call of 'Election' for fags was a serious interruption to the juniors' period of study from eight to ten. It is a sign of the potency of government by senior boys that, even in a school eminent in pride of scholarship, the working time of junior boys was arbitrarily interrupted to serve the convenience of their boy masters.

At Winchester, College was ruled over by the praefect of hall whose powers were in practice almost unrestrained. No single boy, whatever his standing, in the sixth-form oligarchies of Eton and Westminster held a comparable rank relative to the rest. It was said that there were three absolute rulers in the world, the Great Mogul, the captain of a man-of-war, and praefect of hall at Winchester, and his position and the position of his lieutenants, the other praefects, was the outward and visible expression of the authoritarian stress which distinguished Winchester from other schools and characterized the complex severity of her spirit.

The gulf between praefects and the rest appears to be almost one of class, and the classes to be master and slave; those who would at other schools be called juniors were at Winchester called 'inferiors'* and all boys were inferiors who were not praefects. 'Slavery warps the character of both slave and master, and slavery is the only word

* At Westminster juniors were unofficially called 'slaves'.

which summed the three years of experience of a college junior. Its details, whether cruel or grotesque, were all so contrived as to stamp upon the young boy's mind his grade of servile inferiority and his dedication to the single virtue of abject and unquestioning obedience.' These are strong words, but they have a claim to attention in as much as they were written not by some defeated rebel, or misfit with an unredressed grievance, but by a former praefect of hall.

The demands made on the spiritual stamina of Wykehamist boys were racked with conflict. A Wykehamist inferior was expected to be brave but submissive, accomplished yet unquestioningly conformable. 'Nothing,' continues our former praefect of hall,

> was more resented by seniors than the faintest manifestation of independent feeling on the part of any fag. No maxim was oftener cited than the unwritten law that a boy was not allowed 'to think' until he had twenty juniors. Anyone who showed tacit dislike of the degradations he endured, or even a desire to retain, in spite of them, some fragments of that refinement and self respect which he brought from home, was designated 'spree', and to be spree was to be a mark for spite and insult from every one senior to oneself.[8]

Through the agency of William Tucker and another Colleger, Charles Allix Wilkinson – or rather of the aged clergymen these boys grew to be – we are able to get (albeit censored) a sight and sound of daily and nightly life within the walls of Long Chamber, at Eton,[9] where fifty or more senior and junior Collegers slept together in one dormitory, locked up overnight without supervision by any master or adult in authority.[10]

On a winter night, with all its draughts and leaks, lit from top to bottom with fifty 'dips' and two roaring fires, Long Chamber presented a vital and atmospheric picture. Some boys would be at their desks writing or lying down on their beds, with candles standing up in their own wax; some reading; some walking up and down in laughing or earnest talk; others boxing, or fencing with single stick. Notwithstanding the burdens of a junior's life 'there was,' says William Tucker, 'an ease and independence about it indescribable'. But a lower boy with his duties to his master and the sixth and, if he were conscientious, his own work, was lucky if he got to sleep by midnight; he had to rise at six, when Keate's servant, Cartland, came in ringing a bell, and swinging a large horn lantern, ready to give light to anyone who had fortunately preserved a bit of candle from overnight to dress by. The stress was considerable and boys were dozing off in class at nine. Tutors complained to Keate who sought to get to the bottom of the cause, 'with as much chance of success as a Protestant JP would have of probing the secrets of the confessional'.

Tucker, newly arrived in college, was standing by his bed gazing about him when a bigger boy came up to him and posed a mysterious question: 'Who is your master?' With ingenuous pleasure Tucker answered that he was an entirely free being, unpossessed by any 'master'. The next words dispelled the mystery; he was hearing his master's voice; 'You are my fag.'

From that moment life under the Long Chamber regimen began. His prime duties were to make his master's bed, wait on him at informal meals, shop and run errands, care for his best linen and generally look after him, do all he was told and, if he was prudent, a few useful things he was not told. His master, Henry Hatch, the future Rector of Sutton, was severe but not abnormally so. Faults were punished by slapping a fag's face till it was 'red hot', or by 'flaking' his bare hands with a wet towel. The worst crime a fag could commit was, in making his master's bed, to place the rough middle seam inwards, and it was one he was not likely to commit more than once. The offender would be wakened at about midnight and flung out of bed by an enraged master, and driven with kicks and blows by three or four older boys, howling in his night dress to repair his error. On the other hand he might not be in bed at midnight. There was no limit to demands that could be made on him and, at least at night, no escape from them. He could be required to attend on his master at late-night toilet of hair and whiskers, known as 'mowings'. A grand seigneur might be observed seated late at night before the fire, with his feet on the hob, cigar in mouth, a lower boy brushing his hair, while he himself was absorbed in the latest new novel. At such times, and especially when the sixth had to 'sap',* there was 'admirable quiet'. Sometimes a pin might be heard to drop somewhere in the length of the great dormitory, and the warning, 'Be Quiet', was uttered. If thereafter a rustle or whisper was heard it was followed by a sonorous, 'Subbs and Grubbs, epigrams'. This was a command to the culprits to produce four-line verses, which must each contain some wit in play on words, or they were torn up and had to be done again. They could be required in English or Latin.

---

* Study, from *sapiens*.

Wilkinson, a more gamesome boy altogether than William Tucker, when sentenced on one occasion to an 'epigram', produced:

> One Larney, in his frantic hours
> Endowed with great poetic powers
> Last week or else the week before
> Parsed 'Niger Amor' blackamoor!

One clever little delinquent, ordered to produce *eight* verses for impudence on top of noise, sat down and quickly wrote out:

> Carmina, carmina, carmina, carmina, carmina, carmen,
> Carmina quanta vocas, carmina tanta dedi.

'Get me a candlestick' was a frequent and familiar command. None was supplied; the alternatives were to buy or make, and the favourite material used in the latter course was the back of a book, one's own, or another's. A book left lying unattended was deemed 'fair game' and its appropriation quite morally legitimate.

The problem of a college junior by day was where to go when he was not in pupil room or division. To make an appearance in Long Chamber was to commit himself to servitude, for over and above the regular tasks he had to perform for his master, he could be summarily required on sight to labour for any senior boy. Life was hardest when it rained. 'It was rather desolate,' says Tucker. 'We had nowhere to go. – We wandered. Sometimes we made a party under the Thirteen Arch Bridge, out of the way of our great enemies, the fagging masters, raising up funeral piles with crossed sticks and setting on fire.'

A few disgraceful seniors made their fags do 'blackguard' acts like thieving for them, but this was exceptional, and if it became known the offenders might be shamed out of the abuse by the contempt of their equals. A more common and dangerous service required of a fag was the purchase and conveyance of liquor for his master. There was nothing deemed ignoble in this, so there was no inhibition of it, though it was a flogging offence for the boy employed if he were detected emerging from a forbidden bar by a master. The safest resort was the Christopher Inn in the High Street, opposite the entrance to College, because quasi legitimate excuses for having gone in could always be pleaded. If caught, the boy had been in to see some friends from London, or to inquire about parcels and, as W. E. Gladstone told a younger Etonian (Brinsley Richards), masters shrank from provoking these ready lies and a great deal was winked at.

The fagging which was universally most disliked was cricket fagging. The same complaints are heard generation after generation from all the schools. The fags were not allowed to bat or bowl; they were there only to chase and return the ball.

Vying with cricket fagging in unpopularity at Eton was log cutting for Carters Chamber, the other College dormitory, which had no basket, but fire dogs. The lower fifth had care of the fire, and they would not call for service, for that would only cause the potential labour force to disperse in flight, but they would creep up upon a chosen victim and tap him on the shoulder, with the words, 'Come and saw logs.' The smaller the boy the larger the log he was likely to be awarded.

Tea fagging duties for the sixth form in College included the provision of refreshment in Poets' Walk. Heavy deal tables, which had to be scrubbed clean of stains every Saturday, were carried on important cricket days on fags' backs to Poets' Corner, appearing to move on their own volition, until one spied a pair of diminutive legs underneath. There tea was brewed from a cauldron called the 'conjuror' on a 'gypsy' fire. It was a morning's work, cleaning and filling it from wash hand basins in Western's Yard. Tablecloths were rarities, but their appearance was expected, and sometimes in chapel on a saint's day a few black gowns would be seen among the surplices of the lower boys, the absent surplices being at the wash or doing service as tea cloths; or worse, they might appear upon the person of a chorister after having been used to dry up twelve supper plates at night, and boys were known to appear in chapel in a state 'piteous and disgraceful to see'. If his appearance was conspicuous enough, a boy might be indignantly admonished by members of the sixth form whose demands were responsible for his condition.

On winter evenings a fag had to collect and carry two or three pieces of coal in his gown, with the ends clasped over his shoulder, the nightly supply for the upper fireplace. The Liberty, the top twelve boys (Collegers and Oppidans) of the upper fifth who were exempt from fagging and from interference by the sixth form, had a table set and supped near the lower fireplace so there was a debris of bread, cheese rinds, and odds and ends to be swept up next morning if it had not been eaten by the rats.

The relationship of a junior to his fag master and to any member of the sixth form who condescended to notice him could exercise a powerful influence upon his life for several years; and these relationships provide a key to discrepancies of experience between one boy and another of the same age at the same school at the same time. There were all kinds of privileges, protections and exemptions, official and unofficial, which a junior boy, if he happened to be tactful, opportune and diplomatic, could obtain from a sixth form, and the sooner he obtained them the better for his own welfare. The Duke of Roxburghe, an engaging and modest little fellow in his first half at Eton, was returning from the playing fields and was passing a knot of big Collegers who were standing near Lower School Passage just before Absence when one of them, Goodford (Provost of Eton to be), called out to him, 'Hullo! You're a new fellow ain't you? What's your name? Who's your tutor? Where do you board?' Having been answered he said, 'Well, take a basin out of lower chamber and fill it up at the pump.' Roxburghe did as he was bid with a cheerful smiling countenance and returned with the basin looking as if he had really enjoyed the unexpected task. Had he made a bad impression the effects might have continued for a long time. But the great man looked at him and liked what he saw. 'You're a jolly fellow. You may have my name and liberties.' Now this meant an immediate and tremendous boon for the recipient; whenever any other senior boy sought to claim his services as a fag, he could legitimately refuse on the ground that he was already doing something else for Goodford. Most often he might not be doing anything; that was the joy of the privilege. In a single happy moment he had been translated from relative servitude to liberty. A different boy, unwary, or tactless, or vain enough to let jokers make a dupe of him, could forfeit expectation of the 'liberties' indefinitely by careless conduct, uninvited familiarity or insufficient respect, to a sixth form in his first half. The situation is playfully handled in one of the Eton magazines as an imaginary letter home from a new boy:

. . . You know Harry B—, who is a sixth form, and knows papa – well, I went to him as you told me, as he was standing among some other big boys, and said, 'How do you do, Harry, and how's your mamma?' They all laughed and he looked very black indeed, but I couldn't tell why, but suppose it was because he did not recognize me, so I said, 'I'm Tommy Green, and I'm come to be socked the liberties please.' That's what they told me to ask for – instead of shaking my hand, or anything, he looked very proud, and said, 'Well, you're a very pretty fellow, now!' So I said, 'Yes'; because of course I thought he meant it, and sisters sometimes tell me I am, but he laughed in my face, so I ran away as hard as I could, and I shall not go near him again, I can tell you, for all the liberties in the world. . . . Sisters told me it was the best plan to imitate what other boys did, but will tell you that I find it quite a mistake; for there's a rather pretty boy who is a fifth form, and they call him Clara.* He gave me his book the other day to take to his room, and then he said, 'You know my name?' so I said 'Clara', but he boxed my ears. I have to lay my master's things every day; there are three other fags, but they tell me that he likes his breakfast so much better when I lay them that he told them always to leave it to me. . . .[11]

That account was only a slight parody of the truth. In a genuine letter a shrewder boy writes to his elder brother, 15 November 1831. 'I shall be a remove higher at Christmas than I am now. . . . Tunnard will then be Sixth Form and if I can get to know him in the Holydays, it will be a great advantage to me . . . because I shall ask him to get me the Liberties. . . . I should think he would give me his name, that is, when any fellow tries to fagg me I may say I am fagging for Tunnard; but perhaps he would not do these things, and then if I asked him I should be worse off than ever for he would report it to the other fellows, and then I should be the general laughing stock.'[12]

The life of a junior was affected in every way by how he managed his relations with senior boys with disciplinary powers who could extend or withhold patronage and protection. In some cases it might be benevolently negative '. . . they have let me off singing again,'† wrote William Adams from Rugby to his brother, 'as I am great friends with all the big fellows'.

William Ewart Gladstone fagged for his elder brother, who treated him well, unlike the Duke of Bedford at Westminster School, who declared penitently in later life that the greatest sin he had to answer for was his treatment of his brother Lord John Russell.‡ Of his relationship at Winchester with his elder brother, Thomas, Anthony Trollope reports, '. . . he was of all my foes the worst . . . as part of his daily exercise he thrashed me with a big stick'.[13]§

Some boys, like Milnes Gaskell, were destined by their natures to be more bullied than others, and not necessarily those who would be least successful in worldly contests later. Precocity, born of too much

---

* For girls' names in schools, see p. 310 fn.

† 'Lamb Singing', see above, p. 80–1.

‡ Lord John Russell's own experience of school life may have accounted for his course in not sending his grandson and ward, Bertrand Russell, to school at all. Earl Russell was educated entirely at home by tutors until he went to Cambridge in 1890. But he sent his own son, Viscount Amberley, to Harrow.

§ Thomas was acting as his younger brother's 'tutor' (see footnote on p. 98).

and early intercourse with adults, which appeared to a boy's contemporaries to be pretension to superiority, perhaps more than anything else tended to draw upon him the odium of his fellows.

The practical test of the fagging system as a form of governmental control was how far it prevented bullying and oppression which without it would have occurred. Tucker believed that 'If boys are trusted their impulse will be to answer loyally to the trust,' and 'White sheep will overawe and keep under the black.'[14] In good conditions this did happen. Henry Everard, writing home from Eton to his elder brother, Sam, concerning 'the cock of my Dame's', who was a bully, is unperturbed because 'he dare not bully me because I should tell my master, and . . . I know my master will see that I am not bullied'.[15] Yet at the same school in another house Milnes Gaskell despaired of obtaining relief from bullies. 'What would I give,' he exclaimed, 'to be in Chapman's house, or to be in this without Rowles and Law.'[16]

The weakness of the system was its variability, and the extent to which it relied for effectiveness upon the moral qualities of the particular and changing individuals on whom authority devolved. Stability and order could vanish overnight with the departure of a generation of just oligarchs, and be succeeded by a reign of terror.

'The house is quite different from what it used to be when Barnett major* was here. Now there is nothing but riot, instead of which, when he was here, if we made the least noise we were all licked. . . .'[17]

The writer, Fortescue Wells,† in Mrs Holt's house, was personally protected for a time by a strong and kind fagmaster, John Wickens;‡ but when Wickens left he fell victim to two brutal oafs called Ford§ and Bethell** who prowled together in evil partnership, and a

---

* Henry Barnett of Glympton Park, Woodstock, JP and DL, Oxon., and Major, Oxford Yeomanry; in sixth form, 1832. Henry Rowles, a brewer at Kingston-on-Thames, was in the 7th Hussars; in fourth form, 1832. William Towry Law, MA, Peterhouse Cantab, in Army; Chancellor of Wells, Vicar of Narbonne, 1845–58, entered the Church of Rome; in fourth form, 1823.

† Fortescue Wells, born 1820, the son of W. B. Wells, a solicitor of Dursley, Gloucestershire. He came to Eton when he was ten and was admitted to St John's College, Cambridge, as a sizar in 1837. Ordained priest in 1844, he became a chaplain to the Royal Navy, and served in HMS *Albion* and HMS *Cumberland*. He died at Plymouth 13 March 1856 of consumption.

‡ John Wickens, barrister, Lincoln's Inn; Newcastle Scholar, 1833; Balliol College, Oxon. Double first-class honours, 1836. Edited *Eton College Magazine*.

§ Charles Wilbraham Ford, Madras Army, on retirement lived at Bath. Middle division of fifth form, 1835.

** Richard Bethell, Exeter College, Oxford, farmed in New Zealand. Son of assistant master George (later fellow and vice-provost of Eton), whose unpopularity provoked resistance to Keate in 1809.

belligerent strongboy called Macgregor;* and, since the appointment of 'a great blackguard' called Wright† as captain of the house, there was no redress, as 'Wright instead of stopping the bullying in the house, he is the first to create it'.[18] Holt's was a Dame's house, and houses kept by Dames, especially by female Dames, had a reputation for laxer discipline and harsher bullying than houses governed by assistant masters. The worst, in Margaretta Brown's view, was Mrs Atkins's house, where 'the boys do scream so and behave so ill'.[19] There in 1822 a strong and courageous senior boy, Knowlys,‡ when he intervened to stop the sufferings of a victim, was set upon by several at once of those whose power was challenged (including Clive,§ the captain of the house, and a notorious bully), one Pearson attacking him from behind with a poker.[20] Thus although the institution of fagging, at its best, did protect the weak and the young, and chasten the strong unruly, it was liable to precipitous decadence, which only continuous renovation and prevention of abuse could correct.

At Rugby in 1840 George Cotton (the 'Young Master' of *Tom Brown's Schooldays*), who hated bullying and had helped to moderate it in college at Westminster, had the house with the worst reputation for bullying and general demoralization in the school. It was saved and restored to order by the draconian rule of a strong captain of the house called Hodson who later carried his methods to a dramatic climax in India with the summary execution of the Mogul's sons. About the same time, it could be said of a boy with a bad record at Rugby that 'if he had been in any house but Birds he would have been one of the finest and most gentlemanly fellows at Rugby'.[21]

Conditions could vary sharply not only between different houses in the same school at different times and at the same time, but between different bedrooms in the same house at the same time. At Rugby in Melly's time, one could move from civilization to barbarism by travelling along a corridor from one bedroom to another. 'Some,' says Melly, 'were well managed and very pleasant rooms; others were perfect infernos.'[22]

Clearly the selection of boys for office and command was crucial

* Sir W. Macgregor, 2nd baronet (succeeded 1828), captain 93rd Highlanders; died unmarried, 1846.
† Edward Wright, only son of Rev. T. Wright of East Claydon, Bucks; went to Christ Church, Oxford; died in New Zealand.
‡ Thomas John Knowlys of Heysham Hall, Lancashire; in lower fifth, 1820.
§ George A. Clive, St John's College, Cambridge. Rector of Shawardine and Vicar of Motford, near Shrewsbury.

to the quality of the system. 'I believe the system worked well,' said the Wykehamist Robert Mansfield (in College 1834–40):

> It would have been impossible for the masters to have been continually spying after the boys, and the confidence placed in the praefects strengthened their character, inasmuch as for the most part they felt proud of the trust confided in them and conscientiously endeavoured to fulfill their duties.[23]

But some of the names featured in the complaints already cited were of boys in authority. An error in the appointment of a praefect, or captain of a house, might put dangerous power into malign hands. 'The boy made no cry but recorded audibly the hundred and fifty cuts as they fell, then was for some days in danger. His father, a person of consequence interfered and the praefect was disgraced or turned down.' In that report of a 'tunding' inflicted with a ground ash by a praefect at Winchester about 1840, the remarkable circumstances are that a parent did protest at all and that only because the parent happened to be a person of power and influence was any disciplinary action taken against the praefect. William Tuckwell, himself a former praefect of hall, remembered cases of power 'atrociously abused'.[24]

One account of the system in action is, perhaps, more impressive than an indictment because it is offered in a spirit of genial approval. A 'tutor' at Winchester was not an assistant master but a senior boy to whom a junior would be allocated for the superintendence of his studies and moral welfare. Tutors were, we are told, chosen 'on moral and intellectual grounds'; a tutor was 'expected to take a real interest in his pupil's work, not only to purge his exercises of the grosser faults, but to keep a general superintendence over his morals and manners,* and generally 'tejay'† him. Robert Mansfield recalls:

> My old friend Dummy, however, was not fortunate in the selection made for him; he was handed over to a tutor who, by way of taking a great interest in his welfare, prevented other boys from thrashing his pupil by operating on him so constantly himself that they scarcely had any chance of doing so. The tutor was tall, thin, bullet headed and apparently about forty-five years of age, and he used from time to time to conduct his pupil into a quiet corner and with a cheerful smile

---

* 'A tutor was supposed really to look after a boy who was rather friendless.'[25]
† 'Tejay', derived from 'protéger'.

beaming on his countenance, would give himself a few minutes healthy but not too violent exercise. He was not very muscular or the consequences might have been very serious. As it was when Dummy went to bathe a number of spectators always assembled to see his back which from the nape of his neck to his ankles was a network of intersecting bruises.

On reflection the narrator himself found no cause for alarm in the system, for he tells us, 'Dummy's skin gradually got as tough as a hippopotamus's and I don't think it did him much harm.' The sequel, which he tells as an amusing bonus to the anecdote, is not entirely reassuring, as he intends it to be:

At any rate I saw him last year in rude health. He was delighted to see me; and he told me that not long before he had met his venerated tutor at a railway station in Northumberland, looking still about forty-five and apparently a Bishop or Dean or something of the sort, with a Gothic waistcoat and a broad-brimmed hat and altogether so little altered that Dummy's body gave an instinctive shrink as it passed him, in expectation of the never failing blow or kick that used to follow on his propinquity.[26]

A sudden and dramatic change took place in the condition of the boys whose lives at school we have been sighting. They went home at the end of one half, fags and juniors, in some cases harassed and troubled ones; and they returned to find the quality of their lives all at once changed beyond imagining by an elevation of their standing and position. Some boys thought about the experience more than others, but they all felt the translation from subordinate to oligarch. They were aware of having entered into possession of the School. The very air they breathed was charged with the scent of inheritance, and more, the process seemed magically curative of the effects of previous hardship. The pains and tribulations and oppressions suffered not long ago were sublimated now in retrospect into the dignity of honourable trial by ordeal, creditably endured. There might or might not be in later adult life, a critical recoil from this hypalgesia. 'From a timid, unhappy green-horn, sharing no fame, no fun, no nothing, shirking tyrants and bullies and writing doleful letters home,' the little boy felt himself grow wondrously to a different species of being, '*au fait* with all the mysteries and intricacies of Eton customs and slang'. The older boy, George Lyttelton, bears witness that, 'to a little boy, the whole world of school seems large; there are giants of 5ft 9ins and super men of 6ft; his feeling of awe and admiration is increased by receiving an occasional blow from these huge animals, as he creeps about among the few of his own diminutiveness, mightily impressed with the words and mightiness of the race of giants towering above him'. Then, as he grows up, 'the scale changes, he may himself become a giant without feeling one; at least the giants fade away'. The junior who could not stir out of his room without danger of being knocked about or fagged in fifty directions, and heard all sorts of fun going on 'without daring to see what it was, or attempt to participate in it', being now risen to the upper division, 'the whole range of the House is open to him' and he frightens the Lowers with every motion of his finger.[27]

Thus Milnes Gaskell returned after an interval to Eton, braced for the worst, to find life transfigured; the clouds vanished; the sun beamed; Eton was renewed and now his; and the boy who had written agonized protests to his mother upon his ill treatment, burgeons, almost overnight, into the complacent youth who writes to his, no doubt relieved, but perhaps bewildered parent, 'Why do you not congratulate me on the Elysian state of happiness that I, in common with most other Etonians, enjoy?'[28] Even the lugubrious Churton, the most socially uncomfortable boy to have come to our attention, who suffered miseries of disassociation and paralysed emotion at Rugby, declares by 1817 when he is a prefect that he 'cannot help sharing with other boys the impression of considerable regret at the idea of leaving for ever the scenes of thoughtless childhood where perhaps have been spent the pleasantest hours of their lives'. He even goes so far as, 'I may say I have been tolerably happy here, particularly in the Sixth and Fifth form.'[29]

This is all the more remarkable inasmuch as Thomas Churton, although of painfully earnest moral character and the best of intentions, lacked those qualities which commanded respect and obedience from a body of male adolescents. His emotions had been crippled; he could feel, but he could not articulate his feelings spontaneously. 'I am fond of sprightly, exhilarating companions, perhaps because I lack that blessing myself. . . .' he wrote to his parents. 'But there are several little boys low in the school, to whose amiable simplicity and lively and sensible gaiety I owe many pleasant hours.'[30]

Such boys as Thomas Churton and his brother William, who provoked similar reactions, could not escape from persecution through the normal route of seniority. Even as a praefect either of such boys would remain isolated and harassed and, if possible, defied by the pack. 'Last Monday,' William told his father, 'one boy, Stapleton, dared to be riotous and defy my authority, threatening to lick me if I sent him up to be flogged.' This was 'not to be borne' but Stapleton, evidently feeling that a large part of the school was with him, continued his defiance and was expelled. Wrote William, 'Now since that a number of fellows, chiefly in the fifth form have refused ever speaking with me . . . but not one whose good opinion I think worth having. . . . But there is a party whose pride it seems to be to oppose everything that is praiseworthy, and that party I have offended.'[31]

The 'fags rebellion' at Winchester in 1829 was occasioned by the appointment of a new team of commoner praefects, none of whom commanded a personal authority acceptable to the rank and file. It was in an important sense more radical than any other insurrection which had punctuated English public-schools history since the middle of the eighteenth century. Boys against masters was normality. Boys against their own boy masters was a rarer phenomenon. Grave and earnest scholars of their own affinity, however just, were not acceptable as rulers to boys; the haughty heroes of the playing fields, though sometimes capricious, *were* acceptable. The latter were endured as part of the natural order of life; the former were instinctively attacked through a kind of animal osmosis, unless they were so reinforced by superior powers as to render them, in practice, invincible. Such reinforcement of moral merit, rather than physical prowess or boys' own natural selection, was the policy which Thomas Arnold adopted to justify the fagging and monitorial system of school government and, as we shall see, his methods were fraught with contradiction. In the present case reinforcement was not deployed until the damage had been done.

At Winchester in 1829 the new head commoner praefect was George Ward, whom Roundell Palmer, also a newly appointed praefect, described as 'able bodied'.[32] That was an understatement. Ward was a boy of abnormal bodily strength and dauntless moral courage. But he was absentminded and eccentric, the butt of practical jokers, and although the son of the most successful cricketer of the day,* was himself without interest or skill in any game and could never, in a juvenile community which worshipped at the Olympian altar of

---

* George Ward's father, William Ward, of Northwood Park on the Isle of Wight, proprietor of Lord's Cricket Ground, scored 278 in 1820 for the MCC against Norfolk, the largest score made up to that time at Lord's in a first-class match.

games, be 'an object of fear'. By unfortunate coincidence, none of the other new praefects was able to make good Ward's deficiency in athletic prowess, so that there was a sudden and dangerous decline in the moral authority of the presiding hierarchs of Winchester, which occasioned in the breasts of resentful inferiors the temptation to mutiny. If Ward had numbered tact among his qualities of character, a confrontation might perhaps have been averted. But whereas he had neither sought nor welcomed his office, once appointed, he endeavoured to administer the law with strict and unrelenting precision. Some of the bolder spirits among the inferiors decided that the time had come to rise up and throw off the yoke of such despised and decadent rulers. According to plan, a popular and spirited boy, Arthur Malet, defied Ward when called upon to fag in hall. Ward rashly attempted to enforce his authority, there and then, with an ashplant, the rod appertaining to praefects, but this was the signal for attack, and he was suddenly set upon by a pack of furious inferiors, who leapt on his back and tried to pull him to the ground for execution. Only his great strength enabled him to escape from the ambush with the loss of his coat tails, dragging with him a load of boys sufficient, as it seemed to one spectator, 'for an elephant (to which animal the boys sometimes compared him) to carry'.[33]

Malet and five others were expelled and bitter public controversy broke out over the issue of fagging and the rule of praefects. Arthur Malet's elder brother and guardian, Sir Alexander Malet, published indignant letters attacking the fagging system, addressed to the headmaster, who replied very temperately, but refused to vary the order for expulsion. 'The result,' said Roundell Palmer, 'was a long standing breach between praefects and juniors, and loss of confidence between the headmaster and praefects.' Writing to his cousin, twenty-seven years later, who was in his turn a praefect, Palmer told him, 'I think I have never in my whole subsequent life been in a position of anything like equal difficulty.'[34]*

Fagging and praefectorial or senior boy government were the mainstays of the old system. 'The masters from Keate downwards,' said

---

* A piquant element of the matter which no one thought fit to remark on at the time, was that Sir Alexander Malet had himself been a leader of the famous Winchester rebellion of 1818.

Arthur Malet went into the Indian Civil Service and became head of the Bombay Secret Service. He was also the author of an English metrical version of the psalms, *Job, Ecclesiastes and Revelations in English Verse*, and *The Marriage of Solomon with the Daughter of Pharoe*. The praefect he had buffeted, after joining the Tractarian movement and losing his fellowship and degree for publishing *The Ideal of a Christian Church*, became a convert to the Church of Rome and the stormy petrel of religious controversy in later Victorian England.

Tucker, 'never interfered or intervened in any way out of school. We were a self governing community. People who have not known the system have objected.'[35] Some of those who objected believed they knew the system, or part of it. 'This abominable practice,' Southey had called it, 'which suffers boys to establish among themselves the law of the strongest, and reduce tyranny to a system.'[36] Southey had been at Westminster during its worst days, and he tended to be a professional protester. Rowcroft had been at Eton, contemporary with Tucker. It was 'an oppressive and demoralising system' to him. 'Those who have not had actual experience of the fact can have no idea of the length to which this privilege of fagging was sometimes carried.'[37]

There were violent and persistent attacks upon the system in certain sections of the press. 'Fagging,' declared our renegade Etonian, George Lewis, in the *Edinburgh Review*, was 'the only regular institution of slave labour enforced by brute force which exists in these islands'. Its effects he claimed were that 'Corrupting and corrupted, the little tyrant riots in the exercise of boundless and unaccountable power.'[38] The system of fagging, according to another denouncer, was 'replete with mischief' and its effects were 'to subdue or destroy the spirit of the sufferer or to render him when he became a tyrant, a cruel bully'.[39] An anonymous writer painted a lurid picture of little Wykehamist fags, forced to fight for a place in the crowded front of a fire to toast their master's bread and, if they failed to penetrate the mêlée with their toasting forks, being 'lashed by a large brute with a whip'. Evocation of this imaginative spectacle inspired the verdict 'We would . . . abolish at once this odious and demoralising usage.'[40] But we do not know whether this particular allusion was true, or partly true, or false. Certainly acts of cruelty were committed,* but sometimes the reports were exaggerated and at other times invented.

Partisans like Lewis and the unnamed journalists were not engaged in the disinterested pursuit of truth, but in the selective presentation of evidence serviceable in making a case adverse to the public schools. Their objections to fagging, emotive and fashionable in radical circles, were conjured out of a disingenuous confusion of cause with coinci-

---

* Samuel Rogers recounts that Lord Holland was forced by his fagmaster to make toast with his bare hands. His mother sent him a little toasting fork but his master broke it over his head and compelled him to continue as before. In consequence of this experience his fingers became permanently misshapen.[41]

dence. *The fagging system operates in the schools, but cruelty occurs in the schools, therefore the fagging system causes cruelty.*

The vice of argument by syllogism, the fallacy of affirming the consequent when there are different and conflicting propositions from which the consequence might follow, could be seen by reference to schools where the fagging system did *not* operate and where the most savage elements in the school were free to indulge without restraint 'the innate . . . mysterious tendency to abuse personal strength and size, to torment, tease and tyrannize over the younger and weaker'.[42] In the absence of alternative restraints, the withdrawal of the old system merely weakened the rule of law. When John Russell abolished fagging at Charterhouse, bullying at once increased,[43] and the atrocities committed in private schools without praefectorial or fagging discipline were vicious and uncontrolled to a degree unknown in public schools where the authority of senior boys prevailed.[44]

The traditional system was defended and justified, not merely by professed traditionalists, but by men associated with democratic policies. As a chorus of hostile slogans was chanted in obedience to the baton of a political conductor, T. H. Green, a radical social reformer as well as an old Rugbeian, wrote in exasperation to his father, 'The spirit of the age, raving against everything that sounds like oppression, seems likely to establish a worse tyranny in public schools, as everywhere else, for it is impossible for bullying to be stopped except by praeposters.'[45] Arnold himself considered the fagging system the only way to maintain order for a multitude of boys living together;[46] and Gladstone defended fagging against Lewis's allegations as 'one of the most salutary parts of the system'.[47] The 'tyrants' exercised 'a merciful tyranny'[48] and a 'mild jurisdiction'[49] according to two other products of the system; and another testified that fagging was 'of the greatest benefits to younger boys' for 'the defenceless stranger who is immediately apportioned as a fag to some upper boy of the same house, from that moment acquires a friend interested in his well being, willing to guide him in his difficulties and protect him from the aggression of others'.[50] As for the system being 'oppressive' and 'demoralising', 'boys learnt much from being left free to rule and regulate their little world'[51] and an observer admired 'the spirit of manly confidence and fresh fearless self respect' engendered in the 'bold but untrembling look' with which a boy 'gazes on men of every rank and condition', and in a 'distinctive style of independence and ease'.[52]

The fagmaster as a fag's best friend is depicted in many narratives, perhaps most observantly in a long short story called *Collegers v. Oppidans* (1871), which is notable for more reasons than one. The author is an Etonian, intimately familiar with the world of Eton in the 1850s in which the story is set, and the account, written in a vein of whimsical sentiment, but in a sophisticated, sometimes ironic style, utterly unlike the bluff bonhomie of Hughes's *Tom Brown's Schooldays*, is the product of direct experience. It is, in fact, the most graphic and detailed account of life at Eton during the period we cover, with the exception of *Seven Years at Eton* (1883), 'edited' by Brinsley Richards, and it is more than likely that both are the work of the same author, Reginald Temple Strange Clare Grenville Murray, to give him the name by which he was known at Eton, before changing it to Brinsley Richards after the catastrophic scandal in which his father, Eustace Clare Grenville Murray, was involved in 1869.*

Collegers v. Oppidans is the story of the redemption of a wayward and unprepossessing younger boy by a senior boy, whom he serves. In appearance Jickling was dirty, untidy and slovenly. Although he

---

* *The Wellesley Index to Victorian Periodicals* ascribes *Collegers v Oppidans* to 'Grenville Murray' by which is meant Eustace Clare, who must be distinguished from his son, Reginald Temple Strange Clare, also a writer. Eustace Clare Grenville Murray was born in 1824, the natural son of Richard Grenville, the second and last Duke of Buckingham and Chandos. Although illegitimate, he had, as a son of one of the richest peers in England, great expectations. Perhaps reconciled to being a bastard, he was certainly not so to being a poor bastard. But his father, by feats of extravagance and mismanagement amounting almost to genius, succeeded in demolishing one of the great ducal fortunes and was in 1848 declared bankrupt. This catastrophe may explain the bitterness and disdain Grenville Murray later showed for all ranks of English society. After a turbulent career in the diplomatic service in Vienna, Constantinople and Odessa, he returned to England and began to employ his considerable abilities as a writer, first seen in *Roving Englishman* (1854). In 1868 he contributed to the first number of *Vanity Fair* and the following year he launched his own periodical, *The Queen's Messenger*, which was the ancestor of modern satirical reviews, in particular of *Private Eye*, inasmuch as it printed stories which no one else would print. On 22 June 1869 Lord Carrington, with an assurance of moral licence which a modern complainant might envy, horsewhipped Grenville Murray on the steps of the Conservative Club in St James's Street, in requittal of an alleged libel on his father. Carrington was formally prosecuted and technically convicted, but treated by the court with respectful sympathy, while Grenville Murray was himself arrested and charged with perjury as a result of denying under oath in the witness box the authorship of the offending article. Remanded on bail, he fled to Paris and never returned. As a result of the scandal, his son, Reginald, changed his name to James Brinsley Richards. From France, Grenville Murray continued to produce brilliant social satires on English life, notably *Young Brown*, all worthy of rediscovery and buried treasure to the social historian. In my judgement the most undeservedly forgotten English writer of the nineteenth century, Grenville Murray could certainly have written *Collegers v. Oppidans*, but he could not have evoked the detailed texture of Etonian life and the impeccable atmosphere, unaided by someone intimately familiar with Eton. He was not himself an Etonian, but his son was, and later produced in *Seven Years at Eton* the best and most revealing account of Eton around the mid century ever to be written. My guess is that *Collegers v. Oppidans* was a work of collaboration between father and son.

had at least the average amount of pocket money, he was always impecunious and in debt to the Eton cads* and tradesmen. He did nothing well or successfully; everything he attempted seemed to go wrong and he was continually in trouble.

> So there was Jickling, at the very bottom of his division – a boy of about twelve, with lank hair of a muddy flaxen colour; fingers permanently inkstained; Balmoral boots that were never laced; and a curious white face that looked enquiringly at you, out of a pair of eyes so wild, shifty, and defiant in expression, that it was a wonder Nature had not taken them to put into the head of a polecat.

In contrast there was Asheton, who was a 'swell', a designation 'not very easy to explain to outsiders'. A boy was not a swell because he dressed well, or played cricket well, or boated well, or was high up in the school. A display of superlative ability at sport did not alone make a swell. The quality which conferred this coveted status upon Asheton reflects the measure of moral superiority which prevailed in the society of which he was an ornament. It was integrity. He was a consistent whole, in which every part corresponded with every other. 'He was not surpassingly excellent at any thing, but he was good at everything, and *might be relied on in everything*. He pulled a capital oar, without great dash, but conscientiously and in fine form'; unlike most 'wet-bobs' he also played a good game of cricket, while at fives and football he was counted among the best players. But the great merit of him was not superlative excellence at any one sport; it was that '*his play was sure*'.† 'As he played today so he would play tomorrow; there was nothing unequal in him, no wavering, no unexpected breaking at a moment when all the hopes of his friends were centred on his performance.'

As a swell, Asheton was necessarily a personage of elegance. Eighteen years old, lightly built, and rather above middle height, 'his figure was fitly set off by the absolutely faultless style in which he dressed'. His white cravat, speckless linen, glossy hat, and trimly folded silk umbrella 'were things to see admire and copy'.

What puzzled observers in the house was the association of Asheton with Jickling. 'There could have been no community of thought or

---

* Cads: low fellows who hang about the college to provide Etonians with anything necessary to assist their sports (*New English Dictionary*).
† My italics – author.

sympathy' between the two, said the author; but that remark was an artifice of feigned naïveté, for he knew as he wrote, and had already acknowledged, that Asheton, being captain of the house, could have chosen anyone he pleased as his fag; but he had *chosen* Jickling 'who blacked his toast, spilled the gravy of sausages over his trousers and, when sent to carry a note, invariably took it to the wrong place'.

Asheton, after bearing patiently with Jickling's shortcomings for some time, was moved to intervene in the interests of his fag's moral welfare, after the discovery of a number of deplorable practices:

'A fellow who will sell a worthless dog to a credulous schoolfellow at twelve, will sell spavined horses at twenty and be kicked off racecourses at twenty-five,' he exclaimed, pale with anger.

Thereafter Asheton talked to Jickling seriously about his way of life:

'. . . Up to this time, Jickling, your life at Eton has been a failure; and as we all in this house are concerned for our own honour in not seeing you go to the bad, I mean to keep a sort of look out over you this half. Yes, I don't mean to spy over you or pry about you, or anything of that kind; but I shall make an attempt to make you fit for something, as you've hitherto been fit for nothing. Last half, and the half before, you never played and you never worked. You spent your time mooning about with your face unwashed, your lessons unlearned, and no sort of object in life but to catch flies, count the dogs in Fisher the birdman's yard, run into idiotic mucks, and get swished. That won't do. Be anything you please – a sap, a dry bob – or a wet bob – but be something. Going on as you're doing you'd be a confirmed muff,* and perhaps a leg† by the time you're twenty; and then, of course you'd lay it half to me, and say that if Asheton, who was your fagmaster, had done his duty, you wouldn't be where you are. And that's true. If I had a brother here I shouldn't let him follow the road you are treading, so I don't see why I should allow you.'

Cornered and under pressure, Jickling turns at bay:

'. . . You're always badgering me Asheton.'
'I want to see you a good fellow, and on the highway to becoming a man,' answered Asheton, with almost a woman's patience.
'What is, is,' said Jickling doggedly. 'You can't unmake yourself, and you can't do what's impossible.'

* Bungler.
† Swindler, especially on the turf.

'And what's impossible?' asked Asheton.

'Why,' cried Jickling, breaking out, and throwing down the poker with a clatter, 'it's impossible to be this and that simply because you are told to be it; and it's impossible to do this or that, when you've not strength enough. What should you say if I told you to win the football match against the Collegers this year? It seems you're in the Eleven – and they're stronger than you. You know it. So let me alone.'

There was a moment's silence, then Asheton walked straight up to Jickling. He had become very pale, but looked at his unhappy fag with a steady and earnest expression in his eyes.

'I know the Collegers are stronger than we are,' he said. 'But will you promise me' – (he paused) – 'will you promise me Jickling, that if I win the match for our side – you'll change?'

Jickling looked growlingly surprised, and glanced at him with sullen suspicion. 'It's not much to promise,' he said at last, 'for you won't.'

'But will you promise?' asked Asheton.

'Well then, yes,' said Jickling with a dry laugh and a shrug.

'Very well,' said Asheton, and he left the room.

Collegers v. Oppidans being a fairy tale of a kind, Asheton did perform what Jickling had called impossible. In the last moments of a furiously contested match, he scored the only and the winning goal.* Limping and battered, with the blood flowing in torrents from his nose, with 'something like superhuman energy' he bullies the ball down the length of the pitch, seemingly impervious to the kicks and charges of larger opponents. He shoots the ball over the calx line, follows it, raises it with his foot against the wall and touches it with his hand, thereby earning a 'Shy', the right to take a shot at goal. The breathless silence is broken by a mighty shout as the umpire shouts 'Goal!' and the college clock clangs out half past one and end of play.

In the instant before Asheton is raised on to the shoulders of jubilant friends he 'made a step forward, and holding out his hand (the first and last time he had ever done such a thing to a lower boy in public), said, "You see, young man, it *was* possible." '

On the walk back to their tutor's house Jickling is unnaturally quiet, pale and moody, and he kicks a pebble in front of him as he goes 'with a strange almost absent expression'. Saying he is not hungry, he avoids dinner and shuts himself up in his room. When he has not emerged at tea time the narrator visits him and, opening the door quietly, sees Jickling, seated at the table with his head buried in his hands, 'sobbing as if his heart would break'.

* See Appendix, 'The Eton Wall Game', pp. 352–4.

Jickling is now trapped by Asheton's chivalric feat, without any means of honourable escape from the obligation to make himself worthy of Asheton.

As a fairy tale should, it ends well:

> If you ask nowadays of any old Etonian who Jickling was he will probably answer you 'Jickling? Did you mean the fellow who was Newcastle Scholar and in the Eleven. He went to Oxford didn't he? and took double honours.'

Convention did not quite allow the simple conclusion of Jickling and Asheton living together happily ever after; but an acceptable transference is decorously performed. 'And stay, didn't he marry somebody, I think it was the sister of Sir Frederick Asheton?'[53]

SIX

The Liberties

Winchester College lies in a hollow valley between chalk hills through which meanders the Itchen, a clear, limpid trout stream of a river. The valley is green with stately trees, especially round the cathedral and the college which lie adjacent, as if they were one establishment on the verge of the ancient market town, once the capital of England, where the bones of Anglo–Saxon and Danish kings are buried. The river, when it reaches the cathedral, divides into two main branches, one flowing under the college walls, the other in the early nineteenth century being navigable by barges to Southampton. After passing the college the channels subdivide into smaller branches, intersecting the water-meadows below the city with a shining network of streams. The college had, and still has, much of the appearance of what it once was, a monastic foundation. The oldest buildings, sheltered behind a long high wall, are relatively low, rambling, but full of concealed architectural wonders and surprises; sudden openings from dark passages into spacious cloisters and interior courtyards. The two together lying adjacent continue to express through all the vicissitudes of change the cultural unity of the Middle Ages. The cathedral, simple and majestic outside is, inside, a complex of subtle craft. The first effect on the eye is of vast length; and the clustered piers and arches of the nave and the choir, the former vaulted in stone tracery, are so proportioned in the Perpendicular style as to give the effect of soaring celestial height. 'Beyond description sublime' was the impression which Roundell Palmer carried with him for the rest of his life. 'I well remember,' he says, 'the effect on my mind of this glorious building, when I first went with the other boys to the cathedral service. Nothing that I had seen before made a similar impression. It was like a heavenly revelation; as if I had received the gift of a new sense.'

Some account is due of the sudden appearance at Winchester of the boy Roundell Palmer. We left him at Mixbury Rectory after the death of his youngest brother, Tom, in expectation of going to Rugby; and to that school he did go in the summer of 1823. A senior boy called Bloxam 'walking up and down the Great School as Praeposter of the week before lessons observed . . . with great amusement an odd looking little boy chewing a pen and making strange faces while his mind was occupied with intense thought'.

Roundell's little head was indeed strained with intense and anxious thought. He was very unhappy at Rugby. Neither his own shy and fastidious and, if we are to believe him, meddlesome, temperament, nor the idyllic childhood of private freedom in a pastoral wonderland, had prepared him for the jungle of Rugby. He was severely bullied, enslaved for his prolific abilities to write stupid bigger boys' verses, and probably – he hints – harassed in other ways, for he was a pretty child. Mr Palmer, himself a Wykehamist, knew from his own experience that a closed society of growing boys bred moral problems. As Vincent, headmaster of Westminster, had declared with candour in 1802, 'Vice there is, wherever three hundred human beings are collected in a body,'[1] and the boys' letters, without being explicit, did bear witness to their trials. Their father's attitude to the situation seems to have been that certain moral risks and suffering had to be incurred for what he thought was a 'greater good'; and in the context of the times one would not expect him to be less resolute than Mrs Gaskell. When the boys alluded to anything 'disagreeable' he 'advised us,' says Roundell, 'to bear silently what we could not help, unless it were of a corrupting as well as a tormenting kind'.

Why then did Mr Palmer think it 'prudent' after two years to take Roundell away from Rugby? Again, Roundell is not explicit. He could state facts as plainly as anyone when he wished to; but at other times he could be indefinitely illative and equivocal. His brother William, he tells us, was fitter 'morally as well as physically' for Rugby while 'for me,' he says, 'it was certainly best to be removed, though I did not like it at the time'.[2] From this one can gather at least that in making a change Mr Palmer was not acceding to any request of Roundell's to be removed from Rugby. Despite the difficulties of life, he enjoyed the companionship of his brother William and his friends Edwin Martin Atkins, of Kingston Lisle in Berkshire (the 'Squire' of *Tom Brown's Schooldays*) and Edwin's younger brother William. The decision, as one might expect, was taken independently. From what is known of the opinions and conduct of Mr Palmer himself, it seems likely that he would have been influenced in his judgement by the turbulence of current conditions at Rugby.

Mr Palmer treated disobedience to a lawful superior as a sin infective of deadly social corruption. His feelings reflected the fear, shared by many thoughtful gentlemen at that time, that society was in danger of violent disintegration, with consequences of incalculable horror, and that only the exercise of rigorous discipline, as well as prudent benevolence, could avert catastrophe. Rebellion of boys at school was viewed by such a parent with horror, as a glimpse in miniature of the anarchy on a national scale which they dreaded. Charging his sons utterly to repudiate the rebellion, he held out the hope that thereafter they, and others like them, might 'by their learning and good conduct reflect as much honour' upon the place of their education as 'the disgrace and disrepute of others now seems to bring upon it'. On reflection Mr Palmer may have come to the conclusion that it would be 'prudent' at least in the case of Roundell, who was thought 'more liable' than his brother 'to suffer from the contagion of bad example', to take him with his 'learning and good conduct' to a safer depository. He chose his own old school and tried to get him into college as a foundation scholar, bringing Roundell to Winchester for examination by the warden and fellows sitting in conclave. The failure of Roundell to secure a place in college might on the face of it seem strange to those unacquainted with the underlying realities of election. In theory the places were awarded on merit by examination; in practice they were in the patronage of the fellows of Winchester and New College and were conferred upon the sons of friends. By the time the annual 'elections' were held at Winchester, the successful candidates had been chosen. Mr Trollope knew that Thomas would get a place on the foundation because he had a 'poser'* sponsoring him in private; Mr Palmer did his best for Roundell, but his friends were not influential enough to secure the boy a place. The candidates' examination consisted of being asked to construe a very simple sentence in Latin or Greek (known in advance) and being interrupted after two or three lines with the question, 'Can you sing?', to which the reply was spoken: 'All people that on earth do dwell.' That was the end of the interview, and the candidate, successful or unsuccessful, departed.

Thus, in June 1825, Roundell entered as a Commoner a more ancient and more decorous regimen than Rugby, but it cannot be said in truth a kinder one.

Commoners in those days crowded into a barracks-like eighteenth-

---

* One of two fellows of New College who examined at Winchester.

century building of Spartan simplicity in all respects. Their quarters formed, with the headmaster's house, three sides of a quadrangle, a high wall at the back of the warden's stables making the fourth side against which, within the court, grew one or two large elm trees. Opposite that wall was a cloister with a sleeping gallery above it and on the south side were the kitchen and buttery with stairs leading to the principal dormitories, the 'Commoners' Hall', a 'small and inconvenient study for the Commoners' tutors', and 'a smaller still, and even less convenient one for the six senior praefects'. Commoners were even more destitute of privacy than College boys. The three dormitories were closed to them during the day; their only place of resort was the same hall which was used for all meals. It was not well lit 'nor remarkable for sweetness and cleanliness' and for most of the time 'every kind of amusement, noise and disturbance went on, especially in cold weather'. This was the only sheltered place where Commoners could congregate within the walls when they were driven by the stress of weather from the open court or quadrangle, but in Roundell Palmer's view the austerity was justified by the check it imposed upon 'some evils of a serious kind'.[3]

As at Eton and Westminster, a headmaster who wished to make any change at Winchester, however much of an improvement it might appear to be, found himself frustrated by a higher authority than his own, whose watchword was 'No Innovation', even opposed by the very people, the boys themselves, whom the measure was designed to benefit. The conservative spirit of the school towards traditions and precedent was never more characteristically displayed than when Dr Williams decided to improve the service at meals. Meals were not then well managed. Breakfast was too late after chapel and long lessons. Dinner was too soon after the 'visits naturally paid to the pastry cook and the fruiterer during the one hour of freedom which immediately preceded it'. The food, 'not delicately served', was 'no doubt good and wholesome', says Roundell Palmer cautiously; other reports are less flattering. The servants, though civil and patient, were too few, and Palmer concedes that 'the whole accessories were disagreeable to those who were at all nice and fastidious, which boys, even rough boys, are very apt to be'.

The custom of the school had been to serve out from the buttery to every boy his regulated allowance of bread, butter and milk, all other things being extra and supplied by the boys themselves at their own expense, the little boys fagging for those elders who had a right to such service. The service hatch at breakfast was remembered by a participant as a scene of hazardous turmoil, 'we helpless juniors shouting pitiously for trenchers, senior candle keeper and his deputy pitching into us with their sticks'. The headmaster decided to do something to 'add to the comfort of all, especially the smaller boys'. On return to school one autumn after the summer holidays, Wykehamist Commoners found breakfast laid out for them in civilized style, with tea, sugar, milk, bread and butter and 'all needful crockery ready provided, and servants to wait upon everyone'. If Dr Williams expected gratitude he received a disagreeable surprise. On the first morning the boys rose *en masse* in protest and smashed the articles provided for their comfort. The notion of a novelty, especially if borrowed, as they believed, from the practices of despised 'private schools', being interjected into their ancient ways was abhorrent to them.[4]

Compared with Eton, and even with the less tolerant Westminster, Winchester was precise and inflexible in the character and enforcement of its discipline. The gates of College were kept locked and egress was not permitted except on saints' days and whole holidays, other than for officially recognized and organized expeditions on two afternoons of every week. On the other four days the boys were only allowed to go out for one hour between twelve and one, to 'meads', the playing field at the back of College and beyond the walls of Commoners for air and exercise. Boys complained that 'the doors to meads seemed always to be locked' and that it was difficult to 'get the Porter to open them'. On two afternoons a week the entire school, college boys and Commoners together, went for a walk two by two, under the command of the head college boy, the praefect of hall, with an occasional roll call on the way by the headmaster, whose official title was Informator.

At Winchester boys in College had their 'chambers' on the ground floor of three sides of an inner quadrangle comprising seven chambers, heated in winter by log fires. Each chamber where boys lived and slept was allotted a praefect, and a chamber constituted the basic social unit of life in College. In the middle of the chamber was a pillar, hung with surplices, and over the fireplace an iron sconce with a rushlight 'functure' which burned all night. Each boy had a chest which acted as a seat and a little desk with cupboard above, called Toys, where he kept his books and papers; and each boy was allocated his clearly defined share of domestic tasks. College boys enjoyed more intimate living conditions than Commoners, but no Wykehamist ever really knew the meaning of privacy, nor was intended to. Privacy was not a Good Notion.

Some element of pre-reformation monastic rigour, in which the foundation had its origins, seemed to have survived to circumscribe Wykehamist life with a peculiar and exacting type of formality. At Eton it was the normal practice for a boy to choose his closer friends from comrades in the house where he boarded; a boy who did otherwise would be considered a bit odd; but no one would have thought for a moment that he should be forbidden this idiosyncracy. At Winchester such matters were not left to a boy's discretion. What was and what was not permissible, even to social transaction, was laid down and codified into 'Notions'. There were Good Notions and there were Bad Notions, and for a boy to cultivate a preferential friendship with a boy in a different part of the school was a Bad Notion. Juniors had to memorize Notions and answer an oral examination to the satisfaction of praefects. The traditions of the place, 'as inflexible as the Laws of the Medes and the Persians', were more rigorously perpetuated than elsewhere.[5] The ancient Catholic practice of ambulatory prayers, 'going circum', was piously observed.

So were other, curious and sometimes mysterious practices. The origin of the custom of college boys doffing their hats as they passed under the main archway was unknown, but no one thought of abandoning it. News of a vacancy at New College, Oxford, was brought by a messenger called a 'Speedy Man'. He arrived with the appearance of breathless urgency, after a long journey, in brown cloth breeches and gaiters covered with dust. The 'news' was no news, for letters advising the warden of a vacancy had already arrived, but 'with reverence to tradition', the Speedy Man came all the same, journeying on foot. For him, in any event, the journey was well worth making, for he was handsomely entertained and regaled with college beer, which was very good.

Rugby was not quite as tenaciously conservative as Winchester. There was an old song sung traditionally at Rugby at the end of term, the fourth stanza of which went

> Let us now, my jovial fellows
> Shout aloud with youthful glee
> Sing old Rose and burn the bellows.

The third line was later changed to

> Sing sweet home and burn libellos

115

because nobody knew what the original line signified. At Winchester, once the lyric had been consecrated by time it would have been deemed untouchable.*

Life as a Colleger on a public-school foundation was punctuated by traditional and historic ceremonies, some of them more agreeable than others. At Eton there was 'Threepenny Day' when the praeposter, list in hand, accompanied the bursar who, by custom, distributed to each boy a threepenny piece, or rather, in practice, a sixpenny piece to every second boy, which he was trusted to divide with his unrequited neighbour. But, again in practice, the boys tossed a coin 'heads or tails' for the sixpence. When the distribution had first been established each Colleger had been entitled to half a sheep, and 3d was its current value in coin. Some years later, apprised of this historic intelligence, one boy called Branwell, when his turn came, told Bethell, the bursar, that he would rather have the half sheep. He may have spoken abruptly, without a prudent civil preface, and Bethell, not at any time the most amiable of men, flew into a rage and exclaimed, 'I'll tell the headmaster of you, and have you flogged.' And flogged he was.

A more consequential misdemeanour to the school authorities, because it offended against rights of property of others, varied conventionally according to its nature. Money and jewellery were untouchable, and a boy detected in breach of this code would suffer ostracism. But all else – food, drink, clothes, books – were legitimate plunder[7] and trunks and desks were broken into shamelessly. 'I found my bureau broken open. . . .' Fortescue Wells wrote to his father in 1833. 'At Eton stealing is the order of the day. . . .'[8] James Lee Warner, writing to his mother from Rugby in 1849, reported, 'Stealing here is not uncommon and they alter the 8th commandment to "thou shalt steal nothing except. . . ."'[9] The first piece of friendly advice Stanley got at Rugby concerned the security of his hat. 'Put your name on it or you'll have it bagged.'[10]

When they were not oppressing one another, boys at public schools from 1800 to approximately 1860 were free of adult authority to a degree which might seem bizarre to a modern eye. 'Sat up all night with three other fellows swigging wine and playing cards. We had three bottles and a fine ham,' says Charles Minet, aged fifteen, in

---

* The mysterious line alluded to a former Rugbeian called George Rose (later the MP for Christchurch) who, in moments of elation or excitement, used to burst into song and consign furniture within reach to the fire. On the occasion celebrated in the song, the bellows alone remained for sacrifice.[6]

his Winchester Diary. 'Shirked chapel next morning 2hrs sleep. Told looked unwell. But after breakfast much better – Not so Meredith.' Again, 'At four o'clock a great bowl of punch with Sheddersen. At night after tutor had gone round we grubbed a cold goose up in our room, having no plates we eat of the back of our basins which gave it a great flavour, aided by a comfortable bowl of punch.'[11]

Appetite was sharpened by adventurous forays on the enemy, in this case College. 'On Sunday, Oct., got up into Chambers and made about 20 apple pie beds, broke about 50 cups and pots, etc.' A good day's sport to be celebrated illicitly in the taverns 'after which Master Duff was rather top heavy'.

Early morning was not always a time of peace. Thomas Arnold, fourteen years old, writes home from Winchester: 'Dear Aunt, On the morning of the twenty-ninth of the Anniversary of the Restoration, and on the taking of Constantinople by the Turks our Chambers sustained a most dreadful Siege for nearly two hours without intermission I will relate the Particulars of this most memorable Action at full length; and if the Perusal of it gives you as much Pleasure as the Acting of it did me, I shall think myself amply rewarded.'

Thomas explains to his aunt at length that it was the custom of boys to rise early to read and prepare their lessons, and some 'for the purpose of making a noise and disturbing the sleep of others', and on this morning, two boys in his chamber having got up early and gone out, he had deemed it prudent to relock the door after them lest the chamber be invaded by enemies and all of them 'pull'd out of bed'. But the locked door proved only a challenge.

The Noisy multitude out in Court, who already made great Havoc in two other Chambers, when finding our door locked, they had Recourse to Stratagem; & sent out one of those who had got up out of our Chamber to the Window to ask us to open the door, under pretence of getting out a book: In case this had succeeded, they all intended to rush in. – But we were too cunning for them, so having tried the same Stratagem twice without Effect, they commenc'd to attack in Form. Now the beds were disposed in order all round the Chamber and mine was close to one Side of the Window, the head of it being placed against the Wall in which the Window is & as there is over it a Head very much resembling that of the little turn up bed I used to sleep in, I was very secure. Moreover my Bookcase and Desk, or as it is called Wicamise Toys, were on the side of me as shelter, so I defied their efforts. But they deliberately breaking a pane of glass open the Window entirely & rain'd a most dreadful shower of trenchers Bread, Water &c.,

which horrible Din woke us all, & we immediately began to Concert Measures for our Defence. On Top of my Bed I keep my Shoes and washing Box with various other Articles, and as I was thrusting my Nose out of Bed to learn the Cause of such an Uproar, one of the enemy, putting a long stick thro' the Window push'd every Thing down on my Head. I was so much annoy'd at this, that I immediately drew my feet up into the Bed out of Reach of the Shot, as several pieces of Glass had fallen around me. – In the mean Time one of our Men got up on the Top of a Bed on the other side of the Window, in such a Situation that without being touch'd himself, he could annoy anyone who came near to the Window: Here he stood arm'd with Cups of Beer which he pour'd very liberally on all who came near him, to the great Discomfiture of the hostile Squadrons. – But another of our Men coming out in his Shirt to the scene of the Action & not being sufficiently cautious, received such a Wound in his Posteriors from a stone that he fled howling to his bed. In the meantime it was first peal. . . .

The engagement described was in no way exceptional. His chamber is, says Thomas, 'Very subject to sieges'; and he himself, he tells us, lately was 'besieged in his bed by about six Fellows', the cause being his 'getting into bed before the other Fellows'. The assaulting party had a leader:

Lipscomb coming into the Chamber & beginning the Assault & the Forces of the Enemy increasing, I sprung out of Bed, and girding a Blanket about me, & standing up on my Bed gave & sustained a most dreadful Fire – Loaves of Crum of Bread, Washing Boxes, Candles, Candle Sticks, the Broom & every kind of missile Weapon was hurl'd without Distinction; I received a wound on my head from a washing box, but my Pericranium being far harder than any Stone, the Washing Box rebounded; the only Damage I sustained was in my Bed, which was not only pull'd to Pieces entirely, but so covered with Crumbs, Candles &c, that I was oblig'd to make it again completely.[12]

This high-spirited, cheerful boy of action is a distant figure from the sombre headmaster which he became less than twenty years later, obsessed with 'sin' and the almost unimaginable 'wickedness of boys'. At the age of thirteen he described the following encounter in a letter to his aunt:

This morning as we were going to Hills we pass'd, or rather accompanied Eight hundred Souldiers who were all going to the River to bathe; At one place we had to cut through them all, & so both kept advancing, the Hustling was in Consequence great. When they came to the River, I never in my Life saw such a Sight: They all stripp'd and danc'd about the Banks, some jump'd in, all raising the most horrible Cries, as you must know it rain'd the whole Time, – & the Wind was very fresh. – I suppose it was done to make them hardy.[13]

His letters, in their graphic exuberance, are probably the most revealing picture of one aspect of boys' lives – their social freedom – in public school at the beginning of the century to have been written and survived.*

'It seems to us a matter of course,' said one qualified admirer of the system, 'that our public schoolboys should be trusted with liberties which would astonish foreigners.' All the benefits which Gladstone derived from Eton came to him 'from the liberties of the place', and its corollary, the absence of the 'spiritual tyranny' which was exercised over boys by the headmasters of 'the clerical schools on the continent'. The writer felt it necessary to add that this 'spiritual tyranny', the surveillance of boys' private lives by masters, and the enforcement of uniform and competitive recreational occupations, were also exercised by the headmasters of certain new English schools '. . . with no good results'.[14]

At Eton conditions varied widely between King's Scholars and Oppidan boarders. In general the lot of a King's Scholar was from the beginning to the end of his life in college more austere as well as less private than that of an Oppidan, residing in his own little room in a boarding house. College diet was unwaveringly monotonous and, for juniors at least, insufficient to satisfy the appetite of a growing boy.

With few exceptions the fellows, who alone had the power to remedy established wrongs, were unperturbed by conditions prevailing in college, which they had suffered themselves as boys, and now regarded from a comfortable distance with whimsical approval as a salutary experience. '*I* was cold,' Provost Goodall is reputed to have said, 'Now these boys can be cold.' Whether he said these words or

---

* They were all available to Stanley when he wrote his life of Arnold but, except for the briefest passing allusion, he makes no use of them; no passages are quoted. Their unregenerate male adolescence did not harmonize with the final and only posture in which Stanley wished his hero to be observed.

not, he and others acted by them. Tucker, invited to dine in cloisters at Windsor by a venerable fellow, over a good – to him sumptuous – repast, could not resist alluding to the hardships, and especially the 'short commons griefs' of life in college. His host smiled cheerfully and observed that modern Collegers were much better off than Collegers of his day had been, and that he remembered once supplementing his dinner with raw turnips from a field. Tucker restrained himself from reminding his elder that the turnips had not been his to eat.

A Colleger breakfasted at ten at his Dame's, the proprietor of the residence where a quota of Oppidans boarded. Each Colleger also had a Dame allocated to him, to whom he went, if he was ill, to 'stay out', who disbursed his tea and sugar allowance, saw to his washing, gave him pocket money by arrangement and also breakfast daily. The nourishment provided was a half pint of milk in a tin with a loop handle, and a penny roll and butter. A second roll was provided in addition by the 'mercy' of his family; any extras he had to provide himself, and breakfast was consumed for want of anywhere else on the Dame's dresser.

Dinner was served at two o'clock and lower Collegers mustered in an anteroom to the college kitchen, a bare-bricked cellar. When the joints were arranged on a large dresser there was a fierce rush at them by the young servitors, the object being to seize a leg or a loin because they would go first. A procession of boys, each carrying a round pewter dish on which rested plates, then set off up the stairs to the Hall, where the assembly stood in line. The captain of the first mess, consisting of eight boys, stood up and chose a joint, a loin, that was apportioned for eight. The ninth boy was captain of the next mess, their number depending on the size of the joint chosen. Dinner was eaten off pewter plates with 'broad horn-handled two pronged forks, and broad round bladed knives, known as "pea eaters".' The mutton was Southdown and therefore a small animal. 'It was,' said Tucker, 'cooked to perfection.'[15] Not everyone shared his approval of its culinary preparation,* but upon the matter of quantity everyone who passed through college was agreed: there was not enough of it, and the chief sufferers from the insufficiency were the smaller and younger boys. It would be a chivalrous hungry adolescent who stinted himself at table for the sake of a junior, it

---

* '. . . roasted almost to a chip, the dripping being his (the cook's) perquisite'.[16] The allowance of meat in college at Westminster seems to have been even less than at Eton.[17]

would be well-nigh à saint who did so as a regular practice. Everyone carved for himself. A loin was not enough for eight and, says Tucker, 'day after day during my first year I was forced to dine on dry bread dipped in the dish and potatos'. Tucker was rather unlucky, because a year or two later strong pressure from many quarters compelled College to take the matter up and the loin was promoted to serve only six. It would have been difficult for the 'College' to have done otherwise, for the fellows had so much to conceal in respect of maintaining a rich standard of life for themselves and dining grandly with funds properly intended for the welfare of the hungry boys in their charge.* Disputes between the fellows furnished periodic entertainment. On one occasion the disputants were brothers, called Roberts. One Roberts (William) contended that potatoes served to the boys in college should be peeled. 'The boys,' he said, 'had been treated like hogs.' The other Roberts (John Abraham) opposed the suggestion as 'an unnecessary piece of refinement'. For generations to come, long after the origin of the distinction had been forgotten, the Etonian kin of the two Robertses were distinguished as the Hog Roberts and the Peelpo (or Peely or Peelypo) Roberts. With the mutton, college-brewed beer was served, and in summer months a quantity of bread and beer was set out in Hall under the name of Bever. Later in the century the custom was abolished amidst groans and lamentations by late Victorians, old gentlemen who had been Collegers; a remarkable tribute to the force of tradition, because none of them in their time had ever drunk the stuff, except *in extremis*, and had pocketed the bread to supplement private entertainment later and elsewhere. Of the beer, 'I do not think,' says Tucker, 'writing as I do some eighty years after – that any beverage was ever so vile, villainous and detestable.' Complaints were made and, at least once, a fellow made an appearance and went down the tables with an 'enquiring mind', looked at the beer, did not smell or taste it, and went away; that was all; as for the beer, it never improved, never altered.

Supper was served in Hall and consisted of scraps of cold mutton. No other meat but mutton was served as part of the regulation and it was served every day. It is remarkable that, as many Collegers have borne witness, subjection to this regimen for perhaps a decade did not have the effect of disinclining them to mutton in later life;

---

* The retention and private disbursement among themselves by the fellows of substantial fines paid on the renewal of leases on college property, and not shown in the accounts, occasioned strong criticism by the Clarendon Commission (see below, p. 325).

but the serving of mutton for a second time in one day, and cold, seems to have caused what today would be called 'food fatigue', which evinced itself in the form of a taboo against the supper. It was worse than unfashionable, and even hungry boys would eschew it, and despise the few who were unable to do so.[18]* The alternative was private provision, when one's purse was equal to it. The cook at the Christopher Inn made daily a variety of good apple, currant and gooseberry tinned puddings which were cut in half and sold at sixpence each. Roast poultry and other dainties were also supplied at considerable price, which put them beyond the reach of the majority as a regular source of nourishment. 'I have gone times without number,' says Tucker, 'without a morsel of food within my lips from dinner to breakfast, save draughts of water; and I have slept and dreamed of feasts and banquets such as boys of nine or ten can imagine, many a night. . . .'

The sixth were privileged; they enjoyed a hot supper, mutton again of course, in lower chamber, and three lucky juniors were detailed in rotation to wait upon them. Their luck lay in the chance of getting a morsel left over. A loin of mutton was allowed for twelve. In practice it was shared by the first four of the sixth form, who split it into two bones each. The remaining eight ordered theirs to be sent in from the Christopher Inn. As the entire community was locked in at night, orders for food and drink were taken through a grated window by a cad called Swaine. His tip was a chump chop from the roast he conveyed, which he would sell back for a shilling to anyone who wanted it. Superb porter was to be obtained at a shilling a quart from Garroway, the host of the Christopher, which had been brewed at Bulstrode, the Duke of Portland's seat; a more common variety was on sale at 6d a quart. According to etiquette the sixth ate only 'bone meat', the 'flaps' being sometimes bestowed upon a servitor or favourite, who might consume it, or share it with a chosen friend. Occasionally by this declension little William Tucker became possessed of a piece of meat and 'I,' he says, 'in the fierceness of my hunger have gnawed it without bread or salt like a dog – and with a dog's appetite.' Oppidans, unlike Tugs,† dined at their Dames' and had a varied diet. The quality of the diet varied too, from establishment to establishment. Some of the Dames were women of fashion;

---

* The significance of the rejection was misunderstood by Mack who describes as 'absurdities . . . unjustifiable in rational terms' such 'Eton practises' as 'refusing to eat a good supper because the scraps of meat were considered infradig'.[19]
† Short for 'Tug Muttons', a contemptuous allusion to the diet of Collegers.

at least one, Florella Angelo, received her lucrative appointment at the age of eighteen as a mark of favour from the Prince of Wales.

Pocket money and provision from home – what at Rugby was known as the 'home hamper' – could make the difference between comfort and privation to a boy's condition at school. Sometimes parents and friends sent so much that a headmaster had to appeal for moderation, as the headmaster of Rugby, Dr Wooll, did, in a general communication objecting to the boys' receipt of so much 'poultry and other meat' which was 'productive of mischief'.* But, as we have seen, at some schools and times boys who did not receive enough help from home might go short of what should have been recognized as necessities for health. Conditions varied with wild irregularity from, at their worst, too little food, and of a kind which 'delicate boys could not eat',[20] to periodic compensatory feasts, paid for by the boys themselves or provided by their friends. 'At Surley, an immense quantity of wine was drunk,' says Gaskell, 'and champagne from the Ale house . . . the tables were covered with hams, turkeys, pigeons, fowls, geese and everything cold. There was a great abundance of oysters and wine.'[21] But this was a very special occasion, the celebration of Montem, when the Colleger captain had an abnormally large sum of money at his disposal which he was expected, and indeed obliged, to expend on lavish entertainment of his army; and the effects of one meal, however nourishing, did not last for ever. A hamper containing 'the usual amount of sock'† was always acceptable, 'a partridge or two and ham would do nicely for breakfast', just as another boy, a few decades earlier, had written, 'A hare and a barrel of oysters would be very acceptable to me.'[22] In practice many boys were given too little to eat at school dinners; some could not eat what was provided and recourse to hampers and sock was often 'not greed but pure hunger'.[23] The symptoms ridiculed by the Rev. S. Tillbrook in a general letter to Samuel Butler were indicative of malnutrition, not gluttony.‡ Memories of special fare on days

* A single printed page, headed 'Rugby School. The Second Tuesday in June 1812. Temple'. Similar appeals were made by other headmasters of the public schools, including Dr Keate. See letter from an Eton Dame to a boy's father, W. W. Farr, in 1823; *ETA*, no. 122 (7 June 1969), p. 339.

† Etonese for tuck: also, as a verb, 'to treat'.

‡ 'Who could ever hope to satisfy the real or fancied cravings of a hungry schoolboy? I remember a schoolfellow of mine who after dinner drew the wick of a mould candle through his teeth and ate the cold tallow afterwards. Upon this he piled up eight raw turnips and twelve large cooking apples. Besides these he cracked nuts during a walk of four miles . . . and then at night ate toasted cheese and drank a joram of treacle, or ate it so crumbled with bread that the spoon stood erect in it.' Samuel Butler, *Life and Letters*, p. 162.

of celebration were cherished. 'Mock turtle soup, veal cutlets and asparagus and marrow pudding,' the boy Thomas Arnold reported home with rapture of the warden's dinner served after Commoners Speeches, adding, in anticipation of family reaction, 'I suppose you will say I am always caring about my inside. . . .'[24] Disappointments were poignant: 'We were quite cheated out our sock;' and displeasure vigorously expressed: 'Please give Susan a good scolding as a preparatory one, for I will give it her precisely when I get home. She picked out the very worst ham she could find; hardly a bit of lean, and that so musty that nobody can eat it.'* In such situations the hospitality of generous masters was memorable. ('William and I breakfasted with our tutor the other day and he gave us sumptuous entertainment'), while against so much often deserved satire and complaint upon school food must be set a not inconsiderable record of satisfaction and approval of the catering of particular houses. 'She' (his Dame) 'actually gave us a whole and very fine salmon,' W. E. Gladstone wrote to his father from Shurey's in 1822. 'We have tart or pudding every day and always two dishes of meat.'[25] 'We have very good dinners altogether in the dining room,' said Henry Everard, writing to his eldest brother and guardian, Samuel Everard, from Hexter's House, on 13 September 1831. 'Today we had codfish and roast beef, and so on every day. Tea I may not have without an order from you or Rob, but I had as leave be without it as with it. Supper we have about eight o-clock which generally consists of either cold fruit pie or meat, and bread and cheese. In every meal we may have as much as we like, eat just what we like and leave what we do not like. Breakfast about 10 o'clock, Dinner about 1 o'clock, supper about 8, I think I fare very well.'[26]

Such compliments are noteworthy, for, while from the dissatisfied complaints come readily, the well provided tend to accept their state as a just and natural one, requiring no acknowledgement.

To be dined out by good-natured adult friends was always supreme delight. A kind and, perhaps, effortless gesture by an adult to an adolescent of generous feelings may have earned its maker, unknown then to him, a lifetime of gratitude. 'We had been well pouched at Ascot,' says our young acquaintance and guide Charles Wilkinson, making a declaration seventy years after the event, still with the zest almost of boyhood; 'and I would like to record this of some kind

---

* Charles Willington Johnson, 1838; see Faith Compton Mackenzie, *William Cory, a Biography* (1950), p. 8.

friends who always came to the races, always asked about a dozen of us to a capital dinner, and always, when dessert came on the table, shelled out, by the hand of the president, a sovereign apiece on every plate of strawberries and iced cream handed round with a glass of Curacoa after dinner. These three hosts were not even near relations, only distant cousins of some of us, but great friends of our respective fathers, and Eton men to the backbone, and they knew well what pleased Eton boys. I sincerely hope, if there are any of the boy-party still alive, they feel as much gratitude as I do, and honour the memory of such friends to this day.'[27]

Milnes Gaskell, with his interest in politics already rivalling his interest in food, managed to have the best of both worlds by getting asked to dinner by the statesman and gourmet Lord Canning, whose son Charles was his con. He reported the bill of fare and other particulars dutifully to Mamma: 'Soup with espar in it, eels, boiled fish, lamb, veal, beefsteak pie, two tarts, fowls, oranges, biscuits, claret, sherry, port'; and, in reply to a question from the waiter what wine he would take, 'Lord Canning answered, "port".'[28]

For juniors in general, and for a Milnes Gaskell in particular, going home for the holidays at the end of a school half was not only an escape from work and hardship of all kinds, it was a time of eating deliciously every day, or as often as parental means and indulgence would permit. Wilkinson decided to launch the summer holidays on 'election Monday', which was the end of a half, rowing with a companion past Datchet and Staines and feasting al fresco on the then idyllic and unspoilt banks of the Thames, just beyond the Bells of Ousley. Having moored at a perfect spot for a picnic, they disembarked and made a fire and at first all went well. Rowing had made them hungry and the menu was worthy of their appetites: 'portable soup', veal and ham pie, made by 'a lady up town' on whom they could depend and be sure 'it was not made of kittens', a duck roasted over the fire and broad beans; cucumber, tarts and tartlets, cake and fruit, and shandy-cap, and cider-cup in abundance, made with the best ingredients obtainable. But alas, all this was not deemed enough; for at this time no private celebration between boys, especially at the start of the holidays, was considered complete without large Havana cigars, tied with blue ribbon and stamped with the maker's name; and two of these 'royal cigars' they lit up and 'puffed away a good half hour in pleasant chat'. The sequel was a melancholy humiliation. The state of well-being began to change to one of increasing uneasiness then to prostration. They were both 'very, very sick', and they had to be rowed, recumbent in the bows, by their water cad, Billy Fish, down river to as far as Richmond where they arrived about dusk and took a post chaise to London.[29]

Breakfast was a favourite occasion for Oppidan entertainment of friends at Eton; and hospitality was lavish in all things but bread and butter. Consequently on a holiday morning, about ten o'clock, 'one may see divers curious specimens of humanity trotting around college with plates on which are displayed sundry rations of bread and butter'.

'We know nothing so excellent as a really good Eton breakfast,' is the tribute of one young participant; '. . . the great beauty of these breakfasts are the freedom of conversation and utter want of restraint or ceremony, combined with the greatest hospitality which are to be found there.'

The system allowed three or four boys to mess together, constituting a family, a party with guests when invited, a club and a debating society all in one, a delightful arrangement securing for the members a meeting 'of kindred spirits twice a day for a period perhaps of several years, and', said one of many devoted witnesses, 'lasting in some cases (it was so in my own) till death did us part. . . .'[30]

A subsequent Etonian, J. K. Stephen,* celebrated the camaraderie of the mess in wistful verse:

> There were two good fellows I used to know –
> How distant it all appears!
> We played together in football weather
> And messed together for years:

* J. K. Stephen was remembered by Etonian contemporaries as the archetype of the 'schoolboy hero'. Born in 1859, the son of Sir James Fitzjames Stephen, Stephen was a handsome, magnetic young giant of great bodily strength, whose prowess at the wall game was such that later Etonians, nourished on the legends, supposed that he had invented the game. Stephen wrote light verse with facility in Greek, Latin and English; he was an eloquent and moving speaker, and when he went up to Cambridge and into residence at King's in 1878, he speedily became one of the best known undergraduates of his time. In 1881 he was bracketed first class in the History Tripos and was president of the union. In 1883 he was selected to 'read history with', that is to say, to act as tutor to, Prince Edward of Wales, later Duke of Clarence. He lived for a time at Sandringham and became intimate with his royal pupil. In 1885 he was made Fellow of Trinity.

After this not unpropitious start, Stephen's career declined into a strange anti-climax, perplexing to his admirers. He was called to the bar, but made little progress in this profession. He did some desultory journalism and started a magazine called *The Reflector*, which increased in size as it diminished in circulation and came to an end after seventeen numbers.

Nothing he touched seemed thereafter to advance or mature. In particular his relations with women were frustrated and embittered.

In 1886 Stephen was reported to have suffered a mysterious and unparticularized 'head

Now one of them's wed,* and the other's dead
So long that he's hardly missed
Save by us, who messed with him years ago:
But we're all in the Old School List.[31]

The delights of social breakfasts were also sung at Harrow, but there another kind of breakfast, less enjoyable and more constrained, was periodically given by senior boys as part of the duties of their rank. It was a Harrovian practice for mothers of little boys newly dispatched to the school to write to older boys, the sons of friends and known to the family, committing to their protection the newly arrived fledglings. It was quite impractical for a senior boy, moving in an entirely different circle, to keep a close eye on several juniors living in different houses; but duty required from a 'protector', apart from the occasional nod in the street, once a quarter, a *Breakfast*.

A letter of invitation was drafted:

Dear ——

Will you breakfast with me tomorrow if you are not otherwise engaged? I have not been able to see so much of you yet as I could have wished. I hope you will always let me know if I can help you in any way. Please remember me to your mother when you write next.

Yours very sincerely

Several such missives having been dispatched, the host goes off to order plenty to eat, 'for those small fellows do eat a lot'. Next day, after first school, he returns to his study to find it crowded with as large a table as it will hold and 'three or four small boys sitting on the edge of chairs, looking very shy'. Before he arrived they had occupied themselves in examining his books, pictures and ornaments, and peeping into the dishes on the table. The guests having sat down, after needing to be asked at least three times before they did so, the ordeal begins. The gulf between twelve and seventeen is enormous; a conversational morass is entered, and nervous anxiety is likely to occasion blunders difficult to correct. A plate of tongue intended to

continued from page 126
injury' while on holiday at Felixstowe. Thereafter his health deteriorated and he became incapable of regular work. In fact James Stephen was incurably insane and had become dangerous and homicidal. He was put under restraint and died on 3 February 1892, a week after the death of the Duke of Clarence. Michael Harrison has assembled in *Clarence* (1972) evidence in support of his contention that J. K. Stephen was 'Jack the Ripper'.

* Harry Chester Goodhart, Professor of Latin at Edinburgh University, the last survivor of the mess, died in 1895, aged thirty-seven.

serve all the party is passed to the first little guest who nervously places it before him without passing it on, not daring to ask for less, amidst the 'mute despair and deep dumb agony' of the tongueless rest.

There is one happy solution, if it is grasped in time. Once the guests are seated the host receives an urgent summons elsewhere and repairs to a private breakfast with his cronies, leaving the little boys, with plenty of food, comfortably on their own.[32]

In addition to entertaining in their rooms, Etonians who could afford it supplemented their official diet at illicit supper clubs held in the Christopher and other hostelries. Gaskell remembers a rather 'wild' boy called Clarke,* 'intended for the church', eating beef steaks and drinking port wine with Leith. Oppidans sometimes required such supplement to their prescribed diet; Collegers always did, and on one occasion they enriched their fare for a considerable time by an appropriation which passed into Eton mythology. A close description of the proceedings has been given by someone (Crickitt Blake) who was a Colleger in Long Chamber when the abduction was committed:

> A sow, very near her acouchement, had been observed by the boys feeding in *Western's Yard* close to the dormitory; when a most mischievous thought occurred, that she might be made useful to the community. . . . The scheme succeeded admirably . . . by throwing one of their cloth gowns over the old lady's snout, to obscure her vision, as well as to confine her speaking trumpet from giving too much tongue, immediately, by the exertions of four stout boys, and no easy matter either, she was landed on top of a tower attached to Long Chamber, and afforded the captors delicious suppers. . . .[33]

Confirmation of the main particulars of the account comes from several quarters, though with a supplement which the remembrancer would not have relished; for, disassociating himself from the actual performance, Blake writes (still supposing himself invisible in anonymity), that he 'had no hand nor in anyway participated in the sweets' of the operation. Another boy, well acquainted with the event as it was known in Long Chamber, wrote to his father, 'There was once a boy in College named Blake who was a dreadful thief. He once caught an old sow that was just going to have young ones, and he

---

* Baumaris Stracey Clarke, fourth form, 1826, entered the Navy; ordained an appointed chaplain, Madras.

took her and kept her on the top of Long Chamber, out on the leads. He kept her there until she had young ones, and he eat the young ones, and then turned the old sow loose again.'[34]

Alfred Tennyson's Etonian brother brought the story home and the poet worked it into *Walking to the Mail*.

> By night we dragged her to the College tower
> From her warm bed and up the cork-screw stairs
> With hand and rope we hauled the groaning sow,
> And on the leads we kept her till she pigged

Sympathy with the bereaved parent is delicately ennobled with classical allusion:

> We took them all, till she was left alone
> Upon her tower, the Niobe of Swine.

Tucker, although he did not witness it himself, alludes to a 'legend' of a donkey having spent a night in Long Chamber. Collins, in *Etoniana*, is a believer, though a baffled one. 'It is an undoubted fact,' he writes, 'that a donkey – though with what possible motive it is hard to conjecture, as there could be no hope of supper from that quarter – was kept in Long Chamber for at least one night and regaled with unaccustomed luxury:

> At length an urchin said
> The poor ass must not starve, or he will die
> Which would be very sad, and therefore I
> Will share with him my supper – a veal pie

The donkey was no fiction, and during his overnight stay in Long Chamber, his erstwhile master was none other than our friend Charles Wilkinson, now in 1830 grown to the grandeur of Captain of the School. The occasion was the annual carnival and masquerade held at night in College. It was the Collegers' 'liberty night', a saturnalia, or slaves' holiday, when all were equal, and when the sixth form not only allowed, but were the heart and soul of the fun. The beds were all turned up and penny dips, at least two per head, were stuck upright in their own tallow at all the corners. Private dressing rooms were erected by nailing blankets and rugs between two beds, and in these boys transformed themselves into various striking characters (of both sexes) with costumes and make-up, over which sometimes a great trouble had been taken, and which were intended to conceal the identity of the devisers.

This was, in more ways than one, Wilkinson's special night. He resolved upon a role which would be in its way a unique display. During the holidays he had gone to the opera in London and seen a performance of *Elisir D'amore* in which the character of the mountebank had come on to the stage with a donkey and cart. Here was a character he could make memorable in the annals of Eton masquerade. He would go as Dr Dulcamara. A dress with gold braid was hired, a three-cornered wig and pig-tail. The cart was considered dispensable; but the glory of the part which must be at all costs retained was the attendant donkey. Wilkinson obtained some old saddlebags at a pawnbroker's and then entered into negotiations for the procurement of a donkey with the cad, Picky Powell, who would undertake for a fee to procure anything, legitimate or illegitimate, for the boys.

Wilkinson gives an account of the operation:

At the three-quarters I went out to look after my donkey. Picky Powell was punctual to his time, and after wasting five minutes opposite Keate's lane, and seeing no appearance of the lantern, we thought we were quite safe, and we led the donkey – with the judicious persuasion of a bunch of carrots in front of him – across the school-yard, through Lower School passage and up the steps into Lower Chamber.

We had pushed the beast into the captain's study, when the hiss gave notice of Keate's approach. I had just time to throw a rug to the cad, and tell him to hold it over the beast's head, and to rub him and feed him and keep him quiet, for not a sound or movement must be heard. My young brother was just trying on his dress [he was going as a legless, armless, blacking bottle], that is, his wicker-basket, which was tight, and he could not get out, so the boys shoved him, as he was, into another study and stood before the door. In came the doctor, and we were all attention with a vengeance, for our ears were sensitively on the watch for any sound from the studies. I as captain, called absence, leaving my brother to the last, but when I came to 'Wilkinson, minimus,' an extraordinary answer was given from the inside of his basket, through the eye-holes.

'Here, sir.'

'Here, sir,' said old Keate, 'where, sir, come out, sir,' and again that heavy sound broke out once more, as if some boatswain was giving an order through his two hands at his mouth. 'What's this, sir, come out, sir' said Keate; and, as there was no appearance, he walked up to the study-door, and there, about the size of his own little self, stood the

130

brown-paper effigy, with 'Day and Martin's Blacking – greatest wonder of the age,' staring him in the face. He seized it by the cork and shook it, crying still. 'Come out, sir, you fool, sir, come out,' and my young brother, having no hands to make resistance, fell forward into the room and crept out at the bottom.[35]

All breathed again when the doctor, his servant and lantern had retreated into the night. Toleration might not have extended to the presence of a donkey.

When the revels were at their height, Wilkinson and a team of assistants, with much pushing and pulling, gradually boy-handled the four-footed player up the stairs and Wilkinson made a triumphant entry on his steed as Dr Dulcamara, and passed off his wares and sold his saddlebags of gimcracks to a delighted audience. Afterwards there was a picnic supper to which all had contributed according to their means and 'the donkey came in for a share of viands that had never fallen to a donkey's lot before'. Then there were songs 'that might have been heard in the Long Walk'.

Next morning, like all revels, the wonder and delights seemed to have passed away, an insubstantial dream that had never known reality; but its record was safely stored away in the memory of Wilkinson major, to be produced at will any time during the next seventy years in witness of 'the merry days when we were young'.

In Wilkinson's schooldays Eton was, and could be nothing else but, a microcosm, and a conservative and change-resisting one, of the fashionable world outside, a world of hard drinking, ruinous gambling, horse racing, blood sports and prize fighting.

In Long Chamber, Collegers, locked up for the night in their quarters, would engage periodically in a traditional domestic sport of their own, which required the participation of every boy. When lights went out, in the darkness each night the rats came in troops, 'well fed and wary' and could be heard scuttling up and down in their operations all night long. In Tucker's time one old rat, having once been caught in a trap and left one of his legs in it, was recognized for years thereafter by his halting, tripping run. The rats used to come in the darkness not by twos and threes, but, as it sounded, by swarms, to feed upon the refuse of the liberty supper when, besides broken bread and cheese and tart-pastry, bones were thrown out to attract the quarry. A big old rat, jumping from step to step, sounded 'like the step of a heavy man'. On the night of a *grande chasse* traps were baited and set. These were constructed of two 'strawberry pottles' with the bottoms knocked out and an inch or two cut off till they were just wide enough to enable maurauders to creep through easily; the ends were then inserted and tied fast into long worsted stockings, into the top of which fresh toasted cheese had been dropped. The next stage was the most taxing for boys; 'speechless, breathless' silence, in the midst of darkness trembling with the flicker of fires.

When a sufficient host was judged to have been lured on to the killing ground, the longed-for order to attack was given; the boys leapt out of bed, and silence and darkness were changed into the cries of hunters and the glare of torches. The rats stampeded. But all known holes and escape routes had been blocked. Fugitives took refuge under beds and bureaux and were pursued and bludgeoned to death in half an hour's good run of the *grande chasse*. 'It was really glorious fun,' exclaimed Wilkinson, in conclusion. 'Try it, some of you young fellows, if you have the opportunity and the necessary patience to abide your time.'[36]

Wilkinson does not add that the rats were stripped of their skins, which were carefully stretched and dried, and the trophies nailed in rows over the broad fireplaces from the ceilings downwards, a labour left uncompleted owing to the premature departure of the two expert rodent flayers and wall decorators to King's College, Cambridge. One of them returned to Eton as assistant master, but he did not renew his interior decoration of Long Chamber. Wilkinson does add a reflection which suggests that moral inhibitions, however faint, had to be suppressed in the reconstruction of the *grande chasse*. 'Rats,' he says, 'as well as foxes, are such maurauders that they are fair game.' It is unlikely that any word of justification would have been deemed necessary by the boy who had engaged in the sport; but the old man, looking back from 1885, had been subject during the interval of more than half a century to a changing distribution of moral pressures.

SEVEN
Liquor and Violence

In every public school there were periodic drives against drinking, usually when it became too conspicuous by occasioning collective disorder. In 1802, at Eton, Dr Goodall had to be summoned to quell violence which had got out of control in Ragenau's house, due mainly to a boy called Grose;* and in 1814, at Rugby, two boys, Fisher† and Cook, were central characters in a scandal of persistent drunkenness.‡ Thomas Arnold denounced liquor at Rugby, but in general little serious notice was taken of drinking unless it became a threat to corporate discipline. T. H. Green estimated that, when he went to Rugby at the age of fourteen, he was the only boy out of four hundred who was a 'water drinker', that is an abstainer from alcohol.[3]

At Winchester beer was not merely permitted, it was an obligatory drink for the boys. The beverage which incurred official displeasure was tea since, it having been unknown to the founder, there was no mention of it in the statutes. The boys drank it surreptitiously, but it remained in magisterial disfavour until 1838. Friends would form 'tea messes', for it was an expensive luxury; but if they were surprised by a master he would smash their cups with his heavy pass key, saying, 'What are these things, sir? Sir William of Wykeham knew nothing, I think, of tea.'

---

* Edward Grose, commissioned to the Guards, killed at Waterloo.
† John Fisher, Rector and Lord of the Manor of Higham-on-the-Hill, and grandfather of Geoffrey Fisher, Archbishop of Canterbury, 1945–61.
‡ Thomas Macaulay wrote home from Rugby, 'Some boys have been getting into a sad scrape. Fisher is one (the son of Mr Fisher of Higham) and Cook a boy boarded here is an other. . . . Fisher and the others were flogged publickly yesterday. Cook ran away last Sunday and Dr Wool will not take him back again.' Soon after, Thomas's brother, J. H. Macaulay, wrote in confirmation: 'Tom has told you that some boys got into a scrape but he has not told you what about. Its for drinking which has lately got into the school very much.'[1]
  A somewhat different version of the circumstances attending John Fisher's withdrawal from Rugby is given by the Fisher family records, according to which he was removed 'because of the school's roughness' and sent to Oakham School, Rutland. He went to Sydney College in 1815 and died in 1868.[2]

133

Periodically the sixth form in college at Eton regaled themselves with a feast, paid for with taxes collected for cricket overheads, when fags had the additional duty of getting their masters undressed and to bed. To accompany the fine fare sent over from the Christopher there was wine in abundance, claret, champagne, madeira and heady black-strap port.* At the end of the meal the exalted diners, attended by their unfed fags, repaired to tables drawn up in front of the fire in Long Chamber where, according to custom, they caroused on shilling bowls of Bishop – hot port, spiced and with a roasted lemon floating in the middle. Bishop is one of the most potent mulled vinous drinks ever devised.† After a few songs and choruses the boys, large and small, were babbling nonsense, with the juniors, half tipsy themselves, struggling to get the celebrants undressed and into bed.

Facilities for Oppidans were even freer. A typical party al fresco on 4 June is recalled. 'Meanwhile Jackson had been looking after himself in the same way as I had been, and both of us in the excitement of the evening had been drinking claret, champagne and sherry with the most egregious want of discrimination.'[4] When Prince George of Cumberland sent the crew of the first school boat eight dozen of champagne, 'it all went off well', Miss Brown remarked with relief;[5] but on a later occasion she deplored 'the folly of so many people having given the boys champagne'.[6] Her concern did not end with the boys. 'Dear Mr Keate' himself, who drank neat brandy in preference to Madeira on a hot cricketing afternoon was, she felt, 'more éveillé' when he lived sparingly, and less subject to frequent visits of 'his enemy, the gout'.[7]

Sometimes a Dame like Mrs Holt would try to prevent the receipt and consumption of liquor by boys in her house, but it was easy for them to circumvent her measures with the complicity of parents and friends.[8] Gladstone said that his father not only made him a moderate provision of wine at Eton, but insisted upon his drinking it.[9] In any event Gladstone would have experienced no problems of supply, for he lodged in Shurey's boarding house, which was treated as an extension of the Christopher Inn opposite, where boys needing to sober up could obtain a friendly emetic of mustard and water. It was

* Very young and spirituous wood port, bluish purple in its natural colour, which was generally darkened by the addition of elderberry juice to give it a semblance of maturity.

† An historic receipt I have used is as follows: Pour a bottle of wood port, ruby or tawney, into a pan, together with a lemon, cut in half and stuck with one or two cloves, and with a pudding spoonful of sugar. Warm the liquid: it must not boil. When the wine is hot, put a lighted match to the surface and it will flame. Pour into glasses and drink at once.

easy to speed a fag thither for liquor and, when the coast was clear, the boys would return running with his Princeps* full of beer or port. The Princeps, a receptacle of deceptive appearance made out of the covers of an early edition of Virgil, would hold – again our informant is Gladstone – three bottles, and when carried under the arm looked like 'a grave folio'. Keate seems to have had some inkling of its use; hence his otherwise inexplicable prohibition once addressed to all Lower boys (he seems, said Gladstone, 'to have accepted the inevitable from the Upper School'): 'I'll have no folios carried about; if I catch a boy with a folio I'll flog him.'[10]

The danger of gambling was that boys might be given credit far in excess of their means by unscrupulous men in the confidence that parents would honour the debts. 'Keate in a passion addressed the School,' said Gaskell, 'on boys gambling openly and tossing money in the streets on Sunday.' There is a vivid little picture of the shocking progress of the schoolboy gambler (called Frederick Golightly), painted at the time and from the life by a schoolboy:

> The time of Ascot Races was the most important period of the year for our young Blood. His room was literally the betting stand where all the juvenile amateurs of the Turf met to forestall their allowance until the next vacation. At this time you might observe Frederick in the centre of the School Yard, attended by his levee, with a list of high-bred cattle in his hand, which he was discussing, to the great edification of his audience.

Predictably Golightly comes to grief:

> His duns made his life miserable: it was quite impossible for him to walk up town without being accosted with a – 'Sir, you promised. . . .' 'Oh, I was coming down to you Mr Golightly.' 'The smallest trifle would be a consideration.' Pressed on all sides he was obliged to throw himself on the affections of his father who consented to pay off his debts on observing a thorough repentance.[11]

Sensible to the temptations and tone of society, prudent parents, even the richest, insisted in advance that their sons should keep accounts when they were away from home, so that they were always aware of what they were spending. 'I will not fail to be quite regular in my accounts,' Milnes Gaskell writes home more than once.[12]

* Princeps: first folio edition.

Roundell Palmer's father, a generous-hearted man of limited means who had to make a little money stretch as far as possible, felt the dangers of debt to his sons so keenly that he forbade them to obtain anything on credit; and when Roundell's brother returned from Rugby with a gift of two stuffed birds for his sisters, and had to admit that he had obtained them in anticipation of holiday tips from uncles and other adult relatives, he was sent back to school with them immediately, a two-day journey there and back, bearing a letter to the headmaster requesting him to instruct the tradesmen that the Palmers were forbidden to use and must not be offered credit in purchasing anything. But Mr Palmer was abnormally scrupulous.

In 1830 the headmaster of Harrow struggled to persuade more parents to take the attitude Mr Palmer had displayed. In a circular letter he wrote that, 'So long as the shopkeepers can trust the mistaken kindness [of parents] in ultimately discharging the amount incurred so long will he hold out temptation to the boys by giving them almost unlimited credit.' Monsieur Bernard, a French victualler trading at Harrow, sent duns in pursuit of an Old Harrovian, Mr Daniel Griffiths, to obtain payment of a £10 account for delicacies supplied on credit when the gentleman was a schoolboy. The tradesman had evidently learnt his English colloquially from the local natives, and he spelt as they spoke. The items included 'a veal poy, bread and beer – one and sixpence:' 'muck turtle soup and bread – one and twopence:' and 'shicken and toasted custard orgeat – sevenpence'.[13]

But controls were never likely to be stable or enduring at a school like Harrow which, during the next fifty years, after one bad period, became, through the success of Vaughan (and later Montagu Butler), the most expensive school in England. Boys were against deprivation of credit, the tradesmen even more so; and unless the parents supported the policy consistently, there was no chance of enforcing it. But during these coming decades the great public schools would attract the importunate applications for the admission of their sons from members of a new plutocracy and, from such, an ostentatious display of wealth was to be expected as their means of pressing to obtain higher social status. By the 1850s a familiar figure at Eton and Harrow was the over-pocket-moneyed son of an industrial millionaire who 'stuffed a fifty pound note into each of his son's waistcoats in sending him back to school after the holidays'.[14] In 1834 a critic, on the whole very sympathetic to Eton, wrote, 'The greatest moral evil now operating at Eton and which I understand is yearly increasing to a large amount, arises entirely from a mistaken fondness of the friends of the boys and is beyond the control of the Masters. I allude to the means of indulgence afforded by large supplies of money received from their homes.'[15] These 'large supplies of money' were for a minority; the majority of parents never had money to throw away; and many made, as they still make, a designed sacrifice to send their sons to the school of their choice. But at this time the minority was growing in numbers and social influence, and the time was not far distant when money would set the tone at the great public schools, and by taking over fashionable sport, and making heavy expenditure upon costly clothes and extravagant practices a conditional qualification for playing a game, turn into a luxury and a cult those recreational activities which once had been a matter of picking up a ball, or a bat, or a racquet and setting to.

Some modification of schoolboys' self government was implicit in the modifications taking place in adult society. The modern spirit which proscribed duelling and prize fighting was the same modern spirit that would not condone the random hazard to life and limb which in the past had been accepted by those who sent their sons to public schools as part of the natural price paid for the benefits of a 'public education'. In 1730 at Eton a boy called Thomas Dalton had stabbed another, Edward Cochran, to death during a quarrel in their form; the scandal was hushed up, the victim was buried in the college precincts and the killer lived on to enter Trinity College Dublin as a pensioner.* In 1821, Miss Margaretta Brown's 'dear volatile boy' Tom Hoseason made a murderous attack with a knife on a fellow Etonian, Edward Trower, during a quarrel in the School Chapel, and inflicted a deep wound in his thigh. Hoseason received a routine flogging just as he would have received for a common disturbance in chapel not involving the vicious use of a lethal weapon; but had the

---

* The inscription on Cochran's tomb reads:

> Here lyes the Body of Mr. Edward Cochran
> only SON OF ARCHIBALD COCHRAN Esqr.,
> Of the Island of ANTIGUA IN AMERICA
> Who unfortunately lost his life
> By an accidental stab with a
> Penknife from one of his
> School fellows the 2nd March
> In the 15th year of his Age, and
> In the year of our Lord 1730.

But the parish register says 'Edward Cochran murdered by his school fellow, Thomas Dalton with a pen knife'. Dalton was convicted of manslaughter but suffered no penalty.[16]

effects of the stabbing been fatal, as they might well have been, it would have been more difficult to ward off public indignation in 1821 than it had been in the previous century.

Some of the public schools' more disorderly traditional sports were also coming increasingly under censure from the spirit of modern propriety. The affrays between the boys and their town enemies, in particular the battles between the Westminsters and the Skis, and Etonians and the Windsor butchers, in which serious injuries were sustained, shocked the sensibilities of an adult generation still haunted by the spectre of social disorder on a revolutionary scale. In a juvenile self-governing community, risks of grievous bodily harm might be incurred without the involvement of weapons, so dreaded by Dr Butler, and even without what he called 'vindictive feelings'. A sportive recklessness was enough to breed danger. At Eton two boys, Prettyman* and Morson† almost killed another, Liddell‡ (afterwards Lord Ravensworth) by, Miss Brown tells us, 'a most unaccountable scheme' which was to make all the boys in the house lie on top of one another on the floor, then to pull 'a small cupboard bed' from the wall on top of the boys and jump on the bed. 'We are quite alarmed,' she said, 'about Liddell, who was quite breathless from the pressure.'[17] The alarm felt for Liddell did not occasion any serious condemnation of those who had caused it. Boys would be boys; and Morson and Prettyman were so far from being in disgrace that they were guests at the headmaster's table only a few days later. Liddell was reported 'quite well', but not well enough, it seems, to join them.

One traditional practice in the schools which was being viewed with concern from what were called 'progressive quarters' was pugilism.

Up to the 1840s boys battled in bloody combat on any pretext; 'hardly a day passing', according to Gladstone, 'without one, two, three, or even four more or less mortal combats'.[18] The Rev. J. Matthews was marked on the face for life in the battle he fought as a boy at Shrewsbury against another boy, Hughes, to vindicate the unfavourable review by Bishop Blomfield of Dr Samuel Bulter's edition of Aeschylus.[19] The danger of organized school fights lay in their being modelled upon the aims and methods of the prize ring in

* Richard Prettyman, Trinity College, Cambridge; Canon and Precentor of Lincoln and Rector of Middleton Stoney in Oxfordshire; in the fifth form in 1808.

† John J. T. Morson, son of the Hon. Thomas Morson; Rector of Bedale and Chaplain to the Queen; in the fifth form in 1808.

‡ Henry Thomas Liddell MP, Lord Ravensworth 1855; in the fourth form in 1808.

an outer but proscribed adult world. Pugilism, 'the noble art', stood in the anomalous position of being, in its professional form, unlawful, yet highly esteemed by its followers at the top and the bottom of society. The prize ring being the fashion, boys fought in imitation, according to its code and, what was more serious, according to its objectives. The prize fight was the ancestor of modern professional boxing. Superficially the progress of one to the other appears to be punctuated by merely technical amendments, the number and length of rounds, the definitions of fouls, and the use of gloves. But in fact the two are widely separated by morality and purpose. The formal purpose of a contestant in the ring is to defeat his opponent. In the modern ring a contestant wins by a knockout, the traditional and manifestly the most decisive kind of victory, or by a victory on points, awarded by judges at the end of a limited and fixed number of rounds. During the course of the twentieth century moral considerations have imposed a third kind of decision, the technical knockout, or 'stopped fight', when a man appears no longer capable of defending himself, or in danger of punishment that might cause serious and lasting damage. Before this stage is reached a referee may, if a fighter's fitness to continue is in doubt, award a compulsory pause in the form of a count of ten, even if the fighter would not by his own choice have stayed down for any part of the count. Thus by a conjunction of measures the act of the knockout has been made more difficult to effect, and the boxer has been *comparatively* protected from suffering extreme punishment.

In the prize ring the knockout was also made difficult to effect but by very different means and for an entirely different purpose. While the ostensible object of the contest was to defeat an opponent by a knockout, and skill was held in nominal esteem, the qualities which the prize ring was designed to test, and the spectators were primarily interested in seeing exhibited, were those of *endurance*. How much pain and fatigue could a combatant, man or beast, endure and still fight on? The challenge, 'what could be endured', was the incentive behind blood sports like bull, and bear, and badger baiting, when animals of notorious courage were fought to exhaustion in order to test how they would perform *in extremis*. For by such ordeals alone would be measured that quality most admired, which in the eighteenth century had been called bottom. In the prize ring there was no limit to the number of rounds which a fight might last; the fight ended when one of the contestants failed to come for the start of a round. A round ended with a knock *down*, but this, far from preventing a man being knocked out in the modern sense, allowed him to be resuscitated with every means available during the sixty seconds rest, and pitched back into the ring if he was standing and willing to continue. Thus a contestant who would have won on points 'over the distance' in a modern ring, might not have won at all in the prize ring, while a man who might have been clearly defeated on points in a modern ring could, with sufficient determination and stamina, end the victor.

'I say, Horsham,' exclaimed Chudleigh, 'this is a regular slaughter; hadn't you better let him take a hiding?'

'He's only a little bit stunned,' replied Horsham, 'he will be all right presently. I've sent my minor for some brandy, and I expect him back at any minute.'

Later in the same fight, as described in a documentary account by an Etonian journalist, when the other contestant falls unconscious under a barrage of blows, his seconds, in their efforts to revive their man, throw a basin of cold water over him, 'but without effect'. 'Horsham pulled out his watch and looked at the time; five minutes had elapsed, but Chorleigh remained in a prostrate position.'[20]

Such engagements, when stubbornly contested, could go on for hours, without giving offence to 'public opinion', the only power at school capable of regulating conduct in this, or any other activity. The feats of boy pugilist heroes were committed to sagas and passed down from tribal generation to generation.[21] At Westminster, Frederick Walker, 'a very handsome boy, a very Cupid', fought on the Green with George Haggard. The fight lasted two hours. 'Cupid was not recognizable for some time afterwards and had to be attended at home by the doctor.'[22] At the time of the engagement neither combatant could have been more than ten years of age. Again at Wesminster, James Goodenough fought a much taller boy until the latter was carried off unconscious. One little novice who watched the fight was first sick at the sight of 'blood pouring from the wounded', but 'use effects wonderful changes in the feelings'; after his own first fight he had to stay off a fortnight under care until he had recovered.[23]

A giant-killer was always especially honoured. James Harris (later Lord Malmesbury) saw Lacey Yea at Eton fight 'a very desperate battle' when thirteen against a much bigger boy of sixteen, which he 'won by sheer pluck'.[24] Kinglake, Yea's exact contemporary, was later to witness Yea's feats in battle as Colonel of the 7th (Royal Fusiliers) in the Crimea.*

Outstanding fighters of the day were almost canonized by their contemporaries. At Eton, Sanders, Pringle, Rigby, Cornwall, Hillsborough, Savile, Barrow, Waterford, and above all Boudier and Wyvill became the names of heroes whose feats against the school's hereditary enemies, bargees, Windsor butchers and visiting bullies, were enshrined in domestic mythology. Wyvill was famous for the severe beating he gave a notorious bruiser in the Life Guards. The soldier complained afterwards to Goodall, who said, 'My good fellow, how can you expect me to know who the boy is?' 'Boy!' the guardsman exclaimed. 'Why that's the biggest mun in tuttens.'† From that time Wyvill had been known at Eton and probably long afterwards as 'the biggest man in tuttens'.

Naturally it was the victories rather than the defeats in the battles against outsiders which were enshrined in the collective memory. Perhaps the most famous feat of all was the victory of George Boudier,‡ while still a schoolboy at Eton, over the leading pugilist of the day, the Royal chimneysweep, Hastings, in a public battle fought in Batchelor's Acre.

Not all domestic fights among the boys themselves were protracted by the application of prize-ring conditions. The spontaneous flurries of aggression between boy and boy were likely to be curtailed by the demands of school business, or other interruptions; but sometimes more than trivial damage could be inflicted in a short time when a boy like MacDonald 'tuff as iron' clashed with another, or William Kemp, of Liverpool, 'gave Bowring such a licking that he could not come into school'.[26] Even unwilling combatants might sometimes do more damage than they knew, as when small boys who entertained no enmity for each other were compelled to fight, whether as an initiation rite, or for the entertainment of their elders. In adult life Thackeray used to recall the 'scrunch' of the blow landed by his reluctant opponent Venables[27] which broke his nose at Charterhouse.

---

* At Alma. Yea's regiment, on the right of the light division, and his six or seven hundred fusiliers, held a column of fifteen hundred of the Kazan regiment when the rest of Sir William Codrington's brigade had been forced to give way: Yea's 'dark eyes yielded fire, and all the while from his deep chiselled, merciless lips there pealed the thunder of imprecation and command'.[25] Yea was killed at Inkerman on 18 June 1855, leading a brigade in assault on the Redan.

† Tuttens: the 'two towns', Windsor and Eton, separated by the river Thames.

‡ George Boudier (upper fifth, 1838), son of the vicar of St Mary's, Warwick; Rector of Ewhurst, Sussex.

A realistic headmaster knew that until public opinion changed there was no chance of abolishing severe *informal* combat among boys. Fighting expressed the standards of virility of the age, and readiness to fight was the ultimate moral self-justification by a boy in the eyes of his peers. The formal fight, pre-arranged and conducted under the rules of the prize ring, was a more serious and dangerous affair. Seconds appointing such a contest between promising adversaries would choose the morning of a whole holiday 'as giving more time for deciding the superiority of the antagonists,'[28] and in a prolonged period of anticipation partisan feelings had time to grow into a fever of factional hostility. Keate objected strongly to such 'long projected' battles and whenever he had intelligence of a plan for one he prevented it. But in 1825 catastrophe occurred.

In a distraught letter to his mother, Milnes Gaskell wrote home, 'A most awful and horrible warning not to fight in the playing fields happened last night.' Two boys, Charles Wood, and Francis Ashley,* the youngest son of the Earl of Shaftesbury, having quarrelled, their respective friends entered into an engagement for the principals to settle their differences in a fight in the afternoon of 2 March. Reports of what happened vary in many particulars, but what is known for certain is that the two boys – Ashley, aged thirteen, and Wood, aged fourteen but considerably bigger – fought for about two and a half hours and at the end of that time they both collapsed. Wood was assisted from the field; Ashley in a state of coma was carried back to his house by two friends and placed on his bed. He never regained consciousness and died that night.

The enemies of Eton pressed for a prosecution of the surviving combatant and his second; murky rumours began to breed, the most insalubrious being that a factor contributing to the tragedy had been the consumption by Ashley of the best part of a bottle of brandy between rounds. The blame for this alleged imprudence was presumed to be Leith's who was thought to have acted as Ashley's second, and both Wood and he were summoned to appear and stand trial at the Aylesbury Assizes. This was when Etonians closed ranks. Lord Shaftesbury refused to prosecute or offer witnesses for the prose-

* The surname of the Earls of Shaftesbury was Cooper and, in conjunction with Ashley (derived from the first earl's mother), Ashley Cooper (with or without a hyphen). Also, as at Eton at this time, Ashley standing by itself was treated as the surname, Cooper being omitted. The variant forms perplex even the learned compiler, 'GEC' in *The Complete Peerage*, vol. 11, pp. 642–53. In Stapylton the boy is in the 1823 school list as Mr Ashley min[imus], Christian name Francis. He was known to his family and friends by his middle name, Anthony.

cution and accordingly the charges of manslaughter were dismissed for lack of evidence. A number of malicious and inaccurate articles appeared in the press, but the boys who knew most said least, and lay low to avoid notice. Some, including Ashley major, withdrew from school for a period and sought refuge in the seclusion of their parental homes.

Both Gaskell and Wilkinson have left accounts of what transpired, Gaskell in letters home at the time of the fight, Wilkinson in his memoirs written many years later. But neither was an authoritative witness. Gaskell, who hated fighting, saw little if any of the action but retailed such of the contradictory reports as he had received. Wilkinson admits to seeing no more than three of the sixty (it was said) rounds, but this did not deter him from supplying a racy report compiled from what he had seen, what he had heard said, and in this case, I am afraid, what he had imagined.

The boy who knew most of what happened from beginning to end, having been present when the quarrel occurred and then acted in practice as Ashley's second throughout the fight, was Thomas Taunton.* He was a close friend of Ashley's. He had kept silent on the subject of the fatal fight for many years, until, in fact, the publication of Wilkinson's memoirs. This was too much for him and he wrote a detailed refutation† of considerable asperity, correcting Wilkinson's 'tissue of misstatements'.

To summarize Taunton's account. On the last Sunday of February, 1825, Taunton and Ashley walked together from Knapp's house to attend 'Prose', notoriously the rowdiest and most disorderly public occasion of the week. A large concourse of lower boys was already formed, as most of those present were struggling to get as near to the door as possible with the object of securing one of the limited number of advantageous places *behind* the master's desk. Taunton put Ashley in front of him, being himself bigger and better able to resist the pressures from behind. The two friends had by degrees worked their way closer to the door, until they could touch it with their hands, when a tremendous push from behind thrust them forward on top of the boys in front of them and, in the mêlée, Ashley unintentionally kicked the heel of the boy immediately before him, who happened to be Wood.

---

* Captain of Boats, 1828.
† To be exact Taunton left two accounts, one being contained in a letter to his friend and fellow Etonian, J. E. Edwards-Moss, 'Captain of Boats 1827', of Roby Hall, Prescot, Lancs. Both (nearly identical) versions are reproduced in *ETA*, no. 65, 31 December 1936, pp. 225–28.

Wood may have supposed that the kick was deliberate, for he turned and struck Ashley in the face. Ashley returned the blow. The scuffle continued when the doors were opened, until Le Mann, the praeposter, put an end to it. Afterwards a meeting was arranged in orthodox style by the friends acting for the principals.

Before the fight Ashley major put sixpence into Taunton's hand and asked him to buy brandy with it, and Taunton went to the Christopher taking a small medical phial into which the landlord, Garroway, poured brandy to the value of 5d. With the remaining penny Taunton bought a lemon. When he reached the playing fields he found the combatants already there with their supporters. The two elder Ashleys delivered their younger brother into the care of Taunton, who gave him a knee and tended him between rounds and, from the beginning to the end of the fight, 'never left him for a moment'. Leith, the titular second, did not 'back up' Ashley and never came near him during the fight. Taunton was at first under the impression that Leith was Wood's second.

Wilkinson, 'the clerical historian', provoked Taunton to heavy sarcasm, although most of the embellishments he objected to were, at worst, innocent poetic licence of an old man. The boys did not fight, as Wilkinson had said, 'like professionals of the ring, stripped naked to the waist', but 'in their shirts like gentlemen as they were'; neither did Wilkinson see, as he reported, Ashley borne, 'still naked to the waist on the shoulders of four boys' ('like pall bearers') but carried, clothed, by two, Morrell and Taunton. The imputation which Taunton most resented was the alleged consumption of brandy, since this could have affected Ashley's physical condition, and the only brandy had been in Taunton's keeping. The phial containing the brandy was never, says Taunton, out of his possession from the moment he purchased it till the end of the fight, and not one drop of the brandy passed Ashley's lips. The only use made of it was late in the fight when it was rubbed, as was the lemon, on Ashley's swollen hands. Taunton asserts that he asked Ashley major many times to stop the fight and that he refused. His description of the last stages of the fight presents a picture which is in no need of brandy or any other factor to account for its sombre ending.

For the last twenty five minutes neither combatant was capable of striking a blow. They were simply pushed against one another in the last ten rounds or twelve when both fell though no blow had been struck. Ashley fell, and Wood falling forward at the same moment, landed on top of Ashley, striking him with his left knee on the back of the neck.

Christopher Teesdale, Wood's second, gave evidence at the inquest that brandy had been administered internally to Ashley. 'I was not present to contradict him,' said Taunton. 'Having taken so prominent a part in the melancholy affair I became alarmed and went home on the Wednesday and did not return till Easter.'

When Taunton and Morrell got Ashley to Knapp's house it was nearly time for Absence*, and having laid him on the bed they hurried off to answer their names. The boys did not inform the housemaster, Knapp, of Ashley's insensibility, because they thought Ashley was under the influence of liquor and would sleep it off. Later Ashley major and two of his friends, the Booths major and minor,† sat down in the room where the youngest Ashley lay, and played cards. The sound of the injured boy's breathing, which had been heavy, suddenly ceased. Ashley major went to his brother's side and, apprehending too late the gravity of his condition, applied a looking glass to his lips, and cried out, 'Anthony has stopped breathing.' Another boy jumped out of the window in his stockinged feet and ran to call Dr Fergusson for help. All the doctor could do on arrival was to certify Anthony Ashley to be dead.

In the closing darkness, by Wilkinson's account, he could distinguish Ashley major below in the yard crying and wringing his hands. Wilkinson did not say – probably he did not know – that Ashley major's grief was occasioned by remorse as well as bereavement, because he had been the principal cause of the fight's prolongation, urging his brother on to 'one more round, one more, for the honour of the Ashleys',[29] when Wood had been ready to end the fight; nor that the combatants' fathers, Colonel Wood and Lord Shaftesbury, were bitter personal and political enemies.

Lurid libels circulated and were inflamed by the press. It was suggested that Knapp had failed to call Absence in his house that night, and was unacquainted with Ashley's state because he was tipsy, a condition not unknown to him; but we have Margaretta

---

* Absence: a roll call which all Etonian boys were obliged to attend to answer their names.
† Booth major: Sir Williamson, Bart, of Paxton Park, St Neots; nephew of Sir Felix whom he succeeded 1850.
  Booth minor: Charles; brother and heir presumptive of Sir Williamson. Succeeded to Sir Felix Booth's gin distillery.

Brown's testimony – and she was no friend of Knapp – saying 'poor Knapp was unwell that night'.

We also know her opinion of the friends and spectators of the combatants without whose appetite for violence and suffering the ordeal would not have been fatally prolonged.

> I never heard anything worse than the conduct of the boys about poor Ashley. All this – owing to their horrid spirit for prize fighting which has been so patronised; and it is a misfortune that Tom Cannon, the present Champion of England, as he calls himself, was a Windsor bargeman.[30]

The only person to emerge from the wretched affair with his credit enhanced was the headmaster. Keate was not blamed personally for the fight having taken place. It was not then considered part of a headmaster's duties (nor was it possible) to exercise surveillance over the activities out of school hours of boys within bounds at Eton, and even, in practice, 'out of bounds'. A few sports, notably tandem driving, which would have threatened the safety of the public, were proscribed, but for a headmaster to have inhibited fights on principle would have been objected to by Etonians past as well as present as an infringement of the sacred 'liberties' of the boys, which were believed to nourish the free spirit of an English gentleman. Keate addressed the school after the death of Anthony Ashley and his speech made a deep impression on the boys, according to witnesses as different as Milnes Gaskell and Frank Doyle, who wrote:

> I have seldom been so deeply moved than I was by that noble address, full of unflinching courage and steadfastness, delivered by him to the school shortly after the sad accident. . . . 'It is not,' he said 'that I object to fighting in itself; on the contrary, I like to see a boy who receives a blow return it at once;* but that you, the heads of the school, should allow a contest to go on for two and a half hours, has shocked and grieved me.' He then proceeded to express his sympathy with the bereaved parents, in strains of genuine, because it was honest, eloquence, and to urge upon us that, for the future, we should act in such cases with better judgement, and under a deeper sense of responsibility. One and all, after listening to that speech, we trooped

---

* Compare this with Thring's denunciation of a fight between boys as an 'abomination', and his pronouncement of what all the boys must have known to be bluff: 'Now the next fight that takes place, I will flog both the fighters, all the seconds, and everyone looking on.' Skrine, *Memory*, p. 31.

out of the Upper School with a thorough belief and confidence in Keate that Arnold might have envied.[31]

But if Keate's auditors did not forget later, as men, neither did they change their ways suddenly at the time, as boys, at the impact of a fatality. The exposure certainly did provide ammunition for the apostles of reform who were already making the 'liberty' of public-school boys the target of their censure. But actual change, in distinction from anticipation of change, would occur only gradually, and not in obedience to any command or prescription, but in conformity with the unplanned mutations in the morals governing public feeling, which followed their inexorable course, and of which the exhortations of moralists were a symptom rather than a cause, until a time when men looked about them and at each other and exclaimed, 'We have changed indeed'.[32]

Meanwhile the spirit of violence overflowed into games and pastimes which were not formally defined as combat. Even the end of the Hoop season was celebrated at Eton with a confrontation between Collegers and Oppidans which developed into an open battle.* The tendency was notably manifest in the game, or rather, games – for each school had its own variety – of football. James I had denounced football in Basilikon Doron as a pastime 'meeter for laming than making able the users thereof', and up to the 1830s at least football persisted as little more than a free fight between teams of usually equal numbers involving a ball, in which little distinction was made between kicking the ball and kicking an opposing player. The old cry 'hack him over' was heard as late as the mid century in a match between the new schools Marlborough and Clifton.[33] 'My maxim is hack the ball when you can see it near you, and when you don't why then hack the fellow next to you.' That is a mild parody of the old-style, no-holds-barred football player who was already being looked upon as a savage anachronism after 1850, as rules began to be asserted, and a parodied diehard is made to lament the good old days when 'there was none of that underhand shuffling play with the ball that there is now; no passing it along from one to the other, all was manly and straightforward'.[34] Matches between boys and 'old boys' were especially violent: different generations seeking to justify themselves.

---

* Hoops are alluded to in Gray's *Ode on a Distant Prospect of Eton College*; also in H. J. Crickitt Blake's *Reminiscences*, p. 70. Lyte in his *History*, p. 321, writes: '. . . even in the second decade of the nineteenth century the October half was "hoop time" for all boys below the Fifth Form'.

In theory there were rules. It was considered 'opposed to all the principles of the game' for a player to attempt 'to throttle or strangle another' in a maul. But in practice, apart from primitive prohibition to carrying disguised offensive weapons on to the field, anything short of murder was allowed. Broken bones were no infrequent occurrence, and Tuckwell remembers players being carried off to 'sick house' and their places being taken by others in a Winchester 'hot'. The capacity to endure, as well as inflict, punishment was much admired. Tuckwell's own fagmaster, the school's hero of the football field, was known as Pruff, because he was deemed insensible to, or 'proof against' pain.[35]

Variations between the games played in the first half of the century were considerable and fluctuating. Sometimes they were due to physical conditions. At Harrow football used to be played on the gravel in the court which surrounded the old school house on three sides, so that the goals, instead of facing each other, were separated by the building, round which the ball had to be kicked. The gravel cut not only the leather of the ball, but the hands and faces of those who fought for it, in what at Eton was called a rouge, at Rugby* a scrummage, and at Harrow a squash. These marks of combat, when permanent, were esteemed as honourable scars.

At Eton there was a lack of formality in the early days, a freshness and insouciance about play. Etonian boys in the twenties and thirties played football without even taking off their tall Beaver hats which, after the game, were 'all brown with mud and spattered like the felts of the Irish peasantry'. That may have been carrying spontaneity too far, but in the second half of the century there was to be a reversal to the opposite extreme. Another, and yet less formal, type of exercise was poaching. No plunder was more alluring than the poacher's, whether in water, on land, or overhead. Boys regarded game and the cultivated fruits of the earth as their hereditary possessions, bequeathed to them by God, much as the Masai in East Africa regard all the cattle in the world as theirs by divine right. Poaching was a prized pursuit tenaciously followed by generations of public schoolboys, for as a sport it offered the conjoined attractions of hazard, conflict and profit, while the penalties of discovery, however severe, did not carry

---

* William Webb Ellis, who is said to have started the game of rugby football in 1823, by catching the ball in his arms and running with it, entered Rugby School in 1816 at the age of nine. He left in the summer of 1825, two years after his reputed innovation, and went as an exhibitioner to Brasenose (an eminently suitable choice of college), took holy orders and became incumbent of St Clement Danes. He died 'on the continent'.[36]

the faintest stigma of dishonour. The irony of the proceeding was that many of the juvenile poachers were themselves already landowners and were destined to become magistrates.

Samuel Butler nearly lost the end of his nose as a Rugbeian in quest of a sharp-toothed 'great Jack',* a deprivation which he would have found of peculiar embarrassment when, as headmaster of Shrewsbury, he was obliged to become the denouncer and scourge of poachers. Thomas Arnold's most strenuous efforts failed to persuade public opinion at Rugby to treat poaching and foraging as disgraceful offences. A Rugbeian called Mordaunt, fishing in forbidden waters and being surprised by the owner of the fishing rights, Boughton Leigh (with whom successive generations of Rugbeians carried on an energetic feud) made off with his spoils, followed over hedge and ditch by his mounted pursuer. At last they came to a ditch which balked the horseman and Mordaunt turned and threw a fish in his face, bidding him take it home and have his wife cook it. In the sequel of investigation Mordaunt was identified, denounced, and expelled. Soon afterwards he returned to Rugby to a hero's welcome to display himself and be much admired in the uniform of an officer in the Lancers.

The poaching expedition, with the ducking episodes in *Tom Brown's Schooldays*, is based on actual incidents, one of which rocked the throne of Arnold, and caused the expulsion of a number of popular 'heroes' of the day, almost including 'Muscleman' Oswell. A party of boys, among them Oswell, when illicitly fishing, clashed with a posse of keepers, and in the battle which followed one or more of the keepers were tossed into the river. Formal complaint was laid by Boughton Leigh; and Arnold appealed to his sixth form to discover and report the names of the culprits. But this was an occasion when Arnold's elect rebelled against his authority and reverted openly to the ancient tribal laws and loyalties. No names were forthcoming. Arnold summoned the whole of the Upper School and ordered its members to pass in file before Boughton Leigh and his keepers for identification. An eyewitness of the scene was Thomas Hughes himself. 'Arnold's power of ruling,' he admits, 'was never put to so severe a test for the whole school was against him,' and the praeposters of the week made no serious attempt to stifle the tumult. As the boys' names were called and they passed before the observers the keeper identified five, or possibly six, who were all summarily expelled there and then.

* Jack: pike.

Cox, Price, Torkington, Wyniatt, Peters (the cock of the school) and, possibly, Gaisford, the son of the Dean of Christ Church, names which would be 'treasured as those of heroes' by a generation to come. 'A tremor,' says Hughes, 'ran through the school as Oswell, the handsomest and most renowned of athletes, passed out, but he was not recognized.' In later years, David Livingstone said of Oswell that 'he was one who had had more hairsbreadth escapes than any man living'. This might be described as the first of them.

The boys' adversaries numbered not merely gentlemen and landowners, like Boughton Leigh who, however offended, would conduct hostilities according to rules of propriety, but smallholders, some of whom could be dangerously brutal if they managed to catch a boy alone; and these had to be fought with their own weapons. The farmers would have claimed that it was they who had been driven to fight with the *boys'* weapons. There was little moral distinction between the tactics used on either side, and the operations could be vicious, especially in schools set in the shires and perhaps most of all in the new 'public schools' founded around the middle of the century, like Marlborough, which was said to resemble nothing so much as 'a barbaric tribe' who poached and thieved through the countryside and 'collected in gangs to beat frogs with sticks in the wilderness and to fill buckets with their bodies'.[37] A little new boy eight years old was tied to a bench in upper school where there were throngs of boys present and 'branded on the forearm by means of a red hot poker'.*

In addition to the landowners and tenant farmers, the boys' other natural enemies were rival marauders, who made no moral distinction, as the boys did, between stealing game and stealing money. On Friday, 5 November 1819, some Wykehamist Commoners were playing football when, says one of them, they noticed some little 'gigs who were lurking about our coats . . . to steal . . . which they had done before when things were left about the field'. The loiterers were ordered to depart but, whether with felonious intent, or simply for the sake of defiance, they did not obey, and two of the players, Papillon and Elmhurst, broke off from the game 'to lick them', we are told, 'for their impudence'. The 'gigs' took to their heels and a chase ensued. Papillon caught his quarry and duly thrashed him. Elmhurst failed to secure his, but the fugitive was subsequently

---

* Seventy-one years later Cyril Norwood saw the scar, he tells us, extending from the forearm to the wrist.[38]

apprehended by another Commoner, Ricketts, who administered correction.

Later the players were walking home in twos and threes when Papillon was seen some way off, surrounded by four strong fellows, one of them the father of the thrashed boy. The intentions of the newcomers were clearly unfriendly. Papillon was keeping them off with a stout stick, but they were waiting their chance to close and overpower him. An alarm was immediately raised, and with shouts of encouragement to Papillon, reinforcements rushed to his rescue. The two parties now faced each other and after an exchange of discourtesies ('the mob abused us, which roused our spirit') the Commoners attacked, and seizing the father of the boy who was the ring-leader, flung him down the river bank. In the mêlée the man struck one of the boys with his bill-hook before retreating on to 'the wharf where he belonged' and where he evidently supposed himself safe from pursuit, for he shouted insults at his enemies and defied them to touch him. This was the height of imprudence, for all that stood between the boys and himself was the law of trespass. 'We immediately,' our correspondent reports, 'fell upon him and gave him the soundest thrashing a man could well bear.'[39]

One of the more scandalous escapades, or at least one of which records have been preserved (for much was destroyed), was an exercise the boys of Shrewsbury (a school then notorious for brutality) called a 'boar hunt'. A pig, the property of a local farmer, was dragged from its sty, tormented into flight, and then pursued and harried over fields by a pack of 'hunters', whose intention was, after the pig's martyrdom had provided them with sport, to kill it for their commissariat. The beast was not a wild animal, but a tame, domestic creature, bred on a farm and entirely unable to defend itself by flight, evasion or combat. The frantic progress became the pig's *via dolorosa* as the quarry lurched and stumbled, squealing in pain and terror, hither and thither, harried and goaded with sharp instruments by its pursuers. It was an act, said a remorseful participant to his father afterwards, 'most brutal and disgraceful as ever a schoolboy was guilty of'.* It was not possible to convict on evidence any of the leaders of the outrage (including Gretton), for the farmer was too frightened to identify any of the Salopians who had descended on his

---

* The boy, Frederick Edward Gretton, son of the Very Rev. Dr G. Gretton, Dean of Hereford, was then fourteen years of age. He took a good degree at St John's College (he was 7th Classic) in 1826, and became a fellow in 1829. He was headmaster of Stamford Grammar School from 1845 to 1872, when he was made rector of Oddington.[40]

farm, but the records of two boys most strongly suspected as criminals were such that the headmaster, Dr Samuel Butler, ordered their banishment. To his old acquaintance, Francis Holyoake, he wrote to say that he must send home his son George,* who had become 'a proverbial terror' to the neighbourhood, and whose 'whole conduct was a series of continual offences'. Dr Gretton, too, was an old friend of Butler's and as the letters of ill tiding increase in number, they reveal that the most dangerous enemies of the headmaster's peace at Shrewsbury were the sons of church dignitaries.

In 1848, the old wild ways were still in the ascendant. On 23 November of that year, a boy at Rugby was horsewhipped by an old farmer when he was caught trespassing. The following Saturday six of the strongest boys in Anstey's house set out to demand an explanation, but not, they subsequently averred, intending to 'repay' him. At their approach the farmer came out of his house with a son and nephew armed with pitchforks. The boys decided to disengage and await a more favourable opportunity for parley or war, but as they withdrew from the field one of them who was armed – whether any of the others were also armed we do not know – fired a pistol at the farmer's party. This gave the farmer, who seems to have trusted in the principle that attack is the best defence, an opportunity to invoke the law, and he issued summonses against the boys' housemaster, Mr Anstey, as the person responsible for their actions. After a long and bitterly contested litigation, the defendant was fined four shillings. But if the farmer supposed that was the end of the affair he was disabused. Soon after the trial his haystacks were burnt, his fields were ravaged and his hedges broken. This time he kept quiet.[42]

Life did change in public schools, inevitably, to some degree of correspondence with life 'in these sweeping days of reform' outside their walls. There must have been a last time when a boy arrived at Westminster School wearing a wig and sword, and there would be a last time when a boy arrived at any school in a horse-drawn carriage, or riding pillion behind his father's groom. But changes were resisted as long as possible and accepted with grudging reserve, at least for

* George Holyoake was commissioned in the Queen's Own Royal Staffordshire Yeomanry in 1831. He was Justice of the Peace and Deputy Lieutenant for Staffordshire and Shropshire. His elder brother, and fellow 'terror of the neighbourhood', Francis Littleton Holyoake, after going to St John's College, Cambridge, assumed the name of Goodricke in 1833 (probably to conform to the conditions of inheritance), was MP for Stafford in 1835–36, for South Stafford in 1836–37, and Justice of the Peace for Warwick, Norfolk and Worcester, and Deputy Lieutenant for Worcester in 1834. He was created a baronet in 1835 and died in 1865.[41]

the first half of the century. In the second half of the century change accelerated under cover of the Clarendon Commission and a new order emerged overlaying the old like a fresh surface of soil and expressing the character of a different, decorous and broadcast upper middle class. Public opinion had changed.

Late Victorian old gentlemen, looking back to their early Victorian, or pre-Victorian, schooldays, found it difficult to believe that those times of rabid licence had ever really happened and that *they* had been part of them. Records of the less indecorous events might be lovingly, if privately, preserved and cherished. The diary of a Wykehamist Commoner called Minet for the year 1818 survived to be frowned on in later days by the writer's nephew.

Winchester, 30 April. Some fellows came into our room & filled Wigget's bed with glasses, cups, brushes and other things. Afterwards we swilled the fellows in the next room and they returned it with a great slop and put our candle out.
... Bolster match in Floyer's room. 17 fellows. After getting knocked about a little I went to bed much fatigued with my exertions.
Saturday, October 30. Feast in our room, Ducks, a Goose (eaten off the back of our basins* which gave it a great flavour) a large cake, apples, walnuts etc. etc. (window stopped up with a blanket that no light should be seen) ... we set to grubbing most ferociously ... a bowl of Punch crowned the whole. Afterwards, near midnight we amused ourselves with launching† fellows in the two adjoining rooms. ...[43]

A veil was normally drawn over incidents deemed too outrageous for recall. Where a memorialist's self-censoring seemed insufficient, there were usually diligent heirs and executors to perform the pious rites of expurgation on a deceased writer's behalf. But there were the rare mavericks whom even the collective pressure of social proscription could not deter or silence. Froude published, under a pseudonym, *Zeta*, an account of his childhood's wretchedness at Westminster, despite the contumely he incurred from his peers. J. A. Symonds went further. He wrote, but did not – could not – publish, in plain

---

* Minet alludes more than once with relish to the practice, then in vogue with his contemporaries, of eating off the back of wash basins. See above, p. 117.
† To launch, in Wykehamese, meant to cast, from the bed to the ground, mattress, bedclothes and the occupant of the bed together.

language, the particulars of an underworld of vice which he said flourished at Harrow in his time; and he effectively protected the manuscript from those who, given an opportunity, would have caused it to vanish without a trace after his death.

EIGHT
A Little Learning

In theory the distinction between work and play was clear enough. Boys were not at play when they were under instruction from assistant masters or tutors, but in practice even these conditions did not guarantee serious application. The classes, or divisions, were too large for regular control over an individual boy to be feasible. William Johnson, assistant master at Eton, by repute the most inspiring teacher in the public schools during the period under review, had the insight to discern that much of what passed for relatively successful scholastic transactions was partly play, and that when a schoolmaster may have thought boys were 'improving their minds they were merely playing a game ... a game in which the master is the principal player', while 'the boys are making scores as in the playground'. By his reckoning no more than one in a hundred had 'a real desire for knowledge for its own sake ... knowledge apart from imaginative excitement'.[1]

Perhaps the only safe assessment which may be made is that generally a boy worked when he wished to work, and this applied especially to Eton and to senior boys. Giving evidence before the Clarendon Commission, the headmaster of Winchester, Dr George Moberly, affirmed that until recently promotion by tests and 'taking places' had stopped in the senior part of the fifth form, halfway up the school. Up to that point ambitious boys worked very hard, knowing that a fellowship at New College for life was the prize of 'a struggle that ended at fourteen'.[2] Later in the century, a Mrs Haslam, the mother of several sons at Rugby, reported, 'When I asked Mr Knyvett Wilson to speak to Sam about not finishing his copies, he positively refused to do it, saying, "He is in the VIth and may do as much or as little work as he likes." '[3]

A junior worked when his fagmaster, or another boy capable of enforcing his demands, required it. A big boy who could not do verses got hold of a clever little one and locked him up in his room until the required quantity, eight or twelve lines, were done. The extortionist did not mind a few false quantities, in fact they were requisite. M'tutor might have been suspicious if there was none, although it was more likely that m'tutor knew and did not care. Charles Wilkinson as a small boy suffered this fate, and at first he duly got a licking and a warning that he would be locked up again after four if he did not produce the verses. This time he decided it would be more profitable to come to terms with *force majeure* and ran off eight lines of a sort, for which he got thanks and some sock and was free after four. Looking back as an old man he not only bore no ill will against his tyrant, but he did not regret a moment of the time spent on the work because the exercise had had a permanently improving effect upon his abilities.

Stafford Northcote wrote home cheerfully from Eton that he was hardly bullied at all, 'for most bullies are very stupid and I construe them'.[4] The future Marquess of Salisbury, a boy of a different temperament, followed a different course, defied the system and suffered correspondingly more. In May 1844 he wrote to his father, 'I have been kicked most unmercifully since I saw you last for refusing to do a fellow's theme for him. . . . He kicked me and pulled my hair and punched me, and hit me as hard as ever he could for twenty minutes and now I am aching in every joint and hardly able to write this.'[5]

There are other tributes to the bizarre rewards of 'spare time' or 'private business'. 'The long winter nights are everywhere the trial of forced companionship,' said Mozley of life at Charterhouse about 1808. 'As soon as the little boys had dispatched their scanty supper and done in some hasty fashion the work for next day, the word was given, "Open the closet." That I think was the name, but it was the place where things were stowed out of the way. As many as a dozen or twenty would have to go and pack themselves in as close as they could one upon another in a dank hole, the door of which was closed upon them. They managed to entertain themselves in whispers. If the whispers were too loud, the door was opened and the living mass indiscriminately lashed or pounded. My informant declared that these were the happiest hours of his life; that here he made his warmest friendships and here he acquired more information than he acquired in any other way at school.'[6]

The vice of the system was that it was committed to the cultivation of an accomplishment, the composition of elegant verses in Greek and Latin, and therefore, by inference, to the premise that a considerable number of those taught were capable of learning to write elegant verse in these languages. But the reality was that few indeed of those taught were capable of ever learning to write elegant verse in *any* language. The majority, therefore, were condemned to labour towards a goal which they could never reach, however hard or long they strove. The requirement was, in Milman's metaphor, 'a Cinderella slipper': it fitted one foot in a hundred, and the rash attempt to put it on all might cripple the other ninety-nine for life. For boys like Lord Wellesley and William Johnson and Charles Merivale, with a bent for classical scholarship and a creative literary talent, the work gave satisfaction and delight. To the rest, and vast majority, without these attributes (although perhaps with others which were not being cultivated), the process was a conventional imposture in which the masters were accomplices, made possible by an established system of cribs, mutual aid and forced labour.

Few teachers can go on indefinitely demanding and expecting to receive that which they know a boy is incapable of producing. They could go through the motions of pressure and encouragement during the fifty to sixty hours a week of parsing and scanning, to try whether a little stimulation would release hidden springs. In the pupil room, using a pet name for his favourites, an old tutor, Yonge, would pull their ears and pinch them, remarking, 'We must be whipped', with the received meaning of Frederick the Great to an erring soldier, 'My friend, either you or I must be shot.'[7] We have eyewitness reports of the same boys being flogged at Rugby 'four or more times in a week for "failing to perform what was beyond their capacity" '.[8] 'Alas, my English brethren of the scholastic cloth,' said one notably conscientious teacher, 'how long shall we turn rapidly our gerundstones in the vain endeavour to turn sawdust into flour?'[9] Such unproductive and frustrating toil would continue to be sanctioned for as long as the venerable misconception was cherished as an article of academic faith, that all minds of a superior order were by nature potential classics, and that the standards of performance in the study of ancient Greek and Latin grammar and prosody were a reliable, and the *only* reliable, measure of quality applicable to all kinds of talent.

Looking back at his boyhood at Shrewsbury, one former misfit in that classical forcing house recalled,

Nothing could have been worse for the development of my mind than Dr Butler's school, for it was strictly classical and as a means of education to me was simply a blank. During my whole life I have been singularly incapable of mastering any language. Especial attention was paid to verse making and this I could never do well. I had many friends and got together a good collection of old verses, which by patching together, sometimes aided by other boys, I could work into any subject. Much attention was paid to learning by heart the lessons of the previous day; this I could effect with great facility, learning forty or fifty lines of Virgil or Homer, whilst I was in morning Chapel; but the exercise was utterly useless for every verse was forgotten in forty-eight hours.

That boy was Charles Darwin, and looking back he remembers that the best part of his education at school took place in his spare time, bird and insect watching ('I remember wondering why every gentleman did not become an ornithologist'), and working on chemistry experiments with his brother, which earned him a public rebuke from the headmaster for wasting his time on such useless subjects. 'He called me very unjustly,' says Darwin, 'a "poco curante" and as I did not understand what it meant it seemed to me a fearful reproach.'[10]

Except in cases of natural vocation, there was a lack of incentive when the tutor and the boy knew that the latter would soon be joining his regiment, and then his studies would cease to be relevant to the needs of his life except as a social flourish at the dinner table or in the drawing room, or repairing to his estates and his stables when they would be even less relevant. Such conditions made the general academic atmosphere something less than bracing, and productive of the kind of amiable cynicism expressed by a tutor who, finding the low standards of a certain pupil's composition necessitated much labour in correction, said, 'B, you don't improve. If I could not do better than this, I'd be given'; meaning, in Etonian patois, 'I'd get someone else, more able, to do the work for me.'

He was alluding to a familiar usage. The case was known of a boy at Eton* who remained invincibly unable to construe accurately a line – much less write an original verse – of Latin or Greek, and who progressed to the fifth form, a considerable eminence in scholastic seniority, by means of having a clever friend† who sat next to him in their division. When his turn came to 'show up', he invariably received a paper pellet which, when unrolled, revealed an appropriate

---

* General Sir Thomas Westropp Macmahon, Bart, 1813–92, Honorary Colonel, commanding 5th Dragoons.
† Samuel Gambier, Scholar of Trinity College, Cambridge; Wrangler, first-class Classics, 1836: died soon after.

few lines, sufficient in quantity and quality to pass muster, but not so good or so long as to arouse suspicion. This arrangement appears to have worked perfectly up to the time the boy was removed from school by his father who had bought him a commission in the Dragoons. His subsequent career as a soldier was eminently successful.

Cribs and libraries of 'original' verses for all occasions were bequeathed from boy to boy and generation to generation. One example may be given of the captain of a Dame's house c. 1820 who had inherited or acquired a collection of 3000 'old copies', as they were called, a bank of verses for all seasons, even corrected by the original authors' tutors. The unforeseen requirement to produce a verse on the death of George III was not beyond the capacity of this library, for its contents included verses on the death of George II, which with only small adjustment met the demand handsomely.

How good the best scholars were and how great the chasm dividing them in performance from the rest was nicely pointed by Lord John Russell. Speaking later in the century of the great bygone orators, he said that in his early days there were always more than a dozen men in the House who could make a finer speech than anyone now living; but he used to add that there were not another dozen who could understand what they were talking about:[11] 'The best scholars and the idlest and most ignorant came from the public schools.'[12] To most boys who never got near the sixth form, nor desired to, the public schools imparted just sufficient quotations to play into conversation to support their claim for admission to polite society. At the same time they acted as an efficient agent of social exclusivity by providing nothing which could be of the slightest use in preparing them to earn a living in commerce or industry, or in any employment other than the learned professions and select government service, the latter being in any event in the patronage of the friends and relatives of those destined to obtain them.

By the time George Moberly addressed the Clarendon Commission in 1861 the sciences had become militant and the régime of the classics was under attack from men of the fame and eminence of Herbert Spencer and T. H. Huxley. But in the first three and four decades of the century, what Huxley called 'intellectual gymnastics' still reigned supreme as the criterion of 'education'. The kind of parents (or at least fathers) who sent their children to public school still tended to take the *academic* values of the system on trust, for they were often not what the boy was primarily sent to acquire. Mr

Rowcroft, delivering his son Charles to Eton in 1810, disposed of an awkward subject by brisk delegation. 'People don't talk Greek and Latin now,' he remarked to the boy, 'at least I've never heard them; but they are very useful nevertheless in a variety of ways not necessary for me to mention at present because your tutor will explain all that to you.'[13] Offering what he judges a true picture of an ordinary English country gentleman dispatching his son to Rugby in the 1830s, Thomas Hughes has Mr Brown saying, 'Shall I tell him he's sent to school to make himself a good scholar? . . . Well but he isn't. . . . I don't care a straw for Greek particles or for the digamma, no more than does his mother. . . . If he'll only turn out to be a brave, helpful, truth telling Englishman, and a gentleman and a Christian, that's all I want.'[14]

It was commonplace for such a father to profess, 'He will be satisfied if his son never does anything unworthy of a gentleman.' A more worldly, ambitious father might wish 'that his son should advance himself by his talents',[15] but advancement in public life, or in the limited professions and pursuits open to such a son, could still be achieved without specialized study or the acquisition of technical skills. If the effect of schooling tended to make a subject brave, resourceful, confident and chivalrous, at ease with all ranks, truthful and honourable, yet shrewd in judging men and situations, and with such philosophic matter, great or small, in his head, culled from the noblest literature in the history of mankind – that might be accounted the education of an English gentleman, and who could ask for more?

Bustling utilitarians could be repelled with the counter assertion that classical studies were *useful* as enabling one 'to maintain with comfort and respectability the station of a gentleman',[16] or were *necessary* for the achievement of 'the one great purpose for which boys are sent to Public Schools' which was 'to prepare themselves by study for the station of a gentleman'.[17] Educationally this was a society, not of immaturity – far from it – but, despite its vices and brutality, of innocence in decay, and on the brink of dissolution. If society could function on this prescription there was much to be said for it; but society and its needs were changing faster than squires like Mr Rowcroft and Mr Browne, with one foot in the eighteenth century, apprehended; and in practice the system only worked to maturation upon the gifted and industrious. The former were inevitably a minority, and no one was compelled to be of the latter. Wilkinson confesses,

Some did come away, after many years of the curriculum . . . without writing a respectable hand; without being able to spell; without any acquaintance with common geography, not only of the world, but even of Great Britain, scarcely perhaps of England; without knowing whether the sun went round the earth or the earth the sun, or whether the moon was or was not 'made of green cheese', without knowledge of history except the stories they learnt at home in the nursery, of Alfred and the cakes, of Canute and his courtiers on the seashore. . . .[18]

In part the condition was lack of incentive from home. William Johnson complained in 1867, 'In the holidays there is hardly a father who tries to direct his son's mind from dogs and horses.'* But although it was true there were and would long continue to be such fathers in plenty in the classes which sent their sons to public schools, public opinion was gradually changing. It was no longer as fashionable as it once had been to be ostentatiously ignorant of everything other than field sports and the classics. As qualifications for understanding and controlling a changing environment also changed, more men became ashamed of being ignorant of the new knowledge, even when they themselves did not require it for the practical purposes of survival. In 1860 a very modern Old Etonian declared, 'I have a high opinion of successful men and I am not ashamed to confess it. . . .' The defiant tone was provoked because, 'It was the fashion some years ago to sneer at success . . . nay, indeed sometimes to revile it, as though it were an offence, or at best pretentious humbug. . . .'[19]

It is remarkable that, in the prevailing conditions, the number of excellent classical scholars produced was as great as it was. A boy with an appetite for learning had every opportunity for improvement which leisure could provide. If he was lucky he had a good and conscientious tutor, for whom a gifted, even a diligent, boy was an oasis in a desert, delightful to cultivate. But he might not be lucky. The tutors, being themselves products of a system in which graduation was not conditional on any tests, were nearly as wildly disparate in their intellectual quality as the boys. At one end of the scale there were Knapp and Keate himself, both consummate classical scholars; at the other men like Bethell and Green, who, later, as pressures grew – even upon Eton – for amendment, had to be removed, and

* But Johnson also said in evidence before the Clarendon Commission that currently, out of the forty-three pupils whom he tutored, only thirteen were sure to inherit property (Report, vol. 21, Minutes of Evidence, Eton, para. 4349).

could only be removed by being promoted, kicked upstairs to the sinecures of cosy fellowships.

When displeased with such tutors as these, a clever boy would turn work into play. 'All right. He shall have a Greek theme next week and be up with his Lexicon half the night to make it out.'[20] That was fair play; another joke was not, although it gave great sport to the player and his confidants. The method of instruction then in use at Eton placed a boy in direct relation to two teachers, his tutor and the master of his division. When he had written his verses or theme, his tutor first went through the work with him, assessed and criticized it and made such corrections or improvements as he thought fit. The boy then made a fair copy which he showed to the master of his division. The system 'gave every master frequent opportunities of gauging the scholarship of his colleagues'.

These occasions gave one boy in the first ten of the fifth form who, together with the sixth form, were 'up' to the headmaster, the opportunity to display his not inconsiderable skill as a forger. He had particularly perfected imitating his tutor's handwriting and made solecistic alterations and ludicrous insertions in his rough copy as if they were his tutor's work. When Dr Keate came to inspect the fair copy he was confronted by a hexameter ending '*nigrum detrusit ad orcum*' (he thrust him down into dark Hades) in which the word *conto* was substituted for *nigrum*. As he read over the page Keate suddenly jumped with surprise and indignation and glared at the boy.

'What do you mean by using such a word as "conto"? "He thrust him down into Hades with a punt-pole." How dare you write such rubbish.'

'If you please, sir, it was my tutor's correction,' replied the boy, with all the confidence of injured innocence. Keate snarled and continued, amidst roars of laughter from the privileged audience. Success made the criminal bolder, until one day he went too far and came within an inch of exposure. The verses were a translation of the elegy upon the death of Sir John Moore and the forger had had a field day. Almost every line was mined with a fatuous 'correction' and faithful to all expectation Dr Keate obliged with explosions on every line. 'Not a drum was heard' had become '*Jam sonat armorum strepitus clangorque tubarum*', and as the travesty unfolded Keate raged and the sixth form hooted and rolled about with mirth. At last he came to '*lacrymae rubros dedecuere viros*'; *fortes* had been cut out and *rubros* inserted.* Keate was now almost apoplectic, and getting the same answer, 'Not mine, sir, m'tutor put it in,' he roared, 'Go, fetch your foul copy, sir.' It was brought and there were all the corresponding corrections in the lines, apparently all in the same hand, the tutor's, and at the bottom, his initials, and the observation, '*Very bad indeed*'. There followed the silence of breathless incredulity; then, recovering his presence of mind, Keate dilated upon the disgraceful proceeding of a boy so high up in the school having shown such a copy of verses, which his tutor well condemned as 'Very bad indeed'. The forger recognized how near he had come to discovery and never repeated the performance.[21]

Keate should have suspected a plot, if only from the sudden improvement in the fifth former's work. Perhaps he did and thought it better not to disinter a matter which had subsided. But since he never knew the truth for certain, the harm remained unrectified. The tutor was never promoted out of lower school and many times thereafter was superseded by new masters, appointed to upper school over his head.

The tutor of genius, when he appeared, was discerned even by the majority. William Johnson (who later changed his name to Cory) was a teacher unforgettable to those whom he taught. His knowledge was cyclopaedic. Palmerston wished to give him the chair of History at Oxford. But he was above all a classicist. He wrote English prose and verse with sensuous economy, and his apophthegms were famed and feared; but he wrote best in Greek and Latin. A. C. Benson, in his eulogistic introduction to the posthumous publication of Johnson's *Ionica* describes the poet as 'a first rate classical scholar', an observation which provoked Herbert Paul, a former pupil of Johnson who might himself fairly have been described as 'first rate classical scholar', to remark, 'This reminds me of the late Lord Crewe asking Mrs. Gladstone whether her husband did not take a considerable interest in politics.' Professor Munro ('Lucretius Munro') said that William Johnson wrote the best Horatian lyrics since the death of Horace.

On two points those who knew Johnson best were agreed: he was

---

* 'Not a drum was heard,' tendered as clash of arms and blare of trumpet, does not move me to laughter; although I can understand a collection of boys seizing on it as a pretext for levity. But I am baffled by the comic purport of 'tears disgrace red [bloody?] men', unless any deviation from received metaphor and vocabulary in Latin was inherently comic to boys who were taught nothing but classical literature. Peter Baldwin, head of the classics department at the Charterhouse, was kind enough to examine the lines in case I might have missed some hidden meaning; but Mr Baldwin also found nothing there to designate as wit.

incapable of being dishonest or dull. 'Nothing that he taught,' says Paul, 'could ever for a moment, while he taught it, be dull. He never seemed as though he tried to be interesting, but as though he could not be anything else. In scholarship he began where some of his colleagues left off; and I have wondered at times whether he thought in Greek.' There is nothing extravagant in Herbert Paul's conjecture. Johnson's best English verses are his own translation of what he had first written in Greek. 'The pedantry of scholarship he loathed,' says Paul, 'the author with whom he had most affinity was Plato. . . . There was a good deal of resemblance, more than appeared at first sight, between him and Socrates.'[22]

Johnson was too sensitive and too spirited not to be capable of intense happiness and unhappiness; but the conjunction of circumstance and conditions which fate had decreed assured the ascendancy of unhappiness and frustration. For Johnson was at once a paederast by nature, a schoolmaster by vocation, and an honourable man by principle. If this insoluble dilemma were not enough, he was also in aspiration a soldier and an athlete, and was born a myope. He used to say that he had never seen a bird fly. He sculled as best he could; no one who had not been on the water would have written the 'Eton Boating Song'; and he played such games as were possible for him. Arthur Duke Coleridge remembers him playing the wall game, 'a strange figure, that bow-legged youth dressed like an Eskimo in a coarse jersey, blind as a bat, and in constant peril of having his spectacles smashed, for he rushed indiscriminately at friend and foe, like a bull in a china shop'.[23]

A characteristic of Johnson's makes him the indefeasible touchstone in any study of the public-school mystic in this seminal period. For he had a mind, fastidious and rigorously disciplined; but it seemed to be habitually at the service of ancient and irrational tribal sentiments and traditions, which belonged to another age, and might have been supposed to belong to another mind. The dichotomy was not lost on the instincts of boys. 'There were ways,' says Herbert Paul, 'of getting round my tutor, with which no mental process had anything to do. But intellectually I do not think he was ever deceived.'

Johnson had a mind and tongue which cut through humbug and gush and overweening pretensions. His instincts usually prevailed in his responses and, as he himself, being a man without vanity, was morally impregnable, his lash sometimes hurt more and longer than he ever intended. To a clever boy, coming into a lecture late and stealthily not for the first time, he said as a quick, casual aside, 'Why do you bother to creep in? You've established your insignificance pretty well, already.' The boy, psychologically a robust character, used to remember, with a slight shudder, the occasion and impact of the words into his old age.[24]

Johnson was always in quest of the company of his superiors. 'A Schoolmaster,' he remarked, 'must needs get dogmatic or weak in faith or both unless he has some such intercourse with equals or superiors – and it is of infinite importance that they be men of his own age.' Yet the same man was never fully at ease, because never fully happy, except in the company of youth. 'I long for the boys every day,' he wrote, a month after his premature and poignant retirement from Eton:

> I'll borrow life and not grow old;
> And nightingales and trees
> Shall keep me though the veins be cold
> As young as Sophocles.
>
> And when I may no longer live,
> They'll say who know the truth,
> He gave what ere he had to give
> To freedom and to youth.

The honesty and delicacy of Johnson's mind appear in his words to one boy, scholarly and musical, whose sight was threatened. There is no pretence and no evasion, yet abounding comfort. 'It is dreadful to speak of, but as I am told that I may be deaf, so you may bear to be told that you may lose the power of reading books or music and it would be a great blessing to you to have your memory stored with book thoughts as well as with tunes.'

Johnson was never typical of any code or standard. He was exceptional not only in his ability, but in his humility. In an age when the accomplishment in which he was supreme was itself academically supreme, and he needed to look no farther than his own authority for honour, he declared himself ashamed of his lack of education in science and used his prestige to promote its advance in education. Later he was to write,

We teach boys to say in Latin verse, 'Happy is he who hath been able to learn the causes of things, why the earth trembles and the deep seas gape'; and yet we are not to tell them. . . . What would Lucretius have thought of men who knew or might know such things and were afraid to tell the young of them for fear of spoiling their perception of his

165

peculiarities. How would Ovid flout us if he heard that we could unfold the boundless mysteries contained in his germinal saying, 'All things change, nothing perishes', and passed them by to potter over his little ingenuities.[25]

Johnson saw the classics as useful not merely as patterns, but as warnings exposing 'the shallowness of their induction', their 'employment of metaphor instead of argument', the frequent 'breaking down of their rhetoric', their 'countless fallacies of observation' and the barrenness to which they were condemned by the estrangement of their literature from science. He predicted the substitution of French for the Latin language as a vehicle for linguistic schooling, for there was 'enough grammar in French for coercive discipline' and for 'the shampooing of a dull mind', and 'etymology enough to be the foundation of that healthy nominalism which above all else arms us against delusions'. At the same time French had not inherited the vice of the classics, 'the worship of difficulty for its own sake'.[26] As for the present character of classical education, if there was clear proof of its 'frivolity' it was the habitual misconception of the term history, 'its miserable limitation to a tissue of homicide and perfidy stitched together with dates'. Examination questions should be problems, not just a display of received knowledge.

Johnson's satiric criticisms of orthodox practice were indulged as the privilege of proven genius: indulged, but not currently followed; and by the time his Socratic questions had become more obviously relevant, Johnson himself appeared in certain respects an embarrassing anachronism. His career as schoolboy and schoolmaster spans most of the period we cover and, in retrospect, such of his commentaries as have been preserved are invaluable counsellors for, although idiosyncratic in discrimination, they are rigorous in quest for truth, and ready to confront every identifiable fact, however disagreeable its implications. His voice will be heard again.

NINE
The Habit of Rebellion

The boys at English public schools in the period we are covering were engaged in an irregular but continuous warfare against adult government. To some extent the same is true of most boys at all times; but in the 'unreformed' public schools the practice was (like the raids and forays in the tribal belt that separated Afghanistan and what was the North West Province of India) part of an approved way of life, an educational exercise and a display of the spirit of independence prescriptive by honour for all aspirants to the respect of their peers.

Amongst the boys and their dealings with each other and the outside world, the cultivated literary elegance which was one element of their education, and the readiness to resort to violence and battle as the sacred criteria of merit, co-existed in a curious partnership of contradictions. It is not difficult to credit that an adolescent boy could behave barbarously and offensively in public; it is less consistent with patterns of conduct familiar in the late twentieth century that the *same* boy (Lord John Manners), should have been capable of writing an apology, of which Dr Keate's sister-in-law said, 'I never read so perfect a note from any man or boy.'[1]*

Rows between boys and masters, boys and boys, and boys and outsiders were part of the way of life, and the process of trial and growth. After the turn of the century instances of direct conflict between individual boys and masters diminish. One no longer hears of episodes like George Brudenell's swarming up a pillar and defying Dampier for half an hour until pulled down by the praeposters and the birch desk keeper, and then 'under pretence of struggling to evade punishment most wantonly and violently kicking the still weak limbs of the master',[2] who had been suffering from gout. After 1810 one

---

* John Manners, 'an elegant tall boy, stammers so dreadfully as scarcely to be able to utter one intelligent sentence'.

does not hear of a master being flogged in public by a boy, as Heath was by K— with a tandem whip after he had reported him for 'tandem driving'.[3] Even in the great rebellions in Keate's time, there were limits which were not passed. Masters might be threatened, and even pelted, but they were not physically attacked, as their predecessors had sometimes been, while Keate, for his part, never attempted to enforce his discipline by mere force. He required submission, and the boy who would not 'submit' was expelled.

Corporate character varied from school to school. On the whole, senior boys took themselves and their battles with authority very seriously. What distinguished the bearing of boys to masters at Eton was a native spirit of playful irreverence, and absence of deference, a presence of levity and readiness to question and inquire and dispute when pronouncements from above were felt to be fallacious or contemptible. 'He really is the most sneaking fellow that ever I saw or heard of,' Gladstone wrote home of Heath, his division master, on 8 June 1823, having caught the native spirit very quickly. 'Butcher Bethell, so called for the quality of the correction of his pupils' verses, had a favourite and ever recurring phrase which he used with a small variation for long and short verse: for the former, "*sibi vindicat ipse*", for the latter, "*vindicat ipse sibi*". A boy asked by him what he would eat answered, "Sir, I vindicate myself a piece of mutton".'[4]

Edward Coleridge, whose evaluation of his own scholarship was thought by some to err on the side of generosity: 'Not know your Homer, idle boy! Why, were I cast on a desert island I should be content with three only books, my Bible, and my Homer.' Boy: 'And your Lexicon, sir.'[5]

Respect had to be earned by a master, and a judgement deemed malicious or erroneous would not be borne in silence as, for example, it might be borne at more repressive Winchester, until one of those moments of violent eruption when Winchester became the most belligerent and scurrilous of all the schools in the expression of long-nourished grievances. In the rebellion of 1818, the first answer returned to the headmaster's inquiry into the reasons for the insurgence was, 'That you are ugly'.[6]

At Eton contests between boys and masters were more open and customary, and therefore less bitter. Charles Metcalfe began to keep a diary at Eton in 1800, just at the time when he came into collision with his tutor over the subject of an evening service of tea, against which novel practice the tutor harboured an, to Metcalfe, unreasonable objection.

> Monday 3rd March. Drank tea after six in Harvey's room according to agreement. Afraid the plan of bringing in that custom won't succeed.
> Thursday 6th. Tutor jawed about drinking tea after six.
> Friday 7th. Drank tea with Shaw according to our conversation. after six. Tutor jawed with great spirit.

There was no question, as there might have been elsewhere, of concealment.

> Monday 11th. . . . Gave tea to Neville, Harvey and Shaw according to our agreement. Had a most tremendous jaw from my tutor who said nothing but that it was a serious inconvenience but could not bring one argument to prove that it was so.
> Friday 14th. . . . Drank tea with Harvey after six. We have conquered, and my tutor, not finding an argument against us, so obliged to consent: so now we do it lawfully. Had it not been for our last despairing struggle we should have failed.[7]

Dames and tutors with boarding houses sometimes had more cause for concern than Metcalfe's tutor seems to have had. In particular, vigilance was shown at the beginning of the period from Michaelmas to Lady Day when fires were allowed and, to celebrate, little boys with money to spend bought sausages and meat to cook on a new-lighted fire, while the house owners prowled about alert to prevent their chimneys being set alight through an excess of conflagration.

> No dame should then on tiptoe come upstairs
> And snatch a pipkin from us unawares
> As late, when met to eat, with all our might
> Our fill of sausages on St Michael's night.[8]

Not every encounter ended in victory for the challengers. Etonians went protesting to the block and beyond, sometimes more than once over the same issue. An Irish boy was flogged three times in one day for refusing to do a poena which he considered unmerited.[9] Gladstone's fag, George Mellish,* seems to have been unable to get rid of the propensity in after life, to judge from the opinion of, among others, the Lord Chancellor, Lord Selborne (Roundell Palmer), upon his eager 'habit of too freely interrupting the arguments of counsel'.[10]

There was in general no attempt to conceal in letters home the combative and sometimes riotous nature of the transactions between

---

* Sir George Mellish, Lord Justice of Appeal in Ordinary.

boys and their titular adult governors. It was presented to parents and guardians sometimes with glee as evidence of tests and trials of daring and endurance, honourable and appropriate to the progress of an English young gentleman at a public school. In 1830 the high cost of misconduct at the time of the annual Windsor Fair was made the occasion to beg some additional pocket money to finance operations on a worthy scale.

> Windsor Fair Happens Monday Fortnight, and that is the time of larks, crackers flying, China Stalls overturning, Keate flogging, Masters jawing and billing for the first ward missed, Hexter and other magistrates pushing fellows into the Cage, Eton fellows half killing clods, &c. &c. &c. but all this is carried on by the *needful pecus*, which bye the bye has nearly vanished out of my pocket and therefore I (a humble petitioner) pray that that part of my dress may again be filled with *Peck* (there's slang) to enter a little into the spirit of the said Fair.[11]

After the Fair damage to property was paid for, and tradesmen's signs and other coveted trophies acquired by revellers were later hung on display in the 'Eton Court of Claims', a room in the Christopher, where the lawful owners could come to identify their property. It was restored to them with compensation or, if they preferred (which they usually did), purchased outright on generous terms and carried off by new owners to adorn college rooms at Oxford or Cambridge and regimental quarters.

A cheerful spirit of play and healthy insubordination still prevailed four decades later, though moderated somewhat by the advance of Victorian canons of propriety which even 'unchanging Eton' could not entirely repel forever. The atmosphere made chivalrous, even quixotic, gestures possible:

> *Master*: Write out and translate your lesson for kicking Jones minor.
> *Boy*: Please, sir I didn't.
> *After school*
> *Boy*: Please, sir, I really didn't kick Jones minor I only pushed him off the form.
> *Master*: Makes no difference: do the punishment.
> *Boy*: Please, sir, but he's such a beast.
> *Master*: So he is: you needn't do the punishment.[12]

Or again:

> 'Did you use a crib for this translation?'
> 'No, Sir'
> 'Run and fetch it.'

It would have been considered almost indecent to agonize over offences as 'sins'; punishments were awarded for detected breaches of discipline. The eccentric classics tutor, Cooksley, cautioning boys against attending forbidden race meetings, did not descant on the immorality of the Turf. He said, 'Go to Ascot today and you'll get your arse cut tomorrow.'[13]

Cuffing of younger boys by tutors, although forbidden, was widely practised in moments of exasperation. Nobody objected; it was part of the game. But an unpopular master who broke the rules and tried to meddle in matters beyond his province found himself in collision with a combination. After Bethell had objected to certain boys in his division wearing red coats after Montem, a practice licensed by tradition, next day, instead of a small minority, fifty or more appeared together, all in red coats. He was furious, but took the hint.[14]

When a tutor was felt to be applying excessive pressure (which seldom happened) he was described as 'bullying', even 'bullying shamefully',[15] as if he were another boy doing something reprehensible. The skills acquired by years of verse translation (and penal epigrams) could be turned to the service of 'hints' at a later date. Oscar Browning, tactless and greedy, a tutor without malice but not without vanity, was admonished

> O be obedient O.B. to nature's stern decree
> For if you take too much to eat you'll soon be too obese.

As the century advanced a change in public expectation began to be felt. A tendency of government, under pressure from religious and political moralists, to intervene more directly in the private sector of social transactions was reflected in the theatre of the schools. Mozley, reviewing the scene in retrospect, sixty years later, simplifies what proved a long and devious conflict. 'It was,' he wrote, '. . . universally agreed that public education had to be reformed. The old traditions had to be broken. Extravagance and wickedness had to be controlled – at all events not to be taught. Masters had to be masters and scholars scholars.'[16] A new kind of master began to appear, seeking victory in his contests with boy power not for the honourable sake of victory in combat, but in order thereby to alter the traditional constitution, and invade the sacred preserve of boys' social independence. The basic tenets of public-school tradition were openly assailed:

> Boys must not be allowed to form a distinct society of their own: they are not sent to school to form a society for themselves; they are sent to live in a society framed and governed by the intelligence and virtue of a man whose profession is to train boys. Boys are sent to school, among other purposes, to be instructed in the knowledge of social life, not a social life founded on their own notions, but one which shall be a fit introduction to the social state of manhood.[17]

The final words are revealing. It was the 'social state' of *manhood* that the missionaries of the new order wished to change, making it conform with the standards of industry, utility and decorum which they had exalted for reverence. In this design boyhood was seen as too important to be left to boys, and its capture a strategic imperative in the struggle to reform the morals and criteria of the *men* who would inherit authority and power.

Roundell Palmer had warily hedged his approval of fagging with qualification. 'It cannot be easy for a youth of sixteen or seventeen . . . to be honest and keep faith with the masters and at the same time be on friendly and comfortable terms with all classes of his schoolfellows.'[18] This was an uneasy adult's revision of reality. No praefect would then have been much concerned to 'keep faith with masters'; not that he would have wished to break faith with them, but he would not have deemed there to be faith to be kept or broken. Masters were the enemy, claimants to power and authority, and school life was commonly a struggle between two sets of laws and two parties of legislators for dominion. Sometimes, inevitably, there was a formal alliance in the tactical interests of both sides. More often, in the first half of the century, the senior boys, whether sixth form or prefectorial, were seen as contestants advancing the claims of a rival authority, the court of common law against the courts of prerogative, or so a boy might have distinguished the powers in confrontation. On 21 October 1819 Charles Floyer, 'Princeps Oppidanus' of Westminster School, wrote of the headmaster Dr Goodenough:

> Deaf to all remonstrance [he] ventured to infringe upon the established image of the school by flogging a 6th Fellow who had been shewn up for being intoxicated. In consequence of this it was unanimously agreed

172

throughout the Town Boys that in order to bring him to a sense of his misconduct and to cause him to redress the injury done to the Honour of the Sixth he should be hissed on entering into school on the ensuing day.

Roundell Palmer puts a mature finger in retrospect upon a source of prefectorial weakness more frequent than lack of conscientious performance of duty when he alludes to 'foolish assumptions of dignity, unsuitable to his age . . .',[19] to which a boy hastened into a position of power over others is susceptible. Vanity and arrogance are the natural vices attending puerile power; but there were other more serious dangers. An error in the appointment of a praefect might put almost unlimited power into seriously unsuitable hands.[20]

Westminster, once the proudest and most aristocratic of the public schools, having fallen out of fashion, its *ancien régime* had become peculiarly vulnerable to the attentions of neologizing pedagogues, bent on benevolent progress. The Town Boy Ledger, from 1815 to 1862, is an unvarnished record, kept by the Commoner praefects, of the running battles fought between praefects and a succession of masters. The contents were treated as absolutely privileged, to be revealed to no one at the time of writing but the writer's Commoner peers in the sixth. The records of 'circumstances . . . useful or entertaining' were aimed at 'posterity' but often addressed by a retiring head boy to his successors as advice, encouragement and exhortation to keep up the good fight.

Liddell, headmaster in 1851, after being hissed, manifestly on orders from the sixth form, when an established pattern of dates for leaving and returning to school at half term had been changed, 'sent a polite message,' says the Head Oppidan, J. M. Murray,* 'intimating that the captain was to lose his election and that I was to be expelled if any more demonstration of sulkiness was made. I of course, could do nothing but laugh at this empty threat, for I can hardly suppose that he could think *I* should endeavour to impress on the fellows that "Obedience to your masters is your first duty and that whatever your *masters* do, is all for the best" with such like moral effusions to save myself from an expulsion in which for such a thing I should rather glory.' That was the praefect's attitude as honestly as it has ever been presented. 'I really think,' said Murray in the

---

* J. M. Murray, 6th Light Cavalry, died in India in 1856. Some of Murray's observations may have been too strong for a later and tamer generation. Several lines of his entries have been obliterated by another hand.

same entry, 'that we have a right to a voice in a matter which concerns *us* chiefly and I do not see why *we* are to go home and come back at the call of a "fashionable master" in defiance of old rules and customs.' But distasteful as it was to a proud pagan youth like Murray, the changing age was one of growing 'moral effusion' and of an increased zeal among post-Arnoldian masters to intervene in the moral development of boys in their charge. The headmaster was not the only meddlesome intruder. 'To the great astonishment of all,' Murray reports, 'the under master had the cheek to hand Forster, a boy in the Upper Fifth & this being mentioned to Liddell he said he was certainly right. This needs no comment.'[21]

The under master alluded to was T. W. Weare, 'who,' says another entry signed by A. F. Pope, 'has since Liddell left Westminster made it his business to interfere in every way possible with every body else. . . .' The occasion was when Liddell took the opportunity of a collision between Weare and a sixth former called Maples, with the whole of the sixth form backing the boy, to repudiate the traditional privilege of the sixth of immunity from the authority of all masters but the headmaster. 'All boys,' he asserted, 'were subject to *all* masters' whatever the customs of the past. The school appeared to be about to mutiny. Entries in the Town Boy Ledger solemnly adjured the writer's successors to have the order rescinded as soon as they could get themselves a new headmaster. As for Weare, who had said of himself that he was 'loved and respected', 'the truth is he is feared by QS [Queens Scholars] on account of their election and hated'.

A headmaster like Liddell and assistant masters like Weare, and afterwards Marshall, sought not only to curtail the traditional privileges of the sixth form as a class, which made them almost independent of authority and a law unto themselves, but to reduce by appropriation their power, especially their physical power of the punishment of their juniors. 'In consequence of my having shewn up for tanning a fellow (which he richly deserved),' says Pope, 'Liddell told me that the only way a head town boy or Head of a House had of keeping order was by shewing up to the masters. I told him that it had never been the custom at Westminster to do so and therefore I could not think of being the first to break the old rule.' But the headmaster was quite ready to lead the way. 'Where will this stop,' wrote Osbert Salvin on innovation in general, 'I cannot venture to assert but am afraid not until the whole school and perhaps everything else pertaining to Westminster has been converted into a sort of Private

Academy for the education of Young Gentlemen.'[22] These words express the ultimate in the public schoolboys' vocabulary of contempt.

Why Westminster, with its exceptional record of violence through the centuries, did not erupt in open rebellion was due in large measure to the decayed state of the school. From three hundred in 1821 the numbers had fallen to ninety in 1846.[23] What could hardly have been attempted in the days of Westminster's glory – and would have been effectively resisted by a coalition of the boys, their parents, and influential Old Westminsters – had been promoted by an ambitious headmaster (not himself an Old Westminster) from whom much was hoped and feared. The divided feelings which gave him his chance moderated the bias of even as staunchly conservative an Old Westminster as Colonel Clavering, who remarked with little hope and some distaste: 'It is said that Westminster is rather getting up under the new master. It is to be hoped that he will keep up as far as possible the good old customs for which however he may not entertain the same veneration that we do even to fagging which the stupid writers in the newspapers of the present day are endeavouring to drive out of fashion. . . .'[24]

This, then, was what public-school traditionalists meant when they talked of 'freedom': not freedom of an individual to flout or evade the customs and exactions of his peers, but freedom of boys as a self-governing tribe, to live their lives and grow to manhood without prying surveillance and interference by their titular overlords. There had always, of course, been conflict and tension between the powers of masters and of top boys, as between officers of the crown and mighty vassals; but warfare, though vigorously conducted, had been conventional, with limited objectives on both sides. Now the struggle appeared to have become one of independence or subjection.

As the fifth-form prophets of Eton had put it when they drummed up resistance to the new headmaster in 1809, 'If the old rules are to be broken by every master who takes it into his head what are to become the liberties of the school – We might as well live under a pure despotism.'[25] Little did they guess that the man they feared, John Keate, would be remembered as a bulwark and last upholder of the old order against the kind of reforms they dreaded, which were indeed to infiltrate their ancient groves and subvert their hallowed practices. Eton was able to resist standardized reforms longer than other schools and was recognized by reformers as the arch enemy of their hopes, a place where 'nothing is permitted . . . but everything is winked at',[26] and by boys themselves as the citadel of 'boy power', 'a place where boys comparatively do as they will, where they are allowed to commit the unheard of sin of passing their bounds – and where, in fact, the measure of their labours is in a great degree under the control of their own discretion'.[27] Indeed the resistance movement to the imposition from *above* of a uniform moral pattern was never decisively defeated at Eton, despite strenuous campaigns (notably by Warre) to bring the community into line with prevailing fashions in propriety.

The rebellion against Keate in 1810 had been plotted even before he became headmaster. The legacy of the French Revolution was active, and it may be that this generation of boys felt more than any previously an increasing reactionary attempt by adults to encroach upon their social autonomy. Keate was regarded by the militant Oppidan libertarians as a provocative and abrasive meddler with the sacred licence to do unhindered as they pleased which had been enjoyed during Goodall's long and indulgent reign. Councils of war were held to organize resistance. At a private conference between senior and junior boys, certain fifth formers confided to select juniors that Keate might be expected to hold the reins of power with 'more than a tight hand' and that there was reason to apprehend that he would attempt to introduce some new restrictions in respect to 'bounds' and 'absence' which would trench on 'the ancient liberties of the school'. This information was received with great uneasiness, but it was judged on the initiative of the upper fifth that it would be impossible for any headmaster to succeed in any policy if 'all fellows in every form, big and little, would stand firm in their resistance'.[28] Having pledged themselves to what today would be called 'solidarity', they opened bottles of wine and toasted each other with vows that they would live and die together.

Trouble began immediately on the accession of the new monarch, and was occasioned by resentment felt against two assistant masters, Bethell and Green, who were not only bad and idle tutors, but were generally disliked as men. The former received his pinch of immortality in the derisive lines of a versing junior, W. E. Gladstone:

> Didactic, dry, declamatory, dull
> Big Bursar Bethell bellows like a bull.[29]

A boy's-eye view of the restlessness from within college comes from H. H. Milman in a letter to his Harrovian friend, William Harness.

It is not unlikely that we shall have a serious rumpus here: civil dudgeon is growing very high. The best part of the joke is that there is no reason in the world for it except the spirit of the O.P. [Oppidan praeposters]. . . . *Entre nous* if there was as much spirit among the O.P.s as there is among their prototypes at Harrow, we should have flat rebellion, as Jack Falstaff says. . . . One of the assistant masters is the chief object of abomination – a man whom I cannot say I admire; but Keate comes in for a share which is very hard upon him, as he has certainly done nothing to give offence. I believe the rioters think the more noise they make the greater the respect they pay to Goodall.[30]*

The first opposition came when Keate tightened the reins by calling an extra Absence after long Church on 30 May 1810. At first the noise of booing was such that even his voice could not be heard. It took two hours to call the roll, although tutors were stationed in the concourse to detect culprits. Keate placed the blame for the distur-bance squarely (and correctly) on the middle divisions of the school and as a penalty he set the whole of the last remove of the upper fifth and the whole of the lower fifth a five o'clock Absence. At an angry meeting of those affected many boys declared their resolution not to attend, and a high proportion failed to answer their names. Summoned to appear before the headmaster the following day, the offenders marched in a body from the playing fields, through Weston's Yard to the library shouting slogans of defiance. When Keate began conventional execution with the birch, the hooting and yelling became furious; people hearing it in Eton feared a dangerous mob was abroad; the sound frightened Miss Brown, who was a far from nervous woman. As Keate flogged an egg flew through the air and broke on the wall near him. It was followed by another, and another, and then a shower of eggs burst all round him. Keate suspended operations and withdrew. He returned, having changed his clothes, accompanied by assistant masters and praeposters to impose at least physical control and resumed the performance. By eight o'clock, to the accompaniment of unabated hoots of derision, he had flogged all those sentenced.[32]

Having vindicated his authority, the threatened ruler addressed a stern warning against any repetition of disobedience to the tempor-arily subdued, but unrepentant mutineers. Henry Milman, was present:

---

* Goodall had had similar resistance at the time of his own appointment as headmaster, with 'no Goodall' chalked up with other more offensive intimations on the college walls.[31]

Keate talked in a very spirited manner and I must say I think he will be more feared than Goodall, but he will never be so much loved. He has a sharpness in his manner which presupposes most against him and sometimes when he intends to be particularly civil, he looks as if he would knock you down. Moreover – and this was against him – he did not wear a wig.[33]

Nothing could better illustrate the innate conservatism of the public schools than the immediate resistance to any variation, whether of abridgement or addition, in established practice. Wigs had already gone out of fashion in society when Keate became headmaster, but here and there they had lingered within the schoolmastering profession as a visible affirmation of the authority and superior status of their wearers, much as they may have been retained to perform this office for the judiciary and counsel in an English High Court of Justice. When Samuel Butler consulted his mentor, Samuel Parr, on how to strengthen the effect of his presence among the boys, Parr had advised him, 'Wear a wig.'[34] Parr visited Butler at Shrewsbury and listened to the boys' speeches seated on the platform resplendent in a huge 'Buzz' wig and smoking a long pipe, the nobility of the tableau impaired by his liberal use of a spitoon placed before him. But wigs, when they enjoyed anything less than the respect exacted by the majesty of the law, could be subject, as conspicuous and readily abductable articles, to the hazard of outrage at impious hands. There is no knowing in what strange places and on what inappropriate objects Dr Keate's wig, had he favoured one, might not have been discovered.

In the year 1818, by strange coincidence, rebellion broke out in all but one of the public schools. A general restlessness in the atmosphere of political discontent following the battle of Waterloo was a contributory irritant. The masters of the several schools were conscious of a 'disagreeable spirit'[35] amongst the boys and 'an unusual state of turbulence' which was different from the familiar sporadic fits of juvenile rowdiness and bad behaviour.

Warning signals had been in evidence for some time. There had been a full-scale rebellion at Eton in 1768 after the headmaster, Dr Foster, had insisted that the masters' authority must supersede the sixth form's if there should at any time be a difference of opinion, and the sixth form had replied that they were themselves, not the assistant masters, to be the judges of 'the reasonableness where it should be used'.[36] On that occasion order was reimposed due to the firmness and solidarity of Etonian parents. But the conflicting claims had not been resolved.

In 1793 there was rebellion at Westminster, led by Sir Francis Burdett, a puerile firebrand, but on this occasion temporarily extinguished by the cudgel of the muscular headmaster, Dr Samuel Smith.[37] In the same year there was rebellion also at Winchester against the weak and erratic rule of Warton, unfair severity alternating with feeble apathy. In the panic which anything savouring of 'revolution' aroused at that date, three companies of militia were drawn up under arms in College Street, and it was seriously suggested that the 'insurgent' boys should be fired on. The quality of the headmaster may be judged from his concluding a treaty with the rebels and later breaking it, in the eyes of the boys, by privately requesting the removal of boys he had promised not to expel. The betrayal was neither forgotten nor forgiven, and had been nursed into a potent mythology by succeeding generations of Wykehamists. A rebellion at Rugby in 1797 was led by the future General Sir Willoughby Cotton, who later proved more successful at putting down the 'slaves rebellion' in Jamaica than he had been at leading one at Rugby.

The rising at Winchester in 1818 was again over the classic issue of senior boys' versus masters' authority, and was precipitated by an assistant master called Williams, nicknamed 'Puffer' by the boys. Williams was not public-school educated himself and was vehemently opposed in principle and by temperament to the traditional independence of praefectorial government, a custom which, although certainly 'old', he did not regard as 'good', and his determination to interfere in transactions between praefects and juniors led to an open clash between the master and a praefect.

On Sunday 22 March, after cathedral service, a praefect called Goodenough punished a boy, Wade jnr, with a ground ash, for some offence. If Charles Minet's account is accurate the beating was excessively severe by the standards then in use because Wade 'was taken up quite senseless' and the surgeon, perhaps with an eye to future business, 'said that if he had been an hour later he would have been a corpse. It was hurt on the back of his head which occasioned it.' Instead of addressing his observations to the praefects as a body, Williams complained direct to the headmaster, Dr Gabell, and evidently in strong terms, because in the evening Gabell came into the praefects' study and expelled Goodenough privately. Afterwards Goodenough came into Hall and wished the assembled boys farewell when Williams was on duty as tutor. Goodenough then went to

Williams and reproached him in front of all the boys for his perfidious conduct in telling Gabell of what was not his concern. 'They spoke very high,' says Minet, 'and I thought they would come to blows.' Goodenough walked over the table which, it seems, 'put Puffer in a greater rage'. The significant part of this episode is the demeanour of the expelled praefect, not penitent, nor even defiant, but righteously indignant. He considered Williams the offender, himself the injured party. After prayers Goodenough went and talked to Gabell and Puffer. 'He was very impudent to both,' says Minet, 'where I think he was much in the wrong' (a prudential not a moral judgement), 'as Gabell would give him a worse character on that account and prevent him going to Oxford.'

Winchester in 1818 was not ready to submit to direct adult rule outside the schoolroom; moreover, 'Puffer' Williams, as his name might suggest, was not a popular master, and when he presumed to invade the privacy of the boys' lives he started more than he could control. Minet, our boy on the spot, reports, 'Puffer came out of his house and made me go behind him lest I should give an alarm & went up to our bedroom where he detected several fellows out of their rooms & some bolstering [pillow fights], Meredith was one of them. Puffer told Gabell what had been going on – and got Praefects & fellows in for long impots.' That was in April. In the following month, when fires were out and summer clothes came in, 'much talk of a rebellion which I thought would come to nothing'. But the same afternoon, Wednesday the 6th, in the meads, 'we made agreement about the rebellion after which we had a song'.

It all happened fast. The boys 'took to their arms', sticks which they had been cutting that morning and 'a strong party went round to servants hall and another to Hatch, who took the keys from Ethridge, unlocked the gate and went into college where we found them all armed and prepared (never saw a thing done so quickly)'. Having taken the keys from the college porters and locked the servants in the lodge, the boys took possession of the towers and set watches on them while another party nailed up the warden's doors. Williams, who must have realized that this was the day of reckoning for him, 'came in twice', says Minet 'and prosed, but made no effect'. All the fellows and masters 'went into the Warden's house and prosed us from the windows without success'.[38] Juniors were posted as sentries on the middle gate and stood watch all night, keeping awake by frightening themselves with ghost stories. One of them, George Moberly, was to be an important headmaster of Winchester. Neither time, nor the majesty of office, shifted his sympathies, which remained with the rebels.

As usual in confrontations of this kind, the results were varied and inconclusive. The boys, suffering from inadequate commissariat,* laid down their arms and walked quietly away without the authorities having formally conceded anything. There was one ignoble perform-ance when a troop of soldiers was allowed to attack unarmed boys outside the school† and one of the boys had his head cut open by an officer's sabre.

The boys had not expected to achieve the impossible – outright victory – but to draw unwelcome, and therefore probably influential, attention to the strength of their feelings and their willingness to suffer in a just cause, as they saw it. Subsequently twenty-seven boys were expelled, including six College and six Commoner praefects. The boys cannot be said to have escaped without serious casualties, yet a kind of victory was theirs; for the heads of their enemies which rolled on the other side were the heads of the commanding officers. Williams went and, after a decent interval, the headmaster, Gabell, followed him.

At Eton from the year 1815, Keate was conscious of a growing spirit of defiance of authority, more hostile in its expression than the ordinary Etonian habit of playful irreverence, and after a series of offences, including his being bolted out of the college chapel, he felt it necessary to expel an unusually large number of boys, including two for tandem riding through Eton accompanied by women, and five leaders of misconduct for 'insubordination'.‡ The climax came in October of 1818, and the ostensible cause was the introduction by Keate of an earlier lock-up hour in winter, five instead of six o'clock. One boy, Marriot, a popular figure, conspicuously cut Absence, telling his friends it interfered with his social (racing) arrangements; and when convicted, refused to be flogged. To end this deadlock

---

* Surprisingly, considering the amount of catering they regularly did for themselves, the boys were not on this occasion efficient cooks – perhaps due to lack of facilities. The soup, says Moberly, was 'a frightful mess of raw potatoes at the bottom of warm water with two inches of bacon fat on the top'.[39]
† There had been ill feeling between Wykehamists and soldiers stationed locally since a quarrel over rights to bathing places. See Wood, p. 12.
‡ Christopher Musgrave, 14th Light Dragoons; Richard Ravenhill, of Millar & Ravenhill Marine Engine Builders; Charles Oxenden, Rector of Barham, Kent; Robert Bryan Cooke, Canon of York and Rector of Wheldrake.[40] The future Rector of Barham took a sporting revenge for his expulsion from Eton. He managed to get Harrow to take him in, and in 1818 he captained the Harrovian cricket team that defeated Eton by thirteen runs. See D. Hudson, *A Poet in Parliament*. The fifth was a Colleger (see footnote on p. 183).

there was no alternative to expulsion, a prospect which occasioned Marriot no disquiet: he was an orphan, a ward in Chancery and inheritor of a considerable estate. As Marriot continued intransigent, sentence of expulsion was duly pronounced which, predictably, led to instant beatification of the departing boy, and highly emotional feelings of resentment against Keate. Local inhabitants were put in fear by the howling and baying of the boys, 'very loud and riotous' in Long Walk. The windows and house of the hated tutor Mr Green were damaged and threats made against Keate himself so that Miss Brown, hearing the tumult of the boys, like a mob at an execution, shuddered and quickened her pace as she walked home, fearful lest some 'accident' befall him, and was much relieved when he was safely in the house that evening.

Next day, Sunday 1 November, Keate was hissed and jeered at as he was going into two o'clock prayers. Later, he was reading aloud his customary peroration from the works of Hugh Blair in his 'loud, determined voice', when, from the lower desks, where all the fifth form were congregated, arose a 'stentorian voice', 'Where's Marriot?' Keate did not pause or respond to the interruption, but continued his strong, unwavering delivery. Again there were shouts, 'Where's Marriot? Where's Marriot?' and a chorus of booing. He finished his address as if conditions were normal and left the chamber unmolested. Next day, a half holiday, when everyone was breakfasting sociably as hosts or guests, according to custom, five conspirators went by stealth into upper school armed with a sledge-hammer concealed in a gown. Their target was the headmaster's personal holy place, his great desk of office, raised on a podium, and enclosed in a stall by panels and doors, like a stately pew. In a short time the famous object was smashed in pieces and lay on the ground, mute testimony of wrath and reprisal.

At eleven o'clock the sixth and fifth, and the three divisions of the fourth form were assembled. Keate entered through the library in total silence. He stood amidst the wreckage on the site of his former desk, seemingly oblivious of the debris about him, opened his book and called on one of the sixth form to construe as if nothing abnormal had happened. Thereafter all proceeded as usual. But later in the day every form in the upper school was summoned before the headmaster after chapel. Keate spoke in a voice 'firm and calm' without anger, on the folly of supposing a grievance, real or imaginary, could be remedied by violence or subversion of discipline. Then, to the astonishment of the assembly, he named the conspirators and told them to stand up. He identified them as being deeply implicated in the turbulence of the past week, and the perpetrators of the latest outrage against himself, and pronounced sentence of expulsion on the Oppidans then and there* – the two Eltons,† John May,‡ John Jackson, William Pitt, and George Henry White left the chamber without a word.

How had Keate discovered the conspirators? A variety of theories went into circulation, all or none of which might have been true or partly true. According to Margaretta Brown, a young Colleger, 'that idle pickle, Lloyd', had been seen skulking suspiciously in upper school earlier in the morning and, after rigorous interrogation for two hours, broke down and admitted he had overheard the conspiracy being planned. Another version scouts the Lloyd source of betrayal as a convenient cover to conceal Keate's true source of intelligence, his manservant Cartwright who, unknown to the conspirators, had been at work within the false ceiling of the chamber repairing the chandelier, and had witnessed the atrocity.

At all events there was no reprieve for the six. There was even an additional victim dispatched after them for good measure. When Keate, the condemned having departed, concluded his address by saying that he hoped the action taken would be a warning to the boys to behave better, one boy, Sir Lawrence Palk, a friend of the convicted offenders, hot with indignation, turned to his neighbour and exclaimed 'Never!' Ben Drury, abnormally zealous because it had been his house that had harboured Marriot ('the worst place he could be') overheard the fatal word and denounced Palk to the headmaster. Palk's name was summarily added to the order of expulsion.

To the slogans on the rebels' placards on walls and doors – 'Down with Keate. No Five O'Clock Absence. Floreat Seditio' – was now added, in solemn mourning, the names of the departing martyrs, 'May they ever be revered'. There was special sympathy for Palk, whom Tucker thought 'a harmless, popular boy' who 'had spoken impulsively in the heat of the moment' but 'meant nothing'.[41] But Miss Brown cited 'that disagreeable boy Palk' as 'one of the chief inciters of disaffection'.[42] The comedy had a happy ending for him.

---

* The expulsion of Collegers required an order from the vice-provost, which followed on Keate's recommendation in due course.

† Elton major, Robert James, major in the 17th Lancers; Elton minor, William Tierney, rector of Whitestaunton in Somerset.

‡ John May, Exeter College, Oxford, MA; vicar of Ugborough in Devon.

The Duke of York, receiving a pathetically coloured account of his misfortunes from Palk's friends, made him a present of an ensign's commission in one of his regiments and Palk was able to return in a few weeks and display himself in the glory of his new uniform before his Etonian contemporaries.[43]

Gradually, after Keate's drastic course of expulsions, the fever of rebellion subsided. The local inhabitants, who had feared that 'all subordination was at an end' and that serious attacks on persons and property might follow, breathed sighs of relief and took down the shutters from their windows. The truth was there was nothing most Etonians wanted less than to leave Eton prematurely; and when the consequences of insurrection were made plain in examples by the headmaster, the uproar subsided to the normal cheerful rowdiness of Etonian social life. It was, said George Denison, in after years, 'as tidy a bit of sound and wholesome discipline as one could desire to see'.[44]

But the shock had been severe and left the college authorities worried and puzzled, casting about for an external scapegoat to bear responsibility for the aberration. 'It is thought that the present mode of education at home has much to do with these rows at Eton, Winchester, Harrow and other Schools,' Miss Brown confided to her diary. 'Too much money given to boys etc. That they become men too soon and grow conceited.'Although habits of increased indulgence to children may have been a contributory factor of the condition, it could not alone explain the epidemic in general or, in particular, the greatest eruption of violence occurring at a school not remarkable for the wealth of the parents who patronized it.

In November 1818, when life at Eton was returning to normal, Keate wrote to Samuel Butler, the headmaster of Shrewsbury School, saying he was sorry to perceive that the contagion of revolt had spread to Shrewsbury.[45] The symptoms appeared in this school with peculiar virulence. Dr Butler was hated and denounced as a monster of cruelty and despotism by some of the boys; he was not generally liked by the neighbours in the town due in part to an aloofness which he justified as a matter of policy – he was not on speaking terms even with his own lower master,* and when insurrection broke out it was the more difficult to subdue because the headmaster lacked the

---

* The two communicated in the third person. 'Mr Jedwine is sorry to observe that, in default of a seasonable answer to his arguments Dr Butler has recourse to misrepresentation. . . . Mr Jedwine considers the concluding observation as rude and insulting.'[46] The subject under consideration was the division of fees.

allegiance and support of some of the most senior boys, upon whom above all he should have been able to rely in a crisis. Butler certainly had in his early career a reputation for extreme severity; it may have lost him the headmastership of his old school Rugby, when he applied for it.* He used violence against boys to compel them to submit to his will, which no other public-school master of this age did; fugitive Salopians were known to defend themselves with knives against the pursuing headmaster and his servants. One, 'on being secured' was then 'punished with the ordinary school discipline'.[48] Discipline at Shrewsbury was not always 'ordinary'. There is evidence that what jurisprudence classifies as 'cruel and unusual punishments' were in use, including a crude form of 'sensory deprivation'† which would not be approved by modern penologists or courts of international law. Whether the harshness of the headmaster drew reprisals from the boys, or the vice of the boys provoked the headmaster to resented severity, the result was a record of violence and crime without parallel in the great schools of the nineteenth century.

In Butler's correspondence with parents complaints from the public are recorded over such issues as whether the coachman's whip wielded by a boy struck his victims with or without the wielder's intent. The complainants on this occasion were in no doubt that, as their spokesman, Mr Dickinson, 'surgeon', deposed, it was the boys' 'pleasure to use a coachman's whip about them most lustily', and when human targets were out of reach of the whip, 'to pelt them most unmercifully with stones'. An anxious father was urgently concerned whether retribution was to be exacted, as he earnestly desired, by the headmaster, or, as popular outcry was demanding, 'by the common hangman'.[50] In 1817 (the eve of the rebellions) a somewhat sinister development is noted in recorded complaints against the boys. Salopians harassing villages from the top of a coach *en route* between Thornton and Chester, were no longer armed with stones, but with loaded pistols and proved quite beyond the control of the coachman.[51] Local worthies charged Salopians with a catalogue of offences which

---

* Butler's and his friends' unsuccessful efforts to amend the impression are recorded in copies of letters to the trustees of Rugby School. But according to the Rev. Frederick Gretton, who as a boy was often in trouble at Shrewsbury, discipline 'could not be said to be severely or harshly administered'. He testifies that he never saw Butler exceed six strokes for minor offences and twelve strokes for graver offences and 'but once knew him to operate more than once in the week upon the same patient'.[47]

† Rowe's Hole. Named after a frequent occupant, this was a box, slightly larger than a coffin and the shape of a Punch and Judy booth, in which even 'younger boys' were confined for hours, and were sometimes forgotten overnight by the master who had ordered the confinement.[49]

included theft, violence to travellers on the public highway, intimidation, extortion, coining money, consorting with criminals and prostitutes. By the beginning of 1817, Butler seems to have felt in danger of losing control over the savage denizens of his seminary. On 28 January he wrote, 'I do not know how I can either confine the boys more securely at night or provide effectually for their good conduct in the day. I am at present lost in baffling and uneasy conjecture.'[52]

In such an environment, theft between the boys themselves inevitably abounded, and a stage was reached when it was not possible for a boy to put down any article unattended for a moment without its vanishing.[53] As usual in societies of thieves, the word 'steal' was not in polite use. The favoured term was 'knobble', and knobbling went on wholesale. Understandably, the headmaster's most urgent concern was with crime committed against external society, and he attempted to prevent a foreseeable crisis by getting rid as quietly as possible of the worst offenders, who unfortunately included the sons of some of his personal friends.

Open rebellion erupted in November 1818 with a brozier.* The disaffected may have judged food to be a suitable subject for initiating hostilities, as it had always been an issue of painful disagreement between Butler and his charges. Butler strenuously defended school diet in respect of quality and quantity ('the rule is that all boys eat as much as they like')[55] and he officially condemned gifts of food parcels, 'as pernicious indulgence' tempting boys to form 'junketting parties at low houses and exciting to other irregularities'.[56] But the recurrence of complaints over the years cannot be ignored;[57] nor can standards of schoolkeeping economy which Butler received as protégé of Dr James at Rugby. Advising Butler, soon after he had come to Shrewsbury, to keep as few servants as possible because the work can be done by boys and 'servants are for ever eating between meals', James adds, 'nor will servants live on cheese at night, like boys could'. Remnants on plates were to be mixed with bread and served up

---

* If the boarders in any house were collectively dissatisfied with the supply of food (which meant in practice the senior boys as the juniors would do what they were told), an exercise known as 'to brozier' was performed. The boys ate every scrap of food that was served, and then banged on the table with their knives and forks, calling for more and better. When more was brought, they ate that too, and the performance was repeated until, if successful, they had consumed every morsel of food in the house. This broad form of 'hint' was intended to produce amendment, and sometimes did.

Performed with excess of zeal, broziering could have disastrous results, as it did at Westminster in 1821: 'L. G. Parry [son of Major-General Parry Love-Parry], a boy in the fifth form, died in consequence of having over eaten himself in a frolic in which he was engaged with others.'[54]

again so 'nothing is lost for hashes consume all'; and if Butler wished to reduce the portions of meat served to the boys, he should introduce the reduction 'just after the holyday, or when they had money in their pockets. . . '.[58]

The brozier was followed by demonstrations of hostility to the headmaster. Placards abusing Butler and threatening him physical violence appeared in and about school. Butler set in motion a diligent investigation, without success. Boys, bound by what Butler complained of as 'a mistaken principle of honour',[59] would divulge no names. In his record of these bitter transactions, Butler unconsciously reveals the quality of devious and self-righteous duplicity which poisoned, almost beyond cure, his relations with several generations of boys. In this case he had two suspects in mind, but could convict neither. Both boys denied authorship of the published threats and offered their word of honour that they spoke the truth. Butler told the boys that he entirely accepted their word. But afterwards he contrived to get the boys to write combinations of letters used on the placards and conveyed their handwriting to 'persons versed in deciphering'.[60] It does not seem to have occurred to Butler that by boys' code he had done an ignoble act, or that, if to him the boys obeyed a 'mistaken principle of honour', to the boys he obeyed no principle of honour whatever.

Accordingly, the boys next behaved to the headmaster as they would to a cad. When Butler further affronted the sensibilities of the school by appointing praeposter a boy whom the sixth form did not respect and whom he had previously treated with public indignity, a high-spirited and popular praeposter, Thomas Coltman, paid the public town crier and bellmen to bawl satirical observations of the headmaster's choice to a gaping crowd through the streets of Shrewsbury. 'I furnish,' said Butler, 'a subject for the Shrewsbury tea table, without having an opportunity for defence.' Butler took the emergency measure of passing sentence of banishment on Coltman and two other suspected leaders among the 'upper boys' who had been 'diligently instilling insubordination'[61] into the minds of younger boys, and he marked several more for quieter dismissal after conference with their parents. But even extreme measures were no longer in practice reliable remedies. The night before they were due to board early morning coaches to take them home the three broke out and vanished, later reappearing to display themselves defiantly in the vicinity of the school in contempt of Butler's authority. Coltman, considered the leader of the rebels, inspired Butler with a healthy apprehension of personal danger, and when the boy was seen prowling in the headmaster's garden in conference with other boys (in particular with John Underwood,* the son of Canon Underwood) he sent an urgent signal to the mayor requesting armed protection. 'I am at the post of danger here,'[62] he wrote, behind locked doors and bolted shutters. Butler's fears for his physical safety may have been increased by all three boys suffering from what he called 'military mania', which was his way of saying they wished to be soldiers, and therefore were already addicted to firearms.

Coltman seems to have been an impulsive and wilful boy, but his real danger to Butler was that, being popular and admired, he was influential, and there is more than a possibility that Butler deliberately provoked him to a confrontation which would justify his dismissal.

On 11 December Coltman was in Chester, where he had a friend, Mr Scott, who had arranged for him to receive a sum of money, and he may have discovered that Butler had attempted to have this temporarily withheld. That same day he wrote to Butler for the last time, charging him with 'direct falsehood' in telling his father that his opinion of Butler was beginning to alter, for, 'far from having changed, that you are a paltry, despicable pedant are and *ever will be* the sentiments of Thos. Coltman'.[63] At the same time his father was writing despairing letters to Butler as he saw his son not only turning his back on a 'brilliant prospect' at university, but what distressed him most, forfeiting by disinheritance the fortune which would have been his as heir to his rich uncle, Dr Coltman's brother. 'Unfortunate youth! he has played a deep game at which he may have lost Honour, Riches and every valuable consideration in Life.'

Partiality to rhetoric seems to have run in the family. Evidently Dr Coltman was not more able to shake the resolution of his quixotic and wilful son than Butler had been. 'The brilliant prospect is at an end,' he tells Butler, 'and I must descend in sorrow to the grave. . . . I consider him as already embarked in the well known expedition to South America† from whence there is scarcely an atom of chance that he will revisit his native shore. I have partaken largely of the cup of affliction, yea, even to the very dregs, and as for my poor wife she can scarcely be said to be in her senses.'[64]

* John Hammer Underwood, scholar of Brasenose College, Oxford, BA, 1823; vicar of Bashbury in Hereford, 1830–56; prebendary of Hereford Cathedral 1850–56; died 1856.
† Coltman appears to have declared his intent to enlist in a volunteer force bound for Venezuela where civil war had broken out between the Creole rebels and their Spanish overlords.

Yet, after all, Dr Coltman's profuse lamentations proved premature. At the last minute Thomas Coltman changed mind and course, whether on reflection in solitude, or under the influence of another, is not known. What *is* known is that, far from going to join a forlorn hope of 'loyal Spaniards' in Latin America, to die in an obscure corner of some foreign field, he appears at Oxford as an undergraduate at BNC, and in 1822 takes his BA. He must have been reconciled to his father and, perhaps even more important, to his rich and childless uncle, for he next appears as the master of Hadnaby Priory, a landowner of substance, High Sheriff of Lincolnshire (1849), Deputy Lieutenant, Justice of the Peace and a prominent pillar of county society.

In November 1818 Butler wrote a circular[65] giving his version of events and followed it with a second circular, dated 10 December, exhorting parents to impress on their sons the importance of obedience to the headmaster, and earnestly entreating them not to return any boy who was not willing to promise 'cheerful submission' to such regulations and discipline as he might think fit to impose. 'No consideration,' he declared, 'will induce me to receive after Christmas any boy from whose parents I have not a satisfactory answer on this head.'[66] In private communications he also begged particular parents not to allow their sons to return to school in possession of loaded firearms.

The first reaction was that knives and firearms were less openly displayed, and kept hidden in reserve for serious confrontations. In mid-June, 1820, an affray between two hostile factions was narrowly averted by Butler's intervention. On 20 June he wrote to the Reverend James Price, expressing regret that 'your son appears to have been chiefly concerned . . . in a design' by the aggressors 'to attack and severely beat at the moment of departure some boys whom they happened to dislike'. But the 'aggrieved (if I may use that term)',[67] having been forewarned of the plan, were not unprepared and had armed themselves with loaded pistols. Butler wrote severally to the parents requiring a pledge from each boy that he would engage in no repetition of armed violence if he were allowed to return. Of the leader of the bludgeoners* he wrote, 'he is a fine boy, has taste and talent and . . . may distinguish himself highly' but he must learn 'the control of vindictive feelings'. From the leader of the pistoleers,

---

* John Price, left Shrewsbury, 1822; Scholar St John's College, Cambridge; Bell Scholar, 1823; 3rd Classic, BA, 1826.

Thomas Hill, he required through his father a promise that he would never again at school arm himself with a similar weapon.[68]

The parents as a whole conformed with the headmaster's wishes and showed little inclination to palliate the conduct of their turbulent sons; for, despite the odium in which he was held by many of the boys in his charge at this time, Butler was a resounding and growing success who made Shrewsbury attractive to an increasing number of gratified parents. In addition to being an inspiring and meticulous teacher, he was a trainer of genius for particular events, and the first headmaster of a public school to set his sights on university prizes and scholarships not merely as decorative honours, but as primary objectives to be captured. It was the brilliant success of this policy which enabled him to win for Shrewsbury the status of public school. Shrewsbury was certainly not numbered among the public schools when Butler accepted the post in 1798. A famous school in the seventeenth century, it had been in decay for generations, and Butler's predecessors had been at best listless mediocrities, and at worst tipsy idlers who either stole or allowed others to steal valuable books and manuscripts from the school's library.*

By 1820 when, owing to political pressure, Brougham was obliged reluctantly to exclude from the scope of the Bill he introduced in the summer of that year, the 'public schools, Eton, Winchester, Westminster, Harrow, Charterhouse and Rugby', Butler was in a position to claim similar treatment for Shrewsbury. 'If by a public school is meant one to which persons from all parts of the kingdom send their sons for education', he wrote to H. G. Bennet in the House of Commons, '. . . and I cannot conceive any other meaning of the term . . . then I beg leave to say that there is now and usually have been during my mastership, boys at Shrewsbury from almost every county in England and Wales, some from Scotland and some from Ireland.' How had this transformation come about? After an appropriate gesture of hesitating modesty, Butler feels constrained to confess that 'there are more prizemen at Cambridge from Shrewsbury School in proportion to the numbers than from any other school in England'.[70]

---

* Almost worse than theft was the desecration of rare and precious books and manuscripts. On 21 June 1810 Butler wrote to his friend George Gaisford that he had discovered in the school an interleaved copy of a Turnebus edition of *Hephastion* with MS. notes, and he says, 'I have not yet examined them and am obliged to state to you a fact which from its loathsomeness and for the sake of my predecessor, now dead, I could not put into circulation. The book has been used to comb boys' heads into; it is full of dead vermin and other impurities at which delicacy must be appalled and even common cleanliness recoil. The leaves are mangled and a few cut out.'[69]

The argument was unanswerable. The mafia of Salopians, hatched in the dark domestic underworld of bishops, deans, canons and arch-deacons of the Church, might be dreaded by the local community as violent, vicious and dangerously quick with a knife, gun and bludgeon; but they were also to their adversaries dangerously quick with classical scholarships. What William Gover, after a year there, called 'this cruel and foul school',[71] produced an élite of scholastic athletes, superbly coached for particular contests and events. Butler made a professional operation of the business of preparing for a competitive examination. He used his growing influence at the univer-sities to control curricular and marking policy, and he monitored his intelligence service at Cambridge and Oxford by frequent personal visitations. Charles Wordsworth, the Master of Trinity, with a touch of *amour propre* on behalf of his own Winchester, remarked to Charles Vaughan, 'Dr Butler comes here year after year, just as a first class milliner makes a yearly visit to Paris, to get the fashions.'

That was an inversion of the truth; Butler was the creative educa-tional force of his time in classical studies. He did not follow fashions, he set them by his success. In 1818 the academic performance of the school since Butler's arrival was already lustrous, in the next two decades it was to grow dazzling. Still a small school by the standards of public schools – tiny compared to Eton – and later temporarily disadvantaged by the advent of the railways which benefited most schools,* Shrewsbury carried off sixteen Browne Medals, nine Chan-cellor's Medals and nineteen university scholarships in the Classical Tripos established in 1824. In 1841 no less than twenty-eight of Butler's pupils obtained first-class honours.† At Oxford, where Butler was not so deeply entrenched, Salopians gained eleven first classes in *literis humanioribus* and nine university scholarships. A Salopian won the coveted 'Ireland' in 1827, 1828, 1829, 1830, 1831 and 1833. The victor in 1831, Thomas Branker, although entered on the books of Wadham College, was still a schoolboy at Shrewsbury when he defeated, among other competitors, the already grand young Oxonian, W. E. Gladstone, and Robert Scott, the future Master of Balliol and co-editor of the Liddell and Scott lexicon. This was the occasion which inspired Gladstone, never a graceful loser, to the reflection that the result 'had contributed amazingly to strengthen

* Shrewsbury had been on the great coach route to North Wales and Ireland, which began to decay before the new railway system touched the town.
† This particular achievement occurred shortly after Butler had resigned the headmastership on receiving the Bishopric of Lichfield, but it was a legacy of his impetus.

the precedent opinion that the Shrewsbury system was basically a false one'.[72]

Most of these triumphs were yet to come in 1818, but portents were already indicative enough of the future to tear the minds of heads of colleges agonizingly between covetousness of Salopian classicists and dread of the Salopian incendiaries. The Master of St John's College, Cambridge, congratulated him on resisting the 'turbulence and self-will of foolish and presumptuous boys' and expressed confidence that in consequence the school 'will stand as high in reputation for the due subordination and modesty of the scholars, as it does for their improvement in learning'. The compliment was somewhat demoted by the final paragraph of the letter in which the writer tried to persuade Butler to confide to him the names of the more dangerous desperados from Shrewsbury likely to invade Cambridge in the near future; for, he says, 'We have numerous, and, I am happy to say, a most respectable and orderly set of young men. I could not knowingly introduce sowers of sedition among them.'[73]

But Butler was too wily and too conscious of the importance of respecting the interests of parents and even of troublesome pupils, to betray prejudicial information to outsiders. Nor was he disposed in his own interests to advertise that his personal relations with his most senior, and often most talented, boys were so bad that among those he felt it necessary to deny readmission to the school after the Christmas holidays was the captain of the school himself. 'I have the pleasure to send him to you a very elegant and accomplished scholar,' he wrote to the boy's father, 'and whether you send him to Trinity College at once or place him with a private tutor for the ensuing half year it will make but little difference to him.' What mattered to Butler was that the boy should not return to Shrewsbury where he had kept him until the end of the half year only 'that he might leave me ... without any mark of disgrace to himself'.[74] This was intelligence which would not have been passed to the authorities of Trinity College.

Butler's second circular sent to parents on 12 December had the desired effect. There has probably never been another great head-master whose boys were so rancorous in resistance and parents so reverential in admiration, and ready to give him their 'united and strenuous support'.[75] Letters stretching over three decades bear witness to parents' gratitude not merely for the effectiveness of their boys' education, but for acts of kindness and generosity. Mr J. Butterton, on his son, George, obtaining an exhibition at Cambridge,

1. View of Harrow school in Byron's time

2. The school steps, Harrow

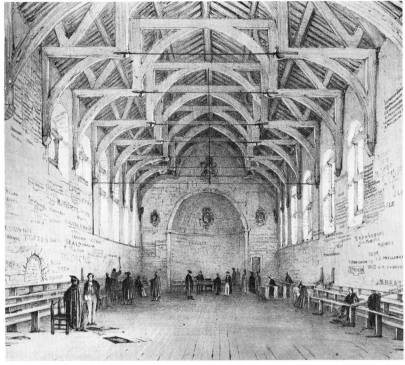

3. (*Facing page top*) Long Chamber, Eton, *c.* 1840, where more than fifty Eton Collegers lived and slept. 'Some of the best men I have ever known ran the risk of becoming the worst from the ordeal of Long Chamber . . .' (*see p.88*)

4. (*Facing page bottom*) The schoolroom, Westminster, *c.* 1840

5. (*Above*) The headmaster of Winchester, George Moberly, and assistant masters, *c.* 1864

6. (*Right*) 'Three Boys in Montem Dress', by the Rev. Matthew William Peters, 1793. 'Montem night, most odious of orgies' (*William Johnson*)

7. 'Hog Lane', by George Cruikshank, 1826. Harrovians loot the premises of a disfavoured tradesman. 'Harrow . . . a small world ruled by the bold'
(*Sir William Gregory*)

8. Staircase to the Upper School, Eton

9. 'Prose Rouge'. This kind of mêlée occured normally at Eton before 'Prose', which was Dr Keate reading prayers on Sunday. It was on such an occasion that the quarrel between Ashley and Wood took place, ending in their fatal encounter (see pp. 142-7)

10. 'Booking for the fourth form', Eton, *c.* 1830

11. A steeplechase and 'Boar hunt' at Shrewsbury, by the Rev. A.T. Paget, 1852 (see pp.151-2)

12. A boy at his 'scob' – a Wykehamist at study, c. 1850

13. 'The Oppidans' Museum or Eton Court of Claims at the Christopher', by Robert Cruickshank, 1824. Etonians often returned from nocturnal revels bearing trophies in the form of objects that had been displayed by local tradesmen. Periodically the tradesmen were invited to the cellar of the Christopher Inn to identify their property and exercise the option of reclaiming it, with the payment of interest, or selling the articles (as most of them preferred to do), in which case the trophy went to adorn the walls of a college room or an army mess

14. The Eton Eight (Eton *v.* Radley), 1858

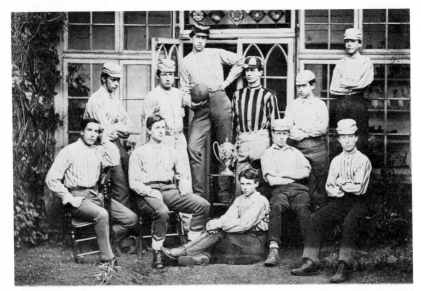

15. 'Happy boys at Drury's', winners of the Eton inter-house football trophy in the 1860s

16. The Harrow Football Eleven, *c.* 1860

writes on 4 September 1823 thanking Butler for 'kindness at a time when difficulties surrounded me which as long as it pleases God to continue my existence I shall never forget'. Once before he had written to Butler, when his business had failed, saying that in consequence of his losses he must remove his son from Shrewsbury, and Butler had replied, 'I have a very high opinion of your boy, and had set my heart on making him a good scholar: with your kind permission I intend to do so still and beg that you will not trouble yourself about the fees.'[76]*

The Rev. Edmund Paley who, after suffering serious financial loss, was never again sent a school bill, writes volunteering to resume payment, 'I have been treated with such unusual and quite unexpected delicacy throughout the whole of the six years ... I cannot sufficiently thank you. ...'

Butler would address parents with caustic candour when he felt an unpleasant truth to be due. 'The boy,' he said to the mother of a new arrival at Shrewsbury, 'has wasted what he has hitherto neglected to make use of – and what he can never recall – the years of his youth. ... I much doubt his capacity and still more his inclination to endure the hardships and difficulties of study after so long and injurious indulgence.'[77]

Keenly sensitive to status, his own and the school's he had created, Butler was quick to resent anything he construed as undervaluation of either. When his 'Dear Brother Archdeacon' Owen tactlessly retailed a parent's expression of interest in entering his son at Shrewsbury because he preferred him not to go to a school of 'greater pretention', Butler struck back, 'To say the truth I have no particular wish to receive the son of any man who has yet to learn that though Shrewsbury School ... is above making any pretention at all, it claims to be on a par with every other principal school in the kingdom in every point connected with the moral and literary improvement of its pupils.'[78]†

But in general his letters to parents and boys alike were decorous

---

* George Butterton did not disappoint Butler's hopes: 8th Wrangler and 3rd Classic in 1827, fellow of St John's College, Cambridge, 1828–37, he was headmaster of Uppingham School, 1830–46.

† The father, a Mr Newton, may have made acceptable amends because Butler relented and, happily for all concerned, the boy, Charles Newton, did enter Shrewsbury. Sir Charles Newton, a classicist worthy of Butler and first Keeper of Greek and Roman Antiquities at the British Museum, did more than any other Englishman in his time to further the cause of classical archaeology. His acquisitions included the Faranese, the two great series of Castellani, the Pourtales and the Blacas collections.

in argument and mild in tone, sometimes, perhaps, misleadingly so in respect of the realities of confrontation with the latter. Butler and his career remain a paradox. He was himself certainly the most *influential* headmaster of a public school in the first half of the nineteenth century. Other headmasters might venerate, or express veneration for, the 'spirit' of Arnold, but they adopted the standards and followed the example of Butler. Emulation became the watchword. 'Whatever Eton and Harrow may be,' said Henry Drury, who was equally at home in both, 'I can safely say that they would not have reached even any moderate excellence if you had not been the agitator.'[79]

Why the price of this success was an extraordinary unpopularity among the beneficiaries of his skill can only partly be accounted for by Butler's unwillingness to delegate authority in the traditional public-school way, and govern through discipline exercised by his senior boys. 'If boys are to decide when and how they are to be punished,' he protested in an appeal to parents, 'or to be guided by the suggestions of their schoolfellows instead of the authority of the master, all discipline will be at an end.'[80] But the members of the Salopian sixth form were, as a class, Butler's chief enemies and, on an occasion yet to come, he expelled the captain of the school and all the praeposters; and then he expelled the captain's successor.[81] 'I hope by this time that Heaven is quiet and that you have expelled the Titans and all their rebellious crew,' his friend, the Rev. S. Tillbrook wrote to Butler on 7 December 1818.[82] The identification of Shrewsbury with heaven might have provoked some sour levity among contemporary Salopians.

Without questioning Butler's energetic goodwill for his boys' interests (which he served devotedly both at school and university and even beyond in securing the needy employment), and admitting his genius as a teacher, one cannot disregard the accumulation of evidence that, justly or unjustly, he was regarded by a seriously large number of boys – and *senior* boys – as worse than an oppressive tyrant, a dishonourable enemy, treacherous, false to his word and revengeful. The boys were taxing him, he complained to parents, 'in the usual strain of schoolboy impetuosity and misconception, with hatred, malice, revenge', which, he said, a 'selfless and well intentioned master' was 'not infrequently accused of'.[83] If the boys' judgement was an error, it was an error committed independently by successive generations of Salopians. The words of the official spokesman of one of the boys' rebellions survive because they were quoted with indignation by Butler. 'I am come, sir, to tell you the opinion of the boys: it is our opinion that you have taken away our characters, and unless you recall all the praeposters who have been dismissed we will not do the punishment.'[84]* The stubborn solidarity of boys in mutual loyalty against him incensed and perplexed Butler the more for its being a *personal* antagonism which he knew he could not have contained without the equally solid reinforcement from the parents. Shrewsbury was never a happy school under Butler. But to him must go the credit of re-creating Shrewsbury out of a decayed, almost extinct relic of the past, and making it first into a conspicuously successful, and next into a famous school, renowned for learning if not for tranquillity.

Meanwhile, however, in our year of reference, 1818, with the departure of Coltman & Co., relief was at hand. After the Michaelmas holidays and the exclusion of the offending 'Titans', the decimation of their 'crew' and the subjection of the divided rank and file to planned parental pressure, rebellion at Shrewsbury, as at the other public schools, began to subside, and life returned for a decade or so to the reduced state of turbulence which was normality. The headmaster's prime concern ceased to be the preservation of his life and became once more the preservation of his wine cellar.†

---

* In that instance Butler had over-reacted, and after face-saving gestures of submission, organized by tactful parents, from the boys (who had rebelled over bad food, 'the Beef Rebellion'), the praeposters *were* recalled. Otherwise the 'Ireland' would not have been won in 1831 by Thomas Branker, for he was one of the expelled praeposters.

† Butler had a taste for good wine and spirits, and so did the boys. The contents of his cellar were by tradition an interest in common, and a letter addressed to an offender's mother concerns her boy's part in sawing through the door of Butler's cellar and stealing wine and rum.[85]

The World of Dr Keate

'I rather expect there will be another row with Keate today,' an Etonian wrote home in times of peace, 'as it has been a standing rule to have a row on Sunday at Prose.'[1] What was called 'Prose' was, correctly, 'Prayers', but it had acquired the substitutive name because that was how the boys said Keate pronounced 'Prayers'. Keate, says Kinglake, 'had a really noble voice, and this he could modulate with great skill, but he also had the power of quacking like an angry duck, and he almost always adopted this mode of communication to command respect'.[2] All the boys were assembled at two o'clock in upper school. Keate had sole charge of the sixth and fifth forms and one praeposter had to walk round and keep the rest of the school in order. Keate's enormously strong voice would be raised to nearly full blast in an attempt to make audible some such noble exhortation as:

> Cultivate, in all intercourse among friends, gentle and obliging manners. It is a common error to suppose, that familiar intimacy supersedes attention to the lesser duties of behaviour; and that, under the notion of freedom, it may excuse a careless or even rough demeanour. On the contrary, an intimate connection can only be kept up by a constant wish to be pleasing and agreeable.[3]

Around this endeavour at dignified recital seethed a ferment of chatter, laughter, hissing, scraping of feet, booing and yelling, 'a noise so great as to arrest the attention of all the passers by in the Long Walk'.[4] Wilkinson (who acted as praeposter) says, 'The row and interruption was so great Keate never got through more than a few sentences of the sermon.'[5] Keate would 'violently stamp his foot, dash his cocked hat on the desk, and call out, "I will declare it immediately"'.[6] But nobody ever made out what he was to declare. 'I was thunderstruck at their audacity . . . thought it amounted to rebellion,' an astonished new boy reported in his first week at Eton, having 'heard something read, could not hear what'. That really is, Wilkinson testifies, 'an exact and not exaggerated account of what used to take place every afternoon' at 'Prose' and it was 'impossible for any man, however resolute to coerce such an assemblage of boys by the mere use of his tongue, however stentorian and voluble'.

Keate was certainly resolute in his fierce idiosyncratic style. Although tiny, he was wonderfully strong and agile. As a boy he had been a noted pugilist at Eton and reputed a 'pocket Hercules'. Familiar as it is, Kinglake's evocation remains indispensable in any account of John Keate. 'He was little more if at all than five feet and was not very great in girth, but *within* this space was concentrated the pluck of ten battalions.' His pugnacious features were eminently caricaturable: '– a red face with a fiery eye', with red, shaggy eyebrows, 'so prominent that he habitually used them as arms and hands for pointing out any objects whatever to which he wished to direct attention'.

> Anybody without a notion of drawing could still draw a speaking, nay, scolding likeness of Keate. If you had not pencil, you could draw him well enough with the poker, or the leg of a chair in the smoke of a candle, . . . wherever from utmost Canada to Budelcund, there was a whitewashed wall to an officer's room or any other apartment where English gentlemen were forced to kick their heels, there, likely enough in the days of his reign, the head of Keate would be seen, scratched or drawn with these various degrees of skill which one observes in representations of saints.[7]

Out of doors Keate's normal posture was one of militant anticipation of mischief on sight of any boy. When he issued out of his front door he became a lone magistrate venturing into a community of malefactors, vigilant, alert and zealous to detect conspiracies and crimes. Fierce as a little grizzled lion amidst an awkwardly large pack of puppy dogs, it behoved him to be wary. Mischief could be open, or it could be concealed and lying in wait. When he approached a corner he gave the cough peculiar to him – Ba-a-affin – a sound that inspired the nickname by which he was known to all. After the cough came the point of the umbrella which he carried even in fine weather, to give further notice of his presence, and to prevent the outrage of possible collision 'by accident', with a boy hurtling round the corner; then followed the cocked hat and the sturdy little body in the 'widow woman's gown'.

On one occasion Keate encountered a very junior Wilkinson who had been dispatched by the captain of m'dame's to purchase and return with four dozen hot sausages, delicacies considered indispensable by any senior, Oppidan or Colleger, when entertaining friends for breakfast.

> These send their fags or little pages
> To Stevens, to buy sausages.[8]

The little boy was hurrying back with his treasures, spitting and seething hot from the frying pan, in a covered receptacle when, on rounding the corner at full speed, he collided with the headmaster himself. Keate's suspicions were ever ready on sight of a boy. 'What have you there, sir?' he demanded in his fearsome voice, holding out his hand. Wilkinson thrust the dish of sausages into the august hand, turned and bolted. 'Stop, sir; here, sir; come back, sir,' he heard called fiercely after him as he ran, 'I'll flog you directly.' But being in Lower School he felt fairly safe from detection.

Keate now found himself, in the interests of dignity and propriety, urgently in need of being relieved of his hot and savoury burden. He first tried to enlist the service of one or two boys within hailing distance, but the blast he directed at them was not encouraging. 'Come here sir; do you hear me? I'll flog you sir.' Averting their faces, they fled. In the end the little monarch was reduced to the indignity of requesting the most disreputable of Eton cads, Picky Powell, of whom he thoroughly disapproved, and whose presence he would not normally have deigned to recognize, to take the thing off his hands.[9] It was a lucky morning for Picky Powell and one hopes not too unlucky for Wilkinson, who would probably have had to make a second journey, for cancellation of a breakfast party was unthinkable.

Owing to the frequency of these entertainments, there were more unlucky casualties than Wilkinson.

I was coming one morning from the Christopher buoyantly bearing a plate of sausages (seven for sixpence) swimming in grease and covered with another plate to keep them hot. Meat for breakfast in Keate's eyes was one of the deadly sins, and when, sailing along in full canonicals, he recognized me, he proceeded to appropriate the spoil. Summoning a labourer who was passing, he was about to give it to him when I said, 'If you please, sir, the plate belongs to the Christopher.' Keate was equal to the occasion. 'Poor man,' he said, 'hold your hat,' which the poor man did, and the ownership of my sausages, grease and all, was thus transferred. The plates were delivered back to me. 'You will stay at eleven' for the first time greeted my ears, and the just reward of my iniquities was meted out in due form a few hours later.[10]

Although Keate himself was never without an umbrella out of doors, no boy was permitted to carry one, whatever the weather; Keate would not have tolerated such degenerate practice even with a certificate from the most distinguished physician living. 'Wet, sir! Cold, sir! Don't talk to me of the weather, sir. You must just make the best of it. You're not at a girl's school.' Ineluctably, on the morning after this particular admonition, a notice board was found to have been detached from its station at Slough and nailed above Dr Keate's chambers displaying the words, *Seminary for Young Ladies*.[11]

But despite the jokes, Keate could have had no more staunch supporters than the boys themselves in the maintenance of traditional practice. Boys were tenaciously conformant to precedent and established usage. At Eton, which was notoriously the freest and least regimented of all the public schools, compliance with certain forms of language and conduct were effectively exacted, not by formal prohibition, but by the power of example and the fear of ridicule. Writing on 7 November to say that 'a great coat would be useful' Henry Everard adds a caution against 'cloaks', as 'those who wear them generally get properly well teased, which does not agree with my constitution'. Again, accepting an offer from him of a supply of tea (a considerable luxury not enjoyed by all the boys), he desires the purchase of tea be authorized, but that in communication with his tutor it shall not be called 'tea' but 'Evening Things', for otherwise 'I should get very much teazed, which I know you nor I would wish for'.[12]

One prank in Keate lore has been celebrated with peculiar piety:

> At dead of night, a form in cassock clad
> With gown and bands; and oh, more strange than all
> In that cocked hat which marked the reverend head
> Of our Magister Informator, stood
> Before the house where that kind despot dwelt
> The very image of its owner safe in bed,
> An 'ere the wondrous sight or apparition fled
> Had painted the green doors fantastically red.

An assortment of witnesses were interrogated next morning by the wrathful headmaster, including the watchmen, who deposed

> . . . we both last night
> Saw him, the Doctor, in his own cock'd hat
> His bands, his breeches and his bombazine
> Paint his own door-post red.

But the Doctor cut them both short 'with one tremendous Noo' (the sound he made when he said 'no', which was often), in a voice which a boy described as a 'brazen trumpet with a cold in the head'. He charged them at once with the suspicion which always came readily to his mind.

> I smell the gin and foul tobacco stink
> Their only round last night was a round a can, I think.[13]

But the watchmen had not seen anything which had not happened; and the reason why the scarcely imaginative antic has received so much attention was that the actor who impersonated Keate was the Marquess of Douro, the Duke of Wellington's eldest son. Years later, when Douro was being entertained to dinner by his former head-master, then Canon of Windsor, he playfully alluded to the episode, intending to confess all, but 'Keate became so red in the face with emotion at the recollection that he thought it wise to desist'.

The practical jokes were hardly subtle – adolescent humour tends to be broad – but they were served up with tireless gusto and when one generation outgrew them, another was on its heels ready to carry on the good work.

An early favourite was locking Keate out of the schoolroom which he entered from his personal suite through a private door. Only he possessed a key, but a small bullet inserted into the lock did the trick and compelled him to go back and make a long detour under the Colonnade. Arrived at his destination and disdaining to take cognizance of any abnormality, he marched impatiently to his desk, the famous object, raised on a dais and enclosed by panelling, with doors on two sides. He made to enter, but the door would not open; it was screwed fast. Foiled, he rushed to the other side and hauled at the other door without success; it was in a like condition. Jubilant booing arose from the spectators, one of whom reports 'that Keate then, his face glowing with rage, like an angry meteor', despite his small stature, 'vaulted over the door, dropping his three cornered hat and sitting down on a seat smeared with cobblers' wax, was unable to rise without rending his silk breeches'.

Five o'clock school in winter was the most trying period because, as daylight faded, opportunities for every kind of mischief increased. A small class Keate could have dominated with his presence; but this was a hundred and sixteen boys – the sixth form and all the upper division – with, audible beyond, the whole of the remove, upper and lower, of one hundred and fourteen boys and one assistant master in the 'lobby', packed, like sardines in a barrel, in a space not large enough for eighty or ninety at the most. The only light was a large chandelier with old moulds, hanging from the ceiling in the middle of the room, and two candles on Keate's desk, which lit his book but rather impeded than otherwise his sight of activities in general occurring beyond. He was continually moving a candle threateningly from one side to the other as he detected, or purported to detect and stared at, some suspect malefactor.

At the time of the Windsor Fair, noisy toys were brought in and operated by stealth, and songs were sung. A song would start on one side of the room and then be taken up by the other. When Keate glared and fumed in one direction the boys under his gaze immediately ceased to pronounce the words of the song, their faces grave, but, without moving their lips or a muscle of their countenance, 'they kept up the sound in grunts to the tune, while the words were loudly continued by the boys to whom Keate's back was turned'. The chorus of one of the songs contained a reference to Charles Wilkinson's elder brother, who had recently been very ill from a fever, had had his head shaved and was now wearing a wig. Another boy of his standing was known to have a favourite cat, and both these and another boy's name and nickname featured in the chorus:

> Wilkinson's wig, Battiscomb's* cat
> Barney Vallencey† and Wilkinson's wig.

One day a neighbour of Wilkinson tied one end of a length of thread to Wilkinson's wig without the latter feeling it; the other end of the thread was passed from hand to hand until it was slung over a candle branch of the chandelier and preparations were complete. The singing began and, on the pitch of the chorus, the wig suddenly rose from its owner's head and flew up to the chandelier leaving the astonished

---

* Battiscomb, K. S. George Frederick Adolphus; King's College, 1827; went into the Austrian Cuirassiers and died in that service, 1836.
† Vallencey maj., George Preston; Lt Col. Portsmouth Rifle Volunteers; later colonel in the Indian Army, and was 'very instrumental in suppressing Thugee' (the practices of the Indian association of robbers and stranglers).

Wilkinson sitting 'bald as a coot'. Keate immediately stormed at the victim for his 'egregious folly', he being the only person concerned who could be identified for certain. Fights were kept up with pellets of bread 'rolled up hard and shot like marbles from one side of school to the other, and if they missed a boy aimed at, they hit an oak panel'.

Morning operations in daylight were more dangerous, and all the more honourable for that. Harry Everard writes to big brother Sam: 'We agreed that everybody should take an empty Stone Ink Bottle with us, and every now and then to drop it; every fellow played his part so well that Keate began to wax very wrath by nine o'clock . . . some fellows say he was (if possible) in a greater rage than on Sunday at Prose.'[14]

Punishments were meted out summarily, almost at random, on suspicion of complicity in any offence, in an effort to retain some degree of control over the bear-garden. On one occasion, at Prose on Sunday, when Keate was giving out the themes for the week to come, and at intervals, quacking angrily for 'silence' above the uproar, a boy, willing to risk a flogging for the sake of getting an offensively virtuous boy the same, gave William Gladstone's arm a sharp nudge which sent his hat flying. Keate saw and pounced. 'Playing cricket with your hat, eh,' he screamed. Gladstone protested that there had been no game, only an accident. 'I must flog somebody for this,' Keate declared, 'find me the boy who gave you the nudge.'[15]

Yet despite appearances and his fearsome demeanour, Keate was not at all a harsh or cruel man; notwithstanding the flogging lore surrounding his name, he was never known to punish any individual boy excessively, and the number of strokes he limited execution to – five with a single birch, or ten with two birches for aggravated offences – was lower than the number inflicted by other headmasters before and after his time. He was 'rough', but in Doyle's words, 'not unjust or unkind to boys'.[16] His constant air of fierceness, his look, as Milman put it, 'as if he wanted to knock you down', was part of his performance in a strenuous game which had to be played. He was under ceaseless pressure and provocation in a society which considered it 'ignoble to submit to rules' and treated successful infraction of them as laudable triumph. 'Nothing but a firm hand,' Tucker remarked, 'would have kept these gentry in hand',[17] and even Gaskell, who went in terror of the Baffin, declared to his mother, 'I do think it absolutely necessary for there to be someone of Dr Keate's disposition and temper at the head of the school.'[18] Gladstone was less cordial. 'Mon. 7th Nov. 1825. Whole holiday for the doctor's recovery. He is *more* savage from his illness.'[19]

The lesson which those who had intercourse with Keate as pupils had to learn, and the quicker the better, was that what he abhorred above all things was the tender of monotonous and overworked familiar excuses, and he seemed to object to them even more, if anything, when they were the truth than when they were a shift. It appeared to incense him as disrespect that anyone should dare to present him with a story which, even if it was true, had no right to be. 'Mind your lying to him,' exclaimed Lord Blachford. 'I should think not; why, he exacted it as a mark of proper respect. I remember getting into some trumpery scrape, and when called upon for my explanations, instead of making the shuffling statement he anticipated, I told him the literal truth, upon which he at once inquired of me, with a great appearance of anger, whether I had been drinking.'[20] Keate's response to any first explanation offered by a boy was one of indignant disbelief. The expressions, 'Go along, sir, go along, no unfair artifice if you please,' and 'I see guilt in your eyes!' were known to every Etonian ear.

It was customary for Lower boys on 5 November to light forbidden fires; Keate waged a stubborn but not entirely successful war against the practice. He had been deeply shocked by a tragic incident when he was Lower Master in 1804. The entry in Miss Margaretta Brown's diary for 5 November reads: 'Poor little Grieve mi. got most terribly burned from some squibs which he carried within his coat and to which Lord Cranbourne accidently set fire.' Grieve died. On one such anniversary, meeting James Colville* with a pile of books under his arm, Keate taxed him indignantly with intending to set fire to these volumes. Colville, who 'would as soon have burnt his own hair as a book' answered that he was going to Hallam's room with Gladstone's books and his own to prepare a lesson. 'I don't believe it,' Keate snapped, 'you and the other two have got some foolish notions into your head about *dulce est desipere in loco*; but school isn't the place for dissipation. You shall all three bring me five of Aesop's Fables written out tomorrow, then I shall know that you have not been up to mischief.' Next day, Keate sent for Selwyn minor. 'Where's your Greek Grammar, boy?' 'Please Sir, it's at my Dame's.' 'Go and fetch it: if you're not back in ten minutes I'll flog you'. Selwyn ran,

---

* Colville maj., Sir James William, MA Trinity College, Cambridge; Chief Justice of Calcutta, 1855–59.

but in his hurry brought his brother's book. Keate was triumphant. 'I knew it. You've burnt your own book, sir. Don't deny it. I see guilt in your eyes.'

As the anecdote is from Gladstone, it is of interest; but as it is from Gladstone on Keate, it must be treated with caution: for in Gladstone's eyes Keate could have done no right. Gladstone even managed to nurse a grievance against the Baffin for having let him off a punishment. One day Gladstone, as praeposter of his division, had inadvertently omitted to mark down a friend who had come late to school. A birch was at once called for and 'Keate magniloquently upbraided as a breach of trust what was a lapse of memory'. William Gladstone raised an objection. 'My praepostership would have been an office of trust if I had sought it of my own accord, but it was forced upon me.' This was the kind of original, unhackneyed point which Keate would readily take, and he excused him punishment; but, instead of remembering the occasion with gratitude, Gladstone denounced Keate for having accepted his 'sophistry'. His defence, he insisted, had been more culpable than his fault.[21]

Keate's wrath could also be turned by a total and unexpected *non sequitur*, and even on occasions by the frank admission of the absence of any excuse whatever. An example of the first, preserved by delighted witnesses, occurred when he had been thundering at a boy who rose and said only, 'You know sir, that I have always regarded you as a father.' After a moment of stunned silence Keate murmured, 'I believe you do', and that was the end of that.

Francis Doyle, among others, suggests that much of Keate's rage was affected. Certainly to those who never saw it, the transformation of Keate the headmaster into Keate 'out of school' was startling. In his official capacity, teaching in division, his features were 'stern, his voice harsh, intolerant of the slightest mistake, captious, rough, exacting'. The moment the lesson was over he became another man, 'low-voiced, courteous, agreeable'.[22] Wilkinson got to know Keate more intimately than anyone else who has recorded his impressions except Margaretta Brown, because, after leaving King's, he had the 'privilege and happiness' of being Keate's curate and 'finding him everything that was kind, courteous, mild, amiable, and', he says, 'what those who did not know him will not anticipate, but those who did know him will fully confirm – both in manners and also in voice – *gentle*'.[23] The fierceness and the 'brazen trumpet' were in private circles unknown. They certainly became well enough known in public life to make him a legendary figure in his own lifetime, all over the world wherever the union flag was hoisted. It was enough for a wag to quack the words 'Don't answer me sir, I'll flog you directly,' to be able to tell by the response whether there was another Old Etonian present.

Tucker wishes that Keate had shown more of the amiable companion to the boys and believed that it would have been to everyone's benefit, but Keate had to be the judge of his own strategy in the war which he had to wage; and whatever one may think of his style and methods, which were in the highest degree traditional in character and original in execution, he had a great deal to contend with. One Etonian boy wished to 'settle the matter' of a disagreement with the headmaster by the honourable process of a duel, but Dr Keate, having already expelled the offender, was disobliging enough to consider the matter already settled.*

Another trial which Keate had to endure at one time was the appearance for sale in public of small plaster-of-Paris busts of himself. About nine inches high, they were declared a perfect likeness of the original in his clerical cassock and peculiar old-world three-cornered hat, and were bought up instantly by Etonian purchasers the moment they were offered for sale by itinerant Italian pedlars, hawking images and busts of celebrities and men of renown, ancient and modern. Far from treating as a compliment his inclusion in a company which numbered Wellington, Napoleon, Shakespeare, Hercules, Venus and Apollo, Keate would immediately destroy any example of what he called his 'personal representative' which fell into his hands. He was booed at five o'clock Absence when he smashed into pieces a bust that was cleverly wedged on the door handle of his chambers. 'It might be called a masquerade,' said the Baffin of the traditional entertainments in Long Chamber, 'but it was great tomfoolery.' Neither one nor the other were ever far from life at that time and place.

It was one of the ironies of this comic-opera régime that, although Dr Keate called the masquerade and the display of his 'personal representative' tomfoolery, he did not give the same name to Montem.

Every ancient school has its traditional ceremonies. Harrow's outstanding distinction was its annual pageant of Archery, unfortunately

---

* Nathaniel Waldgrove Mickelthwaite, Lt Col. Scots Fusilier Guards; died 1856. The boy had given Dr Keate an explanation for his absence which was not true and was not believed. He admitted it was not true, but felt that his honour had been impugned by the headmaster's 'not having believed his assertion' and sent a letter from 'Mr Mickelthwaite' requiring an apology from Dr Keate.[24]

abolished in 1772 by an 'advanced' headmaster.[25] Westminster with its dual traditions of learning and violence, had celebrations as disparate as the annual performance in Latin of a play by Terence and the Shrove Tuesday 'grease', when a pancake was tossed by the school cook over a high transverse bar in 'School' and fought for by a chosen few below, the boy ending with the largest piece as trophy receiving a reward. But nowhere was there anything to compare for sheer effrontery with the institution of Montem, and it is questionable whether any other school would have had the cheek to practise it in the first place and later to sanctify it as a venerable tradition.

Montem was an exercise in begging, pure, but not entirely simple. The beggars comprised all Etonians, Collegers and Oppidans, and the brute realities of the performance were veiled by a procession and pageantry in exotic costumes. Montem, said to have started as a nutting expedition to a wood near Slough on the Feast of the Conversion of St Paul, must have had its origins in religious observance.[26] William Malim suggests in his *Consuetudinarium* that it was concerned with a boys' ceremony of initiation. How the custom crept in and was tolerated of boys begging money* from wayfarers is unknown. Its initial purpose may have been charitable and it may have been performed by a seasonal 'Boy Bishop' and his suite.[27] Nor do we know whose organizational skill converted piecemeal begging into a corporate operation in the interests of one particular boy. But, at all events, Montem, as a benefit for the senior Colleger of the day, known as Captain of Montem, was an ancient custom.

It was celebrated every third year, and the choice of the fortunate boy was, in practice, a lottery. If a sixth-form Colleger did happen to find himself at the Head of the School at the right time of the right year the hazards were not over; for he stood in line for the next vacancy to King's College, Cambridge and a candidate had to fill or forego the vacancy within twenty days of succeeding to it. Therefore if a vacancy occurred at King's College more than twenty days before Montem day he would be obliged to relinquish his place as Senior Colleger and Captain of Montem to the boy next to him in seniority. The heir presumptive only became heir apparent on 'Montem-sure-night', when cheering and ringing of bells resounded through college.

On the great day the procession set out from School Yard and advanced through a concourse of the public, local inhabitants and

---

* The stigma of begging was evaded by the formal tender of 'salt' in exchange for the money exacted, and in the end salt and money became synonymous.

visitors, members of the nobility and gentry, sometimes royalty, and an agreeable profusion of beautiful and fashionably dressed women. The Captain of Montem himself was grand in the uniform of a general; the sixth form attended him in fanciful military uniforms of their choice, waited on by their pages, clothed in silk. There followed the saltbearers, dressed as pirates, brigands or whatever took their fancy, highly responsible officers, with their assistants, twelve runners arrayed in costumes of pink, blue, violet and red, and wearing plumed hats and buff boots. Then came the fifth form marching two by two, their costume being scarlet coat, frock or cut away, with sash and sword, white kerseymere shorts and buckled shoes. Behind every pair of fifth-form officers walked two lower boys wearing blue coats with gilt buttons, white waistcoats, white or nankeen trousers and silk stockings, a costume described by an Etonian naval officer as 'something between a cabin boy and a Lord High Admiral'. These were known as 'pole bearers' and carried plain deal wands, five foot long, which would be severed before the day was out by the swords of their fifth-form seniors. Montem was already approaching decadence, but it was still, at its best, described as a 'gay, lively, good humoured scene'.

The procession to Salt Hill was in fact the ceremonial conclusion of the event; the actual business had been done earlier. Soon after sunrise that morning the saltbearers, with scouts and runners, had been scouring the countryside, posting themselves at strategic stations such as Staines Bridge, Hounslow, Maidenhead and Slough within a radius of twelve miles of Eton and Windsor. All vehicles on the road, public and private, were held up with a summons for 'salt'; and travellers on the Bath and Western or another coach from distant parts, without previous experience of the festival, would be amazed to find their way barred by boys dressed as Turkish pirates or Spanish brigands and other even more improbable picaroons, requiring 'salt' and leaving nobody in doubt of what they meant by the expression. When he had made a contribution a traveller would be presented with a ticket inscribed with the words *Mos Pro Lege* which, fixed in his hat or in some conspicuous part of his dress, secured him exemptions from future applications for money.

'Out upon the eternal hunting for causes and reasons,' exclaimed a sentimental Old Etonian, 'I love the no meaning Eton "Montem", I love to be asked for salt by a pretty boy in silk stockings and satin doublet, though the custom has been called something between begging and robbing. . . .' It was a defensive cry; Montem was already, in the twenties, under attack by the moralists of a new and more decorous order. 'The absurd pageant of Montem,' wrote our renegade Etonian in the *Edinburgh Review*; and other critics deemed it more culpable than absurd. A new censorious neo-puritanism was creeping up through the ranks of society bent on 'reform', reaching even as far as female royalty. At the conclusion of the parade to Salt Hill, it was the custom for a 'parson' and 'clerk' to read a burlesque service in Latin, after which the 'parson' kicked the 'clerk' down the hill. The clowning must have been of great antiquity, certainly pre-reformation, and connected with one of the profaner 'Boy Bishop' charades.[28] It had been enjoyed for generations by spectators as a harmless piece of fun; but when Queen Charlotte saw it she was shocked and used her influence to have the pantomime abolished.

Montem still in Keate's reign commanded an army of staunch defenders. But the social tide was flowing against the indulgence. One of the Eton boys who himself took part in Montem in 1826 made an entry in his diary: '16 May Tues Montem day . . . the whole thing a wretched waste of time and money; a most ingenious contrivance to exhibit us as baboons.'[29] The boy, William Gladstone, when he wrote those words had just finished taking part in the procession to Salt Hill, 'disguised as a Greek in white *fustinelle* and embroidered cap', and had been one of the saltbearers who begged for money for the reigning Captain, Edward Hayes Pickering. Gladstone was not typical of that time, but he was considerably representative of standards to come, and Montem itself had become its own enemy. It was too open to abuse to be healthy. Serious-minded former Etonians feared that the 'vulgar highway robbery called Salt'[30] would before long be challenged and physically resisted by some resentful yeoman and the whole affair shown up to the shame of all Etonians in a public court of justice.

It was the railways that gave Montem its *coup de grâce*. Whatever case the conservationists might have made previously, once the populace had cheap, fast and frequent transport Montem was condemned. In 1841 and again in 1843 the metropolitan multitude poured in by railway, intoxicated, spoiling for trouble and containing a large criminal element which brought serious danger of riots and mass violence to the carnival. In 1847 Montem was not celebrated (to the disappointment of Queen Victoria)* and the following year it was

---

* Victoria was a keen supporter of Montem, attending first just after her accession in 1838, and thereafter on every occasion until its abolition.

abolished by Provost Hodgson, by when, although it had its staunch and unretreating defenders, it had been denounced by as loyal an Etonian as William Johnson as the occasion of 'odious orgies'.

But that day still lay twenty years ahead and almost unimagined by Etonians when Gladstone, Tucker and Wilkinson, Milnes Gaskell and others retired to bed after a day which, whatever their feelings for it were, had been long and tiring. The sum of money involved was substantial. When a gift of, perhaps, a hundred pounds from the king and other generous offerings from rich Old Etonians had been added to the collections taken on the highway, the total might be more than a thousand pounds. Out of this the Captain had to pay for a sumptuous dinner for his army in one of the best hostels, the Windmill where

> Floreat Etona! swelled high on the flow
> Of Sherry and Port and Champagne and Bordeaux

He also had to defray his followers' expenses, mainly damage to private property, which his carousing troops vied with each other to make as large as possible. The fifth form in their scarlet coats and cocked hats used to draw their swords and lop the heads off flowers and cabbages, slash trees and palings, anything that looked of value. But, even when the cost of feasting and vandalism had been met, the Captain was left with a sum equivalent in value to fifteen thousand pounds or more today to set himself up in his university life. In 1826 the purse was exceptionally large and Gladstone was instrumental in enabling Pickering to preserve a larger proportion than usual by organizing a muscular praetorian guard which discouraged the 'liquored Hectors' in their scarlet coats from committing wanton damage in the gardens of the hotel at Salt Hill.

Even after 'lights out' the sport was not at an end for those with the energy and appetite for more. Oppidans who wished to risk their skins broke out from their Dames' houses in pursuit of local, but dangerous, entertainment at Windsor, or made a clandestine expedition to London, catching the old Emerald, one of the fastest coaches of the day, and on reaching Hatchett's and having a wash before going to change into their dress clothes at their tailor's in the 'Opera Colonnade', they settled down in the stalls to enjoy the voice of Catalini in *Don Giovanni*. After the ballet, which followed the opera, there was an oyster supper in the Haymarket; then, unless they were inclined to more nefarious amusements, friends would sit up in the obliging tailor's shop, dozing till it was time to catch the early Bristol coach which would land them at Slough corner in time to reach School Yard for 9 o'clock Absence.

An Old Etonian of Keate's days, John Delaware Lewis, remarked that Eton was not to be regarded as a school for serious business, but rather a crèche where big children were sent by their parents to be kept out of harm's way and to amuse themselves.[31] Amusements were lawful and unlawful, and in between was a broad area of practices which were officially disallowed but openly tolerated.

Certain laws had to be made and enforced for the protection of the public. Gigs were permitted; tandems were forbidden. So the tandem became the symbol of ultimate defiance of authority. The tandem then was the social equivalent of a fast sports car, requiring precise and delicate control; it was dangerous to the driver, to other users of the road and to pedestrians, and Etonians were forbidden to own or travel in one. They were all the rage among the sporting swells, and perfect instruments for playing practical jokes on the Baffin. On a signal given as Dr Keate emerged from School Yard to cross the High Street, a tandem driven by an Etonian disguised by a false moustache and the box coat and cape of a military dandy, and accompanied by two friends arrayed as tigers,* flashed into view and sped towards him, missing the little figure by a calculated hairsbreadth and disappearing in the direction of Spiers Corner.†

Other laws which had to be applied related to private property, and made the pleasures of trespass and poaching irresistible.

> Some bold adventures disdain
> The limits of their little reign
> And unknown regions dare descry
> Still as they run they look behind
> They hear a voice in every wind
> And snatch a fearful joy.[32]

The voice in the wind which Tucker heard one day as he took to his heels was Keate's and it intimated that he had been seen in illicit quest of game. 'Come back! Come back! I know who you are.' Then receding in the distance, the comforting qualification, 'I will discover you.'

---

* Tiger: a servant in livery who rides with his master.
† So called from the name of the three sisters who kept a hot-roll and sock shop opposite the gate of Wren's Yard.

In a society which exploited tomfoolery as profitably as Montem, it was hardly to be expected that the masters, who tended to live extravagantly, should be indifferent to money. Masters, and above all the headmaster, accepted tips from boys at the end of a half in much the same spirit as hotel staff taking tips from departing guests. At Winchester masters claimed 'gratuities' from the boys, and the supplement was added to the bill like a modern service charge, expressly against the statutes but, having become a custom, being allowed by the Visitors. Similarly at Westminster, what had begun as voluntary gifts by boys to masters had been hardened by time, 'the great nursing mother of abuses', into an obligatory practice. At Eton the transactions were conducted with magnificent shamelessness. A two-guinea *douceur* was due to the headmaster from every boy at the end of each half; 'noblemen' – Peers or the sons of Peers – were expected to leave double or more than that sum; and, at the end of his time at school, etiquette required an Etonian to make a present to the headmaster of at least ten, rising later to fifteen, pounds, which he left in the great man's study after calling to say goodbye.[33] Sometimes, to jog his memory, and to intimate the minimum sum which would be acceptable, a dish, by coincidence already containing a couple of ten-pound bank notes (and perhaps suggestively, one of a larger denomination to hint that more would not be repugnant), stood conspicuously on a table by the door on the same principle as that used by hotel cloakroom attendants today.*

Each headmaster played his part in the performances according to his character. Hawtrey (Keate's successor), of somewhat laboured refinement and delicacy of manners, was said to be painfully embar-

---

* A letter dated 21 June 1864, from an Etonian, Robert Pierpoint, to his father, gives an account of his expenses at the end of his last half at Eton.

I am afraid you will be surprised at the amount of money I am going to ask for, but it can't be helped; leaving Eton is tremendously expensive.

Headmaster	£10	0	0	Boat	2	0	0
Tutor	15	0	0	Musketry Bill about	2	0	0
House Butler	1	0	0	Musketry Money	1	0	0
Boy's Maid	1	0	0	Book for Mrs Young		10	0
2nd. Maid		10	0	Journey Money	3	0	0
Groom		10	0	Packing		10	0
Cook	1	0	0				
Kitchen Maid		10	0		£39	0	0
College Butler		10	0				

Then there are I dare say things that I don't remember, and to leave Eton well, I should be glad if you could make this into about £44 or £45. [Equivalent to not less than £700 sterling today.][34]

rassed by the procedure, but he did not refuse the money, he merely affected to be unconscious of what was happening. If it was the end of summer term he would observe, says one Etonian, 'I think it's rather warm, I'll open the window,' and while he did so he gave the departing visitor time to deposit the envelope on the table. The now open window provided him with a cue for giving the next caller an opportunity to be unobserved, 'Don't you think it's rather cold? I think I'll shut the window.'[35] No such coyness inhibited Keate. Archdeacon Denison remembered that in his last interview with the Baffin, being nervous, he dropped the bank note he was holding and when he bent down to retrieve it he found the headmaster's foot 'which had followed the note, and covered and secured it'.[36]

Life at Eton was fraught with curious contradictions. Boys were allowed to be at certain places, but it was an offence to be seen going to them. Etonians were permitted, by the grace and favour of their patron George III, to walk on the terrace of Windsor Castle, but it was unlawful to be on the streets of Windsor by which alone the terrace could be reached. Collegers, on attaining a certain seniority, were allowed by the authorities to rent rooms of their choice halfway up to Windsor Bridge. They would be breaking a fundamental law in going to them. In order to visit the shops where the school tradesmen did business, boys were obliged to go out of bounds. The 'hair-cutter' was out of bounds, so was the Post Office where you might have got a money order cashed; if your tutor gave you an order for a new hat upon Sanders the hatter, or for a new suit of clothes upon Denman the tailor, he knew that you would have to go out of bounds to get the order honoured.

These anomalies could not be resolved by any official amendment because that would have required a statutory change validated by the provost and fellows; but the fellows resisted all change. They may have thought, rightly, that one change tends to lead to another, and also rightly, that change would not be in their interests. So an accommodation was reached by the convention of 'shirking'. Shirking was a 'marvellous invention'; and no description of Eton up to and beyond the middle of the century would be adequate without some account of its operation. If a boy upon an unlawful journey saw a master approaching he simply dodged into a shop or down an alley until the coast was clear. The master might see the boy, but he was not supposed to see him, and it was contrary to the rules of the game for him to take cognisance of the boy's presence. The act of shirking was accepted as an adequate gesture of respect for the law, and admission of its power. Thus the spectacle was commonplace of two or three Collegers lounging by the wall opposite School Yard and, on seeing the headmaster or an assistant master, gradually backing within the school archway and so within bounds, and capping him as he passed, although, as he was well aware, there were sixty Collegers, if not more, with rooms scattered high and low all through the town. A master might be seen walking along the pavement of Eton High Street in the direction of Windsor with, only a few yards behind him, a gaggle of boys walking in the same direction without stealth, but being careful not to overhaul and pass him. Were the master to be inconsiderate enough to turn round there would be an immediate dispersal, boys dodging out of sight into shops and scampering into alleys.

Grotesque as the performance appeared, a boy would have been imprudent not to take his cue and play his part promptly in the proceedings; for 'shirkable' personages tended to be sensitive to what was due to them and treated failure to shirk as a personal affront, reacting rather as adult male Moslems used to react if a female co-religionist unveiled herself publicly in their sight. An occasion is recorded a generation after Wilkinson had left Eton and shirking was still going strong. The kind of procession described above was travelling towards Windsor when one little new boy called Grenville Murray, not yet accustomed to the game or its rules, broke away from his party and skipped forward, passing the master and walking in front of him. Unfortunately the master was 'Judy' Durnford, an irritable and, when roused, implacable eccentric, who now, almost speechless with outrage, shambled after the boy and arrested him with a demand to know what he meant by his behaviour, which was 'utterly, hm, utterly gross'. No explanation, no plea of ignorance availed; the new boy received his first flogging.[37]

In Keate's time the sixth form also had to be shirked (although they themselves had to shirk masters). At this time also, other candidates were competing to get into the act to raise or reinforce their dignity. The provost, Dr Goodall, who might have been supposed to be above such considerations, decided that he too wished to be shirked – fortunately the fellows did not show any interest in the subject – and Mr Hexter, the writing master, although not an assistant master in standing,* applied, on the strength of a permanent

---

* In addition to the classics tutors, there were, attached to the school but not part of the establishment, instructors in supplementary and optional subjects – handwriting, mathematics, French, Italian – who were of lower status to the nucleus of official assistant masters.

appointment, for the honour of a cap and gown, and the compliment of being shirked. The provost replied that as to the gown, he might please himself; but as to shirking, the boys must be allowed to please *themselves*.

The consequences of this régime were to a degree in anticipation of the world of Lewis Carroll. Keate, inquiring after a boy, and being told he was 'on the river', would receive the news with perfect equanimity; although it was unlawful for the boy to go to the river, his journeys to and from his boat were traditionally tolerated, providing he observed the correct rituals and did not court a confrontation with authority. The sight of a boy in a boating jacket at Absence might provoke Keate's ire, but merely as a breach of good manners.[38]

It was part of the system that Keate pretended not to know what happened on the river. On 4 June, the day of the greatest river celebrations of the year, Keate would send for the Captain of Boats and say, 'You know I know nothing but I am told that you know a great deal. As you are in authority try to keep order tonight. Lock up will be three quarters of an hour later than usual; that is your privilege.' Having received the courtesy of this informal acknowledgement, the Captain of Boats would then have to shirk any master he met on his way to the river.

On 4 June 1803, when Keate was still lower master, he himself took to the Thames in a 'ten oar', accompanied by his beautiful wife Fanny,* and her also attractive and accomplished sister, Margaretta Brown, who lived with the Keates at Eton. Miss Brown recorded in her diary, 'We were delighted at seeing all the boys in the boat shirk Mr K. . . .' How the occupants of one 'ten oar' shirked the lower master in another is not disclosed.

In the spring of 1829 a problem arose which made it difficult for the headmaster to keep to his conventional dialogue and led to the liveliest confrontation between Keate and the school since the rebellion of 1818. There had been heavy flooding and, at the time of year

---

* Allusions to Fanny Keate's charms abound; they even feature in a cricketing poem, celebrating the prowess of a noted Etonian batsman called Harding:

> It was a bat full fair to see
> And it drove the balls right lustily
> Without a flaw without a speck
> Smooth as fair Hebe's ivory neck
> It was withall so light, so neat
> That Harding called it Mistress Keate.

when rowing was most popular, the river was judged unsafe for boats. Keate found it necessary to convey to the Captain of Boats instructions that there must be no boating. But how did one forbid the continuance of what one did not admit had ever taken place? Having summoned the Captain of Boats into his presence, Keate addressed him on the subject in such devious and ambiguous peri-phrases that the boy took the gratifying opportunity of affecting not to understand and when the two parted the headmaster was fuming with frustration. The boy summoned his companions and it was resolved that so favourable a situation must not be wasted. Accord-ingly a rumour was 'leaked' that the eight were, after all, proposing to take to the water; and this intimation duly reached the ears of Keate, whose wrath was unbounded.

It being soon after St Patrick's Day, the honour of the operation was accorded to the *Hibernia* and her crew. A good start was made from Hester's boat shed and the crew rowed upstream as far as the 'Shallows' where they turned and a strong current and easy rowing soon brought the *Hibernia* into 'dangerous latitudes', for a consider-able number of the general public as well as a host of boys and assistant masters and enemy spies were assembled about the boating place and approaches to the river. Warned by their own scouts at Bargeman's Bridge that the enemy were at hand in force, each member of the crew fastened over his face a comic mask with a rubicund nose of gigantic proportions and crowned the disguise with a white or coloured night cap. As the crew darted into view through the centre arch of the bridge, a great roar of cheers and laughter was raised in greeting from boys and other sympathizers. Below the bridge the crew of the *Hibernia* turned and gallantly rowed upstream again and when they were out of sight and had reached a point below the cobler,* sheltered from observation, they pulled into the bank and disembarked where eight local watermen were waiting by arrange-ment to take the place of the crew and assume their masks. The change having been smoothly effected, the Etonians made their way briskly by familiar routes back into bounds to be in time for Absence. Meanwhile the *Hibernia* began her return journey downriver.

Dr Keate, apprised of the outrage being perpetrated by masked boys, hurried in person to the Brocas† and arrived in time to witness

---

* The narrow spit of land at the southern end of Romney island, opposite the site of Windsor and Eton railway station.
† A field between the Thames and South Meadow, upstream of Windsor Bridge.

the return of the *Hibernia*. At the sight his fury erupted and he ran down the bank alongside the boat gesticulating and quacking with rage at the masked crew, 'I know you So-and-so: I know you all. I'll flog you: I'll expel you.' At which the watermen raised their masks and gave the Doctor a cheerful salute.* Keate's discomfiture seemed complete when, at two o'clock Absence, every one of the boys he believed to have been behind those masks was present and answered to his name unexceptionably. But Keate was far too experienced a campaigner to be out-manoeuvred by such tricks. If he could not convict the grand offenders of rowing, he would punish those who openly rejoiced in the hoax perpetrated. He promulgated an injunction requiring all those 'who had shouted on the Brocas' when the master had appeared, to see what boys were 'going up in boats', to declare themselves, and he required that the number of penitents for an *auto-da-fé* should not be less than thirty, otherwise he would keep the whole school back for two days of the approaching holidays. After forty-eight hours of uneasy rumination, eighteen offenders grudgingly declared themselves and were flogged; twenty-four others on being challenged refused to attest that they did not shout, and, having no such protection as a 'fifth amendment', were condemned to remain behind for two days after the rest of the school had begun the holidays.[40] These sacrificial offerings were deemed sufficient to save the face and satisfy the honour of authority. Next year, Nature, and with her all else, returned to normal, and boating and shirking went on cheerfully again as before.

William IV, an ardent patron of the river and a staunch attendant at Fourth of June celebrations, in the first year of his reign presented the crew of the 'ten oar' with a gift of twelve dozen bottles of champagne. 'But,' says a contemporary Eton wet-bob, 'the effect was so disastrous that he was asked to reduce his allowance and next year he sent only a miserable dozen.'[41]

The prevailing feeling carried into after life by men who had been boys under Keate's régime was of a marvellous freedom, 'a perfect freedom', as Francis Doyle remembers it, 'physical freedom for those who preferred it, but also intellectual freedom'. A Tory himself, Keate did not endeavour to propagate conservatism; he even gave W. E.

---

* According to an Old Etonian spectator, the substitutes were the well-known cads of the day, Jack Hall, Joe Cannon (the pugilist), Billy Fish, Shampoo Carter, Jack Garraway, Picky Powell and Jem Miller, the latter being a Protestant Irishman of (probably affected) bigotry, who signed a petition against Catholic Emancipation on the grounds that 'when the d—d rogues burnt Cranmer and Riddle [*sic*], they never paid for the faggots'.[39]

Gladstone his first lessons in public speaking.[42] For him 'it was a crime for a boy to write bad Latin verses, but not to hold Liberal opinions'. That is a generous compliment, up to a point well deserved, but too good to be true. It exaggerates one part of the reality and conceals another.

He once remarked affably to Gladstone. 'You belong to the *Literati*,* and of course you say there all that's on your mind. I wish I could hear you without your being aware of my presence; I am sure I should hear a speech that would give me pleasure.'[43] But Keate knew very well that some of what was transacted in the society would have given him no pleasure and some anxiety. As headmaster of Eton, he could not be indifferent to the possibilities of scandal, and the relative freedom which he maintained was not an easy or careless privilege conferred without tension. There were occasions when he felt it necessary to threaten to repeal the liberty and he read his private riot act to the boldest spirits. Arthur Henry Hallam, writing from Eton to his con, William Wyndham Farr, recently translated to Oxford, informs him, 'You must know he [Keate] has been chafing in secret at our fondness for political subjects, which how he found it out, his spies and Jove only know.' A deputation had submitted through Pickering, the Captain of the School, a request for the relaxation of the fifty-year rule prohibiting direct reference to domestic political events less than half a century old. Keate 'flew off at a tangent' and declared 'we had no right to debate anything subsequent to the Revolution, adding by way of a soothing sequel that' he would 'break up the Society altogether!!!'. But these were warning barks. There was no dissolution 'à la Cromwell'. The boys continued to speak their minds, even on the most tender of all domestic subjects, and Hallam next reports, 'By Mercury and all the silver tongued Gods of Eloquence, you ought to have heard our debate last Saturday on the policy of England towards Ireland from the Revolution in 1688 to 1776. . . .'[44]

A foreign visitor to Eton would have found it a bewildering scene, a place where boys, subject to the rod for breaches of school discipline, were at the same time free to write and publish political and moral assertions which would have caused the arrest and imprisonment of an adult presuming to attempt the like in any other country in Europe. In volume two of the *Eton Miscellany*, we find the editor's 'Ode to the Shade of Wat Tyler'. Composed by Gladstone, the grand-

---

* The Literary Society.

old-man-to-be at the age of eighteen, in a fury of revolutionary zeal,
it begins:

> Shade of him whose valiant tongue
> On high the song of freedom sung

and ends with a salutation to his muse, who

> . . . sings of all who soon or late
> Have burst Subjections iron chain
> *Have sealed the bloody despot's fate*
> *Or cleft a peer or priest in twain.*

The political offensiveness occurs in the middle of the ode where
historic gives way to contemporary allusion:

> I hymn the gallant and the good
> From Tyler *down to Thistlewood*
> My Muse the trophies grateful sings
> The deeds of Miller and of Ings.

Thistlewood and Ings had been the leading Cato Street conspirators,
terrorists whose object had been the assassination of Lord Liverpool's
cabinet and certain of their friends, including the Duke of Wellington,
when they were due to dine at Lord Harrowby's house in Grosvenor
Square. The plot miscarried and Thistlewood and Ings were hanged,
but the affair put many prominent parliamentarians into a state of
nervous anxiety. Although it was published, Keate raised no objection
to the Ode.*

Reports of the transactions between Keate and the schoolboy
William Gladstone tend to suggest that the headmaster may have
felt that the boy was a little premature in the respect he paid to his
own dignity and redressed the balance accordingly. The impression
is not effaced by the resentment which Gladstone continued to show
for the rest of his long life whenever the name of his old headmaster,
long since dead, was mentioned. 'A graceless, senseless, cruel little
martinet,' was the opinion, arising in a context of considerable
rancour, to which Gladstone gave circulation, nearly sixty years later;

---

* Compare this with the attitude of Thomas Arnold to a disfavoured independent view. See
below, p. 260.

and when he said those words he knew he was saying them for publication.

As a youth W. E. Gladstone was taken by his father to hear Edward Irving preach. Mr Gladstone had prudently reserved a pew in the gallery, 'from which honourable vantage ground' the boy Gladstone looked down with 'infinite complacency and satisfaction' upon the struggling crowd below. Then, to his amazement, he espied the figure of Dr Keate, 'the former master of our existence, the tyrant of our days', buffeted in the throng below, like any mere mortal. 'Pure unalloyed, unadulterated rapture.' In a long public life, richer than most in triumphs, Gladstone cherished that sight among his most precious memories. 'Never, never,' he declared, 'have I forgotten that moment.'[45]

The longevity of his feelings is as remarkable as their curiosity, for many who fulminated against Keate and fought him as their hereditary adversary as *boys* grew to cherish as men their memories of the Baffin. One among innumerable anecdotes expresses the general attitude. Soon after Waterloo, Keate was seen eating ices at Tarloni's in Paris 'on the boulevards', and as word got round several Old Etonians then in Paris decided to give him a dinner at Beauvilliers, 'the best dining place in Paris,' (says Gronow) 'and far superior to anything of the kind in the present day' (1863). The hosts included Lord Sunderland, who had been expelled for firing a small cannon on Keate's private lawn on 5 November. They ordered an excellent dinner and 'never witnessed a more jovial banquet'. The Doctor 'paid his addresses in large bumpers of every description of wine, and towards the end of dinner expressed his delight at finding that his old friends and pupils had not forgotten him, concluding a neat and appropriate speech with *Floreat Etona!*'. After drinking his health, the hosts took the opportunity to chaff the guest of honour with accounts of clandestine escapades which had occurred in their time at school; fights with the bargees, poaching in Windsor Park, illicit suppers in the Christopher, nocturnal expeditions in tandems. . . . Keate took the 'revelations' in good part and told them that, if he had any regret, 'it was that he had not flogged them a good deal harder', but he said he felt it had done them good and concluded by paying them all 'compliments in a few well turned phrases'. His address was applauded with cheers and the company 'parted on excellent terms, highly gratified with the evening's entertainment'.[46]

Even Gladstone was touched on one occasion by the strength and unity of the devotion shown to Keate by generations of Old Etonians assembled at the Eton anniversary dinner of 1849. When Keate's name had been announced, 'the scene', said Gladstone, 'was indescribable. Queen and Dowager alike vanished into insignificance. The roar of cheering had a beginning, but never knew satiety or ends. Like the huge waves at Biarritz the flood of cheering continually recommenced. . . . When at last it became possible, Keate rose, that is to say, his head was projected slightly over the heads of his two neighbours. He struggled to speak. I will not say I heard every syllable, for there were no syllables; speak he could not. He tried in vain to mumble a word or two, but wholly failed, recommenced the vain struggle and sat down. It was certainly one of the most moving spectacles that in my whole life I have ever witnessed.'[47]

Perhaps one short anecdote condenses the central human element which endeared Keate, despite his bark and birch, to generations of his charges. It was the almost medieval chivalry with which he conducted his battle to limit the transgression of his turbulent subjects. At night college used to post sentries against a surprise visit from the headmaster. The duty devolved upon juniors. In winter the station could be an uncomfortable one. The headmaster, of course, was not supposed to know of the practice. In cold weather Keate would send a message to the Captain of the school intimating that the headmaster would not be visiting college that night, so that the little watchboy could be relieved from his chilly post.[48]

When Keate retired in 1834 (shortly after the last rebellion), he was presented with, among other gifts (which included £3000 sterling, equal in value to about £50,000 in 1982), a Warwick vase from the boys, bearing the inscription:

Presented
By the Existing Members of Eton School
To the Revd John Keate D.D.
On his retirement from the Headmastership
30 July 1834
As a testimony of the High sense they entertain
Of his Exquisite Taste and Accurate Scholarship
So Long and so Successfully Devoted
To Their Improvement
And of the Firm yet Parental Exercise
Of His Authority
Which has conciliated the Affection
While It Has Commanded the Respect
Of His Scholars

The Unspared Rod

'There was a terrible amount of flogging,'[1] said the author of *The Public Schools* in 1857. As the Rev. Lucas Collins had been at Rugby in 1833, he knew what he was talking about; but he might have been describing any of the public schools. Dr George Moberley, who also had personal experience, and in the very school of which he later became headmaster, giving evidence before the Clarendon Commission, testified that twenty a day might be recorded in a school of 150 boys and 'nobody cared about it'.[2] H. C. Adams corroborates Moberley. On the day a friend of his arrived at Winchester in the early years of the century there were 198 boys in the school, and 278 names were cited for flogging.* Walter Charles Calverly Trevelyan, at Harrow in the Christmas term of 1812, reports on 2 September, 'Sent up by Mr Roberts . . . because I could not construe my Tursulline and flogged by Dr B. for the first time. After tea walked by Turnpike and cricket ground.' But far from the occasion producing constraint or ill feeling on either side, next day Trevelyan was a guest at the headmaster's table and records with appreciation hospitality received: 'Supped with Dr Butler. Eat Mock Turtle soup, Hare, Partridge, Pye, custard and trifle, and three glasses of wine.'[4]

Gaskell estimated that Keate, at Eton, flogged about ten boys a day,[5] except on Sunday, which was his day of rest, as far as flogging was concerned. On some days the number was larger, perhaps as much as forty;† when there had been collective delinquency, it might be even larger. 'The boys, the first time the new Absence was to be called, unanimously refused to go,' Josiah Wedgwood reported to his friend Francis Coleridge, 'so that what did he do but that same

---

* Our witness, the Rev. H. C. Adams, pauses in his testimony to certify that the figures he quotes are not an error. A proportion of the boys had been cited for more than one offence and were therefore due more than one flogging.[3]

† Gaskell estimated (23 June 1824) that if the praeposters had put every name they were given in the bill the number of those parading daily for execution would have been about thirty.[6]

evening he took a little exercise and wore out a little birch in flogging about eighty fellows'.[7]

In view of Keate's reputation as the busiest flogger in the public schools since Busby, it is only fair to reaffirm that the legend was due more to personality than performance. Keate did not flog more than some of his predecessors; but he was an original and unforgettable. The strength of his diminutive form was not in doubt, but there was never the slightest suggestion made against him, even when resentment of his discipline was at its strongest, of excessive *severity* of punishment; in fact school opinion rated his successor, the mincing dandy Hawtrey, as a harder hitter than the Baffin, except when the latter was roused by the seriousness of an offence.[8] With young and frightened convicts, he often did not, as Wilkinson put it, 'so much as imprint the college arms on them'.[9]

Much of the function of flogging was in the nature of a public ritual of humbling submission, exacted from offenders who had treated authority with disrespect, defiance or contempt, or merely looked as if they were about to do so; and, indeed, the posture assumed on the block was not unlike the posture of appeasement required of subordinate members of a simian society before dominant senior members, male or female. It is part of Etonian lore that when Charles Fox returned to Eton after a stay in Paris with his father, where he had been accorded the freedom and respect due to an adult, Dr Barnard took the first opportunity to flog him, to reduce him from feelings of precocious self-importance to a healthy sense of his juvenile status.[10]

Some boys might pass through school without ever being flogged; but others would more than make up for their omission. Harry Everard sends as interesting news to his brother at the beginning of one half, that 'a new fellow named West* has been swished seven times and had a first fault'.[11] Charles Keate, the headmaster's embarrassingly delinquent nephew, was flogged almost every day and one day twice.[12] It was not uncommon for a boy to be flogged twice in a day.[13] The lavish and almost promiscuous exercise of the birch is not in question. The uncertain factor is the degree of force and number of strokes applied.

There is strong evidence from the eighteenth century and earlier that corporal punishment in schools was severe. In this the schools only corresponded with conditions in the adult world. In an environ-

---

* John Temple West, eldest son of Admiral Sir John West; Lt Col. Grenadier Guards.

ment where men convicted of crime were branded and mutilated, flogged (sometimes almost to death), tortured with crushing weights if they refused to plead, and taken down alive from the gallows and disembowelled in public as punishment for treason, it was inevitable that some appearance of these standards would be found also in the lives of juveniles. For a long time before the period treated here, schoolmasters as a class had borne an unattractive reputation for cruel and perverse exercise of their power over the young committed to their charge. The western archetype of the tyrant pedagogue is Horace's Plagosus Orbilius, but his Christian successors yielded nothing to his example in harshness, to judge from the reports of former victims, and the mainly unheeded protests of a notable minority of benign and humane teachers from Anselm to Ascham. Tudor Etonians were known to run away from school 'for fear of beating',[14] and in Tusser's verse we are told that more than fifty strokes might be given for a trivial offence.[15] Practice seems to have varied considerably, and in some schools the number of strokes that might be inflicted was limited by statute. Samuel Harsnet, Archbishop of York, decreed when he founded Chigwell School that 'correction' be restricted to three strokes of the rod.[16] But whether such a decree was in practice observed is uncertain. The prevailing impression received from Tudor school records is of fierce severity:

> My master hath bette my bak and syde whyles the
>   rodde wolde holde in his hand
> He hath torne my buttocks so that theyr is left no hole
>   skynne upon them
> Y wales be so thycke Y one can stand scantly by
>   an other.[17]

In the following century popular reports were still lurid enough for the prospect of his being sent to Eton to fill the boy John Evelyn with terror.[18]* The new regulations in 1623 of Farnworth School, near Prescott, mention that other masters had so misused the children that they had been in danger of losing their sense, lives and limbs.[19] In 1682 Roswell, the headmaster of Eton, resigned when, it was said, a boy had died after a notoriously severe beating.[20]

---

* E. S. de Beer (ed.) in John Evelyn, *Diary*, whose opinions always command respect, suggests that Evelyn's fear may have been of the exacting standards of scholarship, rather than of physical severity. I am not persuaded that a boy aged about ten would be put in terror from a distance by anything as abstract as study.

Parents seem to have been on the whole, by later standards of concern, remarkably indifferent or, more likely, resigned to their sons' sufferings at school, treating their ordeals as an unpleasant, but necessary introduction to the harsh realities of the human condition. Occasionally, tender-hearted parents would rescue an unhappy boy. 'John, though of good parts,' was unable to bear the severity of his master, Mr Denman, 'very able and excellent of his faculty but exceedingly austere' and in consequence grew 'so out of love with learning' that his parents took him home.* But such conduct was remarkable as a curiosity. As late as 1802 a respected educationalist quoted with approval the account (which he attributed to Locke) of the mother who 'beat her daughter seven times to break her obstinacy' for 'had she stopped at the sixth correction her daughter had been ruined'.[22]† The Duke of Sussex frequently described the treatment he and the other royal children of George III received from their tutors as 'barbarous'.[23]

Yet it would be an oversimplification to conclude that the treatment of juveniles, before the mid-nineteenth century, was uniformly severe. In discipline, as in all else, there were trends and reactions. There is at least some evidence to support the hypothesis that conditions in schools became easier in early Caroline times, and reverted to severity after 1636 (particularly at Eton)[24] and that the government of all subordinates tended to harden after 1660.‡ There were always theorists and practitioners of miscellaneous systems of educational novelty doing business in private schools and so-called 'academies', some of whom disavowed the use of corporal punishment; but it is fair to say that Mr Fairchild was still, in 1818, following the guideline of moral propriety when he took 'a small horsewhip' and flogged a little boy, held down by the footman, for having failed to learn his

* His brother, who stayed on at the school, was less fortunate; he was permanently injured and deafened in one ear by the same master.[21]

† For some, magisterial authority in personal relations endured indefinitely. 'When his daughter, aged forty, ventured to disagree with him,' Dr John Plumptre, Dean of Gloucester, 'said gravely as one who means what he says, "Tryphena, you are not too old to be whipped." ' See Kegan Paul, *Memories*, p. 84. Plumptre was an eccentric, but it was the popular man of the people, Charles Dickens, who said, alluding to Mrs Gaskell, in the postscript of a letter to his subeditor, William Henry Wills, 'If I were Mr G. how I would beat her.' The original letter, dated 'Eleventh September 1855' is in the Huntington Library and has been reproduced twice: once in Walter Dexter (ed.), *The Letters of Charles Dickens* (1938), vol. 2, p. 687, and again in R. C. Lehman, *Charles Dickens as Editor; Being Letters Written to William Henry Wills* (1912), p. 173; in both cases without the postscript and without indicating the omission. See Annette B. Hopkins, "Dickens and Mrs Gaskell", *Huntington Library Quarterly*, vol. 9, no. 4, August, 1946, p. 376, fn. 33.

‡ At present I can go no further than to suggest this as a line of inquiry. J. C.

Latin lesson. 'It is my pleasure that you should learn Latin,' said Mr Fairchild, and 'I stand in the place of God to you whilst you are a child.'[25] It was not until the third decade of the nineteenth century (when Mr Fairchild and his ways were still going strong) that any concerted challenge was offered by dissenting opinion in the press to the long-prevailing postulate that without the rod 'not a single scholar was ever made'.[26]

Unrestricted licence to whip, invested as inevitably sometimes it was, in callous or vicious hands, could generate fear in the weak and hatred in the strong, the effects of which might outlast the physical scars which occasioned them. The unknown author of a seventeenth-century protest, *The Children's Petition*, alludes to innocent children 'being brought many times to their wit's ends; and ready to make away with themselves rather than endure the iteration of these torments, whereof they can see no reason, and wherein they can hope no ends. . .'.[27]

A fifteen-year-old Etonian, Pierce Taylor, writing home to his mother, near the time of the 1768 rebellion against the hated Dr Foster, reports:

> He [Foster] called up several boys to repeat their Homer, a thing unprecedented, and if a boy missed a word I will not say he whipped them, but he butchered them, he cut one of the boys so who was with me that he was quite raw, and he had got his lessons as well as he could I am certain. . . .[28]

But towards the end of the eighteenth and the beginning of the nineteenth centuries, a moderating change did occur.

Without exterior legislation or interior decree, the number of strokes inflicted at one time upon an offender became in practice limited, by custom and public opinion, if not by formal regulation, to a maximum of twelve. This number, or less, could be in effect a painful chastisement, as it was meant to be, yet not more than a normally robust boy could suffer safely and without any ill effects on his health. But the same number of strokes, administered with lenity, could produce an effect which not only was not dreaded by the subject, but, as we shall see, could result in consequences widely at variance with the object of the operation.

The diversity of factors affecting the proceedings made corporal punishment in practice a lottery. There was the difference in force used by one executioner and another. There was also the difference in the quality of the instruments. The traditional Winton rod at Winchester was a mere plaything compared to the birch at Rugby, in the opinion of Roundell Palmer, who had experience of both.[29] Then there were the differences in sensory reaction of the flogged, and the effects of habituation. Frederick Marryat, who is usually to be relied on over practical matters, compared his first 'taste of the birch' to dropping of molten lead; but later says he has no doubt that Eton boys will confirm that 'after a certain quantity of flagellation the skin becomes so hardened as to make the punishment almost a matter of indifference',[30] and indeed abundant confirmation is forthcoming. 'I acquired it [indifference to flogging] to such a degree,' says one witness, 'that I deemed the penalty so trivial that I henceforth enjoyed a delightful sense of freedom and independence.'[31] A summary flogging he received from his master for being discovered drunk 'just warmed my backside and I slept beautifully,' said H. Wheelwright in a newsy letter to his friend Henry Everard. 'The next [day] I jawed him and was flogged again. The other fellows were flogged. One was very impudent and got in 2 days 50 cuts in different floggings.'[32]

In the first three to four decades of the century, flogging in the public schools was part of a conventional charade, ritual comedy, with the headmaster, in the role of fierce and irascible Punchinello, struggling to subdue and chastise a multitude of obstreperous Harlequins. Henry Everard, on the eve of the holidays, sent home to his beloved brother, Sam, a jocular declension:

> Put him in the bill Genitive, kneel down on the block, Dative. Hold him tight, Accusative. Give me a birch, Vocative. Oh, it stings, Ablative. Never let me see you again. I think I know the singular number now and I will tell you the plural when we are drinking tea together.[33]

This was before the Victorian code of the 'stiff upper lip' had arrived to inhibit the free style of the players. Far from a dignified silence under punishment being *de rigueur*, the occupants of the block often vied to produce the loudest clamour to unnerve the executioner with their cries. One gang of junior desperados in the 1820s, known as the dervishes[34] and notoriously fearless of and impervious to the birch, used to raise piercing howls which could be heard in the High Street, merely to try to embarrass the Baffin. To gain distinction as a performer a touch of imagination was required. A boy who could imitate in his halooings on the block the braying of a donkey, the squeal of a pig, or the yelping of a puppy received loud applause from an audience of 'sporting coves'; and sometimes it would happen that Keate would turn and catch by the cuff some spectator whose uproarious enjoyment of the proceedings had made him rashly conspicuous, and order him to follow the last victim to the block.[35]

Executions were public, and attendance varied in size according to the reputation and standing of the condemned. When on one long-to-be-celebrated occasion the whole of the sixth and upper-fifth forms were indicted and convicted of passing off epigrams composed by only four of their number but used with small modifications by all, seventy-two senior boys went to the block. The library was crowded to capacity with excited viewers exulting to see their masters humbled and whipped. The floor was covered with victims, the tables and benches with spectators. It was an occasion of carnival, and the proceedings were treated as a joke by all, including, it appears, by Keate. Among those present was William Tucker. 'Flogging in that age,' he reminisced, eighty years later, 'seemed to have been considered a pleasant pastime . . .', and it was astonishing, says Wilkinson, 'how light were the nominal six cuts for a common school offence'.[36]

The collegiate authorities themselves cannot be said to have discouraged the piquant atmosphere of *opera bouffe* in which the enforcement of ritual discipline was conducted, when it sustained such holy rites as the presentation to the first boy flogged by a new headmaster of the instrument used and a dozen bottles of champagne. The latter part of the transaction had fallen into desuetude by the 1850s, but Bracebridge Hemyng alludes to a claim to the birch being successfully made about this time by a boy (whom he calls Chorley) who had the trophy 'suspended over his mantelpiece on the horns of a stag', and everyone in college came to admire 'Chorley's twigs'.[37] Even more persistent was the complementary ceremony of presentation to the headmaster (and lower master) by the captain of the school, upon the death of the provost, of a virgin birch rod, elegantly bound in light blue ribbon, and one bottle of champagne.[38]

Nourished at the springs of such exhilarating tradition, the lore of the birch flourished marvellously. Among the unnumbered anecdotes of this period is one concerning the prank played by a young peer upon Keate's successor, Charles Hawtrey. The boy, who was something of a gymnast, engaged a professional acrobat at Windsor fair to teach him his *pièce de résistance*, a high leap into the air from a stationary position. Once he had mastered the trick he waited until he next incurred the classic penalty and then issued pressing invitations to all his friends to attend the performance. At the appointed hour there was standing room only in the library. As the headmaster delivered the first stroke, the recipient rose in the air with the levitation of a grasshopper and landed several feet from the block. Instantly, Hawtrey was all solicitude. 'I beg your pardon, my lord. Touched some nerve, no doubt. Go home and be quiet. Better send for Mr Ellison.'[39] A few minutes later 'my lord' was celebrating on the river and receiving the congratulations of his friends.

The most thoughtful joker on record was the boy who, in expectation of a flogging, commissioned an artist to paint a likeness of the headmaster on the target area of his person. Thus when, at the *toilette des condamnés*, the shirt was lifted according to custom, the high executioner was confronted by a portrait of himself, greatly to his and his attendant officers' surprise. It was said at the time that, with the aid of two birches, the headmaster succeeded in obliterating all traces of the work of art.

But the climax of Etonian birch lore was the raid on the library carried out by a party of visiting Old Etonians, in 1838, and the abduction of the sacred object, the block, itself. The marauders were led by a former frequent occupant of the block, Lord Waterford ('that reckless boy, Waterford')[40] who had devised the aquatic follies of 1829.* Accompanied by his old cons, Lord Alford and James Heenage Jesse, Lord Waterford crept along the narrow stone ledge over the colonnade and entered upper school by an open window. We have the surprised victim's own account of the ensuing rape.

> One night when flogging o'er
> (I think 'twas fourth of June) wide ope'd the door
> A band of miscreants upon me tore
> Headed by one who used to feats of arms,
> And rows, and sprees, and all sorts of alarms
> And rebel deeds; who often at my shrine
> Had knelt unflinching to receive his nine
> Hard, unrepenting when deculloté
> Seemed made of stone when'er Keate flogged away.
> Headed by him they bore me from the room
> I hoped t'inhabit till the day of doom.[41]

The trophy was carried off in triumph to Waterford's seat at Curraghmore.

* See below, p. 215.

The new age, inquisitive and censorious, was bent on 'improvement', moral and economic; indeed, to the new men, the two were indivisible. When the nature of what was done at the public schools in the name of discipline was circulated in the outer world it caused a shock of disapproval which was quickly registered in periodicals. In the previous century Cowper had included the form of corporal punishment in use in his strictures on the public schools.

> The management of Tiroes of eighteen
> Is difficult, their punishment obscene.[42]

Nobody who mattered had taken the slightest notice. But now a new generation of social radicals, prudish, aggressive, contentious and disrespectful of tradition, was given a lead by the renegade Etonian, George Cornewall Lewis, in the *Edinburgh Review*.

'For all offences except the most trivial,' he informed his readers, 'every boy below the sixth form, whatever his age, is punished by flogging. This operation is performed on the naked back by the headmaster himself,' adding, as if the circumstance aggravated the offence, 'who is always a gentleman of great abilities and acquirements, and sometimes a high dignitary in the church.' Nothing, he asserted, 'but habit, which deadens the minds of honourable men to the impropriety and indecorum of the exhibition could have concealed from them the inexpediency of the mode of punishment itself'.[43] His tone was quickly adopted by writers in other journals of the progressive press. Greatly daring, the editor of the *Quarterly Journal of Education* footnoted, 'Those who know nothing of our public schools cannot well express their surprise when they hear for the first time the manner in which punishment is inflicted in these schools, and sometimes inflicted on boys of the age of seventeen and eighteen.' Having tiptoed demurely round the practice he concludes, 'It is difficult to say what custom will not reconcile us to; there can be no doubt that this indecent exposure, which would shock one not used to it, produces little or no effect where it prevails.'[44] The writer appears to be unaware that boys at public schools were familiar with the sight of each other's nudity, especially at Eton, where as late as 1859, and probably later, boys bathed naked at Cuckoo Weir and other public places.

The protests of outsiders to the birch were without effect upon the public schools themselves, but they circulated sufficiently to make a topic of morning conversation between the young Queen Victoria and her venerated Etonian guide and counsellor, Lord Melbourne. Melbourne said of his own tutor, 'I don't think he flogged me enough, it would have been better if he had flogged me more.' The queen entered in her Journal: 'I said flogging was so degrading; he said it was never thought so by the boys. I observed they did not like it. "Didn't like the pain of it" he replied.'[45]

This exchange was in the nature of a game. Melbourne's feelings on the subject were complex, and the queen was playing devil's advocate. She was herself in practice a strong approver of corporal punishment, and was to apply it in her own family more than Prince Albert, whose ideas of discipline were in sympathy with those of George Cornewall Lewis, approved. When, in 1839, she was hissed at Ascot and the chief offenders were identified as the Duchess of Montrose and Lady Sarah Ingestre, the queen's first reaction was to go scarlet and wish she might have them flogged.[46] Lord Melbourne, who would have liked nothing better than to perform in person his sovereign's wishes, no doubt explained to her that such summary measures were no longer practicable.

There was considerably more that could have been said by the opponents of flogging whom the queen had quoted, but the zeal of the reformers was, in practice, inhibited by prudery. Some suspected, others knew for certain, that flagellation could be a Paphian pleasure. (This was an aspect over which for centuries had been drawn a decorous veil. Unceasingly active, it was seldom alluded to.) A rare and early outburst of candour appears in the unique tract, *The Children's Petition*, and the anonymous author wonders that the subject is not brought up in parliament, 'where are so many gentlemen of excellent parts and ingenuous reflections, and why some of them are not so old as to forget what was unhandsome' at school. Yet nothing is said, nothing revealed, and so, nothing corrected.

The occasion of beating, the author asserts, is not the pretext made, but 'an unquenchable fire in the appetite of the master'. Why, he asks, is the boy or girl 'retired from their fellows, and why so long a preachment made over the[m] bare in a corner'.[47]

The writer could hardly have put the case more explicitly; but his argument was quietly consigned to oblivion. The pattern was already familiar. After Udall, the notorious Eton flogger, had been convicted of paederastic offences against boys in his charge, this record did not prevent his becoming, later, having served a term of imprisonment, not only a successful literary pundit, but headmaster of Westminster School.

The reticence our seventeenth-century moralist deplored became a prevalent convention. It was seldom broken, and the rare instances were smothered in silence and quickly buried. Indeed, almost the only open allusion occurred when pedagogues fell out. Bagshawe, Busby's assistant at Westminster, rebutting one of the charges made against him 'that he strangely delighted in whipping', protested that Busby 'seemed to take it ill that I did not use the rod often enough'. Counterattacking his accuser, such kind of punishment, he declared, was fit neither for him to inflict nor for any scholars to suffer, and he returned to the charge against Busby's own nephew, 'a worthless and Infamous person ... John Busby by name ... who did abuse the Liberty of whipping to such an excess and Extravagance of severity that I do grieve for the practice, but I blush to think of the cause of it and I do in behalf of the school much wonder that the thing being so Notorious was neither complained of nor thought fit to be reformed'.[48]

Satires on the figure of the birch-addicted pedagogue were not lacking, but they were kept very dark and they changed nothing. Perhaps the most brutally explicit is the *Rodiad*, which is pseudo-satire, in fact pornography:

> Oh, how that comes too late and goes too soon
> My day's delight – my flogging hour at noon.[49]

It was slyly ascribed by its real author to George Colman (mis-spelt Coleman), who had incurred much odium by his repressive and corrupt conduct as a censor of plays,* but who also, it was hinted elsewhere, was interested from an early age in flagellation.†

---

* Colman the younger was, said Joseph Knight in the *DNB*, 'disorderly, if not profligate in his writing and in his life', and 'himself the author of some of the least decent publications of his day, he shewed himself squeamish beyond precedent in the task of censor, his proceedings being at once tyrannical, futile and rapacious'.

† The Rev. William Lucas Collins recounts an anecdote of Colman, when a boy at Westminster, misunderstanding the intimation that, if the Duchess of Kingston were convicted of bigamy, she might be subject to corporal punishment. The penalty, which was in fact remitted on the lady's pleading the rights of a peeress, was a relic of more savage days, and would have entailed a symbolic branding on the thumb with a cooling iron. But, says Collins, 'Colman and his friend who attended the trial, could only conceive of corporal punishment in the form inflicted by Drs Vincent and Smith at Westminster, and much relished in anticipation the spectacle of a peeress being treated after this fashion, and great was their disappointment on discovering their error.' By introducing the allusion to punishment as inflicted by Vincent and Smith at Westminster Collins gives a sly twist to the anecdote which is not present in Colman's own, original version.[50] It is, like the deliberate misascription of the authorship of the *Rodiad* to Colman, an indication of what was thought of him.

Scabrous writing like the *Rodiad* was, of course, clandestine, but evidence of the cult was breaking through on the surface of 'respectable' publications for those capable of interpreting it.* The following passage introduces a tremulous rhapsody which was printed in the prim *British Annals of Education*.

> I know no method of inflicting pain so excellent . . . for when you take a rod of suitable size and flagellate the skin, even with some degree of severity, you may not only avoid all danger of injury to any vital organ whatever, but you run no risk of stupifying him. Indeed his sensibility increases rather than diminishes so long as you continue to inflict the blows.[51]

One of those who could interpret the evidence in such a way – exasperating to the censorious – as further to inform the informed without breaching the innocence of the innocent, was Thackeray. He describes dining with three gentlemen who had been at Eton under Keate and who regaled him and each other for an hour with reminiscences and 'lively imitations' of their floggings; 'the very *hwish* of the rods were parodied with thrilling fidelity', the climax of the anecdotes being their account of the night when squad after squad of boys were called from their beds and whipped the whole night.† 'All these mature men laughed, prattled, rejoiced, and became young again, as they recounted their stories . . . indeed their talk greatly amused and diverted me, and I hope, and am quite ready, to hear all their jolly stories over again.'

There was no lack of willing witnesses like Thackeray's friends, a type sketched in fiction by Grenville Murray as the Rev. David Guy, Rector of Muchmore-cum-Pluribus in Berkshire, called 'Snipe' at Eton, and second in flagellation honours to none of his contempora-

---

* In 1870, a few years after the end of the period we are covering, a correspondence on corporal punishment began in the columns of the *Englishwoman's Domestic Magazine* and quickly gathered such momentum that it threatened to appropriate the whole periodical. The letters were subsequently published in a separate volume entitled *Supplemental Conversazione* (April–December 1870).

† An allusion to Keate's suppression of the last full-scale rebellion at Eton, in 1832. Keate, effectively using the tactics of *divide et impera*, summoned the delinquents who had shirked Absence, from their beds late at night, in small batches, so they could not combine in a common policy of resistance; flogging went on for several hours, the praeposter on duty being our friend Wilkinson, who stood by, supplying the Baffin with fresh birch for each operation. One of those invited with exquisite courtesy by his tutor to leave his bed for a late-night interview with the headmaster, recorded that after his flogging, being now 'wide awake' and 'at liberty', he adjourned to a neighbouring Dame's house, and in the room of a friend enjoyed a convivial supper.[52]

ries excepting Mr (afterwards the Duke of) Beresford. 'After dinner, over a glass of fine old Madeira, when the ladies had retired, he loved to recount the story of his floggings.'[53]

Old Boys revisiting school who felt satisfaction even looking 'on the old flogging block'[54] – 'What would they give for a real live flogging to convince them that it was a dream they were indulging'[55] – had no need to long. Renewals could be arranged. After being carried off by Lord Waterford, the Eton block was not consigned to an obscure corner of Curraghmore and forgotten as a superannuated relic. It was no part of the abductors' intentions to retire their trophy from active service. At ceremonial dinners of The Block Club it occupied the place of honour in the centre of the table; after dinner it became the scene of rites congruent with its office. Gentlemen, finding that they missed the accustomed give and take of flagellation might, without necessarily always going to a Waterford's length of stealing an endeared block, import the rod as a tonic auxiliary to Eros into the bedrooms and boudoirs of wives and mistresses, or resort to it in the confidential establishments run by ladies specializing in the cult.* Lord Abingdon used to hold parties at which he impersonated Keate and his performances at the block; guests participated in the roles of culprits and holders down. Descriptions of some of the voluntary activities suggest that they may have sometimes been more rigorous than the overtly punitive executions at school.[57] In Hornby's time flogging at Eton was said to have become 'a farce',[58] sustained only by the demand of boys and masters alike.

Boys were keenly aware of the element of secret – or manifest – pleasure in the performances of certain masters and boys. It was commonly believed at Rugby that James 'delighted in it';[59] and E. C. Austen Leigh, a subsequent lower master (nicknamed The Flea) at Eton, was openly known as 'a jolly old sadist, naked and

---

* Among the more fashionable practitioners were Mrs Collet of Tavistock Court, Covent Garden, and later of Portland Place and Bedford Street, Russell Square, who had royal and court connections; her niece and successor, Mrs Mitchell, of 22 (afterwards 44) Waterloo Road and then of St Mary's Square, Kensington; Mrs James (a former maid of Lord Clanricarde) of 7 Carlisle Street, Soho; Mrs Emma Lee (real name Richardson) of 50 Margaret Street, off Regent Street; Mrs Phillips, of 11 Upper Belgrave Place; Mrs Shepherd, of 25 Gilbert Street. Perhaps the most notorious of all were Sarah Potter and Theresa Berkley, of 28 Charlotte Street, the latter because she gave her name to the useful apparatus, The Berkley Horse, so designed that a 'rider' mounted upon it was accessible simultaneously, fore and aft. Even the names of some of her principal fair assistants have survived.[56]

unashamed'.* One boy, indifferent or addicted, hired himself out as a whipping boy at 6d a stroke.[61] The understanding prevalent was revealed, probably in innocence, by an intelligent and articulate boy, George Lyttelton, when he was about to receive his first flogging. He says, 'To this flogging I looked forward with a certain degree of pleasurable anticipation.'[62] It does not matter that Lyttelton discovered that the experience was not for him a pleasurable one. He was transmitting the message he had received from those who had become addicted, and recording his expectations.

A first experience which begins by being equivocal is described by 'Charley Norton' (or rather, the Rev. C. F. Johnston), the narrator of the autobiographical *Recollections of an Etonian* (1870). The exact date is not stated, but the author was at school in 1859, and the headmaster would have been Goodford. The age of reticence and the 'stiff upper lip' had now penetrated even into Eton, and not only the headmaster, but the condemned also, comported themselves with as much dignity and decorum as the circumstances permitted:

> I loosened my breeches, and biting my lips tight, knelt down on the block. I was resolved that at all events no cry should escape me, and for the sake of my own glory among my schoolfellows, intended to suffer as a hero. But the difficulty of repressing my feelings I found to be in reality by no means so hard as I had anticipated. The first cut, indeed, stung me a little, and I felt at that moment almost as if I was being lashed with a nettle; but after this the sensation seemed deadened and the rest of them felt comparatively harmless. Even before the six were completed, I had made up my mind that there was nothing very terrible in being flogged, nor were my ideas altered by the tingling sensation felt afterwards. . . .[63]

The boy then adjourned to the room of one of his friends to discuss at leisure the enthralling subject of flogging.

How many people from the public schools and others were concerned with what a recorder of nineteenth-century sexual life called 'the propensity which the English most cherish',[64] it is not

---

* Wingfield Stratford describes how, when Austen Leigh flogged, there was a large concourse of appreciative boys enjoying the performance outside the window of the execution chamber, who 'roared with delight' at the sounds of infliction. ' . . . hardly had the last of the strokes been recorded when the door was flung open and the Flea himself appeared, birch in hand, in a state of pleasurable excitement, to make a short waddling rush at the now almost riotous crowd that stampeded in all directions – this last item providing a highly appreciated finale to the entertainment'.[60]

possible to calculate; but at least enough to generate the extensive underground literature of flagellation.*

The abolitionists, although vehement in expression, were wary in pursuing their quarry into the perilous regions of sensual ambiguity, and preferred to base their objections on the grounds of the indecency of the operation, and the barbarity and ineffectiveness of its consequences. They feared the subversive effects of bringing into disrepute honourable and innocent members of an important profession, and the possibility of the accusers themselves being damagingly implicated in scandal of their own raising. When *Punch* directed its indignation at the traditional defender of birch discipline, it presented the issue as one of common sense and decency.

> Is he not plainly incorrigible. If he were not we would recommend him to get himself corrected by submitting once more to the degrading infliction which he advocates with such gusto and the idea of which is so disgusting to everybody else that can be disgusted by anything.[65]

No one could have inferred from that style of blunt sarcasm that the most vexing obstacle to the abolitionists' good intentions was the number of people who found 'the idea' of 'degrading infliction' the very opposite of 'disgusting'. 'To touch a single twig of the hallowed birch is regarded as a kind of sacrilege,' said Sir Leslie Stephen warily, at a later date. 'From the moment the accolade has been laid – not across your shoulders – you are a member of a sort of strange order of Chivalry.'[66] This was as far as he was prepared to venture along a path, the end of which lay out of bounds

The defenders of the old discipline tended to treat reformers as impractical and muddled cranks, 'rosewater reformers who would substitute moral suasion for the birch'[67] and who schemed to discredit a system of discipline, venerable, satisfying and convenient in its simplicity without being able to substitute anything else that worked. Flogging, 'indecorous and unseemly' as it might appear, was 'absolutely necessary' and the best means that could be devised for 'the

---

* Among the many books in this class published during, and shortly after, the period we cover, are the following (dates withheld when they are uncertain): *The Terrors of the Rod*, from *Donum Amicus*, Frances Newbury (1818); *The Merry Order of St Bridgit*; *Madam Birchini's Dance*; *Mysteries of Flagellation*; *The Romance of Chastisement, or Revelations of School and Bedroom* (1870); *Sublime of Flagellation*; *Quintessence of Birch Discipline* (1870); *Seduction of Sontag* (Dugdale, 1860); *Exhibition of Female Flagellants* (republished by J. C. Hotten, 1872); *Experimental Lecture* by Colonel Spanker (1836); *History of the Rod*; *Curiosities of Flagellation*, vol. 1 (1875); *The Yellow Room*; *Fashionable Lectures Composed and Delivered with Birch Discipline by Certain Beautiful Ladies.*

prevention of delinquencies in boys of honourable and intelligent mind'.[68] Thus, notwithstanding an air of belligerent candour, the parties showed, for different reasons, a common interest in suppressing part of the truth, and were engaged in a conspiracy of disregard.

Incipient scandals were usually smothered or disguised, and in the first half of the century few people of importance whose opinions exercised influence wished the subject managed otherwise.

Nevertheless, occasionally scandal did break loose and reach public attention before it could be extinguished. In 1815 Lieutenant-General Sir Eyre Coote, a distinguished military commander, a Knight of the Bath and Member of Parliament, former aide-de-camp to the Prince Regent, was discovered by a 'nurse' of Christ's Hospital in the company of boys and in circumstances which aroused in her suspicion that he had been behaving 'very improperly and very indecently'. A lively exchange at once took place between them of which she gave her own account:

> I . . . saw a gentleman uncovered as low as his knees from his breeches – was closing his trousers – I asked him what he was doing there – no harm, I assure you upon my honour – no harm, he repeated – I said that cannot be, sir, I will have the Beadle – Don't have the Beadle, he said – Again he repeated, I am doing no harm, upon my honour – I was only flogging those boys – I said I am a mother, and I will have a Beadle, fetch me a Beadle – I am also a father, he said – worse and worse, I said – do let me go, you don't know who I am, nor what I am – I said who you are I do not care, but what you are I plainly see. . . .

At Polly Robinson's insistence the general, though unknown as such, was conveyed by beadles to the compter, where he refused to give his name. Subsequently he appeared at the Mansion House before the Lord Mayor and Mr Corp, President and Chief Clerk of Christ's Hospital. If Polly Robinson had expected her zeal to be welcomed she was soon undeceived. It is doubtful which of those present, the accused, the judge, or the President of Christ's Hospital, was the more embarrassed. The latter, who might have been mistaken for defending counsel, declared after 'scrupulous examination' of the evidence that the accused had solicited boys to flog and be flogged by him and had paid them at the rate of one and sixpence to two shillings for six strokes at a time, that 'nothing could be traced beyond an act of unguarded folly'.[69]

Unfortunately for all concerned, 'insinuations of a most disgraceful nature' began to circulate, and the commander-in-chief of the army, the king's brother, His Royal Highness Field Marshal the Duke of York, felt constrained by pressure to convene a court of inquiry, composed of a lieutenant-general and two major-generals, to examine and report on the evidence. A formal comedy of feigned mystification was then enacted, everyone from the commander-in-chief downwards seeming not to understand the significance of the bizarre practices described, although the prince regent himself, certainly, and possibly those acting in the judicial charade, resorted to Mrs Collet's establishment in Tavistock Street, Covent Garden, and others like it, to engage in flagellation parties with her young ladies.[70] Wellwishers were torn between alternative presentations of the general as an innocent man cruelly wronged, and as a brave soldier sadly deranged in mind due to the many taxing ordeals he had undergone in the service of his country.

Polly Robinson had learnt a lesson and, perhaps on instructions, moderated her testimony before the military commission. 'My agitation was so great I do not reckon myself a competent judge.'[71] But prudence required a public gesture of rebuke to be seen, and Sir Eyre Coote, having been acquitted by a civil court, was nevertheless deprived of his military rank through extraordinary exercise of the prerogative of the Crown, by his old friend and brother flagellant, the Prince Regent.

Much of what happened remains buried and hidden, as it was meant to do. It was an age of reticence (and would become increasingly so) concerning the private lives of the eminent. But what had been disclosed tends to support the affirmation of Henry Spencer Ashbee in 1879: 'The secret sexual propensity which the English most cherish is undoubtedly flagellation.' He goes on, 'This is a fact, and did not discretion forbid it would be easy to name men in the highest position in diplomacy, literature, the army, etc. who at the present day, indulge in this idiosyncracy, and to point out the haunts they frequent.'[72]

It was not until a century later that Philip Ziegler's research into the Panshanger MSS. revealed that Melbourne was an obsessive flagellant[73] and that at least two of the women in his life, Lady Brandon and Caroline Norton, were implicated in his practices. How he must have relished his own joke when he said with mock gravity to Queen Victoria that 'flogging had an amazing effect'[74] on him. We learnt from the publication of the *Gladstone Diaries* that Gladstone scourged himself and recorded at least some of the occasions by entering a flagella symbol in his diary. Flagellation was not an uncommon discipline for High Church pietists to use at this time in imitation of early church practice, for the mortification of the flesh. Newman scourged himself (with a somewhat brutal instrument, perhaps to be on the safe side).[75]

Apprehension of the dangerous consequences of disclosure was a powerful deterrent. Men who disobeyed the code might be destroyed by it.* Yet here and there a maverick did appear who seemed able to break the rules with impunity. The one in our field of vision and perhaps the most stubborn iconoclast to be bred in a public school was, to Eton's chagrin, an Etonian and, *horribile dictu*, a former assistant master at Eton. His school life falls just within the end of the period we cover; but his adult activities cannot be overlooked, for he was backward- as well as forward-looking. Henry Salt was a walking, talking and writing incongruity. A Colleger and Kingsman with a good academic record at Eton (where he was up to William Johnson), and at Cambridge, a more than respectable classicist, a gentleman, and a good and conscientious tutor, he had translated Virgil and Lucretius, pursuits of unexceptional propriety; but he was also a socialist, an agnostic, an anti-blood-sports agitator, an anti-corporal-punishment activist, and – most repugnant of all – a vegetarian. It was difficult to dislike Henry Salt for the sake of his offensive opinions because he was honest and utterly sincere, true to his principles, unselfish and without vanity. How he exasperated Eton! If he had been an outsider he could have been ignored. But he wasn't an outsider, and he waged a lone crusade without malice but without compromise against most of the images which Eton held dear, saying aloud and publishing what other men might say privately, in safe company (like Thackeray), or not at all.

Salt asked awkward questions, volunteered awkward answers, and passed unseasonable and less than respectful observations upon sacred subjects like Christianity, cricket, riding to hounds and the use of the 'morally edifying' and 'wholesome birch', in the face of 'the well known fact that the instrument of discipline has associations which are something worse than unwholesome'.[76] The disclosure of

---

* Grenville Murray was hounded out of English society for his satire in the *Queen's Messenger* on Lord Carrington's record as a banker. William Stead and Henry Vizetelly both served terms of imprisonment when imprisonment was a condition incomparably harsher than it is today and when it carried the additional and subsequent penalty of social ostracism. Their crimes were publication of matter repugnant to orthodox opinion – one, factual information, the other, a novel by Zola.

such flagitious particulars was proscribed in mid-Victorian society, and it is a measure of the innate virtue of Salt (while it reflects credit on Eton too) that he was not hounded out of Eton. Perhaps it was felt that he deserved pity rather than censure, and had already been punished sufficiently by fate, for he had married the daughter of the most conservative of Etonian tutors, a lady half German and wholly Lesbian, who refused to consummate their marriage, but was prone to infatuation with a succession of female psychopaths, some of them dangerous, like Mrs Frances Adams, who boasted that she had helped to kill her own husband, and seemed to be hoping for further employment of a similar nature.[77]

Salt cannot be ignored now, because he was, both in his aims and prejudices, generations in advance of his times. Most of the causes which he espoused are today tame platitudes, obediently worshipped by multitudes in response to the stimulants of envy and the dreadful spectre which cannot be laid, inequality. In his own time he was treated as another, rarer kind of eccentric, almost as a harmless, resident madman of a small community. His one triumph in his battle against the birch was when he refused to have a boy flogged at the express demand of the boy's mother, who said she had *sent her son to Eton to be flogged*. The exchanges were all very gentlemanly. Salt even described the much-flogging Austin Leigh, whose tastes he could not have approved of, as 'a thoroughly upright and kindhearted man'.[78]

Outside Eton he was not supported by the avowed opponents of corporal punishment because few of them were willing to follow him into the more scandalous areas of objection which he indicated. Parents also, even when they had grounds for complaint, were seldom willing to make their sons conspicuous before the latter went to public school, and within the public schools themselves the code of reticence made open controversy a rare event.

But sometimes personal interest and indignation overcame customs of reserve. The Platt–Stewart dispute at Harrow was one such occasion. This was good, clean sport all the family could enjoy. There was no hint of prurient undertones, but simply strong human conflict in a setting of privilege. In November 1853 Platt, a monitor at Harrow, punished Randolph Stewart, a boy in the fifth form and a son of the Earl of Galloway, for insults on the football field by a 'whoping'. This was the most serious and severe punishment given by a monitor and on this occasion Platt used a cane which was more than an inch in diameter, considerably thicker and heavier than the monitorial cane normally in use. He administered thirty-one cuts 'as hard as ever he could' across Stewart's shoulder blades. Stewart gave no indication by the slightest sound or movement of the pain he was suffering, but after he left the room he was escorted in a near-fainting condition to the school doctor who was shocked by the state of his back and, after putting him under treatment in the sick room, called on the headmaster and presented a report on Stewart's injuries and the acts which had caused them, of so serious a character that Vaughan summoned Platt and told him that in the light of the evidence of excessive and cruel punishment he must demote him by six places in the school, which deprived him of monitorial status.

Naturally both boys wrote to their parents; the parents wrote to the headmaster, Lord Galloway expressing grave concern over a system which permitted abuse potentially productive of permanent injury, physical and mental, to a young and sensitive victim:

> The spirit of the times in which we live has, in this country, not only done away with excessive corporal punishment, but in the army and navy it has placed restraints on officers in the exercise of their authority. It appears to me that, if this kind of monitorial authority be needful for the discipline of a public school it ought also to be under some guards against the abuse of it by boys of tyrannical disposition. . . . I would urge on your consideration, as the head of a great establishment during the ensuing vacation, whether there must not be something faulty in a system under which such enormities can be perpetrated?

Mr Baron Platt also wrote to Dr Vaughan, and protested that his son had only done his duty in the office to which he had been appointed, and was now being made the victim of an artificially induced scandal, for

> . . . until the contumacious boy [Stewart] smarting with resentment and the mortification of wounded pride, had walked to the doctor, shown him his bruises, and obtained the doctor's formidable prognostication of prolonged injury (which however does not seem likely to be realised), they [the other monitors] did not consider the proper limit had been exceeded. The facts as they now stand convince me that my son's conduct was unexceptionable. May I, therefore, implore you to reconsider the matter, for the sake of his family, for the sake of Harrow, and, with sincere respect I add, for the sake of yourself.

There was a scarcely veiled threat of publicity in those last lines, and the Platt supporters, finding themselves met by a regretful but firm confirmation from Vaughan of his decision to demote Platt, took the drastic course of breaking the unwritten law of privacy, and publishing their correspondence, which meant, in effect, bringing the controversy into the public domain and making an appeal to popular opinion. Lord Galloway and his party then judged that they could not allow these misrepresentations to stand without rebuttal, and published their edition of the correspondence with their version of the facts. The whole scandal burst out into the open with the press in full cry, in pursuit of a rare and favourite quarry, indiscretions from a public school, and every member of the public who chose free to join in the sport. The hostile exchanges between the two parents, delivered in stately broadsides of measured prose, became public property, as did the unconscious parodies of adult rhetoric in the stilted correspondence addressed by the boys to their fathers and to each other,* now printed and circulated like a commercial magazine to entertain the vulgar.

The opportunity to make the Platt–Stewart case a rod to beat the public schools was not missed by the normally frustrated enemies of the system, and the commotion they raised was such that the Prime Minister, Lord Palmerston, a loyal Old Harrovian, wrote to seek reassurance from Dr Vaughan. In reply the headmaster of Harrow broke his silence, and addressed (probably by arrangement with Palmerston) an open letter to the prime minister putting the case for monitorial authority and the fagging system. It is probably the most lucid and authoritative argument made in justification of the method of government then operant at Harrow and, with local variations, at the other public schools, and did much to reassure the worried, and strengthen morale in the faithful.

Having once decided to break his silence, Dr Vaughan produced a statement which was strikingly candid and unevasive. He began by stating that the authority of senior boys 'is the universal rule in Public Schools, the distinguishing feature of Public as contrasted with Private Schools'. If he were to consult his own ease and present popularity he would abolish that power forthwith for, he conceded, 'the tide of public opinion is setting strongly in that direction. Corporal punishment of *any* kind by whomsoever administered is inconsistent with modern notions of personal dignity and modern habits of precocious manliness.' It needed, he was aware, only a few

---

* In a published letter addressed to his father Platt denounced their adversaries' employment of 'Paley's infidel doctrine of Expediency'.

cases of excess to direct against the practice a storm 'too violent to be resisted'. Yet he still affirmed with confidence that the system was 'capable of great good and impossible to replace by any efficacious substitute'. He quoted the opinion of his own headmaster, Thomas Arnold, on the objections to corporal punishment which were already, in the 1830s, being canvassed with fervour and indignation. 'I well know what feeling this is the expression of; it originates in that proud notion of personal independence which is neither reasonable nor Christian, but essentially barbarian. It visited Europe in former times with all the curses of the age of chivalry and is threatening us now with those of Jacobinism.'[79] Reverting to his own less dramatic, but not less persuasive, tone, Vaughan said that there were 'in every Public School, minor offences against manners rather than morals – faults of turbulence, rudeness, offensive language, annoyance of others, petty oppressiveness and tyranny' which lay outside the cognizance of the masters. There were even graver faults which might long escape the eye of a really vigilant master. How were such perpetual problems to be engaged? There was the foreign schools' and private schools' method. 'You may create a body of ushers, masters of a lower order whose business it shall be to follow boys into their hours of recreation and rest avowedly as spies, coercing freedom of speech and action, and reporting to their superiors what such observation has gleaned.' This policy was consistent and intelligible, but 'ruinous to that which has been regarded as the great glory of an English public school – its free development of character, its social expansiveness, in short its *liberty*'. Alternatively ten or twenty or thirty of those boys who were, generally speaking, 'the elder, at all events the abler, the more diligent, the more meritorious, and on more intimate terms than the rest with the master' and 'largely influenced . . . by his principles of judgement and discipline' who '. . . might be invested with authority to act as the eyes and ears of the headmaster in the interests of justice and order'.

But no real *power* would be entrusted to this élite, no power to enforce obedience. Such a system, Vaughan asserted, would be 'nugatory or worse'. The headmaster's elect would be treated not with the respect due to authority, but with hatred and contempt, as spies and informers, the headmaster's creatures. No boy with the ordinary feelings of the son of a gentleman would accept such an office.

But in the monitorial system in force at Harrow, monitors, said Vaughan, while independent and free in the ordinary exercise of their authority, knew that authority emanated from the authority of the headmaster and that in their decisions and acts they were responsible to the headmaster. Thus, in practice, only the gravest moral offences were referred to the headmaster, and in the monitorial system a social discipline was provided acceptable to a community of boys. There was degradation in submitting to the kicks and cuffs of an equal or inferior – none in rendering to a constituted authority 'that submission even to personal correction which may be one of the conditions of the society in which you are placed'. In this system the monitor must feel he could depend on the support of the headmaster, 'providing he stops short of inflicting injury', and parents who send their son to a public school know that 'he will be subjected to discipline *as established*'.[80]

Vaughan's letter calmed and reconciled many interested parents and friends of Harrow and other public schools who had been disturbed by the Platt–Stewart scandal, and it confirmed the impression Vaughan had already made in public life as an administrator – calm, firm and tactful, a natural choice for future high office in the Church. It did not, of course, convert the committed anti-public-school and the anti-corporal-punishment faction, nor did it satisfy their diametrical opponents, Harrovian fundamentalists, who resented Vaughan's importation of a degree of Arnoldian accountability by the monitors to the headmaster, and canvassed for the restoration of full independence for monitorial authority.[81] But the latter was an unrealistic expectation, at variance with the prevailing tide of deontology, and Vaughan was, above all, realistic. Despite his eloquent justification of the system, and his affirmation of faith that 'ten young men, acting under such responsibilities, are not likely to come to an unjust decision or exercise their sentence with undue severity', as soon as agitation had died down and tension was eased, he introduced new measures redefining and restricting the authority of the monitors by more precise regulations. Not more than ten strokes were to be administered to any one culprit sentenced to punishment, and the upper fifth were exempted altogether from corporal punishment by the monitors. In the Vaughan Library at Harrow School I discovered a fragment of irreverent doggerel vamped together by a jubilant hand:

> And though we write in Magazines
>   things to show
> That we act the best for other boys
> Which they themselves can't do

And though we ask repeatedly
Is't not a noble thing
For little boys to fag for us
Like Slaves to tyrant Kings?

And is it not a noble thing
That we should wield a cane
To knock about the little boys
And make them feel the pain

Of being in so low a form
When they should be very high?
Yet people won't believe all this
But say 'it's all my eye'.

Yea all these degradations
Stir up our inmost marrow
But, still our characters we give
A sacrifice to Harrow.*

The Platt–Stewart affair was the first scandal of an abuse of boys' self-government in a public school to explode on a national scale. Part of the charge which Lord Galloway and, even more, Dr Vaughan, had not wished detonated, had been the growth of popular emotive objection from outside the schools to the traditional use of corporal punishment to enforce discipline. The restraints introduced by Vaughan must have moderated the practice at Harrow, yet G. H. Rendell, who became captain of the school during the decade which followed Vaughan's amendments, remembered the boys in office in his time as 'strenuous and ruthless' disciplinarians.[82]

How little and slowly customs were allowed to change by the resistance of the boys themselves may be judged by the fact that the second major public scandal of excessive punishment of one boy by another occurred exactly twenty years after the Platt–Stewart trouble and reproduced most of its main particulars, even to the number of strokes, thirty, which were inflicted. This time the school was Winchester. In spite of the cautionary example of Harrow twenty years previously, there was still, in 1872, no limit to the number of strokes a praefect might inflict at 'tunding'.

The force of public opinion was sufficient to constrain the governing body of Winchester College to hold an official inquiry, the members

* Platt, in a published letter of 28 November addressed to his father, had volunteered to offer 'my character as a necessary sacrifice to the welfare of Harrow'.

of which, in the discharge of their 'difficult task', were exhorted by the press to approach it 'imbued entirely with *the spirit of the present age*'. The same newspaper, *The Globe*, indicated the kind of result it expected by declaring, 'No one who has not witnessed it could believe it possible that anything so odious, demoralising and brutal [as tunding] could exist in these days.'[83]

But the governing body, while ready to reprobate 'excess' and suggest ways of discouraging its commission, had no intention of passing sentence of condemnation on Winchester and the public-school system. 'With respect to the principle' of prefect rule, they said in their report, a record of which is preserved in Winchester College library, 'we do not hesitate to express our conviction that it has borne excellent fruit' and 'assisted to create and keep alive a high and sound tone of feeling and opinion, has promoted independence and manliness of character and has rendered possible that combination of simple liberty with order and discipline which is among the best characteristics of our great English Schools'.

If the urbanity of the report's prose has a familiar cast this may be because one of the governors sitting on the board of inquiry was Dr Vaughan and, being the man he was, he would have had an influential hand in drafting the report. The result, which left frustrated protesters still fuming in the press, nevertheless demonstrated that the schools did change, but they changed from within. Boys' self-government persisted because men who had experienced it as boys emerged with a predominantly favourable impression of the system.

Apostles of the gospel of human dignity might agitate with a ferocious fervour (equalled only by adversaries of blood sports) for the abolition of corporal punishment, but Eton cheerfully flogged on. In its own time and its own way, it registered modifications of response to internal change. Gradually flogging ceased to be a literally public entertainment. From crowding into the library to witness the fun, intending spectators had to view or hear the proceedings from outside the door. Then, from about the 1860s, the door was shut and execution became a private event (though not yet in lower school), to be glimpsed only at their peril through a keyhole by the boldest *voyeurs*.[84] The frequency of flogging abated spontaneously without design or decree to this end. In Hornby's time the amount of flogging was less than it had been in Goodford's and Hawtrey's, and much less than in Keate's days. By 1847 the Old Etonian lamenting that flogging no longer went on 'in the wholesale manner it used to do'[85] was a familiar, almost a stock figure, in an Etonian chronicler's repertoire of types. In the second half of the century modern mid-Victorian gentlemen became rather more coy and reserved in their allusions to the details of the operation than their predecessors had been or, at least, less prodigal in recounting autobiographical experiences of the block.

M. D. Hill writing, in his old age, of having acted as 'holder down' at the execution performed on his subsequent neighbour, Lt Col. B. C. Donaldson Hudson DSO, High Sheriff of Shropshire, remarks, 'I hope he will not resent this disclosure.'[86] Such a thought would not have crossed the mind of Thackeray's friends who had been at Eton in Keate's time. The tendency to a discreet reticence was the complement of the clandestine promotions which multiplied in number and grossness as the surface formality of respectable society became more strictly decorous.

The birch was an instrument revered, not only by those who administered, but by those who received it, the agent of mysterious sanctity in a ritual of initiation which qualified its graduates for admission to that 'strange order of chivalry'. 'To have been flogged,' observed Leslie Stephen, 'in accordance with traditions laid down from our antiquity . . . by Dr Keate or Dr Arnold was to receive an indelible hallmark, stamping the sufferer for ever as genuine metal.' He defied anybody once admitted to shake off the impression. 'By no effort of the imagination will he divest himself of a share of conscious superiority over his dearest friend who has not shared his disciplinary experiences.'[87]

The games of adult obliquity, like the pullulating, monotonous fantasies of Algernon Swinburne,[88] are too removed from the genesis to reflect school experience. The truth, writ small, but faithfully, is to be found in authentic school records. One entry, short, simple, to the point, yet more or less innocent, appears in the diary of a very intelligent schoolboy:

> *March 3* I was worked off* very gently by Chute for throwing a pellet in hall last Thursday. He said I was going to throw more. He could see it in my eye. It gives him a great deal of pleasure and does not do me much harm.[89]

The writer's name was Maynard Keynes.

---

* College term for *beaten*.

TWELVE

Higher Thoughts and Thomas Arnold

To the question, 'What name first comes to mind in connection with English public schools of the nineteenth century?' the majority of answers would probably be Arnold of Rugby. What Thomas Arnold is credited with having achieved is more variable in assessment. When, in 1827, at the age of thirty-two, he answered an advertisement in *The Times* inviting applications for the vacant headmastership of Rugby, his friend Edward Hawkins, Provost of Oriel College, Oxford, said in his testimonial that Arnold 'would change the face of education all through the Public schools of England'.[1] Many men had no doubt in his lifetime and after, that Arnold had fulfilled the achievement predicted. If we examine the changes which reformed the character of the English public schools in the course of the nineteenth century we shall find that they may be summarized as the broadening of the curriculum, with the displacement from supremacy of the classics, the promotion of the study of sciences, the introduction of compulsory, organized games, uniformity of dress, and stricter social discipline, with close moral surveillance of the boys by the masters.

To one of these objectives Arnold was opposed; to another he was indifferent. He had no wish to disturb the supremacy of the classics in the curriculum. Arnold was himself a classic, not a superlative one, but a classic, and he believed that 'The Greek and Roman languages' were the 'instruments' by which the human mind should be formed in youth. It is true he made some unflattering remarks on the practice of composing original Latin verse;[2] but that was because he had himself no talent for composing Latin verse; he wished the emphasis of study to rest upon prose writers, orators and philosophers. For science and its works – what today would be called technology – the railways and engineering, he expressed admiration and approval enough to qualify as a man of modern mind, but he would never admit science to be 'education'; it was 'only fit for earning a livelihood, of no educational significance as a preparative for power'[3] and he used guile to put obstacles in the way of its study at Rugby in 1835, when at the last moment he required boys wishing to attend science lectures of D. F. Walker to produce written permission from their parents or pay the fee of a guinea.[4]*

Arnold was not unorthodox for a man of his time in his evaluation of curricular studies. What made him different from others was the supreme importance he accorded in his stated order of values to a schoolmaster's duties other than cultivating the mind, and to qualities other than learning. In this he did anticipate the growth of emphasis on the formation of character (he would have said 'a cure of souls') as the prime objective of the teacher's vocation. 'Do you see those boys walking together; I never saw them before; you should make an especial point of observing the company they keep – nothing so tells the changes in a boy's character.'[6] The words are Arnold's, spoken to an assistant master, and they mark a change in profession if not in effect, an assumption of moral intervention as a schoolmaster's duty, which previously would have been despised by most – and would long continue to be despised by many – public-school masters as dishonourable prying, unworthy of a gentleman. Games, the means by which moral control was destined to be exercised over generations of boys to come, had neither interest nor value for Arnold.

He felt and sensed, rather than thought and calculated, the still imperfectly understood needs of rising middle classes and the social future they pre-figured. There were parents who desired an improved education for their sons, and with the advent of railways they were able to send them further afield with more expediency than ever before; these aspired to social status promoted by public-school associations; but at the same time they feared and reprobated what they considered the profanity, extravagance and frivolity, the lack of moral earnestness and religious zeal, ascribed to the very classes with which they supposed it was necessary for their sons to consort for social advancement. They wished *their* standards to supplant those of their social superiors. Arnold understood and responded to the need. He was by temperament a crusader, puritan and autocrat; by profession an evangelist, moralist and reformer, and thus in fervent

---

* Two years before his death he showed signs of a change of opinion with the words, 'I do really think that with boys and young men, it is not right to leave them in ignorance of the beginnings of physical science.'[5]

sympathy with the revivalist spirit in the low-church party in the Church of England, and even outside the Church, in Methodism.

In a sense, Arnold did change the face, if not of all the public schools, certainly of Rugby. For the face of Rugby seen by the outside world was the face of Arnold. To the great mass of the public Arnold *was* Rugby, and a very acceptable face he provided for the radicals in the middle classes striving to effect a redistribution of wealth and political power. Here was the headmaster of a public school who talked their own language with impatient eloquence, who desired all members of society to be property owners, who asserted the import-ance of classes coming together in sympathy, and reducing the gap between the ways of life immediately above and below the upper middle classes,[7] and who seemed ready and willing to castigate their adversaries' sacred cows. It was music in their ears to hear trumpeted from one of the bastions of 'privilege' the words, 'There is no earthly thing so mean and despicable in my mind than an English gentleman destitute of all sense of responsibility and opportunities and revelling in the luxuries of our high civilization and thinking himself a great person.'[8]

There were parents – Albert Pell's father was one – who would not have sent their sons to any public school but Rugby, and only to Rugby because Arnold was headmaster. Inevitably what recom-mended Arnold to one wing of the community, compromised him to another. There were parents with mixed feelings who sent their sons to Rugby in spite of Arnold, and those who refrained from sending theirs because of Arnold. 'Am I performing the part of a father,' asked 'John Bull', 'in exposing my son to the fascination of such a talent as Dr Arnold possesses, when I know he will be taught the language of heresy and be nurtured in the cradle of radical reform?'[9]

But in practice neither political wing would have found Arnold a satisfactory ally. His striking rhetorical utterances seldom expressed a stable conviction, but were an immediate emotional response to mood and circumstances, and they could vary like a weather vane. The same man who on one occasion denounced the 'evil' of 'excesses of aristocracy in our whole system, religious, political and social',[10] on another proclaimed the country's 'great means of blessing' to be 'the *Aristocracy* and the *Christian Church*'.[11] For when Arnold was not denouncing the delinquent aristocracy he was affirming that 'the world never saw a race of men better fitted to win' influence 'than the nobility and gentry of England, if roused from the carelessness of undisputed ascendancy'.[12] There was in fact nothing irreconcilable in these two attitudes, and he declared himself, 'No man wishes more earnestly to see them (the Aristocracy and the Church) reformed; and . . . no man would more deeply grieve to see them destroyed.'[13] But the erratic and tendentious shifts of emphasis in his rhetoric, and the extravagance of his emotion made an impression of inconstance and anomaly.

The same man who praised the study of law as 'glorious, transcending that of any earthly thing', also fulminated against 'the moral nastiness in which a lawyer lives and breathes'.[14]

Arnold was a 'star performer', his stage was the pulpit, his captive audience the boys, but he aimed to carry his influence far beyond the school by the publication of sermons, essays and articles in the press. An egoist tormented by a will which craved to impose itself remedially, as he supposed, upon others, 'His hand was against everyone,' said Edward Churton, 'and utterly without reverence for what was time honoured.'[15] To Arnold this painful process was 'love', for 'My love of any place or person, or institution, is exactly the measure of my desire to reform them.'[16] In unguarded moments of exhilaration he betrayed the true nature of his feelings and view of himself. 'The work here . . . I like it better and better; because it has all the interest of a great game of chess, with living creatures for pawns. . . .'[17]

There was always an air of dispatch and urgency about Arnold, but usually more seemed to be happening than in fact was taking place. Due to his 'star' quality, boys susceptible to it received more of personality than meaning, and when his pronouncements were not fraught with unintended contradictions his actions might contradict his pronouncements. When he spoke of what should be, ideally, he made it sound as though it was a practical policy in force, whereas in practice he might be travelling ruthlessly in an alien direction.

'Mere intellect and acuteness,' he said, in one of several much publicized statements to the same effect, 'divested as it is, in too many cases, of all that is comprehensive and great and good, is to me more revolting than the helpless imbecility, seeming to be almost like the spirit of Mephistopheles.'[18] On many other occasions he affirmed with emphasis and dramatic simile that the generation of his scholars to which he looked back with the greatest pleasure was not that which contained the most instances of individual talent, but that which worked steadily. He was, he declared, unfeignedly delighted by the university honours obtained by pupils, but he never laid stress upon them and 'strongly deprecated any system which would encourage the notion of their being the chief end to be answered by school education'. 'A mere plodding boy,' Stanley tells us, 'was above all others encouraged by him', and he rejoiced 'when an inferiority of natural powers' had been 'truly and zealously cultivated', for, in Arnold's own words, 'It is the effort a hundred times more than the issue of the effort, that is in my judgement a credit to the school.' Knowledge (especially scientific knowledge) without godliness was devilish.[19] 'Rather than have it the principal thing in my son's mind, I would gladly have him think that the sun went round the earth and the stars were so many spangles set in the bright blue firmament.'[20]

It would be reasonable to infer from such emphatic iterations of principle that an honest, willing boy, a little short on intellectual endowment, would receive more patient and sympathetic encouragement at Rugby than at the other public schools. Anyone making such an inference would have been disabused, for a boy at Rugby who did not reach an academic level satisfactory to the headmaster within a period of time determined by the headmaster, was obliged to leave the school. It was at the more traditional institutions of Winchester and Eton that backward boys were protected, for the wrong reasons and too much and too long, in the view of certain critics.[21] 'The first, second and third duty of a schoolmaster is to get rid of unpromising pupils.'[22] That draconian declaration was uttered by Thomas Arnold, and it indicates, more faithfully than his moralizing sermons and journalism, the pattern of his practice. He was in performance ruthless and, it seemed to others, often arbitrary and cruel. Expulsion, he thought, should be practised much oftener than it was.[23]

We can see now something of what Arnold meant and why he presented the unresolved contradictions. He thought that the exaltation of the intellect alone, without regard to moral and religious values, was a dangerous course; at the same time he felt that the retention at school of big older boys who were dull-minded, probably bullies, but, perhaps, good at games, was a bad and morally subversive example to younger ones. In practice difficult accommodation had to be attempted. But Arnold did not say this; or he said on separate occasions contradictory parts of what together did not make a consistent whole. To those who heard these variable pronouncements and observed his conduct, he often seemed to be saying one thing and doing another. In his early days as a headmaster he declared himself against raising fees. 'I am confirmed in my resolution not to do so lest I should get the sons of the very great people as my pupils whom it is impossible to sophronize.'*[24] That he *did* in fact raise the fees quite soon afterwards was not in itself a betrayal of policy; economic factors may frustrate the best of intentions; but he also ran down the lower school to extinction in order to exclude the children of local parents, although it was to serve their needs that the founder had endowed the school, and the lower school provided the only means by which local parents of modest resources could fit their children by preparation in the classics for admission to the upper school.[25] We do not know how Arnold, with his tender conscience, contemplated a class of little anxious boys, toiling to achieve what he knew he had himself made it impossible for them to do, by committing them to the charge of men incompetent to teach the subjects required.† The truth as it appears from the record of his conduct is that, notwithstanding moral litanies to the contrary, Arnold was ambitious in a natural, worldly sense for himself and the school, and was, in practice, primarily interested in clever boys and in the fruits of success. It was a normal choice for a diligent head-master to make.

But Arnold's zeal for the regeneration of religion and moral nobility required him to *appear* different. Moreover it required his *boys* to appear different. Every Rugbeian boy was expected to develop a special relationship with God, whatever his honest feelings might be. 'You can make a point of speaking to him every day; of forcing yourself to do it if you cannot do it willingly.'[26] But boys were not long in discovering that, if all Rugbeians' relationships with God were 'special', the headmaster's was more special than others. Disagreement of a boy with a headmaster not unnaturally tends to end in submission to *force majeure*; but disagreement with Arnold led rapidly towards the intimation that the disagreement was with God.‡ Thus, disagreement with Arnold could not be friendly, for the authority he asserted, with a puritan's personal mandate, was not temporal, but divine.

While he was by profession the headmaster of a public school and a teacher of boys, he regarded both the institution and his charges with distaste, because a public school was a society of boys, and Arnold heartily disliked boyhood as a state 'riotous, insolent and

---

* An Arnoldism meaning to enlighten.

† J. Sale, form I, unqualified; Louis Pons, form II, unintelligible and without control.

‡ Wishing as a 'commonwealth' partisan to express his own disapprobation of Prince Rupert's cavalry in the Civil Wars, he called it, 'men most hateful and contemptible who have ever thwarted the will of God and goodness'.[27]

annoying to others, like the gaiety of a drunken man'.[28] The unsanctified exuberance of boys was to him 'a spectacle almost more morally distressing than the shouts and gambols of a set of lunatics'.[29] He distrusted and felt aversion to apple-eating animals as a species, his own haunting recollections of schoolboyhood informed him, of 'monstrous evil'.[30] He volunteered confirmation of John Bowdler's notorious but unoriginal remark (borrowed without acknowledgement from Fielding in playful mood): 'I am afraid the fact is, indeed, indisputable. Public schools are, indeed, the very seats and nurseries of vice'[31] and 'none can pass through a public school without tasting too largely of that poisoned bowl'[32] (of 'low base and mischievous principles'), while good qualities brought from home were 'partly corrupted at a public school within a month'.[33] What he saw and felt, with intense personal reminiscence, as the 'evil of boy nature', made him always 'unwilling to undergo the responsibility of advising any man to send his son to a public school',[34] and tempted him to prefer a 'good private tutor',[35] an educational role he had himself essayed.

How were these opinions reconciled with his profession of headmaster of a public school, and with his choice of sending his own sons to the public school, Winchester, which he had attended as a boy? There was, in practice, no reconciliation, nor did hc feel there could be one, because in Arnold's view *all* boys, in their unregenerate state, were wicked as a genus, and a collection of boys was more wicked than the sum of the parts; therefore *all* schools were seats of vice, and private schools tended to be worse than public schools by lack of an ameliorating élite of redeemed senior boys endowed with authority. The régime of a private tutor also had limitations and demerits of a different kind, manifest in a tendency to overprotect. Subjection to a public school was thus – like life itself – a trial fraught with dangers, from which one might emerge marred or made, for the experience could prove, in the end, irrevocably depraving, or, to a suitable combatant, uniquely beneficial. 'I am a coward about public schools,' Arnold wrote to his friend, Richard Whately, of Dublin, '. . . for I am inclined to think that the trials of a school are useful to a boy's character* and thus, I dread not to expose my boys to it; while on the other hand, the immediate effect of it is so ugly that

---

* Not in every case. Arnold had Whately's own son, Edward, removed from Rugby, 'Having been found totally unfit for the place in every respect.'[36]

like washing one's hands with the earth one shrinks from dirtying them so grievously in the first stage of the process.'[37]

Arnold's way of treating this unfortunate part of 'life's current', over which there hung a 'special cloud',[38] was to apply measures to shorten it, and 'anticipate the common progress to Christian manliness'[39] by accelerating the process of maturity. He was much exercised by the problem how best to get the odious state of boyhood over as quickly as possible.[40] His lack of sympathy with boys' feelings he construed to be a merit, not a defect, in his vocation, so that for much of the time he was in conflict not merely with people but with human nature. In particular he was unable to accept as natural and inevitable what every schoolmaster must accept if he is to maintain contact with reality, that in the state existing between boys and their governors the former will sometimes resist the designs of the latter, when these, albeit for the most benevolent of reasons, are devised to prevent the gratification of their present desire. When boys took measures to avoid detection and punishment for breaches of an unpopular order, Arnold fulminated against them as if they were guilty of heinous and unnatural sin. They endeavoured, he bitterly complained, 'by all sorts of means – combinations amongst themselves, concealment, trick, open falsehood, or open disobedience – to baffle his watchfulness and escape his severity'.[41] Strive as he would, he never seemed able, in that 'great game of chess', to checkmate his adversary, 'the Devil'. Or was it that those stubborn pawns persisted in refusing to accept the role of passive obedience to the hand of their Grand Master, to which he had assigned them?

Sir Francis Doyle, reviewing the changes in public schools seen in his lifetime, managed to put in a few words in tribute to the Baffin, who, like the rest of the old order of pedagogues, had been 'overshadowed and banished into darkness by the widespread renown of the late Dr Arnold, whose avatar is supposed to have reorganised English public education'. After a polite flourish of compliments to the admirable qualities of this 'eminent personage', Doyle ventured to point out one qualification for a headmaster 'which Keate possessed and Arnold did not'. 'I mean,' he said, 'the knowledge of God Almighty's intention that there should exist at a certain time between childhood and manhood, the natural production known as a boy.'[42]

It is difficult to resist the conclusion, on the evidence, that Arnold's much-publicized pronouncements made more impression on the outside world than they did on the school as a whole. His reputation worked, in the end, mainly to the advantage of Rugby, but W. C. Lake, although he admired Arnold's 'idealism', had to confess that conditions at Rugby when Arnold ended were much the same as when he began, and that 'it would be a mistake to suppose that his influence materially changed the character of school life for the ordinary boy'.[43] Even the worst excesses of bullying, 'buffeting', 'chairing' and 'clodding',* were put down about 1815,[44] before Arnold's time. For the rest, conditions at Rugby continued to vary according to the character of the reigning boy overlord and his lieutenants. One bad house was reformed into a very good one by the hard justice dispensed to wrongdoers by a newly appointed head boy, William Hodson, not a disciple of Arnold's,[45] who later performed in the same spirit, effectively but controversially, in India. Part of the main plot of *Tom Brown's Schooldays* concerns the problem raised when members of a strong sixth form leave the school together, and rogue bullies in the fifth form take advantage of the inadequacy of the official successors to impose their own criminal tyranny on their juniors. This is presented as an abuse outside Arnold's control, and Arnold himself admitted that it was one he was helpless to correct, except through the continuity of a strong and responsible sixth form.[46]

Arnold sought to control and to change, and his chosen medium was not compulsory games, but compulsory religion. He has been described as 'the first headmaster who made the school chapel the centre of the school'.[47] He certainly put the chapel, with himself in it, at the top of the school, but that is not the same place as the *centre*. It is true and well known that Cotton – the 'young master' in *Tom Brown's Schooldays* – wrote and published a book of prayers especially for use at Rugby school. It is also true and less known that copies of the book were in regular indoor use as substitutes for a football and kicked to pieces up and down the corridors.[48] A boy could not keep a copy even if he wished to; the demand was unremitting. Weeping with emotion Arnold drove himself to the verge of a breakdown in the pulpit, dilating on the subject of the congregation's guilt for Christ's sacrifice. The boys to whom he appealed for funds for the chapel responded with buttons in the offertory and sometimes

---

* Buffeting: running the gauntlet up and down the great schoolroom through two lines of the upper remove using handkerchiefs tied into what were called Westminster knots. So far from this practice being unknown to the authorities, junior boys were remembered obtaining permission from the writing master for leave to go and watch a buffeting.

Chairing: hoisting a boy in a chair and pinching him in the 'most sensitive parts of his body'.

Clodding: pelting (of novitiates in the fifth form) with hard balls of dried slime from a pool.

cheques for £1000, drawn upon the 'Bank of Elegance'.[49] The same boys, to his chagrin, raised £15 cash by the quick circulation of a hat, towards the making of a steeplechase course. 'A Rugby schoolboy religious,' exclaimed a sporting Old Rugbeian in derision. 'It's not in his nature, and when he pretends to be so, he resembles many of his elders who find their profit in the pretence.'[50] At the same time that Arnold was lamenting that he had known 'boys of eight or nine years old who did not so much as know what would happen to them after their death',* considerably older boys at Rugby would have echoed the sentiments of a former Rugbeian for the school chapel, 'if the devil had flown away with it it would have been a matter of no concern to me'.[52] Under Arnold boys at Rugby who knelt to pray at their bedside were liable to be taunted and pelted with boots and slippers, at least in some houses and dormitories.[53]†

The hostility felt for Arnold could be expressed openly by parents and Old Rugbeians. On a Speech Day after the distribution of prizes a crowd of old boys and parents went off to dine separately at the Spread Eagle, rather than eat the headmaster's food.[55] At a Founders' Day dinner held on Thursday, 29 October 1835 at Rugby, after Arnold had announced his intention to attend, only nine other people made an appearance. One absentee wrote a letter to the *Northampton Herald* to say, 'I know for certain that more than a hundred would have attended if it had pleased the autocrat to have remained at home.'[56]

Animosity was often exacerbated by Arnold's high-handedness, when a little tact might have shown a controversial action to have been warranted. Arnold may have been justified in expelling the boy, Marshall, who had humiliated three prefects attempting to chastise him, by resisting them successfully, grabbing their stick and making off with it. But he put himself in the wrong by expelling Marshall peremptorily, without hearing his account of the case, and completed the miscarriage by an act of gross discourtesy to the boy's father, by refusing to see him when he made a long and uncomfortable journey to Rugby especially to meet the headmaster. By this time the majority of the trustees were his docile servants, so his decision was safe from reversal, but in the press he was vilified in terms for which there is

---

* The heathenish ignorance of some of the younger Rugbeians was such that 'they thought that after they were put in the ground they would lie there forever, and should never feel anything more either of good or evil'.[51]

† Wykehamist style of authoritarianism solved the problem in practice by the rule that *all* boys must kneel in silence by their beds for five minutes, which was called being 'in course'.[54]

no parallel in the history of relations between headmasters and parents. Six lines from the diatribe printed in the *Northampton Herald* on 25 November 1837 are enough to convey the hatred he aroused:

> Not thy angry resolve – nor thy changing decrees
> Not thy toadying serfs – nor thy trembling trustees
> Nor thy rod clotted thick with an innocents gore
> Nor thy letters that pierce parents hearts to the core
> Not expulsion of children too youthful to reason
> Nor thy Prize-books, explaining the beauties of treason[57]

It was unfortunate that the case of Marshall had occurred while the case of March was still fresh and painful in the memory of Rugbeian parents; and it was to the case of March that the lurid third line of the verse quoted made allusion. Like all other public-school headmasters, Arnold used corporal punishment to maintain discipline. Unlike other headmasters he professed to dislike its use and expressed a desire to avoid it, 'keeping it as much as possible in the background and by kindness and encouragement attracting the good and noble feelings of those with whom he had to deal'.[58] Soon after his arrival at Rugby he wrote, 'There has been no flogging yet and I hope there will be none . . . flogging will only be my *ratio ultimo*.'[59] Yet when a brutal abuse of corporal punishment was discovered – a small, delicate boy, with a record of ill health, having been flogged to dangerous excess – the perpetrator was not one of the old-style, traditional wielders of the rod, but the enlightened Dr Arnold of tender scruples and delicate conscience.

One day in 1832 Arnold, on a routine tour of supervision accompanied by James Prince Lee, stopped at Mr Bird's class to test prepared work and asked the boy, March, to construe a passage from Xenophon's *Anabasis*. The boy said the passage lay outside the section ordered to be prepared. Arnold sent to inquire of Bird, who returned that the note was right and the boy wrong. But March persisted in his contention. The atmosphere became inflamed with Arnold's righteous indignation. In the boy's firmness he saw himself confronted by naked evil. Crying out, 'Liar, liar, liar!', he there and then inflicted eighteen strokes of the rod on the offender in front of the class. After execution March was off school sick for two days. This added malingering to his sins in Arnold's eyes and the headmaster ordered him extra work on his return.

We do not know exactly when the first uneasy doubts began to trouble Arnold's mind, but the evidence, slow to emerge, was irresistible when it did, and showed that March had been right and telling the truth and that Arnold had been wrong and misinformed. Had he been more careful and less hasty the truth could have been ascertained at the time the accusation was made. Arnold apologized to the boy in private and in public; but the gravest part of the offence could not be atoned for with an apology, because it was not morally conditional upon the boy's innocence or guilt. Arnold in his passion had administered twice the maximum number of strokes that Dr Keate would have given the most robust and contumacious Etonian delinquent. It was indefensible to inflict a flogging of such severity upon any small boy, and more culpable to do so upon one of known physical weakness.* Arnold had lost control of himself in one of those fits of incontinent rage which rendered him by temperament singularly unsuited to be the governor of young boys.[60]

How arose the mythology of the 'hero schoolmaster', the idealist paragon of Christian virtues surrounded by adoring boys? In part it was due to the timeliness of Arnold's appearance and the attractiveness of his committed tone and posture to a pressing and vociferous complex of political and religious 'liberal' interests. Also, there was a measure of truth in the picture. He *was* an idealist, and was seen to be strenuously concerned with moral issues, even if his declarations, emotional and vehement in tone, tended to be equivocal and ambiguous in meaning.† His 'ideals', when they were translated into an explicit policy of action, revealed unsublimated preoccupation with 'sin' and 'guilt', rather than adaptability to the practical service of 'hope' and 'charity'. The dangerous suggestion, that God might bestow gratuitous forgiveness upon repentant sinners with a long record of performance, agitated him with resentment, and he trained from the pulpit his indignation at this unworthy reflection upon the nature of Divine Mercy.[62] He did say that 'Society, if it deserves the name, must provide for the welfare of all whom it receives into its pale.'[63] But – from the general to the particular – in the case of convicts and the children of convicts colonizing Australia, 'welfare' did not imply social integration or equality before the law. 'The stain' of convict origin 'should last not only for one whole lifetime but for more than one generation that no convict or convict's child should

---

* March suffered from a hernia.

† '. . . the great objects of interest in Dr Arnold's life, namely his theological sentiments. What these really were in many important particulars we can by no means clearly discover from the Life.'[61]

ever be a free citizen; and even in the third generation the offspring should be excluded from all offices of honour or authority in the Colony . . .' for 'it is a law of God's providence which we cannot alter, that the sins of the father are really visited upon the child in the corruption of his breed, and in rendering impossible many of the feelings which are the greatest security to the children against evil'.[64]

In 1832, when political feelings were running high and 'our poor', he declared, 'at this moment have the name and rights of freemen while their outward condition is that of slaves,' he exhorted, 'the aristocracy in every place to come forward manfully to state fairly the amount of their past neglect and their hearty wish to make up for it'; and he avowed his 'most earnest wish to see the working classes raised in everything that there may be one hearty feeling of brotherhood between us all'.[65] But when 'brotherhood' was frustrated by, as he admits, 'the badness and foolishness of the government' and the 'aristocratical constitution of society', and the 'working classes' gave vent to their frustration in a little rioting, or 'popular demonstrations' as they would be called by political sympathizers, the Duke of Wellington could not have prescribed a more drastic remedy. 'As for rioting, the old Roman way of dealing with *that* is always the right one: flog the rank and file and fling the leaders from the Tarpeian Rock.'[66]*

Thus there were always 'ideals', of one kind or another, in orbit about the head of Thomas Arnold. It was partly true, also, that he was surrounded by adoring boys. The immediate circle of his sixth form constituted an elect, a school within a school, almost as separate from the rest of Rugby as he was himself, and it was mainly by his partisans in his sixth form that the mystic was nurtured and propagated of 'the character of Arnold, a power unique and irresistible in the history of English Education'.[67] It was upon his sixth form, his élite of chosen few, that Arnold directed the beam of his will to 'change' as evidence of love, and those susceptible to his magnetism became, at least for the time being, his uncritical admirers. Stanley and Vaughan used to nudge each other with anticipation of delight when they saw Arnold prepare to ascend to the pulpit[68] and Stanley quarrelled with a fellow undergraduate who was bold enough to suggest that Arnold was not infallible.[69] 'Loving him and admiring him as I do to the very verge of all love and admiration that can be

---

* Matthew Arnold, *Culture and Anarchy* (1869; Cambridge 1960 edn). The quotation was excised from later editions, probably in deference to objections from other members of the family.

paid to a man,' Stanley confessed, 'I fear I have passed the limits and made him my idol, and that in all I may be serving God for man's sáke.'[70] Clough, another sixth-form apostle, when Arnold paid an unexpected visit to his study, could hardly look at his trigonometry for the rest of the evening, and seated beside Arnold in the library 'he would look up into his face with an almost feminine expression of trust and affection'.[71]

The author of that sketch of Clough was his contemporary in the sixth form, and the note of mildly quizzical reserve reminds us that not every boy elevated to the lofty atmosphere of the Rugbeian elect surrendered himself entirely to the charisma of the master. The position of a candidate for the sixth form who desired to maintain his honesty and independence of mind was an invidious one. He knew that to be received into the sixth form, with the advantages of prospect its status bestowed, he must succeed academically; that was a basic necessity; but it was not enough; he must also appear morally acceptable in the eyes of the headmaster who looked for zeal and fervour in his chosen, for 'moral thoughtfulness', and, although he did not say so, for the surrender of judgement which might conflict with his own. In theory, honest expression of independent thought was the privilege of the sixth form, reflective of their maturity and responsible character. In practice it was imprudent to speak one's mind unless it coincided closely with the mind of the 'hero-school-master'. A boy who quoted in an essay the aphorism of Joseph Fouché, disapproved of by Arnold, that the murder of the Duc d'Enghien 'was worse than a crime, it was a blunder', received dark looks of displeasure as if he had shown grave moral turpitude by choosing the quotation; and the incident was not quickly forgotten or forgiven.[72] Jokes could be dangerous when the most trifling matters were referred to the awful conscience of a ruler who, as a not unfriendly Etonian commentator put it, 'never ties his shoes without asserting a principle and when he puts on his hat . . . founds himself on an eternal truth'.[73]

The story was told of Arnold and the boy who, in answering roll call, uttered his name in tones which made the windows shake and excused himself with the plea that the volume of sound was involuntary due to a nervous disposition. Arnold, instead of acknowledging the joke and charging the player fifty lines as its price, solemnly went and consulted a physician to ascertain whether such symptoms could be genuine.

An authentic illustration of the kind of pressures applied to a boy's conscience is provided by William Gover, who genuinely admired Arnold and much of his work, but was not willing to make feigned acts of contrition. Gover, when he was in the sixth form, received a visit from a friend, Edward Wheatly, who had recently left the school and, returning as an old boy, invited Gover, and another sixth form, 'H', to dine with him at the Eagle. There was plenty of time to dine and return before lock-up, and in any case both boys supposed that, being in the sixth form and in theory trusted to use their discretion, they did not require permission to stay out on a special occasion after lock-up. At table Gover had one glass of sherry, one of port, and tea after dinner. When they were about to leave, the waiter told them that an 'excellent lecture on the microscope' was about to be given in the inn, and they stayed on to hear it. Afterwards they walked together back to their house, and the housemaster, Bird, asked why they were late. They told him, but he thought fit to report them to the headmaster and Arnold sent for them. They told Arnold frankly what had happened, having nothing to hide. Arnold expressed surprise and disapproval that they should have gone out to dine with a boy of their own standing who had only left last half. Gover said he did not see what was wrong with that. 'Such circumstances,' said Arnold, 'might easily have led you into excess.' Gover looked straight at the headmaster and said, 'I took no more than I would have done at my father's table.' After a pause, Arnold said, 'Abstinence is easier than moderation.' Gover took this to impugn his truthfulness and reaffirmed his account of the evening. Arnold repeated his admonition, and the interview ended inconclusively.

Up to then the encounter had been a commonplace one of misunderstanding between authority and one subject to it. The boy had supposed himself entitled to a degree of liberty, to which the headmaster now said he was not. An admonition and rebuke would have defined the limits of freedom for future occasions, and that would have been the end of it. But a few days later (probably after waiting for an approach from Gover) Arnold signalled for the two to remain after class. He was grieved, he said, by what had happened, but there was a way of showing the sincerity of their regret. Next Sunday the Lord's Supper would be administered, and the two could come to it as a sign of that regret. Apart from the consideration that in Gover's family the sacrament was partaken of 'rather as a preparation for death than as a means of strength for life', Gover felt that, in the way Arnold was putting it, he was being asked to confess that he had done something 'morally wrong', and that in coming to communion, therefore, he would be 'acting one thing' while he 'felt the opposite'. Gover felt that he was unable in good conscience to go. H, a lewd and cynical boy, went in complete insincerity and was thereby discharged from the headmaster's displeasure. After another pause of a few days 'Arnold,' says Gover, 'again spoke to me and said as I had not shown by meeting his suggestion any sorrow for my conduct he must set me an imposition to show his disapproval of it.' Arnold did this 'gravely' and seemed 'to impose it reluctantly, with pain to himself'. Gover did the imposition and handed it to Arnold, who took it and looked at him 'with brows a little uplifted', still waiting for capitulation. Gover said nothing and Arnold took the papers, though they were not what he wanted. The following Sunday, 13 November 1836, he preached a sermon[74] on 'relations which must exist in school life to the law and the necessity of subjection to it'.[75]

This was a case not of obedience exacted from a subject, nor of discipline vindicated by a ruler, but of a boy being pressed by a man to do violence to his own understanding of truth and falsify his own conscience for the sake of the other's version of 'righteousness'. Thomas Arnold was capable of saying, when headmaster, 'I never disguise or suppress my opinions but I have been and am most religiously careful not to influence my boys with them.'[76] Whether naïve or disingenuous in origin, such deformed reflections of reality could only have the effect of cultivating a measure of hypocrisy in his charges, expressed, for self-protection, in calculated displays of moral concern.

Arnold aimed by spiritual rehabilitation to reform the character of his pupils in depth, but what commonly ensued was not a change in character, but a change in posture, and not a change which could be maintained indefinitely under stress. He conveyed to his elect the message that they were destined for some high mission, but left them without any clear indication what it was. Like an inspiring but confused military leader, he did not know where his ideas would take people, or himself. The most perceptive contemporary estimate came from Walter Bagehot. 'He pounded belief, or, at any rate, a floating, confused conception' into young boys 'that there are great subjects and that there are strange problems, that knowledge had an indefinite value, that life is a serious and solemn thing.'[77] But 'the precepts,' as one subject exposed to the method observed, 'were more weighty than boys could assimilate without incessant pretentiousness'.[78] The result was to put a boy who strove to meet these exalted but imprecise demands in danger of becoming a deceiver or a dupe, or both, with a morbid scrupulosity sustained by probably inappropriate expectations. Boys exalted by the system could be carried away by the intoxicating delusion that they were no longer adolescent boys, but priests and prophets wielding in the name of righteousness not a praeposter's penny cane, but 'the sword of the Lord of Gideon'; nor would they be likely to wield the rod of office more justly and modestly for supposing that they were the bearers of transcendental authority; for 'how can it be a vulgar incident to lick your fag for not toasting your sausages when every motion of the tongue, hand or foot involves the idea of $\eta \acute{o} \lambda \iota \varsigma$, and asserts the identity of the Christian Church with the Christian state?'[79]

'A succession of beardless sages',[80] marching on the universities and regiments, 'feeling their moral muscles' and dutifully ready to be responsible for their neighbour's conscience as well as their own, was not, when prolonged, an endearing performance.

Pearson, as a Rugbeian, feeling at liberty to put the case brutally, observed that 'before long Rugby was known at Oxford as "the disagreeable school" ', adding, 'Its reputation in the army was, I believe, even worse.'[81]

The great majority of boys at Rugby were almost as apart from the holy communion between the headmaster and his sixth form as the boys of a different school might have been. But high-minded prigs, making heavy weather of small temptations, were produced by the régime in sufficient numbers to feed the reputation established. The tone, at its most pretentiously insensitive, is conveyed in the few lines of commiseration from a young zealot called Thornton to his father, in response to the news that his parents had suffered serious loss:

Rugby, 9 April 1831. My dear Papa, After reading your letter, I could not but grieve for the calamity so distressing to yourself and Mamma, but the thought struck me immediately, that it was the work of the Lord. Therefore let us hush our repinings.[82]

Disenchantment, when the spell was broken, could be disabling. One victim, talked into an imaginary vocation by Arnold, found his clerical collar strangling him and fled to become the founder of the Primitive Positivist Church, which has been described as consisting of 'three persons and no God'.[83]

The most conspicuous and cautionary example of the effects of the method was the career of Arthur Clough, one of a succession of the elect who worshipped Arnold, sat on his right hand, and in turn was mythologized into heroic stature by a culture of adoration from below. On his arrival at Rugby, a future dean of Westminster was greeted by the future commander of Hodson's Horse with the remark, 'What a fool you were not to come a week earlier – because then you could have said that you had been at school with Tom Clough.'[84]

Meanwhile Clough, having issued out of the citadel of Rugby, was receiving at Cambridge the first of a succession of blows which nothing in his training had prepared him to meet. The news that he had received a second and not a first-class honours degree left him stunned. Dr Arnold's son, Tom, remembers him panting, his face turning from flushed to pale, saying 'I have failed.'[85] Once begun, the process of disillusionment in a romantic is unarrestable. Each doubt, as it hardens into denial, admits a new doubt and the doubt whether professional authorship could be his true vocation if it 'led to insincerity, the unforgivable sin', shrank into irrelevance before the bleak suspicion that 'writing was the thing he did best; and that he didn't do it significantly well'. By the time he came to write *Dipsychus*, the sense of high destiny had evaporated, leaving behind a residue of inhibiting scruples, and the poet breathes through his uncle, who, in the dialogue, blames Arnold for having 'spoilt' the public schools: 'How he used to attack offences, not as offences – the right view – against discipline, but as sin, heinous guilt, I don't know what else beside. . . . Why didn't he flog them and hold his tongue?'[86]

In his lifetime and after, the personal glamour of Arnold, the 'reformer' and Christian crusader, continued to be propagated to a public who found the image what they wanted to see. 'Why had I not Arnold for a master?' complained Thackeray;[87] and Dickens rhapsodized, 'I respect and reverence his memory beyond all expression. . . . Every sentence you quote [from a Life of Arnold] . . . is the textbook of my faith.'[88]* Even the Etonian, Lionel Cust, not usually disposed to look beyond the 'sleepy hollow', was beguiled to remark that Arnold 'was able to stimulate and mould the minds of an exceptionally gifted circle of pupils'.[90] If we consider who these were, we find the names of Stanley, Smith and Vaughan. Stanley's position in the Church was never secure; his success and support

---

* Dickens was not aware of Arnold's disapproval of his own publications as trivial and time-wasting distractions which spoiled a boy's taste for 'good literature'. Arnold also complained to the Wordsworths that the boys thought of 'nothing but Boz's next number'.[89]

were mainly courtly as a favourite of the queen's; this and his social connections gained him reasonable preferment and kept him from being hounded out of the Church of England for his latitudinarianism. Henry Smith entered Rugby at the age of fifteen, a year before the death of Arnold, and later made himself the greatest English mathematician by striking out in a direction for which Rugby was no preparation. Charles Vaughan was, on results, the most accomplished of Arnold's favourite pupils, and followed in his master's footsteps by becoming the most notable headmaster of his day, raising Harrow from a state of depression near to death, to unprecedented heights of success and repute. He himself was a probable candidate for the Primacy; but even Vaughan, as has since been discovered, had hidden defects of character as cleric and headmaster which arrested his rise in mid career. This is not an impressively long list (even if I have overlooked one or two who should have been included) for fourteen years of the most famous living pedagogue. Subsequently Rugby, as Pearson admitted, under another headmaster, turned out many more distinguished men, over a shorter period of time, whose number included Lord Justice Bowen, Henry Sidgwick, and, above all, Lord Goschen. The truth is, Arnold did not have a particularly gifted set of boys to work on and he had to deal with what he had. Rugby began to profit after he had left from his impact on the outside world; but at the time he was determined to make his chosen few, at least his sixth form, shine and radiate his kind of moral effulgence. 'The best Rugby men were no better than the best set from any good public school, Eton, Harrow or Winchester.'[91] Their difference was that they had been trained to be self-consciously and demonstratively righteous; and, in order to obtain advancement at school, they had responded, with sincerity or affectation, or with something of both.

When he died suddenly in 1842 from an attack of angina it was said in the *Gentleman's Magazine*, 'Dr Arnold was remarkable for the uniform sweetness, the patience and the forbearing meekness of his despotism,' a tribute which even his most loyal pupils, having known the passion, and the 'wild and staring eyes', the 'utter contempt' and the 'bitter abhorrance of those who disagreed with him',[92] might have found worthy of a smile.

Arnold was different from other public-school headmasters of his time, not in what he achieved, but in the directions he pointed. He was a conspicuous public figure who dramatized *Life* as the Christian's battle against *Sin*. In his allusions to social justice and his political rhetoric he appeared to be leading the vanguard of progress in education. But, in fact, the future of the public schools did not lie in the direction he approved. Arnold wished to abridge boyhood, and to induce early maturity in youth.[93] Later Victorian upper-class mythology romanticized boyhood (first, ironically, in a novel eulogizing Arnold) and retarded the development of adult maturity in public-school males.

It should not surprise observers of Arnold's fierce combat with the profane spirit of boyhood that the first enemy to be feared had been his own retarded juvenility. Arnold himself had been guilty of horseplay at Oxford. 'Backs were mounted and chairs and tables upset within the grave precincts of Oriel Common Room itself; and in these matters,' Lake remembers, Arnold 'grew the worse for getting greater.'[94]

Arnold placed no importance on games. Games were to become in the public schools the guardian deities of all manly virtue. Arnold taught that 'it is only moral and religious [Christian] knowledge which can instruct the judgement'[95] and that religious knowledge was the one thing needful for a Christian to study; and he did not wish non-Christians to be eligible for British citizenship or admission to universities.[96] His successors shifted the balance of the contents of religion to alter its character from his theopathic crusading zeal (which some saw as unhealthy and even mischievous in potential) to a kind of sanctified, but discreetly manly, social discipline. In its cruder manifestations this became known as 'muscular Christianity'.[97]*

The part of the public-school system which Arnold justified most consistently was fagging and its corollary, government by the power of senior boys, to which, both during and after his lifetime, most of the critical objections raised by educational revisionists were addressed. But although fagging and prefectship survived, usually under increased adult surveillance, and were even piously planted in 'public schools' founded after Arnold's death, they were not used as agencies of moral and religious proselytism of boy by boy – Arnold's dream – but as well-tested disciplinary arms, and sometimes, unofficially, as headmasters' intelligence agencies, when a headmaster's

---

* The expression 'muscular Christianity' first came to the notice of the general public when it was used by James Fitzjames Stephen in the *Edinburgh Review* of January 1858, with allusion to the ideas of Charles Kingsley, in the course of a review of *Tom Brown's Schooldays*. But the term was invented by Stephen's friend, T. C. Sandars, of the *Saturday Review*, according to Henry Pearson.

authority was strong enough to overbear the misgivings of the prefects. Later nineteenth-century educationalists were conscious of what they saw as the dangers, as well as the benefits, of boys' self-government.

THIRTEEN

Nearer to God

When Thomas Arnold died in 1842, nothing material at Eton, Winchester and Harrow had changed since the beginning of the century. Writing of those sinful old days, Moberly remarked that the tone of young men at the university, whether they came from Winchester, Eton, Rugby, Harrow, or wherever else, was universally irreligious. 'A religious undergraduate was very rare, very much laughed at when he appeared, and I think I may confidently say, hardly to be found among public school men.'

The prevailing standards in the twenties and thirties, and even the forties, were a world apart from those which rose noticeably in the sixties as orthodoxy, to remain till the end of the century and beyond. Well might Moberly observe, 'A most singular change has come upon our public schools – a change difficult for any person to understand adequately who has not known them in both these times.'[1] An observant witness like Moberly who lived through the transition saw, at one stage, the two worlds, the old and the new, co-existing in mutual contradiction. While Thomas Arnold was declaring with fervour that the business of a schoolmaster, no less than that of a parish priest, was the care of souls, Lord Melbourne was exclaiming with quizzical distaste that things had come to a pretty pass when religion was allowed to invade private life. These were not merely expressions of religious and political disagreements, but of radically different ways of life.

The figure of an earlier time who did most violence to evangelical sensibilities was the 'sporting parson', for he was the very antithesis of religious 'enthusiasm'. Winchester, in Thomas Trollope's time, enjoyed a notably rich example of the breed. His *pièce de résistance*, enjoyed by those closest to him, was a double act whereby he alternated the chanting of the psalm with, under cover of the response, a report to his neighbour on his current record in the field. The counterpoint would produce something like this.

Who smote great kings, for his mercy endureth for ever;
[and aside] On Hurstley Down yesterday I was out with Jack
Woodburn
Sehon, King of the Amorites, for his mercy endureth for ever.
My black bitch Juno put up a covey almost at our feet
And gave away their land for an heritage; for his mercy endureth for
ever.
I blazed away with both barrels and brought down a brace
Who remembered us when we were in trouble; for his mercy endureth
for ever.
But Jack fired too soon and never touched a feather.

In his comments, Thomas Trollope is at pains to stress that, in these bygone blends of the sacred and profane, no disrespect was intended; neither the parson nor the boys thought there was anything improper or incongruous in his performance; he was, in fact, according to Trollope, 'a kind, conscientious man and a good pastor after his fashion'.

It should not be assumed that, because the old profane pleasantries and plain speaking receded, and a more demure, if less elegant, system of manners reigned, the prescriptions of evangelical enthusiasm, and its dilution for popular consumption to 'muscular Christianity', were accepted and swallowed as staple fare by the country as a whole. Moberly, while approving in principle a more sober and sedate attitude to religion than had been customary in his own youth, was not therefore prepared to be converted overnight into a Calvinist puritan or a Wesleyan enthusiast and had serious reservations respecting the nature of the sources from which a public agonizer like Thomas Arnold drew his inspiration. Religious enthusiasm run amok could become a vice, productive of, at best, prigs, and at worst, fanatics, and England's collective memory of the despotism of the Protectorate, although two hundred years old, was still influentially alive in the minds and judgement of men of Moberly's class and traditions. Having paid formal tribute to the 'improvement' in tone, upon which the mid Victorians never ceased congratulating themselves, he added, from the heart, 'Have a care of excessive church going, of over long services, of very frequent communions or suggested confessions for the young. The recoil is apt to be more serious than you expect.'[2]

The whole condition and induction of 'enthusiasm' with its concomitant 'ecstasies', its cult of the 'hero', and his exaltation, was regarded by classical traditionalists with cordial distaste and suspi-

ciòn as, at best, vulgar hocus pocus, with socially mischievous pretension. We are 'content to have pupils,' said William Johnson, raising
a fastidious eyebrow in the direction of Arnold, 'and do not aim at
having disciples'.[3] In respect of Winchester, Moberly could claim
with satisfaction that his boys did learn 'a modesty, a practical good
sense, and a strong religious feeling, being of a very *moderate, traditional*
kind'. The prescription of John Pelham, a sturdy middle-of-the-road
Church of England bishop, for the good life was '*piety without lukewarm-
ness, and above all without enthusiasm*'.[4]

In the more traditional and higher-church schools, the aversion to
the enthusiasm of puritan evangelism was no posture merely of the
masters and fellows as interested parties; the boys themselves felt
militant objection to suspect zeal. Thomas Churton, an abnormally
serious and religious boy, writing home from Rugby bewailing that
'religion scarcely ever gains anything but mockery, and sacred texts
are handled for witticisms', yet finds comfort in the existence of some
laudable attitudes; for instance 'an abhorrence of methodism and
ostentation. . .'.[5] 'Eton, we hope,' remarked a characteristic mid
Victorian gentleman, 'disclaims any such unsound teaching as to
send into the world precociously pious youths.'[6] The questions he
deemed it requisite to ask were, 'Are they Christian boys? Are they
humble? Are they to be trusted? Are they ready *to respect the offices of
religion*?' The pragmatist Keate's reaction to the issue was succinct
and positive along predictable lines. Informed by an assistant master
that a boy was showing abnormal religious excitation, he declared,
'I'll flog him. It's all conceit. That boy, if he is a bigot now, will
sicken of religion and become an infidel when he leaves school.'[7]

It might reasonably have been supposed that the atmosphere
prevailing at Eton at that time was more than sufficient counterweight
to the spiritual delusions of anyone lacking a true vocation. The
Etonian renegade, Henry Salt, talked of 'the pleasant heathenism' of
'free pagan Eton'.[8] Tucker remarked that the religious tone at school
was of a very light character';[9] and Brinsley Richards that 'there
never was amongst us what is called a strong religious movement'.[10]
They were all alluding to a condition that did not begin to change
until nearly midway through the century and that at first changed
slowly.

Reading authentic accounts of life at the public schools during this
period, one could be forgiven for treating particulars of religious
worship with scepticism, if they were not corroborated from too many
different sources to leave room for much doubt or error. In the first

place there was no religious training whatever,[11] not even for boys intended for the Church, unless one might describe as such the exercise for three weeks at Easter of the lower classes at Winchester reading the Greek testament instead of the usual Greek authors, and the upper classes reading Lowth's *Praelections on the Sacred Poetry of the Hebrews*. Charles Merivale confirms a similar picture at Harrow where once in his school life he was set with twelve other boys as a punishment for some unremembered offence the task of learning by heart the Collect 'Lighten Our Darkness'; but he positively declared that was the only fragment of religious instruction he received from his tutor in seven years.[12] As we know, the education at public schools consisted exclusively of the study of classical, but pagan, poets, philosophers and dramatists. Thus a boy intended for ordination as a Christian priest left school at eighteen or nineteen as thoroughly versed as his tutors' efforts and his own intelligence and industry could make him in the spirit of Homer, Sophocles and Pindar, and the elegance of Virgil, Horace and Ovid.

Attendance at divine service was exacted as a gesture of obedience and acknowledgement of orthodoxy. It was an obligatory 'Church parade' and was treated as such by the boys. Wilkinson admits with candour that their conduct during services was at times 'abominable'.[13] The boys had no prayer books and did not know the words of the psalms. When their lips moved they were making social communications in song to their neighbours. On 8 May 1824, we have Milnes Gaskell writing to his mother, 'A clergyman read prayers for about 20 minutes but was perfectly inaudible on account of the noise made by the boys.'[14]* Wilkinson concedes himself to be perfectly willing 'to give away in a measure to the horror which, in some regulated minds, these recollections may have called up'.[16] 'We were often very naughty boys in chapel; no one denies it.' Their 'naughtiness' began with total inattention to the service, but no one expected them to be attentive to the babble which the cleric officiant was providing at an indecent speed.

Speed was commonly a 'marked characteristic of the performance', for school and college chaplains often held profitable appointments elsewhere, the obligations of which necessitated the expeditious discharge of their school or college duties. At Winchester, in the rapid intoning – or gabbling – of the prayers, no time was allowed for the choir to chant 'Amen', and by the time its tones had died away the

---

* This was after Goodall was said to have 'introduced decency into the chapel'.[15]

priest was already through two or three lines of the next prayer. The fastest of several fast clerical performers in Thomas Trollope's time at Winchester was known as the 'diver'. It was his practice in conducting a service to continue intoning rapidly without pause to the limit of his capacity, then while he recharged himself with air, he continued to read silently so that when he 'reappeared' – on the surface – he was several lines further down the page. This was called 'diving'. At Eton, the form of rival performers was compared; wagers were laid and handicaps determined on who could cover the course in the fastest time by various permutations of dovetailing psalms and responses. It was said of one popular champion that he could give any of his colleagues to 'Pontius Pilate' and beat him. Another celebrated performer was Furse Vidal, 'whose lungs and legs were such', it was said, that 'if the lessons were short he could be in a fives court at a quarter past three, after saying "When the wicked man" at three precisely'. The efforts of the Rev. Furse Vidal were especially appreciated by the boys because the breakneck speed at which he galloped produced a number of happy spoonerisms: 'Rend your garments, not your heart,' was long and tenderly cherished.[17]

The masters themselves – as few as nine of them at Eton in charge of 500 boys – would have found it difficult to be attentive to the service, for their attention upon the congregation was required if the proceedings were not to plunge into total anarchy. After the initial sport of trying to trip the verger in his dangerous walk back alone to the ante-chapel, some boys settled down to playing 'Eggs in the Bush', a favourite game of marbles, while the naturalists of the school produced, for display and comparison, favoured species from their private menageries: rabbits, rats and mice, as well as newts and snakes. One noted collector habitually concealed one of his exhibits in his hair, and was never in chapel without the company of his dearest pets, two mice who lay perfectly still and quiet, until he stroked them when they uttered a 'mournful whine'. Not all his pets were as docile, and a future bishop who knelt in front of him in chapel was accustomed to finding a snake in his pocket.

'Church sock' was a favourite indulgence, the practice of feasting on nuts, cakes, bulls' eyes and other delicacies, which originated among Collegers, and later was taken up as a special cult by Oppidan noblemen to celebrate the elevation of one of their number into a vacancy in the stalls reserved for Etonian peers and the sons of peers. Almonds and raisins were distributed by the host to the entire sixth form, and sometimes to all 'in play', which it was *de rigueur* to finish eating in chapel under the nose of authority.

Social business was transacted during the singing of the psalms. One boy gazed innocently into the eyes of a suspicious master while he chanted, 'I've got a four oar; will you come out with us this afternoon?' His respondent, with no less devout expression, sang, 'No I can't for we have got a match of cricket.'

Over this concatination of clerical patter and choral decoration, blurring, but not suppressing, the elusive hum of voices beneath, presided Dr Keate, the member of the congregation who above all was unable to attend to any part of the service, prayers, anthem, or sermon; for 'his whole being' was on the talkers. First he 'nailed' a recognized offender; then he scowled, to signify his displeasure. If that was 'innocently' ignored, he would produce like a conjurer his memorandum book with his left hand, and in his right poise his pencil 'in an attitude of writing', a prelude which was invariably successful for the moment, and gave him time to pirouette and give his attention to another offender deserving of it in a different part of the chapel. On a certain occasion one of the bolder naturalists brought into chapel and released two large wild rats, which he had captured in a trap. As soon as the congregation were on their knees at the confession, the rats were let loose. Suddenly boys in succession began to jump up and down and shout; masters bobbed about frantically at their desks, 'nailing' on all sides, but to no effect. The commotion swept in a curious, irregular progress through the chapel, at last advancing towards the elevation occupied by the headmaster, who was himself by this time also jumping up and down, but with rage, bobbing and nodding like a jack-in-the-box, 'shaking his fingers, hands and arms at the boys to kneel down, threatening, and in his ire, doing everything but shout'. Then a boy landed a kick on one old rat as he passed, which knocked him into the middle aisle, and all was revealed. The rat did not linger to display himself to the admiring concourse, but set off at full speed down the aisle, passing Keate's elevated station flat out like a racehorse passing the grandstand and, followed by his less fleet companion, vanished down the chapel steps into the hidden underworld whence he had come. When the hoots and the laughter had at last subsided, the prayers which had been in progress during the spectacle became once more partly audible.

The artistic quality of the choral service varied according to whether the singers of the St George's Chapel, Windsor Castle, were available on loan, as they sometimes were, from the royal establishment. The visiting singers not only raised the quality of the singing, they disguised some of the frailties of the resident organist, an eminently charitable man, it was said, 'for his right hand knoweth not what his left hand doeth'.

Feelings for the choral services were mixed in all ranks of the school. Those who enjoyed music, from the fellows to the younger boys, welcomed them. Others found them less agreeable, and bitter complaints were sometimes expressed that the genealogy of the first gospel was inflicted on the congregation in a musical form which was, as well as protracted, improper; for 'while the bass was holding forth about the existence of Abraham, the tenor, in defiance of nature and chronology, was begetting Jacob, and the trebles begetting Jacob and all his brothers'.[18] Some element of this resentment may have inspired the notorious incident which centred upon the person of a celebrated tenor, John Hobbs. The voluntary had ended. The congregation rose and the instrumental introduction to Handel's *Messiah* was played. All waited with silent attention for the opening notes of the voice. 'Co-o-mfort ye, my people' rose in thrilling tones into the air; again and again the noble phrase was repeated, and a fourth time it was being sustained to a climax, when the exquisite sounds were distorted into a shriek of agony. Amidst subdued commotion, John Hobbs was seen to be assisted, limping and moaning, from the chapel by solicitous attendants. It was supposed that the great man had suffered a fit; but what had happened was that, as he reached his top note for the fourth time, one of the confirmation candidates had driven a pin into the calf of his leg. It is not unlikely that the perpetrator became a clergyman, perhaps even a prelate, for Eton, during Keate's time, produced above its average of bishops.

A contemporary, who does not pretend to have been himself an innocent, recalls, in mitigation of the spirit of irreverence which prevailed, the atrocities of a different kind which the boys had to suffer from the pulpit. The sermons preached may have been good or bad, appropriate or bizarre, but their quality was usually irrelevant, because upon one circumstance there is overwhelming agreement; they were, with few exceptions, almost totally unintelligible. Inordinately long, apolaustic pedantries, or whimsical eccentricities were mumbled and grumbled by ancient fellows with smothered voices and grotesque mannerisms, into their waistcoats. One ancient ecclesiastic was famous for his monosyllabic texts, the general favourite of which was 'Shout'.[19] Another provoked a brief spasm of curiosity, not to say levity, when a sentence he uttered was distinguished as, 'When you pray, you need not wait for fixed times and places; make a closet of your bedroom; make a closet of your railway carriage.'

Certain boys, instead of abandoning interest entirely, treated the inaudibility as a challenge, and competed and collaborated to extort some sense from the effusion. Some shut their eyes tight (the better to hear), others opened them wide and fixed them on the mouth of the speaker in the hope of reading from his lips what they could not receive from his speech. There was an occasion when one experienced and conscientious player of this game, although he strained all his faculties, could only make out one word of an entire sermon, and that sounded like 'shoe-strings'. He did distinctly hear that word three times, but was unable to establish any context whatever.

One of the most conscientious of the sermon tasters was William Gladstone and his frustrations are recorded in his diary.

Sunday, October 9th, 1825. Plumptre preached on lying. . . .
Sat. October 16th. Plumptre preached . . . could hardly hear.
Sunday 4th December, Sermon from the Vice Provost – Prepare ye the way of the Lord. Very little of it audible.

How little and how slowly things changed at Eton may be judged by the perpetuation up to and beyond the halfway mark of the century of this orthodoxy of clerical obscurantism. Goodford was a boy at school with Gladstone. Later, when as Provost he read prayers, only one word, Wuffaw (wherefore) was generally intelligible. Whenever in the conduct of a service, Wuffaw was heard more than once, an audible groan went up, for it meant that he had strayed back to the beginning of the prayer. Goodford's voice was a distinctive mixture of a languid Cambridge drawl and a residual West Country burr. On a memorable occasion he preached on the text 'Remember Lot's Wife'. That was about all that was heard, but Lot's wife was remembered, and in after years Old Etonians who had been present could give exact imitations of the sounds, if not the import, of the peroration.

In Keate's and Hawtrey's time the favourites for any award for eccentricity in a gallery rich with candidates would probably have been Green and Plumptre. Green was remembered pacing the cloisters and praying aloud impassionedly for the defeat of the Reform Bill. He it was who addressed a congregation of little boys with the words, 'The subject of my discourse this morning, my brothers, will be the duties of the married state.'[20]

Eton fellows in the shelter of 'sleepy hollow' were licensed to grow curious shapes of personality, and not infrequently became by degrees if not quite mad, at least exceeding strange. Plumptre* used to begin his discourse with a roar emitted from one side of his mouth, which moved in declining sound to finish in a whisper from the opposite side of his mouth, pursued with earnest fidelity by his squint, or 'rolly polly' eye. Such fragments of his lucubration as could be interpreted were in great demand retail, and boys used to sit with pencils poised to capture the occasional flash of lucidity and compare their gleanings in the hope of achieving an intelligible composition.

One juvenile reporter kept into old age his notes of a Plumptre sermon: 'And his mother made him a little coat.' Some sentences later, 'Wash.' Later, 'Thou art Peter.' And again, 'Where were white, green and blue hangings, fastened with cords of fine linen and purple to silver rings and pillars of marble.' Finally, 'This thing was not done in a corner.' This auditor compared his salvage with that of another small boy who later became a bishop, and was able to augment it with the phrase, 'Nine and twenty knives.'[21]

On the ledge of the pulpit was a huge cushion and Plumptre's first requirement, on entering the pulpit, was to plant his cap upon it and conduct a protective investigation. First he turned up each end of the cushion and peeped under it, as if he expected to discover some lurking foe; then he planted his head in his cap and glared with his swivel eye at the congregation. In summer he seemed peculiarly subject to the attention of wasps, against which, defending himself with his spectacles, he appeared to be playing a miniature game of racquets, back-handing and volleying with his tormentor. Occasionally a sentence shone through entire. Describing the happiness of the English people under their young Queen Victoria he intoned, 'And the land is at peace and every man sits in his own garden of cucumbers.'

In the case of the Greens, eccentricity may have been hereditary. W. C. Green, the son of the fellow, and deemed, like his father, a curious being, absentmindedly burnt his own church down. Canvassing friends for subscriptions towards the cost of building a new one, he discovered that one of those he was writing to had also burnt

---

* Plumptre disliked change so much that his contemporaries found it difficult to understand how he had ever come to get married.

down a church in the same county, and he was moved to address his appeal to this correspondent in verse.

> Now look how both by fate's decree
> Two Suffolk fires have lived to see
> You burnt a Rectory at Creeting
> I Hepworth Church, like doom repeating.[22]

Joynes, a somewhat rigid but gentle scholar, tried to comfort the boy Algernon Swinburne when he was frightened and unhappy by reading him the psalms, without notable success. He had better results at the headmaster's dinner table, seated between two guests to whom he had not been introduced, when he kept himself well entertained amidst the noise of conversation, by singing his favourite songs, and telling himself his favourite stories.[23]

Winchester yielded to Eton in the quantity, but not in the quality, of her clerical eccentrics. Dean Rennell, when he preached, used to wear a square of velvet on his head, which in the heat of discourse he would use to wipe his face and then clap it on his head again. The same worthy was wont, having changed into evening dress to go to a party, to retire instead, thus arrayed, to bed, unless prevented by the vigilance of his wife.

These curious ornaments of the public schools, of which each successive generation seemed to produce its share, gave peculiar offence to Benthamite utilitarians, by 'their utter ignorance of human nature and childish incapacity for business' and 'those moral eccentricities by which great scholarship has so often been accompanied and degraded'.[24]

The change, when it came, to a new emphasis on preaching, and simple preaching with a direct contemporary relevance, entered the public schools on the example and influence of the evangelical revival, by way, at first, of Thomas Arnold. The pulpit was Arnold's special domain. He preached with fervour upon subjects which his opponents deemed deplorably unsuitable, controversial, even party political; and he published his sermons. Although he would not have been averse to elevation to a bishopric, he expressed the spirit and assumed the postures of puritan evangelism in which militant preaching had always been paramount. His outstanding follower as a headmaster in holy orders, Charles Vaughan, also distinguished himself in the pulpit and laid great emphasis on preaching; and Arnold's other outstanding disciple, A. P. Stanley, won the ear of Queen Victoria from the pulpit.

The incidence of the intense, but not infrequently forced and shallow fervour of 'muscular Christianity', joined to increasingly utilitarian demands in education, was most conspicuous in the new, or reconditioned, public schools, like Marlborough, Clifton, Wellington and Uppingham, which, in their headmasters' zeal to succeed, naturally reflected the popular trend of the day. The trend was most effectively resisted, after their respective fashions, by Winchester and Eton: Winchester by argument, Eton by bland disregard for as long as possible of change uncongenial to her own *persona*. Eton and Winchester were bound to resist the evangelical current, for its impulses originated in what they regarded as the dissenting enthusiasms of bigotry, irreconcilably alien to the spirit of what religion meant to them, a temperate sacerdotal discipline grounded on obedience to hierarchical authority and conformity to the Thirty-Nine Articles.

Of course certain individual Wykehamists and Etonians went with the current which Arnold had anticipated and accelerated. One writer signing himself 'An Etonian' in an open letter to the Provost of Eton expostulates, 'I think I am not wrong in designating the present age as one of strong religious excitement.' His complaint is that Eton seems unwilling to change with the times, and he urges his 'conviction that the religious energy of any public place of education, must at least keep pace with the general movement going on in the national mind'.[25] William Johnson recognized and acknowledged in 1842 that men in public life were no longer 'indifferent to religion'[26] as they had been seven or eight years ago. As usual he used just the right words and no more. He did not say that they were more 'devout' or 'pious', or 'godly', but that they were 'no longer indifferent'. They could no longer afford to be. This does not mean that the new generation of professed Christians were all hypocrites, but it does mean that if they were by nature, or ambition, or economic pressure, conformists to fashion, they adopted different postures to those still prevalent at the beginning of the century. There are vogues and fashions in religion and in the Church, no less than in the arts and politics; and their influences are complementary and interactive. Men who aspire to advancement in a profession where conformity – even when disguised as non-conformity – is an asset, put on new moral attitudes as easily and 'sincerely' as a fashionable woman puts on new clothes. One must distinguish between posture and practice; but postures are themselves of significance.

'Oh Walter I can't die,' says Charlie of St Winifred's to his friend, in the middle of a conventional gothic storm. 'I can't die yet; and not out on this black sea, away from everyone.' 'From everyone but God, Charlie,' Walter replies, 'and I am with you.' Charlie lives to grow up to become a missionary in distant and savage parts, and in the course of duty is killed, and presumably eaten, by cannibals. But meanwhile the author requires, for the purpose of emotional excitation, a scene of languishing decline from sick-bed to death-bed, an *obbligato* indispensable to his evocation of school life. To the sound of tremulous platitudes a sainted lad, Daubeney, passes decorously away, and his demise is made the occasion for an unctuous rhapsody from the school chapel pulpit. 'The fair sweet purple flower of youth falls and falls, my brethren, under the sweeping scythe of death, no less surely than the withered grass of age. Be ready! Be ready with girded loins!' And so on.[27]

No schoolboys at any time or anywhere may have spoken the stilted cant with which Frederick Farrar, the author of *Eric* (1858) and *St Winifred's* (1862), endows his cast of prigs, young and old; but his books do at least record the attitudes and sentiments which had gradually come to be expected by a substantial public. Their popular success led down to a bizarre basement culture which had begun to evolve, in imitation of supposed reality, when the public-school mystic became an element of social status, materializing as books on life at upper-class boarding schools for boys, written by authors who had never been to such schools. The result was a never-never-land pastiche, compounded of garbled fragments of anecdote retailed at second or third hand, agreeable to the mawkish fancies of readers without the faintest knowledge or experience of the reality. *Reminiscences of School Life* (1864) is a ripe specimen of the genre. The boys and masters who make their appearance in its pages stand in relation to real boys and masters, much as 'pirates' and 'red indians' in Peter Pan stand to the authentic pirates and red indians of history; they are mannikins, tame and spurious. Almost no solecism is left uncommitted. A boy's mother even refers to one of her son's contemporaries as *Master* Jones, but the prescription was manifestly acceptable to the market for which it was designed. A bad boy, Bunkum, accustomed to bullying Digby, is frustrated by the intervention of the chivalrous Rivers, and he revenges himself by pulling a chair away at the moment when Rivers is about to sit on it. In consequence Rivers suffers unspecified injuries which require his withdrawal to the sanatorium. This time the injured party does slowly recover, but the influence of Farrar, already degenerate but still proliferating, is stamped on the scene when Bunkum pays a visit to the invalid in convalescence.

> As he crossed the threshold he started convulsively, for the sight of the darkened room, the long array of medicine bottles and the thin pale face by the bed quite overcame him and changed his indifference to a feeling of contrition.

Bunkum, however, quickly recovers his nerve and enters the room, supposing himself immune to any recurrence of conscience. This is the cue for the conventional dénouement, which, to impart its flavour, is quoted in full:

> 'Ah, Bunkum, how are you,' said Rivers, holding out a thin white hand.
> 'How are you,' was the gruff reply as the boys shook hands.
> 'It is very kind of you to come and see me.'
> 'Well the governor made me come, so I had no choice.'
> A silence ensued, then Harry said – 'You don't look very well, Bunkum. You seem pale.'
> 'Yes, I ain't quite right; I have been sent to Coventry since I – that is – since you had your accident.'
> 'Oh, we won't talk about that. How's the school going on? you have had no cricket since I left.'
> 'No, we have not had any cricket,' was the short, gruff reply; for Bunkum determined not to say too much.
> 'Ah, well then, I have not missed much; but I have been very ill indeed, Bunkum.'
> The sight of Harry's thin face as he said these words almost overcame the boy; he felt a rising in his throat as he murmured, 'Have you?'
> 'But now tell me, Bunkum, was it not meant as a joke when you pulled the chair away from me?'
> 'Of course it was,' said the lad, coughing softly, and speaking in a quivering voice.
> 'I knew it,' replied Harry, smiling; I told M. Blanc so. I said you could not be so wicked; so let's shake hands, Bunkum.'
> This was too much: Bunkum could stand it no longer.
> 'Oh, Rivers, forgive me,' sobbed Bunkum, grasping with both hands the weak little hand which Rivers held out. 'Forgive me, I'll change. I've had a hard part to play. The boys all hate me, – they hate me, and you hate me, I'm sure.'

'No I don't, Bunkum; we'll be friends henceforth; you will change your mode of behaviour I am sure, and all will go well.'

'Oh, thank you, thank you,' said the delighted boy; 'those are the first kind words I've heard since I came here. You know my mother died when I was young, and I've had no one to look after me, so I've done just what I pleased; but now I'll change, I'll try to work, and may yet be able to do well.'

'Bunkum, you shall, my good fellow. We'll be friends; we'll sit together, and I'll help you, and you won't bully Digby again?'

'No that I won't; I'll do whatever you like.'

'Listen, then Tom; I have taken to think more than I did before I was ill, and am inclined to believe that we boys are not quite so religious as we ought to be. Please give me that Testament, and we'll read a chapter together.' Bunkum knelt down at the side of the bed, and when M. Blanc came in, Rivers was repeating these comforting words, –

'Joy shall be in Heaven over one sinner that repenteth, more than over ninety and nine just persons, which need no repentance.'

The evangelical cult of promiscuous religious excitation did not go unopposed or unquestioned. William Johnson discerned from the beginning that this supposedly purifying wind of change carried with it the seeds of other vices of its own, and that to browbeat little boys into 'faith' and to strain a juvenile conscience could cause injuries which might not become visible until much later. 'Over excitation of the religious sense' resulted, according to Clough, Arnold's disillusioned prodigy, who himself suffered it with disastrous consequences, in 'irrational, almost animal irritability of conscience'.[28] We have already heard Moberly's similar warning against 'excessive church going' and all that it entailed.[29] But the spirit of puritan evangelism, though it achieved some spectacular popularity, never really prevailed within the Church of England, in the nineteenth century, any more than it had done in the seventeenth.

That a radical separation between the past and the present had taken place in life and literature, a scholarly purist like James Lonsdale was poignantly aware:

> 'Alas, alas! great Pan is dead'
> And from our land the glory gone
> And pleasant sounds, while still wag on
>   Words rashly flung
> And the unbridled talk of glib Gladstonian tongue.

Although he was too humble in spirit ever to press anyone to agree with him, Lonsdale had no doubt of the direction his approval pointed:

> If that your mind is set upon
> Contrasts, read Burns and then Tennyson
> The first is clear, to nature dear
> The second – Well, he is a peer.[30h10]

There was a separation also in religion, as manifested in the public schools, a distinction of two primary devotional tempers which had been co-existent and unreconciled for centuries in English society: one an ardently protestant evangelical puritanism; the other a reticent, sacerdotal anglican catholicism, subdued even in its expressions of piety. Richard Hooker and Walter Travers had preached alternately from the same pulpit in the Temple, so that the pulpit (said Thomas Fuller), spoke pure Canterbury in the morning and Geneva in the afternoon.

Two hundred years later the gulf remained unbridged. The Act of Uniformity had enclosed but never conjoined the partisans and, as the nineteenth century progressed and the ambling accommodations of the previous century were repudiated in favour of fresh militancy, the old distinctions were asserted with a new sharpness, especially in the field of education, and clergy of different persuasions within the Church of England engaged in long and sometimes bitterly contested disputes over issues of doctrine and forms of worship. It was inevitable that some reverberations of the hostilities in the adult world should act upon the schools. The divisions at the top were fairly clear cut. It was as unlikely that a high churchman should be chosen as headmaster of Rugby as that an enthusiast wth evangelical sympathies should be appointed to command Winchester; unlikely, but not impossible. Later in the century the minds of Old Rugbeians would be exercised over how to get rid of a headmaster who was showing distressing signs of moving too far to the right in liturgy.*

But when the fullest allowance required by the evidence is given to the revival of religion so energetically canvassed by its adherents in the first half of the century, the generality of boys was affected only mildly by the adult propaganda, much less than arch crusaders like Arnold, and later Cotton and Thring, desired and sometimes

---

* Edward Meyrick Goulburn (an Etonian), headmaster of Rugby, 1849–57.

believed. Boys of all ages have tended to view any exceptional demonstration of religious zeal by their contemporaries with suspicious
scepticism. The collective response of schoolboys of many generations
dwells in the remark which slipped casually from one Victorian
chronicler of Eton. 'Although Reginald Purfoy was rather more religious than most of the boys in his tutor's house he was not disliked.'[31]

FOURTEEN

A Demon Hovering

In the 1830s, and as late as 1860, when men used the words 'vice' and 'immorality', they were not taken to be alluding in particular to *sexual* vice and immorality.* Thomas Arnold was continually engrossed by questions of 'Sin' and 'Morality', but in all his recorded homilies there is only one reference, and that a brief and passing one, to sexual offences. The six deadly sins of school life Arnold cited as *profligacy*; *lying*, 'the systematic practice of falsehood'; systematic *cruelty*, as the bullying and persecuting of the weak and vulnerable; *disobedience*, which comprehended all the rest – the spirit of active resistance to, and hatred of, authority; *idleness*; and finally, the *bond* – the spirit of combination and companionship – *in evil*.[2] In respect of 'profligacy' and 'sensual wickedness' his main concern was for drunkenness, which he regarded as a major problem at Rugby; and with drunkenness he conjoined 'other things forbidden in the scriptures'.[3] Arnold's distribution of emphasis was not due to delicacy, nor to unworldly ignorance of the nature and effects of lechery. He knew their character well enough from domestic mishaps. His elder brother, William Arnold, had married a prostitute and Thomas himself had an illegitimate half-brother.[4] While he would have condemned fornication, he saw before him moral and social problems more serious and more urgently in need of his redemptive zeal than sexual irregularities.

When Milnes Gaskell worked cunningly on his mother's feelings by declaring, with a martyr's resignation, that, at her behest, he was willing to 'stand up against the torrents of vice which at every Public

---

* In 1860–61, Harriet Martineau declared that 'a large proportion of the public' as well as herself had been 'amazed and shocked' at recent disclosures 'of the sensual cast of mind of the boys in a great Public School'. The 'disclosures' had been made in *Tom Brown's Schooldays*, and the 'sensuality' revealed, which would make their parents 'dread to expose their sons prematurely to the grosser order of temptations' was the schoolboys' delight in *food*, their daily thinking with sinful 'eagerness and passion of sausages, kidneys, a treat of beef and mustard for supper or good eating of one sort or another'.[1]

School, must more or less threaten all',[5] the term comprehended every practice under moral censure from cruel sports to gambling. And when Miss Margaretta Brown learnt that her protégé, Tom Hoseason, had been seen retiring into the woods off the riverside in company with the 'Hunt girls' known to be 'of loose character', she was not pleased, but neither was she stricken with any sense of monstrous wickedness or disaster. She and other women of her time accepted the nature and appetites of young males as a fact of life, to be contained as far as possible by the discipline of moral training, but not in its manifestations occasion for shock or undue surprise. Miss Brown was incensed by periodic revelations of seduction of young boys by 'nurses' employed in boarding houses;[6] older boys did not conceal their hungry interest in pretty girls accessible in Windsor, and did not hesitate to report in letters home their attraction to a particular quarry.[7]

Up to the 1840s there was no attempt to conceal, or embarrassment evinced at, the illegitimate birth of a considerable number of Etonians. Even the parentage of boys born in wedlock was often in doubt. Creevey and Greville took it for granted that Melbourne's father was not Lord Melbourne, but Lord Egremont, and the Countess of Oxford was so addicted to amorous variety that her children were known as the Harleian Miscellany.

Such an environment encouraged certain censurable qualities, but humbug was not one of them. There was no pretence that boys did not sometimes find initiation in sexual experience with young whores, who came from as far away as Coventry to solicit at Rugby School, and with local girls of light virtue. When an officious assistant master at Shrewsbury declared that 'immorality with women was very common in the School', Butler did not deny that 'it existed and would exist' at least among a few older boys, and that all a master could do was to keep it under and check it to the best of his ability. Butler told his trustees that the church was a place where assignations were made by signal between local manufacturing girls and his senior boys. More worrying to headmasters and parents than 'an unnecessary facility for fornication'[8] was the contingency of a romantic attachment developing between a boy and an attractive and presentable but unsuitable girl, and a boy might be precipitously removed from school on the advice of the headmaster to protect him from an act of folly. The fortune of one of the major clerical dynasties of the age was laid when Charles Sumner obliged Lady Conyngham, the king's mistress, by himself marrying the Swiss girl with whom his pupil, Lady Conyngham's eldest son, had become infatuated, thus saving him from a fate worse than vice.

The extraordinary change in moral postures, affecting almost all levels of society, which became conspicuous as the middle of the century approached, and gathered impetus thereafter, may be seen in an incident at Wellington College in 1871. During the holidays, three foundationers had seduced or, more likely, been seduced by, a fourteen-year-old servant maid employed in the house of one of them. The incident was only discovered because one of the boys was unlucky enough to contract a venereal infection. The headmaster, E. W. Benson, decided that all three must leave the school. He could not expel them formally without reference to the governors, but he could and did arrange for their removal privately with the agreement of the boys' parents. The mothers, widows, acquiesced under Benson's pressure, but one of them, on consideration, repented her decision, and appealed to the governors. The governors, headed by the second Duke of Wellington* (who did not approve of expelling boys for 'immorality') judged that the boys had been somewhat harshly treated and summoned the headmaster to inform him that they had decided that the two uninfected boys should be received back by the school 'as an act of grace by the headmaster'.

This was a confrontation of the old world and the new. The headmaster was wrathful and appalled by heinous wickedness and evil: the aristocratic governors were amused and indulgent to a boyish escapade; when Benson pointed out the purity of the school to a governor, John Walter, the latter 'scoffed at him and indulged in distasteful reminiscences of his Eton days'.[9] Benson had to obey or resign but he knew that the bias of modern society inclined in his favour. He asked for time to consider, and wrote to the headmasters of the great public schools, putting the case without mentioning the decision taken. The answers were unanimous that the boys must go.

At his next interview with the governors Benson presented the letters and stated that if the board insisted on the boys' returning to Wellington, he would ask that it be done on the governors' authority and not on the headmaster's. By now the governors saw that further publicity might damage the reputation of the school and decided not to reverse the headmaster's policy. They clearly were worried about the predicament of the widowed mothers and probably did something

---

* He who had painted Keate's door red; see above, p. 200.

to help them. 'The governors had acted like a pack of cynical, hoary old sinners,' said the Rev. C. W. Penny, whose voice, in this case, may be taken to be the unofficial voice of the headmaster, 'who looked on youthful immorality . . . as a sort of juvenile complaint like measles'. Neither Penny nor Benson had understood. The governors had not looked on the boys' conduct as a distemper, but as a natural stage in male maturation. 'It is a cheap charity,' said Benson, 'for them to reinstate the boys on the Foundation because they are poor, without regard to the evil.'[10]

The incident is revealing. In the interval dividing the early and mid-century, a feverish anxiety, especially in the middle classes, to prevent or abridge sexual experience in the young grew to the dimensions of a collective neurosis. Pusey, expatiating on 'that sin' which 'fifty years ago . . . was unknown at most of our Public Schools', declared that 'now, alas, it is the besetting sin of our boys; it is sapping the constitutions and injuring in many, the fineness of intellect'.[11] By the mid-sixties, and increasingly after, when a speaker used the words 'vice' and 'immorality' without making a contextual distinction or association, he meant, and his auditors understood him to mean, apertaining to sexual misconduct.* 'I have not charged him with *immorality* in the ordinary sense of the word,'[13] Hornby was reported to have said over his dismissal from Eton of Oscar Browning.†

Schoolmasters, educationalists, and self-appointed moralists agonized in hesitation between the alternative dangers of keeping silent and risking the peril of undiscovered abominations growing in secret, or saying too much and planting thoughts and temptations which were not there before. Even a qualification which made meaning explicit could be painfully embarrassing. 'Immorality, used in a special sense, which I need not define,' said J. M. Wilson, later headmaster of Clifton College, addressing the Education Society, 'has of late been increasing among the upper classes of England.'[14] But George Moberly considered that by 1848 the 'inner life' at Winchester

---

* This contraction of meaning in popular usage has persisted. In 1913 Dr David, the headmaster of Rugby, was censured by a senior member of the staff (Bradby) for lack of severity to 'moral' offences. Vehement, but inexplicit, Bradby wrote, 'We should recognise the significance of symptoms, the deadly peril of the disease to the community. . . .'[12]

† Oscar Browning had incurred the headmaster's animosity by indiscretion and disobedience. Good-natured, but irritatingly arrogant and incurably troublesome, he was in personality what today would be called 'camp'. He kept a house at Eton and was conspicuously preoccupied with the moral welfare of his charges, in such a manner that many observers became uneasy about the nature of his influence. Hornby, by stating so openly that he was *not* dismissing Browning for immorality, made it, and meant to make it, clear that moral issues *were* in his mind.

had improved from the condition he remembered as a boy in the second decade of the century, when it had been 'outrageously impure' and 'profoundly secret'.[15] What reasons Pusey and Wilson had to believe that there had been an increase in 'immorality in a special sense' since the earlier part of the century, we shall never know for certain, for neither of them tells us. Wilson continues, 'This is not the place to give details of evidence.' A few minutes later he baulks at another fence. 'I shall pass over this very important point without going into detail.'

Wilson was not, as those quotations taken alone might suggest, a cowardly or timid man. On the contrary he was unusually bold and daring in public utterance for a man of his age. But he was subject to an almost intolerable repugnance in contemplation of physical sexual desires, and he found it virtually impossible to speak to a boy individually on the subject in a friendly, comfortable way. He had to steel himself to make aggressive, but barely intelligible, reference to the subject in sermons from the school chapel pulpit to his juvenile charges. This embarrassment, which he shared with many of his contemporaries, he managed to interpret as a sign of superior moral merit. For, it was 'so utterly repulsive to our nature' to give 'this teaching' on sexual life to boys and girls, 'that men and women of high character and refinement could not and would not do it'. Indeed, what sort of man would he be who would face a class on such a subject? Wilson cited the case of a doctor who, having advised other parents to instruct their sons in the nature of male sexuality before sending them to public schools, found himself 'absolutely unable to begin'.[16] A chorus of corroboration followed these depositions. Frances Lord bore witness that she had never met one grown-up person who had thought about sex without the effort costing 'distress amounting in some cases to such paralysed feeling that made thought useless'. 'E.L.' affirmed that he knew 'more than one father' who thoroughly appreciated the need to give a warning, yet 'nothing could bring him to give it'.[17] E.L. was Edward Lyttelton, and one father he had in mind was his own, George, Lord Lyttelton, whose career we have followed since boyhood at Eton.

Silence, therefore, was to this school of thought, or school of feeling, the ideal course, if it worked. Ignorance, 'total ignorance' of sex 'should always be the rule',[18] according to the chief medical apostle of anti-sex, Henry Acton, and he held up Rousseau's 'hideous frankness' as a dreadful warning of what happens when a man 'pries into his mental and moral character with despicable morbid minuteness'.

288

'Freedom of conversation', Wilson insisted, was an 'incalculable moral evil' and he exhorted parents to give devout thanks for the 'priceless boon' of 'school games' as a subject of conversation. Those who thought that games occupied a disproportionate share of boys' minds should be thankful for it; and he added with crushing finality the question, '*What do French boys talk about?*' Wilson wished that girls could share more of the advantage of a little more of such talk of games. 'Lawn tennis is doing something for them, perhaps,' he added without conviction. In any case, he – the new mentors as a whole – did not wish girls in the vicinity of boys' lives. The ideal way would be 'flight from temptations' for 'there is no other way of dealing with them'.[19]

The perfect course was for the boy to remain entirely innocent and inexperienced of all that pertained to sexual passion until he met his wife-to-be, when, by some mysterious, but natural and wholesome process, all, or rather as much as was necessary for his good, would be revealed, and, if he were fortunate in his choice, this need not be very much; for Dr Acton and others bore the glad tidings that 'love of home, children and domestic duties' were 'the only passions that the best of wives and mothers were capable of feeling'.[20]

But did silence perform its office? Did the proscription of the forbidden subject truly exorcise its fearful allure? The very utterances of headmasters like Benson and Wilson and Cotton demonstrated that it did not. They might, and they did, make it increasingly more difficult than it had been in the freer old days for boys at school to have access to girls. But this separation, instead of putting anxieties at rest, only raised other, different, but no less dreadful, apparitions. Secured from the company of females, what might not boys be incited by the devil to do, alone, or to each other? In the quandary whether to speak or keep silent, when either commission or omission might be the occasion of mischief, the overheated conscience of the new breed of pedagogue–moralist devised a form of self-protective compromise. He did speak, in language stern, earnest, and incomprehensible to all but those boys who already knew more than he wished them to know.

The neurosis was contagious. When Thomas Hughes published *Tom Brown's Schooldays* in 1857, it glowed with an animated portrayal of sides of life in a public school which had never before been presented for public appraisal. On the subject of sexual life, there was not the faintest hint or disclosure.* The kind of Dickensian suppression used in *Oliver Twist* to disguise the real nocturnal activities of Nancy was used in *Tom Brown's Schooldays* to conceal some of the real activities of Flashman and his like at Rugby. But the author well knew of their existence and, thirty years later, when the emotional pressure had risen, we find him publishing anonymously a pamphlet addressed to boys on the subject of depravity. He begins as if he had not changed his attitude by saying that 'immodesty is not in calling a spade a spade, but in alluding to a spade at all without necessity'. But alas, the necessity has arisen. He gives notice of concern with a subject which is 'of the gravest import' but which 'I can scarcely do more than hint at in the most general manner'. He resorts to Latin (*scelus Onanis*) to warn his boy readers that 'the most fatal results' can follow in after years from a practice which he does not otherwise name. 'I could tell of souls hopelessly besmirched and befouled by this deadly habit. More I dare not say; this much I dare not suppress.'[22] This was genteel restrained stuff. Others went much further with greater heat, without achieving more light or a clearer message.

The strain upon the uneasy moralists was considerably relieved by the gratifying revelation that the proper and appropriate persons to instruct boys in elementary facts of human sexuality were not men, but women. While no decent man could be expected to communicate the dreadful details to a boy, the case of a mother, it seemed, was different. In the first instance, a 'good', a 'virtuous' woman, it was well known, was unmoved and untempted by sexual desires† and 'there was no influence to compare with that which the mother possessed in so remarkable a degree'. Suddenly it became 'false delicacy' and 'cruel mercy' for a mother to keep silent. Mothers became

* This statement must be qualified. There *was* a hint of paederasty in his attack on the practice of 'taking up', in which he described a younger boy who had become the favourite of his elders: 'one of the miserable little pretty white handed curly-haired boys, petted and pampered by some of the big fellows, who wrote their verses for them, taught them to drink and use bad language, and did all they could to spoil them for everything in this world and the next'. In the 1871 edition, evidently as a result of protests that the 'taking up' practice could be innocent and beneficial, Hughes added a footnote, part apology, part justification, which ends, 'I can't strike out the passage; many boys will know what I mean.'[21]

† Edward Lyttelton did not go as far as to assert that decent women did not take pleasure in the physical relations of sexuality, but he spread the good news that 'animal desire is stronger in the male than in the female, at least in England'. Edward Pusey seems to have been less sanguine; Honey tells us that Mr A. R. K. Watkinson, of Pembroke College, Cambridge, has evidence that, under Pusey's influence, girls discovered practising (or, more likely, I conjecture, suspected of) masturbation, were referred to a London surgeon who performed (*c.* 1850, presumably without anaethestic) clitoridectomy as a remedy.[23]

290

the conduits through which were discharged much vehement expostulation from troubled men who baulked at themselves addressing boys. Mothers were instructed how to terrify boys into 'virtue' with warnings of lethal danger and to tell them that those who indulged in 'wrong acts' became weak and sickly and unfit for playing games, that they often 'die young or become idiotic', that 'forty years ago a boy who indulged in this sin suddenly went mad and has been in a mad asylum ever since'.[24]

Some of the fantasies which burgeoned from the medical 'science fiction' school of Henry Acton in 1857, and were presented as tested 'facts', were even wilder and more lurid.* One quotation from a favoured 'grand guignol' style of cautionary tale, to be given or read aloud to a boy under suspicion, will represent the genre:

> The fool, the little, inexperienced easily led, flabby brained boy listened. He listened and fell. He allowed the tempter to show him what he meant, to induct him into the knowledge of evil, to work out the devil's end. . . . So the signs began to appear by degrees, the thin lips, the pale cheeks, the haggard features, the irritable temper, the dank and cold hand, and much sleeplessness. Change of air was tried, but the disease had too long a sway; other signs of exhaustion developed themselves, the weak knee and ankle, the bloodshot eye and crimson lower eyelid, and a hard, short cough. And still the victim continued to wreck himself to pieces, the friction now required being so long as to cause the throes of pleasure to be shocks, working terrible havoc on the nervous system. He died suddenly at eighteen, the coroner and twelve men saying it was due to heart disease. But we know better. . . . He left behind certain notes and letters from which the above facts are taken; and perhaps it was as well that he was taken away so soon for, had he lived, who can say what would have been the limit to the disease? . . .

Worse was to come in a scene of vampiric Transylvanian dissolution:

> . . . Vital exhaustion, convulsive spasms, epilepsy and a paralysis – blighting, withering, blasting though they be – fade into mere insignificance beside that other doom – muscular atrophy: in which the victim dies molecule by molecule, inch by inch, till he becomes livid, then the

---

* 'Indulgence is fatal. . . . The pale complexion, the emaciated form, the slouching gait, the clammy palm the glassy eye and averted gaze indicate the lunatic victim to this vice.' Acton was swallowed neat by some headmasters and regurgitated in school sermons. 'The wretched victim either sinks down to a lower level and lives on, or often finds an early grave, killed by his own foul passions.'[25]

process which in other men takes place in the grave sets in, accompanied by childish babbling, and succeeded by manic ravings, while the frame is racked with pain and the imagination tortured with horrid dreams.

After such energetic application of the stick comes, at the end, a sudden carrot of comfort:

But if the vicious habit be left off in time Nature soon puts all to rights again.

With older boys and young men the tone became even more frantic. The Rev. Richard Armstrong exhorted a young captive audience to treat any manifestation of libido in themselves as a woodman treated infection caused by a bite from a poisonous snake. 'No dalliance, no waiting.' He seized his axe and 'with one blow severed his finger. . . .'[26] It seems that what he had in mind was 'plenty of cold water, plenty of brisk exercise', not surgical mutilation, but the advice could have been misunderstood.

Such immoderate and fanatical effusions occasioned a man like Edward Lyttelton, who was a gentleman and no fanatic, embarrassment and uneasiness, for he knew that when boys once discovered that a fraud had been practised on them they would reject, not merely the fraud, but much else tainted by it. He was prudent enough to confess ruefully, at a later date, 'athletes at Public Schools are never above the average standard of virtue, but often below it',[27] for he knew that boys would be likely to find that out for themselves.

A distinctive feature of the new zeal, because it set the pattern also for changed relationships at school, was that the parent (mother) was urged to keep her male children under close surveillance for signs of illicit sexuality from an early infancy. 'In a state of health, no sexual impression should ever affect a child's mind or body',[28] Acton told all who would give him attention. 'Early voluptuous ideas . . .', said another public counsellor, 'transmitted from parents' who have been 'the victims of unbridled lust, may give rise to a dreadful set of circumstances'. If little boys were seen 'to have a predilection for girls and (to use a Hunterian term) toying with them, they should be watched'.

'*Watch*', was, indeed, the watchword of the new order. It was alien to the spirit long venerated in the public schools, but now, in the name of moral purification, it began to be used to invade that social independence of boys which was the sacred centre of the old public-school tradition. The changes in the public schools came very slowly, were strongly resisted and little manifest up to the end of our period. But they were moving towards the stage when Wilson would call with righteous urgency for 'incessant watchfulness', a concept as odious to the old style of master and boy as the notion of 'immorality' – 'in a special sense which I need not define' – was to Wilson. 'We ought to watch for the slightest inclination' of immorality, 'a look, a smile, a gesture' and help the boy at the right moment; the 'help' he had in mind being that 'any offence would be followed by a whipping'.[29]

Whether the new régime did, in fact, reduce what Wilson meant by 'immorality' is uncertain. Lyttelton, looking back on his own experience, was doubtful. 'I admit many boys improve, but some only appear to do so. They learn wariness and decorum more easily than virtue.' Even improvement might be a secret, and as undetectable as recession. There were no open data to work from, only heavily censored memories and subjective impressions and conjectures which could vary so widely that Sir W. Jenner estimated that eighty per cent of boys were implicated, a university physician put the proportion at sixty to seventy per cent and a school physician said that in his experience 'immorality' was 'very rare'; he 'had hardly known any'. An American admirer of the public schools received a very positive impression from his inquiries. 'Throughout the Public Schools a vice is prevalent which is so shocking that it is never mentioned except among those most familiar with the life which the boys lead. And although the Masters have tried and keep trying to suppress it by every means in their power, there is as yet no real public sentiment against it.'[30] This independent view is corroborated by an increasing frustration of zealous schoolmasters in the second half of the century, who complained that, in the words of a typical deponent, the practices were 'in very many cases so completely hidden from the Masters that, what ever they may suspect they can get no proof' and that until 'public opinion among schoolboys' is conquered, 'schoolmasters will fight (as they mostly do splendidly) at a serious disadvantage'.[31]

It did not seem to have occurred to any of the best-intentioned moderns of moral reform that their prescription for a cure of supposed vice might, without achieving its intended effect, do injury to existing virtues. The drying up of the springs of spontaneity and openness was a high price to pay for good intentions of dubious efficacy. In 1758 Lady Caroline Fox had no objection to each of her sons Stephen and Charles sharing a bed with her sister's, Lady Kildare's sons, so

long as they were agreeable – it was, after all, the general custom*
– and when Lord Offaly and Charles were separated it was merely
because they were restless and kicked the bedclothes off.[33] Before the
middle of the following century the suggestion that two boys share a
bed would have been unacceptable at Eton,[34] and would have been
treated as scandalous at some other schools where new brooms had
been introduced. Tolerance of the ancient habits was not due to
naïvety or ignorance. 'Something very unpleasant has happened at
Dupuis. . . .' Miss Brown entered in her Journal on 9 May 1826.
'Lord Lindsay (Lord Balcarre's son) and Deveraux are the boys
concerned. . . .'[35] Such contingencies were accepted and dealt with as
one of the many, but by no means one of the graver, hazards of
school life, and the boys were presumed to be, on the whole, as
competent to regulate this element of their social lives as any other. In
practice the vigour of their execution sometimes needed restraining.
Francis Cust, at Eton, wrote to his elder brother that when a man
came down and tried to pick up boys 'to take a walk with him' in
the playing fields, a party of boys seized him and would have thrown
him into Barnes Pool, if Dr Keate, having been apprised of the
proceedings, had not hastened to the scene and rescued him for
delivery to the constable and presentation to the justices of Iver.[36]

This pragmatic treatment of sexual transactions appeared shock-
ingly casual and careless to later moralists, but it did keep the subject
in a temperate and practical zone of consideration and prevented a
natural element in the human condition from being inflated into a
morbid obsession, with masters described as living 'over the crater
of a volcano',[37] and boys melodramatically exhorted from the pulpit
to venerate the spirit of the great departed Pastor,† who, when he
had spoken of the dreadful menace, 'his brow gathered blackness and
his eyes fire, as he looked into the air, as though he could almost tear
from it him whom he called "the hovering Demon of Impurity" '.[38]

That principle of agonized 'incessant watchfulness' not only eroded

---

* Up to at least the end of the eighteenth century a single bed was an extra charge on the
parents. Some boys enjoyed company, others preferred privacy. W. Grant wrote to his mother
from Rugby on 8 November 1793, requesting her to pay for a study and a 'single bed', if not
a single room, at a cost of 'six guineas' a year. In a satire on schools and schoolmasters, the
master is counselled, 'The more you put in the bed the better also; it will endear them to each
other and prevent their playing wicked tricks.'[32]

† Samuel Wilberforce, 1805–73; Bishop of Oxford and Winchester; third son of William Wilberforce; acquired the sobriquet 'Soapy Sam' from a speech of Lord Westbury's in the House of
Lords on 15 July 1864, in which the bishop's synodical judgement of *Essays and Reviews* was
described as 'a well lubricated set of words, a sentence so oily and sebaceous that no one can
grasp it'.

the character of independence and freedom which was the peculiar heritage of the public schools, but it generated a prurient preoccupation with the very subject it was intended to subdue. Instead of banishing 'impurity', 'watchfulness' infected innocent, and perhaps valuable, relations with suspicion. The time was coming in the seventies and eighties when a man would need to think very carefully whether he might not be seriously misunderstood, before he said, as a dying friend said to Henry Hart, 'Now that I shall never see you again I do not mind telling you that I loved you; loved you as you deserved, as one seldom loves more than once, with my whole heart.'[39] By then, even at Eton, where old liberties died hard, affection between boy and boy, and indeed between man and boy also, was inhibited and disfigured by apprehension not less uneasy for being unjustified, of the 'hovering Demon', and an older boy could not show an interest, however innocent or generous, in a younger, without its being remarked on, and a tendentious construction being put on it.[40]

But in the fifties and sixties the spirit of continuity and resistance to the character of the new order was still robust and effective at the *old* schools. At Harrow a much-loved housemaster used to make his rounds at night wearing hobnailed boots. At Eton a tutor on tour of his house might have, on going into a room where boys looked suspiciously studious, his own private opinion of what had been going on, but it would have been contrary to etiquette for him to express it. The utmost he might do was to make some ironical remark to show that he was not so simple as those he visited should like to think.[41] A tutor, a decade or so later, whose sense of propriety had been so far subverted by the new zeal to pry, or worse, to suggest that a senior boy might act as a spy, was sharply called to order. The captain of a house, writing home to his sister, Susan, alludes to such an approach made by his housemaster.

He actually had the impudence to say he thought I ought to make a periodic visit to the Lower Boys' rooms to see that they were not committing any transgression. So I just up and told him straight out that I was as keen for the reputation of the House as he was himself, and was quite with him in doing anything to keep it up in reason, but if he wanted anyone to go sneaking about like a detective on the system of always expecting to find something wrong, he must get someone else to do it.[42]

Except in specialist publications where the subject was raised in abstract and sterilized terms, sexual life of boys in public schools, although it increasingly preoccupied adults concerned with the education of youth, was seldom alluded to openly in print. Even sophisticated writers like Brinsley Richards and Bracebridge Hemyng avoided reference to what they well knew existed,* although the latter was capable of writing, in another context, of adult sexual relations and prostitution.† They knew that in a society where childhood was sentimentalized in art, while child prostitution flourished as a favourite stimulant for the jaded, the subject of juvenile sexuality was too dangerous for exposure to be tolerable. An editor either would not publish particulars or, if he did, would risk calumny and possible prosecution.

But the very forces which inhibited genuine inquiry promoted the cultivation of scandal. As early as 1840 social sensitivity was keen enough for potential blackmailers to spread rumours of 'immorality' at Eton, with the object of extorting hush money from the headmaster.[43] While the surface of 'respectable' life became more rigidly decorous – and vulnerable – the hidden world, ostensibly recognized by those who paid for and used it, became darker and more depraved. In the underground products of pornography, more joylessly brutal than anything preceding them, it was possible to say anything; but there, because it *was* pornography, it would not be the truth that was sought or found, but the provision of bizarre invention to gratify the secret appetites of men of public probity and principle. Thus, a book like *The Adventures of a Schoolboy: or the Freaks of Youthful Passion* (1866) will tell the historian little, or nothing, of actual life which is valid. The private conversations between men in which we know, from allusions in private diaries, that the realities were discussed in detail have passed away, in the main, unrecorded. Such records as were kept were liable to suffer the fate of Lord Byron's and Sir Richard Burton's papers at the hand of a conscientious friend or widow.

Occasionally, however, someone who could say much to the point from personal experience made an unwelcome and embarrassing interruption of the ordinarily harmonious voluntaries and responses offered up by the Purity Alliance and other self-appointed proctors. The correspondence which followed the publication of J. M. Wilson's lecture on 'Immorality in Public Schools' in 1883 proved more than one reader could allow to pass unchallenged. Refuting the primary

* Except when they wrote anonymously, as I suspect Richards did as 'Olim Etonensis' in the *Journal of Education*; see below, p. 297.

† Bracebridge Hemyng was a collaborator of Henry Mayhew's, and contributed 'Prostitution in London' to Mayhew's *London Labour and the London Poor* (extra volume).

hypotheses and the conclusion of the moral agitators which had hitherto been treated as sacrosanct, he shrewdly requested the editor to publish his letter, unless 'only similar views to those already expressed are to be admitted', since he entirely differed from Mr Wilson and others who had written on the subject.

Calling himself 'Olim Etonensis', this correspondent supported his opinions with memories of his own school life, which internal evidence suggests had been *c.* 1855. He argued that no schoolmaster – and most of the previous correspondents were schoolmasters – knew much about the subject of immorality in his school because he was the last person who would be informed; and a schoolmaster was often as easily misled by evidence as by lack of evidence. Discovery did not in itself imply prevalence, and lack of discovery was no guarantee of immunity. He remembered that in his own schooldays sexual relations were most active when masters were congratulating themselves on the moral purity of tone in the school; and that at another time agitation and harassment were at their most intensive when there was least cause for them. As for the suggestion of enlisting the aid of 'leading boys' as 'confidential friends' of the masters', who were to be, in fact, informers, the suggestion was 'absolute rubbish'. If such a boy never told the master what really went on, the 'confidential system' was useless; if he did tell he must deny it to his schoolfellows, or what was almost worse, act as though he did not tell, and live a lie until he was discovered and rejected with loathing and contempt as a traitor and spy.

However, 'Olim Etonensis' had good news for the distressed moralists. The results of the 'evil' they feared had been 'ludicrously misrepresented'. He had in his mind's eye a long list of those of his school contemporaries who were most addicted to this as opposed to other 'vices' such as drinking, bad language, stealing, bullying, idleness. What would he expect, from Mr Wilson's view, to find had happened to those boys as men? He would have to point to mental and physical wrecks, men who had 'dragged hitherto a miserable existence, preys to consumption and atrophy and insanity, or else outcasts from all good society'. But instead he had to report that these very same boys were today happy and successful men, cabinet ministers, army officers, country gentlemen, clergymen and active members of the other professions, and that they were nearly all of them, 'fathers of thriving families'. There was nothing, in his opinion, in the moral conditions of schools that called for extraordinary measures. Indeed a particular friend of his, a man eminent in public life, a peer, the lord lieutenant of one of the shires, and the father of a public schoolboy, said that he dated his 'self respect and attention to his appearance' from the time when he was 'taken up' by an older boy at school. He therefore invited the previous correspondents to take comfort from the news that 'happily an evil so difficult to cure is not so disastrous in its results' as they had been misled into fearing. His advice to schoolmasters was 'Let well alone.'[44]

Predictably, the letter gave great offence to those who had been raising the alarm. Not only was 'Olim Etonensis' attacked personally (or as personally as a sobriquet permitted) and warned that there was 'a God in Heaven' (by someone calling himself 'An Oxford First Class Man'), but the editor was censured for having put the whole controversy on 'a lower footing' by publishing a letter which treated 'a painful and terrible subject' with 'easy flippancy' which was 'enough to make all right thinking men, as well as angels, weep'. The writer most hostile to 'Olim Etonensis', nevertheless agreed with him that the best policy was to let well alone, because, he confessed, 'for my part I should as soon think of explaining such things to my own daughters'. The way to deal with the fault was 'instant expulsion'.

'Olim Etonensis's' reference to the benign effects of an older boy 'taking up' a younger was tantalizingly brief; for that had been the most controversial, the most justified and the most criticized, element of the traditional system. Highly emotional friendship between an older and a younger boy, though, of course, without a hint of physical attraction, was presented by Thomas Hughes in *Tom Brown's School-days*, as a noble and commendable association, favoured and encouraged by Dr Arnold,[45] who himself had had, and spoken openly of, an intense and emotional intimacy with another boy at Winchester.* At the time when 'Olim Etonensis' was at school, Frederick Farrar, an assistant master at Harrow, was writing on the subject of temptation and sin at a public school in *Eric, or Little by Little* (1858). Farrar did not object to emotional friendships for he himself was as tremulous and prodigal in emotion as a nervous, romantic spinster:

> At last Eric broke the silence. 'Russell, let me always call you Edwin, and you call me Eric.' 'Very gladly, Eric. Your company has made me so happy.' And the two boys squeezed each other's hands, and looked into each other's faces, and silently promised that they would be loving friends forever.

* The boy's name was Liscomb.[46]

But the 'taking up' of a younger by an older boy was a different matter, which Farrar, like Hughes, regarded with worried disapproval:

> 'Your cousin Upton had "taken up" Williams,' said Montague to Russell one afternoon as he saw the two strolling together on the beach with Eric's arm in Upton's.
> 'Yes, I am sorry for it.'
> 'So am I. We shan't see so much of him now.'
> 'You mean you don't like the "taking up" system?'
> 'No, Montague; I used once to have fine theories about it. I used to fancy that a big fellow would do no end of good to one lower in the School and that the two would stand to each other in the relation of knight to squire. You know what the young knights were taught, Monty – to keep their bodies under subjection. To love God and speak the truth always. But when a boy takes up a little one, *you* know pretty well that those are not the kind of lessons he teaches.'

Farrar's little prigs, for ever trembling and blushing, and clutching each other convulsively, preach indefatigably to each other, except when, in a crisis, their author interrupts to harangue them personally like an anxious coach on the touchline:

> 'Now Eric, now or never! Life and death, ruin and salvation, corruption and purity, are perhaps in the balance together, and the scale of your destiny may hang on a single word of yours. Speak out, boy! Tell those fellows that unseemly words wound your conscience; tell them that they are ruinous, sinful, damnable; speak out and save yourself and the rest. Virtue is strong and beautiful, Eric, and vice is downcast in her awful presence.'

The carnal consequences of the indulgence into which Eric is tempted are described in sepulchral rhetoric:

> Many and many a young English man has perished there, the jewel of his mother's heart – brave and beautiful and strong lies buried there. Very pale their shadows rise before us, the shadows of our young brothers who have sinned and suffered. . . . May every schoolboy who reads this page be warned by the waving of their wasted hands, from that burning marle of passion, where they found nothing but shame and ruin, polluted affections and an early grave.[47]

Whatever life was like at school, it was not like that, past, present

299

or future. Farrar was a freak and a joke in his own time at Harrow; teasing him was so rewarding that a great deal of skill and management went into the sport. It was carried far beyond mere classroom fooling. Harrovians set up an intelligence circuit with Marlborough and fed their correspondents with mischievous accounts of the torment to which Farrar was reputedly subject at Harrow. The Marlburians played their role in the game by writing solicitously to inquire of the victim how he was surviving the cruel persecution. Farrar's response to the bait exceeded the conspirators' most sanguine expectations. He wrote off at boiling point of indignation to his friend Beesley at Marlborough:

> My dear Beesley, I am perpetually annoyed by letters from the boys at M[arlborough] speaking as if I have been subject to personal violence by the boys here, and today I have been informed that I had been tied by a great coat and pelted with cinders!! I can't tell you the ineffable disgust which these preposterous rumours give me, and as they are as grotesquely and groundlessly and absolutely false and as diametrically the reverse of anything possible as they can be, I do wish once and for all that they could be authoratively corrected. Whence such absurdly and gratuitously nonsensical tittle tattle can have originated I cannot even dream unless some Harrovians have been humbugging one of the M[arlborough] fellows. The idea! I wonder whether you all think me made of straw. Likely that I should be roughly handled [by] every one and all of whom instantly obey my slightest order and who are in a complete state of subjection. . . .[48]

The effects of these humiliating experiences upon Farrar are seen in his attempts to depict in fiction the character of sinister and mischievous juveniles. He is here describing the kind of boy at Harrow whom he dreaded, while yet unable himself entirely to resist the spell of the bad boys' allure:

> I am sorry to write of this boy. Young in years, he was singularly old in vice. A more brazen, a more impudent, a more hardened little scapegrace – in school-boy language 'a cooler hand' – it would have been impossible to find. He had early gained the nickname of Raven from his artful looks. His manner was a mixture of calm audacity and consummate self conceit. Though you knew him to be a thorough scamp, the young imp would stare you in the face with the effrontery of a man about town. He was active, sharp and nice looking, and there was nothing which he was either afraid or ashamed to do. He had not a particle of that modesty which in every good boy is as natural as it

is graceful; he could tell a lie without the slightest hesitation or the faintest blush; nay, while he was telling it, though he knew it was a lie, he would not abash for an instant the cold glances of his wicked, dark eyes. Yet this boy . . . was only thirteen years old. And for all these reasons Wilton was the idol of all the big bad boys in the school . . . for the boy had in him the fascination of a serpent.[49]

But his is a view from the outside; for Farrar was never inside a public school as a boy, and what is offered as a likeness is largely the fruit of his fancy.

What then *did* go on in the schools, which so agitated the moral sensibilities of the Victorians? The broad answer is that, as in the outside world, there was no uniformity in depth, only a spurious superficial uniformity. There was innocence and there was depravity, and all the intervening gradations of distinction. Hallam was loved at Eton almost to the point of adoration by his intimates, but, although there has been speculation to the contrary, I should be very surprised if there had been any element of conscious sensuality in the relationships. At the same time in the same school another circle of boys was engaged in practices similar to those in the male brothel in Cleveland Street of subsequent notoriety. Romantic, sacrificial friendships and rabid sensual lusts all went on in the same community together. It was possible for a boy to go through school without having an inkling of what was going on under his nose. Stanley said that when he read *Tom Brown's Schooldays* he discovered a world the existence of which he had not even suspected when he was at Rugby. If that is true, then more had been happening at Rugby, in his time – and very close to him – than he dreamed of, even *after* reading *Tom Brown's Schooldays*. He was destined as an adult to learn something of that hidden world in dramatic and shocking circumstances. It was a world virtually impenetrable to an adult save by betrayal from within. Boys were prohibited by one stern code from revealing what they knew: men were deterred by another from uncovering what they remembered. Occasionally a serious accident occurred and, after a muffled explosion, a list of casualties was posted.

1859 was the year of the purge at Westminster, when five notabilities among the senior boys and athletes were condemned to banishment. Execution was quiet and discreet, but there was no disguise attempted in the entry in the Town Boy Ledger, which was intended only for the eyes of the writer's peers and his successors. 'Senior boys were surprised by being called out of bed late at night and summoned singly before Scott and Marshall and questioned as to immorality in the school in general and in College in particular.' Investigation went on until 3 a.m., the boys being isolated and allowed no communication with each other before interrogation. The sequel was that five senior boys were sent away. They were the following: Henry James Frederic Pratt, future sub-deputy opium agent (in Bareilly); James Thomas O'Brien, second son of the Bishop of Ossery, Ferns and Leighlin: commissioned ensign in the 43rd Foot; promoted major; the circumstances of his departure from Westminster did not prevent a memorial brass being erected to him in the school lobby; Charles William Spencer Stanhope, Vicar of Crowton, Cheshire; Charles Robert Henderson; Worcester College, Oxford: died Port Perry, Ontario, Canada, 2 September 1866; George Upperton, ensign 3rd Foot; died 1875. Five others were rusticated and eleven lesser offenders 'were operated on in the library'.[50] The zeal of the inquisition and the scale of the sentences were signs of the times. Ten years earlier there would have been no such solemn and strenuous audit of transient paederasty. But in the new climate of moral intensity, masters felt obliged, in the rare event of a confession, to use the intelligence obtained to make a cautionary example of great delinquents. It should not be disregarded that the increased anxiety about suspected moral 'impurity' of boys corresponded with the increased sequestration of boys from the company of the other sex. Not long before, it had been perfectly understood that an adult woman might take a romantic interest in an adolescent boy, and the beautiful Eton Dame, Florella Angello, had written to a friend in verse on her sense of loss at the imminent departure of two of her favourites:

> I'm left quite alone
> For Coleridge* and Evans† my favourites are gone
> Such elegant figures such charming young men
> I never shall look on their like again,
> However of late my examining eye
> Has fixed upon one their loss to supply
> And that one is Townsend‡ such douceur such grace
> So slender a waist and so smiling a face
> His figure delights me he must be my beau
> In short I will have him to breakfast just so.[51]

* Probably Coleridge maj., Henry Nelson; Kings, 1817; barrister. Known for his Introduction to *Greek Classic Poets*.

† Evans maj. KS; Kings, 1817. Later prepared boys for Eton at Stoke Poges, near Slough.

‡ Townsend KS, Lord George Osborne; brother of the marquess. Became a clergyman; fellow of Kings.

Shortly before the Westminster purge there had been a lesser disturbance at Harrow. The accused were treated leniently; nobody was
expelled, from which it might have been supposed that the culpability
had been trivial or doubtful. But out of sight a more serious drama
was in preparation. While 'Olim Etonensis' was still at school, a
contemporary of his at Harrow, who must have known Farrar as
assistant master, was taking observation for that stark portrayal,
which was lacking, of the 'hidden world' alluded to by baffled headmasters. However strict the code of silence of a secret sodality, it is
never entirely free from the hazard of admitting a natural betrayer,
that is, a betrayer who follows his course, not in submission to a
contrary allegiance, nor entirely from motives of ambition, but in
obedience to a deep-rooted instinct to betray.

Such a natural betrayer was the boy, John Addington Symonds,
who arrived at Harrow in the spring of 1854, at the age of fourteen.
The son of a prosperous medical practitioner, John was an intelligent,
observant, unhappy, introspective child, on his own admission 'neurotic'. His mother, he suspected, with a constitution inadequate to the
strain of childbirth, had 'transmitted neurotic temperament to certain
of her children'. He was also what today is called 'homosexual', a
person not only physically attracted by members of his own sex, but
incapable of maturing intimacy with a member of the opposite sex
in the role of mate. The category of homosexual was not recognized
in Symonds's youth; he himself helped to promote the concept, if not
the term, in the field of psychopathological diagnosis. Previously,
love between men had of course been recognized and celebrated with
approval in literature and art. The occurrence of sexual lust between
males was treated not as an abnormal alternative to heterosexual
relations, but as a supplement to normal sexual intercourse, indulged
in by profligate sensualists in quest of increased variety.* A sodomite
was identified by his acts, not by the nature which caused them. The
boy Symonds was thus to find himself a mystery to himself; for he

---

* A. C. Benson alludes to a high-minded acquaintance of his who 'formed a very devoted
friendship with a younger' and 'a singularly attractive boy', but one who, beneath his charm,
had 'an unworthy and brutal nature, utterly corrupt at bottom'. Finally the truth is revealed
to the elder, but innocent, of the two and, says Benson, 'I can hardly picture to myself the
agony, disgust and rage [his words and feelings about sensuality of any kind were strangely
keen and bitter], loyalty fighting with a sense of revulsion, pity struggling with honour when
he discovered that his friend was not only yielding, but deliberately impure.' In correspondence
between the two youths before the sinister discovery, 'Arthur's letters were,' says Benson, 'so
passionate in expression, that for fear of causing uneasiness, not to speak of suspicion, I will
not quote them'.[52] A severe distinction was made, and professed practicable, between passionate
platonic love – *virtuous* – and sensual attraction – *sinful*.

feared and was repelled in its physical reality by what excited and disturbed his imagination, and he did not at school perform the forbidden acts, which others did out of sheer animal exuberance, but his mind dwelt on them with a mixture of revulsion and fascination. Like many other little boys before him, Symonds arrived at his public school in a state of bleak loneliness. 'I felt,' he said, 'as though my heart would break, as I crunched up the ground beneath the boughs of budding trees.' He nerved himself for the long ordeal that lay ahead by recalling the formula he had heard adults use to account for his fate: 'I have to be made a man of.'

Symonds was not a boy with qualities likely to endear him to other boys. Timid, shy and unsociable, he was physically feeble, deficient in vigour both of body and mind, incapable, he felt, of asserting himself; he was also subject to boils, styes and colds. These unattractive blemishes would not have raised insuperable barriers if he had played any game well, or merely possessed the redemptive grace of a little charm. But he shrank from all games as if constitutionally disabled. He could not throw a ball or a stone like other boys, and, to his especial chagrin, he could not learn to whistle like them; and at the centre of his timidity was not an imprisoned generosity, but a brooding arrogance which required time 'to stand aloof to preserve the inner self inviolate, to await its evolution'. Conceiving himself, when he was merely disregarded, 'perpetually snubbed, or crushed, or mortified', he felt his 'inner self harden after a dumb kind of fashion' and he kept repeating, 'Wait, wait. I will, I will.' What he was to wait for and what he was to become he did not ask. But an impulse to revenge through an act of destruction in the exercise of power was gathering, and it was a force all the more dangerous for being unconscious.

In school work – and that of course meant classics – John Addington Symonds did well, and he enjoyed the benefit of study under the best classic ever to have been the school's headmaster. Charles Vaughan had ruled Harrow ever since in 1844, 'a smooth faced boy', he was advised by Turton* when the headmastership of Harrow fell vacant not to waste himself on the school. Harrow had suffered more and recovered less than any other public school from the depredations of the rebellion era. Some of the older buildings only survived because James Richardson had dissuaded the insurgents from burning them down (at Byron's instigation) 'since they

---

* Thomas Turton, Dean of Peterborough; subsequently Bishop of Ely, 1845–64.

would be destroying their own fathers'' names carved on the wood panelling.[53] In 1844 there were only sixty-nine boys left in the school, and these were in a state of such indiscipline and insubordination that Vaughan, on being chosen as headmaster, was advised by the Vicar of Harrow, who was also a school governor, to expel the lot, and have back only such as he chose, on his own terms.[54] The favourite sport of Harrovians was then throwing stones at living targets, and practice had made their aim accurate. Not a dog could live on Harrow Hill. Tradesmen feared to bring their carts near the school lest their ponies were maimed or blinded.[55] Within two years order reigned under a Rugbeian monitorial system; the number of boys had risen to 200 and continued to rise, until in Symonds's time it reached 469, while the reputation of Harrow soared from its lowest level to unprecedented heights.

We first met Dr Vaughan as a schoolboy at Rugby under Arnold. 'Monstrous cute' was how 'Muscleman' Oswell had described him in a letter to his mother,[56] which was Rugbeian slang for 'very clever'. From being 'monstrous cute' and sitting on the right hand of Dr Arnold in his sixth-form convocation, Vaughan went on to become one of the two scholastic celebrities produced by Rugby in Arnold's time, the other being his closest friend and future brother-in-law, Arthur Penrhyn Stanley, 'Two of the most remarkable men of our time', said the historian, George Rawlinson.[57] Vaughan went to Cambridge and Trinity and was first Classic of the university, collecting also the Porson Prize and the Chancellor's medal. He was elected Fellow of Trinity College and in 1841 became incumbent of St Martin's, Leicester. In 1842 at the age of twenty-six and looking less, he was considered by the school governors (by one vote) too young to succeed his former master, Thomas Arnold, as headmaster of Rugby. Two years later he was offered and accepted the post of headmaster of Harrow.

Old Harrovians and parents of Harrovians were keenly aware of the debt they and the school owed Dr Vaughan. Even the Earl of Galloway, at his most indignant over his son Randolph's treatment by the monitor Platt, went out of his way to pay tribute to 'the fostering care of so gifted a Master and so excellent a man as Dr Vaughan, whose character and admirable qualities have raised Harrow so high in general satisfaction'.[58] The most exacting of a headmaster's critics, the assistant masters, prized the privilege of serving under his leadership. Of his strength of will, 'perfect self possession' in 'calm repose of power' and purpose, there was never any doubt. 'We all knew,' said Montagu Butler, first assistant master and destined to be Vaughan's successor, 'we had at our head a strong ruler who was not to be trifled with.' The 'impenetrable meekness' hiding 'an iron will and determined resolution'⁵⁹ and a softness of voice and manner, at first almost startling, never left any illusion with boys and masters alike as to his penetrating insight or resolute strength.⁶⁰ There was something mysterious, almost inhuman it seemed to some, about Vaughan, which lay in the co-existence of his 'inelastic softness of voice' and 'unruffleable suavity of expression' together with severe and sometimes ruthless performance. It was told of Vaughan that he indicated the termination of a particularly severe flogging by saying to the recipient in dulcet tones, 'Thank you, my dear boy, I won't trouble you any more today.'⁶¹ Vaughan himself said he found it an advantage that 'the more angry I am with a boy, the calmer I am in appearance'. 'In truth,' said an Old Harrovian, 'there was no art to find the construction of Vaughan's mind either in his face or his voice. There was an element of inscrutability in him.'⁶²

Another element in the paradox was what Sir George Trevelyan called Vaughan's 'abundant drollery, carefully suppressed in uncongenial company'. Under his official air of solemnity was an exquisite sense of the ridiculous and his soft-voiced irony could sear. Montagu Butler, speaking 'from clear personal recollection' put it with tactful understatement: 'his bright wit and sense of the ludicrous were not always untinged with sarcasm'.⁶³ To a self-important mother who said that before she entered her son for the school she must ask the headmaster whether he was particular about the social antecedents of the boys accepted, he is said to have replied, 'Dear Madam, as long as your son behaves himself and his fees are paid no questions will be asked about his social antecedents.'

Vaughan was an exact scholar who wrote English with the same limpid economy with which he wrote Greek, but he was not in the least what today would be called an 'intellectual', in the meaning of someone who traffics in modish concepts of political or social philosophies. Matthew Arnold, who was very much an 'intellectual', said that Vaughan – they had, of course, known one another since boyhood – was 'brutally ignorant',⁶⁴ which meant, at the least, that Vaughan did not read the books which Arnold read or, more damning still, those which he wrote. It may also have meant that Arnold had been in collision with one of those strokes of what G. W. E. Russell called the 'remorseless sarcasm and mordant wit' which Vaughan concealed 'under the blandest of manners', never returning from a visit to the Athenaeum of which he was a member, without 'leaving behind him some pungent sentence which travelled from mouth to mouth and spared neither age nor sex nor friendship nor affinity'.[65]

Montagu Butler was devoted to Vaughan both as Harrovian boy and later as assistant master; but when Butler came to succeed Vaughan as headmaster, Henry Sidgwick remarked of the appointment that he 'only wants experience to carry Vaughan's system of disinterested and unremittingly careful management thoroughly well; and he will add this important advantage that nobody will ever fancy him insincere'.[66] In such occasional, fleeting allusions a faint but tenacious suggestion of uncongenial mystery persisted, the more baffling for being indefinable, for there was nothing evasive in Vaughan's public personality.

Being headmaster of Harrow and in holy orders, Dr Vaughan necessarily preached from the pulpit of the school chapel. He once continued to preach with gentle, unbroken composure while a boy in the congregation was in the noisy throes of an epileptic fit. His sermons, sometimes terse, never prolix, often elegant, always well organized and coherent (which could not be said of all his fraternity's emanations), were models of homilies for boys. He even managed to preach with dignity on 'The Excitement of Sensuality'. John Addington Symonds must have been one of those who heard this address, when it was first delivered from the pulpit at Harrow, beginning, 'It is a great thing, my brethren, early in life to fight it out with the body; to settle the question once and for all, whether the body or the mind and soul shall be master.'[67]

Symonds may even have pondered the words when he returned to his house (Rendall's) where 'the body' was, at that time, notably masterful, as he tells us in his manuscript autobiography:*

Every boy of good looks had a female name and was recognized either as a public prostitute or as some bigger fellow's bitch. Bitch was the word in common usage to indicate a boy who yielded his person to another. The talk in the studies and dormitories was incredibly obscene. One could not avoid seeing acts of onanism, mutual mastur-

---

* Phyllis Grosskurth first drew attention to the contents of the school section of J. A. Symonds' autobiography in her biography of him, *John Addington Symonds* (1964). She was inhibited from transcribing any part for reproduction and might only make short notes for reference under the terms of the controls then operant. What follows is the first reproduction, to my knowledge, of any part of the autobiography since the restrictions were raised in 1977.

bation and the sport of naked boys in bed together. There was no refinement, no sentiment, no passion, nothing but animal lust in these occurences. They filled me with disgust and loathing.[68]

They also filled him with a curious feeling of fascination, even for the acts and players whom he most protested to loathe. The times and occasions he professed to detest attracted him 'in fancy' and always found him contiguous and hovering. Two of the chief lechers in what appeared to be a particularly bad house were called Currey* and Clayton.† The latter he could dismiss as a 'brutal clown', 'stupid, perverse and clumsy', but Currey, 'a clever Irish lad', troubled him, for although he was 'dirty in his dress and person, filthy in his talk, shamelessly priapic in his conduct', he was also a better scholar than Symonds himself, and, as Symonds discovered to his bewilderment, there were 'really fine intellectual and emotional qualities beneath the satyric exterior'.

Another in the same set, Barker, 'was like a good-natured bugimands ape, gibbering on his perch and playing ostentatiously with a prodigiously developed phallus'. A minion in the same house who at one time or another served all three of 'the Beasts as they were playfully called', was a boy called Cookson‡ whom Symonds describes as 'a red faced strumpet with flabby cheeks and female mouth – the *notissima fossa* of our House'. Cookson's fate may illustrate the ways in which the warlike sodomites used terror to defend their secrets. Symonds did not know what Cookson had done to incur the displeasure of his erstwhile protectors but, whatever it may have been, he saw its effects in the kind of displays which were omitted from *Tom Brown's Schooldays*. Symonds says, 'I have seen nothing more repulsive in my life – except at the Alhambra Theatre when I saw a jealous man tear the earrings out of the ruptured lobes of a prostitute's ears and all the men in the saloon rose raging against him for his brutality – than the inhuman manner in which the poor creature Cookson came afterwards to be treated by his former lovers [*stallions*

---

* William Edmund Currey, Rendall's, Easter–Midsummer, 1854; son of F. E. Currey, Esq., Lismore, Ireland; monitor, 1857; Lyon Scholar, 1859; Scholar of Trinity College, Cambridge; 4th Classic, BA, 1863; fellow, 1865. HM Inspector of Schools. Died 1908.

† Richard Clayton, Rendall's, January–Easter 1853; son of Rev. R. Clayton, Newcastle-on-Tyne; Cricket XI, 1858; Football XI, 1855–56; left, 1858. Joined 68th Light Infantry, served New Zealand War, 1864–66 (medal), retired captain, 1871. Banker in Newcastle-on-Tyne.

‡ Norman Charles Cookson, Rendall's, Easter–Midsummer, 1855; son of J. W. Cookson, Esq., of Benwell Tower, Newcastle-on-Tyne; left, 1858; Coalowner, lead manufacturer, etc., of Oakwood, Wylam-on-Tyne. Well known as orchid grower. Died 1909.

is crossed out].' After he had been rolled on the floor, indecently exposed and violated in front of spectators, Currey, Clayton and Barker took to 'trampling' on Cookson whenever they encountered him in the passages and in the court through which they entered the house from the road; 'they squirted saliva and what they called "goby" upon their bitch, cuffed and kicked him at their mercy, shied shoes at him and drove him with curses whimpering to his den'.[69]

Meanwhile Symonds conducted his own love life on an entirely different and ethereal plane, as he supposed. He formed infatuations for remote and unattainable figures, such as the 'big and powerful' boy named Huyshe,* whose hymn book he stole from his seat in chapel; but he never spoke to him. The one who caused him to shudder and quake with a mixture of longing and dread was Henry Dering,† whom he likened to a 'handsome Greek brigand'‡ with a 'body powerful and muscular, lissome as a tiger'. Symonds confessed, 'The fierce and cruel lust of this magnificent animal excited my imagination.' Dering was in The Grove, but he used to come into Rendall's 'after a plump, fair-haired boy called Ainslie,* whom we dubbed Bum Bathsheba because of his opulent posterior parts'.[70]

The energy and number of Dering's activities got him into trouble. It was one of his adventures which occasioned the brief disturbance on the confident surface of Harrow, to which reference has been made. 'Dering,' reports Symonds, 'sent a note in school to a handsome lad, O'Brien,† who went by the name of Leila. It informed him that he had a good bed ready and asked him to come there in the interval between 3rd and 4th School, that is from 4–5 p.m.' The note fell into the hands of the form master who gave it to Vaughan. The entire school was summoned to the Speech Room. The headmaster, without the other masters in attendance, read the letter aloud, strongly

---

* Francis John Huyshe, son of General A. Huyshe CB, of Denfield, Exeter; left, 1866; Brasenose College, Oxford; BA, 1864; MA, 1867; Vicar of Wimborne Minster, Dorset, 1881. Honorary canon of Salisbury. Died 1905.

† Henry Nevil Dering, The Grove, September–Christmas 1852; son of Sir E. C. Dering OH, 8th Baronet; winner of Rackets Championship; left, 1855; entered Diplomatic Service, 1859; 2nd Secretary, 1870; Secretary Legation, 1882; Agent and Consul General at Sofia 1892–94; Minister at Rio de Janeiro, 1900. CB, 1896; KCMG, 1901; JP of Kent. Died 1906.

‡ Time tames even a Byronic 'Greek brigand'. Lt Col. Sir Rupert Dering, the 12th baronet, told me that all he could remember about his kinsman was 'a rather dull diary that he kept while in attendance at the Congress of Berlin'.

* Aymer Ainslie, Rendall's, January–Easter, 1854; son of Rev. Dr. G. Ainslie, Master of Pembroke College, Cambridge; winner of Rackets Championship; left 1859; Pembroke College, Cambridge; University Rackets Player; J.P. for Lancashire. Died 1901.

† Edward Arthur O'Brien, son of E. E. O'Brien, Esq., Dublin. Left 1857. 'Financial business USA' 1865–82. Subsequently newspaper manager in London.

condemned the use of female names for boys,* and pronounced sentence. Dering was to be flogged; O'Brien had lines set him, how many Symonds did not remember.

Another of those present also remembered the scene vividly, and published an account many years later, omitting, of course, the names and details which Symonds recorded in his unpublished auto-biography:

There must be those who can recall the summons of the whole School to the Speech-room (in the Old School building) where the boys sat on raised tiers of seats, filling every corner and the Masters with the Headmaster in the middle sat on a platform. Dr Vaughan entered the room last of all, and as he reached his central chair the door was closed. But there were occasions when special offences may have been committed and the closing of the door and the Headmaster's sitting down, with a murmer [sic] which was quite awful in its calmness and solemnity of address which created the profoundest impression, are things to be remembered.

One particular occasion can be recalled, when he alone, without the Masters, met the School in this way, and had the great assemblage of boys, it is not too much to say, in the hollow of his hand. The stillness was phenomenal, and the impression produced by the words, addressed to the School in general and to the culprit in particular, cannot be exaggerated. Dr Vaughan had a way of pushing back his chair when the business was concluded, which seemed to say better than words that all was over.[73]

Symonds was left puzzled by the lenity or, as he put it, 'inadequate form'[74] of the punishment. Several years later, when he was a monitor, he was consorting with another boy called Alfred Pretor,† a Lyon Scholar and as good a classic as Symonds himself. Pretor was quite different from Symonds in temperament: volatile, extrovert, and much more active socially. Symonds accounted him an inferior being to himself, resented such successes as he might obtain, and viewed

* There was nothing necessarily sinister in the use of female names to describe pretty or elegant younger boys. It was a jocular and playful practice, and long established. Vaughan knew this very well. His own brother-in-law and closest friend at school, A. P. Stanley, had been called Nancy at Rugby.[71] 'At Harrow boys with a very fair complexion usually received a feminine name, e.g. Polly, Suckey, Fanny, Dolly. . . .'[72]

† Alfred Pretor; monitor, 1857; Lyon Scholar, 1858; left 1859; Scholar of Trinity College; Cambridge; BA, 1863; MA, 1868; Fellow of St Catharine's College, 1871. Classical lecturer and author of *Ronald and I*. Edited classical texts. Died 1908.

him with a mixture of envy and contempt.* Yet evidently they had something in common without either of them understanding clearly what it was. What they had in common was a feminine cast of male homosexuality, with barbed tensions of rivalry which might exist between female adolescents of marked vanity.

In January 1858, when Symonds was approaching the end of his time at Harrow and looking forward to translation to Balliol College, Pretor wrote to him in high excitement to boast of a new lover to whom he had given himself. It was a letter, given the moral climate of the times, of stupendous folly and indiscretion, for it identified his new lover by name as their own headmaster, Dr Vaughan. Symonds's first impulse was to disbelieve, but he was unable to resist the evidence of a series of 'passionate letters' from Vaughan to Pretor, which his schoolfriend showed him, at the same time binding him to secrecy. Once he was convinced of the truth of Pretor's boast, Symonds's feelings were violent and confused. He told himself he was 'disgusted' to find such vice in a man 'holding the highest position of responsibility, consecrated by the Church, entrusted with the welfare of 600† youths', etc. How far these were postures of convenience would appear later. The real spring of emotion was jealousy. Symonds felt insulted by Vaughan's 'taste' in having preferred Pretor to himself. He discovered that he had never liked Vaughan; now he began 'positively to dislike him', although his own inclination, which he could not ignore, prevented him from 'utterly condemning Vaughan' and, mixed with his righteous indignation and resentment, was a 'dumb, persistent sympathy'.

Brooding on the headmaster's 'clandestine pleasure' produced, he says, an 'indescribable fermentation' in his brain. He began to suspect that Dr Vaughan, when they were reading Greek iambics together in his study, was making tentative physical advances to *him* and he considered whether to confront Vaughan with his information and ask him what the whole thing meant. In fact he did and said nothing for the time being, but he enjoyed 'a terrible new sense of power', and he meditated in solitude a future course of action. A scheme of betrayal was already being plotted.

Symonds waited until he had left Harrow and was an undergraduate at Balliol. To be acceptable, any move to ruin Vaughan had to

---

* Pretor, says Symonds, was 'vain, light headed and corrupt without intellectual or moral foundation', but he was 'superficially bright and attractive', so Symonds 'got into the way of passing time with him'.[75]

† Symonds exaggerates the number a little. In 1858 there were less than 500 boys at Harrow.

shift responsibility for the deed from himself on to someone who could be relied on to exert moral *force majeure*; Symonds could then appear to himself and, he hoped, to others as a reluctant informer, a mere dutiful medium of evidence rather than an exulting prosecutor. The first step was to confide his knowledge to an older man, a member of the university in a position of authority who could be expected to take a severe and censorious view of the events. He chose John Conington who had been elected in 1854 to the newly founded Chair of Latin Language and Literature. As he had foreseen, Conington (a repressed homosexual)* was scandalized by the account and insisted that Symonds had a duty to 'Harrow, English Society and the Established Church' to disclose what he knew to his father, which 'annihilated all considerations of confidence between boys *in state pupolaggi*'. This was just the pressure Symonds was waiting for and he responded in sympathetic compliance. 'My blood boiled; my nerves stiffened when I thought what mischief life at Harrow was doing daily to young lads under the authority of a hypocrite.' Once Conington was told, 'the matter could not stop there'. It had 'virtually passed out of my hands', Symonds was able to tell himself as, with a reluctant air, he carried the incriminating evidence to his father.

'I played the part of a candid and irrefragable witness,' he wrote, then crossed that out and substituted, 'The evidence was plain and irrefragable'. Not so plain, however, that he did not have to lay aside the mask of passivity. 'It took a little time to convince my father . . .'; so he went through the business of exposure, 'painfully but steadily'. Then he stood back and examined the protagonist in the opera: himself. 'Wait, wait!' he had exclaimed, when the little world of Harrow had treated him with insufficient respect. Now they would all learn what they had waited for. 'It was a singular position for a youth of eighteen,' he reflected. 'I had become the accuser of my old Headmaster, a man for whom I felt no love, and who had shown me no [*special* inserted as an afterthought] kindness, but who was after all the contemporary ruler of the petty State of Harrow: my accusations rested solely upon the private testimony of an intimate friend

---

* 'A repressed and unconscious paederast,' Phyllis Grosskurth calls Conington. Unconscious or otherwise he seems to have effectively repressed the forbidden forces; 'Scrupulously correct in his own conduct,' says Miss Grosskurth, 'he was sympathetic towards the infatuations of younger men as long as any physical element was suppressed.' But he made Symonds a present of a copy of William Johnson's *Ionica* (written for Charles Wood, later Lord Halifax), and Symonds wrote to his sister, Charlotte, 'I had all the enigmatic facts expounded. . . .'[76]

whose confidences I violated by communicating the letter to a third party.' To complicate his feelings there was this deep feeling of uneasy sympathy – in fact sympathetic guilt – for Vaughan which, instead of acting as a deterrent, 'determined me to tell the bitter truth'. But the bitter truth was the truth of himself as much as of the man whom he plotted to destroy.

Once his father was convinced, Symonds knew the matter was truly out of his hands, or rather, that his hands were no further required to consummate the plot he had set in motion. Dr Symonds did what was expected of him. He wrote to Dr Vaughan intimating that he had proof of his correspondence with Alfred Pretor, but promised not to make a public exposure provided he resigned the headmastership of Harrow immediately and sought no further advancement in the Church. Otherwise 'the facts [*story* deleted] would have to be divulged [*published in The Times* deleted]'.[77]

On receipt of the letter Dr Vaughan travelled from Harrow to Clifton and called on Dr Symonds; he inspected Pretor's letter, accepted the terms. Then and afterwards he seems to have behaved with impersonal, almost inhuman, composure over the sudden blight of a flowering career. We do not know what was in his mind on the journey to Clifton, but there is a passage in his celebrated sermon on 'Excitement' which that sardonic irony of his may have recalled.

There is the excitement of sensuality in all its forms; an excitement so strong, and for the moment so pleasurable that he who has once yielded to it soon forms the habit of such indulgence, and he who has once formed the habit, always persists in it till his sin is his ruin.[78]

Mrs Vaughan, Stanley's sister, followed her husband to Clifton and implored Dr Symonds on her knees to withhold execution of the sentence. She had been aware of this 'weakness' of her husband's, but it had not interfered with his usefulness in the direction of the school at Harrow. Dr Symonds 'suffered at the sight but could not accede. . .'.

In subsequent negotiations with Symonds, Vaughan was represented by his brother-in-law, Dean Stanley, and another friend, Hugh Pearson, afterwards Canon of Windsor. Whether Stanley had known or suspected previously, he certainly was privy to Vaughan's secret from then on.

Vaughan announced his decision to retire from Harrow to an unprepared and astonished public. 'It was with feelings akin to consternation,' said a contemporary, 'in both Town and School that the news came that he intended to resign.'[79] He managed the sudden alteration with perfect self-possession and seeming ease, with 'consummate skill' remarked Symonds, torn between resentment and admiration. All efforts to persuade him to reverse his decision were met with a gentle but inflexible constancy. 'Fifteen years of headmastership,' he said at a banquet in his honour, 'was as much as a man's strength could stand, and quite enough for the welfare of the School he governed.' Of course there had to be a farewell sermon in the school chapel. It was entitled 'Yet Once More'.

> Yet once more. The expression implies it is here said, an approaching change. Whenever we speak of doing a thing once more, of visiting a place once more, of seeing a person once more, we imply that there is about to be, after that one act, after that one visit, a cessation, a removal, a separation, the thought of which is already casting its shadow over it and us.[80]

To the outside world, the 'shadows' in the story were a mysterious paradox. No sooner had Vaughan left Harrow than the Prime Minister, Lord Palmerston, offered him a bishopric, the see of Worcester. He declined it. His friends appealed to him not to refuse further preferment and honours as there was no limit to his prospects in the Church. He was thought of as having qualities of strength needed by a primate capable of representing the interests of the Church against men like Gladstone and Westbury.[81] Palmerston offered him a second see, that of Rochester. This time he seemed about to accept, then, at the last moment, he refused that bishopric also. In the interval he had received a warning shot across his bows in the form of a telegram from Dr Symonds. Thereafter he firmly put from him all consideration of the high offices which from time to time the prime minister continued to press on him, and he resisted with patience and tact the continued appeals of his baffled friends not to waste himself in retirement to a comfortable but obscure incumbency at Doncaster. 'I value your kind words about the Bishopric,' he wrote on 1 November 1862 in answer to a remonstrance from W. C. Lake and others. 'It grieves me to vex my friends by seeming waywardness in such matters; they must do their best to believe that I would not act thus except from a strong sense of its being right for me.'

Two years later, when Palmerston tried to tempt him yet once more, this time with the bishopric of Ely, he had once more to meet the disappointment of his friends. 'Do not think I act from whim or caprice in the course which I have taken and to which I feel I must adhere.'[82]

The apparently unworldly example given by a man of Vaughan's attainments and status had an effect unforeseen by the Symonds, father and son. Vaughan became, in the eyes of the world, a noble exemplar of Christian humility and disinterestedness in a Church of preferment-hungry prelates, 'the one living instance of *nolo episcopari*, who refused bishoprics one after another to hold upon his quiet way'.[83] The more he turned away honours the more he was sanctified. 'The motives of his disinterestedness,' said Trevelyan, 'were not of this world',[84] and other reports of his admirers suggest that in adversity he lost none of his satirical sense, even when the joke was against himself. Of his refusals to accept any of the succession of bishoprics offered him, a reverential witness remarked, 'Various reasons have been ascribed for this, but probably the best of all is to be found in the reply he made when asked why he had refused to be a Bishop. "I was afraid," he said, "of ambition." '[85]

Canon R. R. Williams, knowing nothing of the drama which led to Vaughan's renunciation, shows an almost uncanny sensitivity in divining the *quality* of the experience, through a choice of biblical quotation. 'The men laid hold upon his hand, the Lord being merciful to him and said, "Escape for thy life; look not behind thee, neither stay thou in all the plain, escape to the mountain, lest thou be consumed." '[86] The influence he exercised without any official standing was great. The Lord Chancellor, Lord Herschell, said that when Dr Vaughan recommended a candidate for preferment to his notice, he considered that recommendation 'equivalent to a Royal Command'. It became a cult for men training for the ministry to resort to Doncaster to sit at the feet of the illustrious Dr Vaughan. His kindness and generosity to the young men, 'the pick and flower of the Church of England'[87] who came to study under him were proverbial. One of his most faithful disciples, the Archbishop of Canterbury (Edward Benson), remarked, 'For a man to gather round him a set of pupils, year after year, not coming to him because of any official position that he had, or because of the membership of any corporation, College or Society – that I believe to stand absolutely alone, at all events in modern history.'[88]

It was decided to commemorate Vaughan's services to Harrow by building a Vaughan Library, and the foundation stone was laid in 1861 by Lord Palmerston, who said 'that it was fitting they should commemorate the School's greatest Headmaster with a building in which the love of learning could be gratified'.[89] A full-length portrait of Vaughan by George Richmond was hung in the library and it hangs there today, described, when it was new and fashionable, as 'one of the most impressive portraits of modern times', conveying an expression of 'goodness' and 'simple holiness' which was most striking.[90]

From his observation post at Oxford, Symonds peered incredulously at the scene of public acclaim. The betrayal of Vaughan and of his own friend Pretor had been, he felt, 'a severe strain on my nervous and moral strength', and the contrast between the fidelity of his report of *events*, and his self-deception concerning his own *motives* was such that he was unprepared and bewildered to find himself treated as a pariah by Pretor and those former Harrovian friends who knew what he had done. While he plotted the undoing of Vaughan 'painfully and steadily', he was able to apply at the same time an entirely different set of standards to himself, searching avidly for knowledge of the history and justification of the practices which he denounced in another. From the grapevine of Oxonian crypto-paederasty he learned that one source of authoritative information and sympathetic counsel was William Johnson. After reading with fascination *Ionicus*, he wrote to Johnson expressing 'the state of my own feelings and asking for advice'. The answer was, he says, 'a big epistle upon *paederastia* in modern times, defending it and laying down the principle that affection between persons of the same sex is no less natural than the ordinary passionate relations'.[91]* Under Johnson's 'frank exposition' lay, Symonds felt, 'a wistful yearning', and the state of 'disappointment and enforced abstention'.

It was the next phase of partial self-knowledge for Symonds. From Oxford onwards he pursued the subject of paederasty in theory and in practice; for the resistance he had felt at Harrow proved to be the fruit, not of virtue and modesty, but of vanity and coyness. Before long he was cultivating Percival, the headmaster of Clifton College (situated near his home) and fishing for invitations to address the sixth form in order to facilitate his designs to seduce a chorister called Willie Dyer.[92] The incongruity of his own private life and his recent moral rhetoric in justification of betraying a friend's confidence does not seem to have touched his sensibilities until his father, who had

---

* This letter may be a clue to the nature of the mysterious 'indiscretion' which later led to Johnson's sudden retirement from Eton in 1872.

become aware of his son's propensity, but took an indulgent view of it, counselled caution.*

In the course of his subsequent career as a writer, Symonds resided much in Mediterranian countries, especially Italy, for 'reasons of health', and the pleasure he took in the company of young Italians of humble station never seemed to pale. His tastes were no secret from contemporary English men of letters. They were not a subject which would be alluded to openly in print, but Victorians knew how to put the knife in quietly. Richard Garnett observed, 'Notwithstanding his habitual association with men of the highest culture, no trait in his character was more marked than his readiness to fraternize with peasants and artisans.'[94]

The interior glimpse our perverse spy has given us was of Harrow. But the scene might equally well have been of Eton or Winchester, or any of the other public schools; we know enough in general terms to know that; we also have cause to believe that what Symonds recorded was merely part of a whole, of which at least another, and probably greater, part was innocent of the practices which he described. How many comparable dramas were acted out of sight it is impossible to guess; for, without a chronicler to reveal and with a sedulous fraternity of censors to conceal, much must have been kept hidden and buried in darkness without leaving a trace. We do not even know whether the sudden and mysterious departure from Eton of William Johnson was due to the discovery of an illicit act, or merely to the expansion of a hyper-prudery in the latter part of the century. It could have been the latter, for conduct which would not have attracted critical notice in the forties had become, by the seventies, sinister indiscretion. In the case of Vaughan there were those who had their suspicions that all was not as it appeared. One was the ubiquitous 'Soapy Sam' Wilberforce, Bishop of Oxford, he whose hands had clawed the air in search of the 'hovering Demon of Impurity'.† After Vaughan had retired from Harrow and refused preferment, Wilberforce sought out Hugh Pearson as the one man

---

* Symonds says, 'the arguments he used were conclusive. Considering the very delicate position I stood with regard to Vaughan, the possibility of Vaughan's story become public, and the doubtful nature of my own emotions, prudence pointed to a gradual diminution or cooling off of the friendship.' Suspicion would be sharpened by the social discrepancy of the friends. '. . . my father made me see that under existing conditions of English manners . . . friendship between me (a young man gently born, bred at Harrow, advancing to the highest academical honours at Balliol) and Willie (a Bristol chorister, the son of a Dissenting Tailor) would injure not my prosperity only but his reputation'.[93]

† See above, p. 294.

who was sure to know what there was to be known, and tried to extort information with threats. 'I am certain that Vaughan had some good reason for leaving Harrow and refusing two mitres. An ugly story must be behind. You had better make a friend of me. If I discover the truth I shall be an enemy.' Pearson refused to be drawn. Some time later Wilberforce returned in triumph to say that he had learned 'the whole secret' from a lady next to whom he was placed at a dinner party. 'And what have you done?' said Pearson. 'Oh, I have told the Archbishop of Canterbury and the Prime Minister.'[95] The intelligence made little difference to the prime minister, who continued to try to persuade Vaughan to accept high office, and it seems likely that effective pressure was put on Wilberforce to curb his tongue, for despite that one dinner-table indiscretion, the 'whole secret' was so well kept that even friends of Vaughan's like his successor at Harrow, Montagu Butler, and W. C. Lake, seem, by the continuance of their lavish public expression of admiration and affection for him, to have remained ignorant of the true cause of his enigmatic renunciation.

After the death of Dr Symonds in 1871, Vaughan felt able to accept the honourable but inconspicuous appointments of Dean of Llandaff and Master of the Temple. For the rest of his life he was seldom seen in a public capacity. Occasionally he consented to serve on a commission of inquiry when his qualifications were of special value. On the death of A. P. Stanley, he preached the funeral sermon in Westminster Abbey, at the express request of Stanley himself, 'because he has known me longest'. The boys of Westminster School were in attendance. 'My dear Mater,' one of them wrote home, 'my black trousers will be some use after all as I will be going to the Dean's funeral.'[96] Dr Farrar, who had preached in the morning, 'broke down' in mid-sermon 'but Dr Vaughan did not at all' and preached 'a very nice sermon' taking as his text 'blessed are the pure in heart for they shall see God', the last text which Dr Stanley had preached on. If there was anyone in the congregation who knew the story that lay behind Vaughan's arrested career, the last compliment he paid his dead brother-in-law and school friend would have had an oblique confessional import. 'I,' said Vaughan, 'who for half a century have been his companion, his confidant, his friend, at last his brother, can say of him as I lay him in his grave tomorrow, never, never, never, did I know him other than pure.'[97]

What made this man of prudence and discretion in, it seems, all known matters but the one that led to his undoing, write self-incriminating letters to a vain and meretricious youth? The only answer may be, after all, that some even of the wisest of men commit acts of ruinous folly under the influence of erotic desire. The verdict of the Archbishop of Canterbury, who knew and admired Vaughan, was, 'no living man has laid the Church of England under a greater obligation'.[98] A more personal tribute came from Canon R. R. Williams, who had never known Vaughan personally, but said of his sermons, 'after a hundred years they make me want to pray'.[99]

When, in 1894, it was Vaughan's turn to approach death, he welcomed 'the decay of the humiliating body', yet hoped it was 'not wrong to love the world as I leave it'.[100] Some of the words he spoke from the pulpit before Symonds's damning discovery – perhaps when he was involved with Pretor or some other boy – are startling in their relevance and candour. In a sermon on 'Loneliness' he considers the loneliness of repentance and loneliness of remorse, 'which is repentance without God, without Christ and therefore without hope'. The end has a personal quality almost of private confession. 'If repentance is loneliness, remorse is desolation. Repentance makes us lonely towards man, remorse makes us desolate towards God . . . from such loneliness may God in his mercy save us through his son, Jesus Christ.'

As he lay dying, messages of gratitude for his kindness to them came from Old Harrovians. From his bed he replied, 'Tell them I wasn't *half* kind enough to them.'[101] At his express injunction all his letters were destroyed and no biography of him was written.

FIFTEEN

The New Order

When on 18 July 1861, by letters patent, a Royal Commission, thereafter generally known as the Clarendon Commission, after its chairman, Lord Clarendon, was appointed to inquire into the administration, finance, studies, methods, subjects and extent of instruction at Eton, Winchester, Westminster, Harrow, Rugby, to which were added Charterhouse, St Paul's, Merchant Taylors' and Shrewsbury, the privileged administrators of the former institutions tended to react like Lord Bathurst at the passing of the Reform Bill of 1832. 'Ichabod,' he had said, 'for the glory is departed.' Balston resigned the headmastership of Eton rather than be a party to the operation, and one of the fellows, Dupuis, prepared to repel unwelcome visitors with dog whips.[1] The radical press, in particular the *Westminster Gazette* and the *Quarterly Journal of Education*, exulted in anticipation of the triumph of its principles. But the apprehensions of both parties were misconceived. The changes, when they came, were not as prescribed by the radicals, nor even as favoured by the Commissioners, but in correspondence with the changes occurring in society, or in that part of society, at least, which patronized the public schools and would necessarily, in the end, determine their character.

Life and society had themselves been changing. Roughly synchronous with the accession of Queen Victoria, the intemperate licence and wild escapades which had characterized public-school life began to become an anachronism in a world of increasing orderliness and standardized public propriety. The principle of juvenile liberty which the public schools perpetuated was obnoxious in theory and scandalous in practice to the prophets of a moral order which had recently given birth to the police force. The public schools, by the strength of their independence and the power of their friends, had kept at bay the tide of moral change.

The influence that at last began to tell on the schools was the changes in the outside world affecting competence for admission to the services traditionally reserved for gentlemen. As technical factors increased in number and importance, even the army began to require some special knowledge and skills in addition to courage and a gentlemanly deportment from its officers, and the introduction of examinations materially changed the functions which the public schools were required to perform.* Upper-class parents began to be conscious of an inadequacy in their own understanding of scientific advances and they – at least enough of them to matter – wished their children better educated than they had been to engage the resources of the new world.

These and other factors were skilfully exploited by two writers in particular, of a very different kind from the usual run of political malcontents. They were Matthew Higgins and Henry Reeve, both gentlemen of independent means, and wider foreign experience than most Englishmen; one, Higgins, an Etonian, although – predictably – of short duration; both well informed on Etonian history and contemporary conditions; and both accomplished (especially Higgins) in the art of ridicule. Higgins, who wrote in the *Cornhill* as 'Paterfamilias' and 'Jacob Omnium', was a friend of Thackeray's.

Writing in a series of three 'Letters', with the ingenuous air of a man commenting on the changes he observes on returning to England after a long absence, Higgins applauded the improvement in the education of the poor, but wished that a comparable improvement could have been seen in the education of the rich, which seemed to have remained stationary and inadequate. Aiming at Eton in particular, he complained of the insufficiency of the number of masters to boys as 'dishonestly small', 'upwards of eight hundred boys taught by nineteen masters'[3] and no limit on the number of boys a tutor might take upon himself',† with resultant rewards ridiculously in excess of merit. Pounding the always vulnerable flank of privilege, finance, he contrasted the remuneration of an Eton tutor who could earn up to £3000 a year with that of an important public functionary such as the director of the British Museum who received only half that amount, and a quarter of what the headmaster of Eton

---

* The pressure is registered in a woeful verse:

> Perhaps I was ambitious
> Perhaps I was an ass;
> But I was really happy once; before
> I joined the army class.[2]

† Balston, having given evidence before the Commission that he himself had had as many as seventy pupils at one time, and being asked gravely whether he was able 'to be a father to that number', replied with with equal gravity: 'That is a rather puzzling question.'[4]

received who put at least £7500 a year into his pocket:[5] all this not as a reward for distinguished achievement, but merely because headmaster and tutors were all Colleger Old Etonians and former fellows of King's. The corollary of the undeserved rewards of the teaching staff was the undeserved deprivation of the pupils, and he called for reform of this 'bad and expensive education' in order 'that the governors of this country should be at least as well educated as the governed'.[6]

Reeve, writing anonymously in the *Edinburgh Review*, covered the same ground with similar arguments as Higgins to reach the conclusion that 'a boy may leave Eton with credit and be quite unable to pass the common tests of the Civil Service Examination'.[7] The article was ostensibly a review of three books on aspects of public schools but, as Reeve confided in a letter to the veteran adversary of Eton, Lord Brougham,* he had been preparing 'a regular mine under Eton College' and he was about to detonate it. 'Keep my secret,' he said, '. . . Eton is still very little improved and the depredations of the Fellows go on with shameless audacity. I mention this to you because your committee has been of so much use to us; but I wish to keep the thing quite dark till the next number of the Review makes its appearance.'[8] Some light relief was provided by Reeve's 'mine' in the attention given to the statutes and the absence of any copy of them on display and accessible for perusal in Eton College, contrary to the express direction of the founder. The original copy had been long ago removed by the Provost on the plea that the scholars used to write improper words on it. But the real reason, Reeve slyly suggested, was that its admonitions were not conducive to the fellows' dignity. They included 'not to loiter in hall after dinner; not to hunt or use nets, not to keep dogs, ferrets, hawks, monkeys, deer, foxes or badgers; not to frequent taverns or raree-shows, not to grow immoderately long hair or beard, not to wear green, red or white breeches, not to annoy those below them by urinating out of the window or emptying slops on their heads'.[9]

Both Reeve and Higgins were too sharply polemical and partisan to sway the main body of moderate public and political opinion. But another exposition, couched in very different language and delivered by a supporter of the public schools, and of Eton in particular, succeeded in doing what the enemies – abolitionists or radical refor-

* At this time Lord Brougham's two nephews, the elder his heir, were at school, and the school to which Lord Brougham had chosen to send them was Eton.

mers – had failed to do in half a century. This was a speech, afterwards published, made by Sir John Coleridge in September 1860, at Tiverton. His primary purpose was to call attention to the dangers of the 'higher orders' relaxing into sloth and neglecting their duties when 'the irresistible tendency of the times' was to 'bring into activity the political power of what are commonly called the lower classes of society'. It behoved rulers by duty and inheritance to be diligent in the education of their children. It would not do to rest on traditions. His great personal affection for Eton did not blind him to her present faults, prominent among which was a degree of 'liberty which trembles not infrequently on the edge of licence'.[10]

Coleridge was just the right man to command the attention of moderate men of substance who shared with him a sympathetic interest in the future of the public schools. There was nothing extreme in him or his opinions. He was a High Court judge, a respected public figure, and, far from being hostile to the public schools, he was known as a loyal Etonian. He struck just the right note of concern for the justification of the ruling classes and the exercise of stricter moral control over the young, which were fashionable and appealing policies to those who thought of themselves in 1860 as serious, thoughtful modern men and women. When a man of his temper and record suggested official intervention, the government had reason to feel that there would no longer be the force of opposition, in and out of parliament, which once had frustrated the intentions of their predecessors. On 18 July 1861 a Commission of Inquiry was appointed under the chairmanship of Lord Clarendon, and its first meeting took place four days later. Besides Lord Clarendon the commissioners numbered Sir Stafford Northcote and Lord Lyttelton (both Etonians), Edward Twistleton (Wykehamist), the Earl of Devon (Westminster), Halford Vaughan (Rugbeian), and William Thompson, Professor of History at Oxford (educated privately).

The chairman's opinion of his colleagues was less than flattering. 'Devon is weak, Northcote pedantic, Thompson idle, Twistleton quirky, Vaughan, mad.' But he allowed that 'they all had merits and have worked well together'. For Lyttelton he had positive praise.[11]* Perhaps it was one of the others who retaliated with a remark which went into circulation that the chairman had gone to no known school.†

* The only member of the commission who did, in fact, die insane.
† The admission to St John's College, Cambridge, described him as educated at Christ's Hospital, because his private tutor, who taught there, was allowed to take his pupil to attend classes.

Witty, incorruptible and of brilliant achievement in the diplomatic service, Clarendon had not, it is true, been subject daily to the relentless measure of quantities and drill of construe which was the academic all in all of a public-school régime. Once, when speaking in the House of Lords on public schools, he had quoted a line of Martial, but unfortunately he misplaced the last two words of a hexameter, thus:

'*Sunt bona sunt quaedam mediocra, sunt plura mala*' at which, according to Goodford, who was present, the bevy of headmasters on the steps of the throne shuddered as though the end of the world had come.

Etonians in general were not happy at the choice of the two Etonians selected to serve on the Commission. Lyttelton they regarded as altogether too impartial to be safe, while Stafford Northcote was 'eminently cautious'. Of the latter, Gladstone, who, whatever else, was a devoted Etonian, said, with that circumlocution which tended to become more convoluted when he was evasive, that he was 'a man in whom it was a fixed habit of thought to put himself wholly out of view when he had before him the attainment of great public objects'.[12]

As witness followed witness to give evidence, the glimmering of a world began to appear through a glass darkly, as strange and improbable to most of the observers as reports of the exotic tribes discovered by explorers like Speke and Stanley in remotest Africa. 'The evidence,' said a reporter, 'was as interesting as a book of travels in a new and unexplored country,'[13] but much of it was 'not intelligible to those who have no personal experience'[14]* of the mysteries.

Inquirers who had hitherto known nothing authentic of the interior life of a public school were puzzled by some, and shocked by other, revelations, especially those concerning practices at Westminster where, at this time, despotism drove further into stylized cruelty than

---

* The cognoscenti insisted that no understanding of the mysteries was possible without the personal experience of initiation. 'One seldom picks up a book on the most ordinary matter without meeting some crude, undigested and equally indigestible remarks about Eton, Harrow, Winchester or Rugby. These are the offsprings of prejudice or of ignorance; and it is impossible to enter into the feelings of those who are connected with the great schools without having participated in the education, so as to appreciate the delicacies of apricot jam by a description of onions and bacon. . . . Good sense has nothing to do with it. . . . Clever men have tried and failed; and so they will fail (unless they have themselves gone through the mill). . . . Men unconnected with the system cannot give credit to the exceptional phases of school life, the fagging, the discipline (as by prefects, monitors or preposters), the apparent absence of hard work and the necessity of hard play, the cribbing, the mutual help and the peculiar code of honour that goes so far to making the man, by the exercise of character in a world of boyhood. It would be difficult to conceive the mistakes which able men have made in discussing these points, were it not palpably before us in the daily pages of reports, weekly and monthly publications, and in the ludicrous inanities of our contemporaries.'[15]

at any of the other schools. At Westminster a boy might be fagged round from the hall to pick up a book lying at the feet of a reader seated on the fender of 'inner Chiswick'.[16] Well might a former prefect look back wistfully in middle age on a luxury of command greater than any privilege enjoyed in subsequent adult life, recalling the time when he and other Westminster grandees rested in 'those armchairs by the upper, under and middle fires, and by the single word "Election", as surely and almost as instantaneously as Aladdin by the aid of his ring, summoned round them youthful genii to do their utmost bidding – whatever that bidding might be'.

The uninitiated heard with incredulity that a fag's duties included rising at 3 a.m. and working for his masters until he called them at 4 a.m. and thereafter at increasingly frequent intervals. They learned with surprise that juniors had to move at all times at the double, but the intelligence that the boys of the two under elections were obliged to touch the ends of the rods as they passed the monitor's table on their way up or down school[17] might as well have been a description of the superstitious rites of some heathen denizens of a distant jungle. The account of punishment inflicted by older boys on younger (who had to adopt a regulation posture with one foot in a washbasin) by kicking them, sometimes in specially heavy boots,[18] so outraged even the public-school members of the Commission that, after subjecting the headmaster, C. B. Scott, to an uncomfortable examination, which he did not come out of well, they entered in their report on Westminster a specific recommendation 'of entirely reforming the present system of punishment in use among boys and especially putting down . . . the practice of kicking'.[19]

There was scandal and curiosity enough to provide a banquet for the press. It was revealed that, despite the strictures of Brougham when he had interviewed Goodall, the Provost and fellows of Eton were still, nearly fifty years later, unlawfully appropriating and dividing amongst themselves the fines imposed on the renewal of leases;[20] and it was rewarding to hear that 'the constitution of Eton was so tangled that it can only be rivalled by that of the British monarchy itself'.[21] Some of the venerable pedagogues and fellows in giving evidence fulfilled the most hopeful expectations of connoisseurs. Dupuis (he who had meditated repelling unwelcome visitors with dog whips) protested in the course of his testimony that at Eton they were *not* against reform: 'The question of the greater frequency of puddings has already been thought of and discarded.'[22] The public appetite was both fed and provoked by hearing that at Westminster the masters had no control over the monitors, who treated them with contempt,[23] and that a boy given permission from a master to leave the room was not free to do so until he had obtained leave from at least three boys in authority: a monitor (sometimes more than one), his immediate senior, and the 'lag'* of the second election. They marvelled on learning that the Captain of College struck the head boy of the election on the face and said in Latin, 'You be free – all the rest be slaves', and thereafter acted on this decree; and that, when a 'slave', inquiring of his masters whether they wished to order any further provisions before the porter went off duty, said, 'Any orders, John is going off,' all was well; but if he varied the words by the slightest deviation, such as, 'John is about to leave', he was liable to summary and severe punishment.[25]

Despite the strange and sometimes startling disclosures, the prophecies of imminent dissolution which had been volunteered by the radical press were not realized. 'Instant decomposition', an impatient educational revolutionary had hopefully predicted for Eton, 'would follow a few well-directed blows of some Anglo-Saxon parent.'[26] But the irksome paradox was that even some of the most prominent critics of the public schools, and men who professed themselves to have been unhappy at their own schools, when the time came, sent their own sons and wards to the very institutions where they had themselves suffered.

As the whole picture was revealed bit by bit it made a deep, and mainly favourable, impression on the Commissioners and the press and, through them, on the general public. The public schools might not prepare the boys to engage modern Victorians' science and technology; that was a superficial defect which could be corrected easily by curricular adjustment. But the schools did, and were seen to, prepare boys as no other schools (except the Royal Navy) seemed able to do, to meet the eternal testing realities of human social intercourse. Its effects were to produce to a greater or lesser degree, according to the material, men who were resourceful and adaptable, calm under pressure, and practical in judgement. As William Johnson put it with his customary acuteness, 'Boys under private tuition are preparing to live, in public schools they live.'[27] Sir James Fitzjames Stephen, who said he was thankful to leave Eton, declared, 'We do not believe that any system was ever invented so real, so healthy and so bracing to the mind and body' as a public school; and the reason

* Lag: the last person of a sequence.[24]

THE NEW ORDER

for its excellence was 'the entire absence of any restraint or supervision, except during the hours actually passed at lessons' which was
'the best possible security against' boys 'forming illusions about the
life which lies beyond their own observation'.[28] A public school boy,
he affirmed, 'has been brought into contact from a very early age . . .
with real men, real passions and real things . . . when he hears or
speaks of them his associations are with realities and not with mere
words or books'. He learned that 'talents and accomplishments do
not govern the world' and he learned to estimate, as well as virtue,
'the power, whatever he thinks of the merits, of a hard coarse temperament'. To those who knew how to use it, a public school was 'a sort
of grammar and dictionary of human nature'.[29] He learned, as a later
English protagonist put it, in entitling his autobiography, *The Art of
the Possible*.[30]

The case for the public schools was put in plainest terms in the
Saturday Review, in reply to the much publicized speech of Sir John
Coleridge which had led to the appointment of the Commission. The
writer (probably Goodford), intimately familiar with his subject, does
not claim that life in a public school is perfect, but he does assert
that, with its imperfections, it is the best of preparations for the
dangers of the imperfect world beyond:

> To the boy or the community alike, the constant reliance upon another
> for aid in difficulties, guidance in perplexities, shelter from temptations,
> fatally weakens the fibre of the character. Boys, like nations, can only
> attain to the genuine stout self reliance which is true manliness by
> battling for themselves against their difficulties, and forming their own
> characters by the light of their own blunders and their own troubles. . . .
> The object of a public school is to introduce a boy early to the world
> that he may be trained in due time for the struggle that lies before
> him. It is to initiate him into a little of its deceits that he may not be
> hopelessly green or soft when he reaches the age at which the passions
> begin to drive him, and at which a false step is attended with results
> more serious than a flogging. It is to teach him something of its
> vicissitudes and troubles, that, when they come upon him in good
> earnest, the surprise may not cow him or cast him down. But how is
> this to be, if there be no world – if there be nothing but a mock Utopia,
> produced by the incessant drilling of omnipresent ushers?[31]

The inquiry lasted three years and it signals the end of our story. It
was not intended to be an end and, of course, in a sense it was
reinforcement by adaptation. The end of sail was not the end of the

navy, but it was the end of a nautical culture. No one willed or desired that this culture should retire into history and private pastime, but this was what happened in the nature of the change, which no one, however much he loved the world of sail, could arrest. The change to come in the public schools was less obvious, immediate and dramatic; not less consequential. The course which lay ahead was not to be discerned from the report of the Commissioners, which was in general terms more favourable than either the friends or enemies of the schools had expected. They recommended reforms of administration, but not of *character*, and gave the system as established the firm stamp of their approval. Their verdict was much quoted in the press in England and beyond the seas:

> It is not easy to estimate the degree to which the English people are indebted to these schools for ... their capacity to govern others and control themselves, their aptitude for combining freedom with order, their public spirit, their vigour and manliness of character, their strong but not slavish respect for public opinion, their love of healthy sports and exercise. These schools have been the chief nurseries of our statesmen. ... In them ... men of all the various classes that make up English society, destined for every profession and career, have been brought up on a footing of social equality and have contracted the most enduring friendships and some of the ruling habits of their lives; and they have perhaps the largest share in moulding the character of an English gentleman.[32]

Scarcely could higher praise have been bestowed. But, in practice, no commission had the power to determine the future character of the public schools. The operation of broadening the curriculum by having other studies 'grafted onto Greek and Latin' was designed, said one commentator, to bring the public schools 'more into connexion with the world at large'.[33] But that in itself implied a virtual reconstitution, for the changes in the world at large had been fast and drastic, and were accelerating. The public schools had been artificially conserving the standards of an order which could not but change, however reluctantly, as the world changed.

It was clever of Disraeli to choose Eton as the scene of Lord Monmouth's valedictory strictures upon the drift of society:

> 'Good-bye, my dear Harry,' said Lord Monmouth, when he bade his grandson farewell. 'I am going abroad again; I cannot remain in this radical-ridden country. Remember, though I am away, Monmouth

House is your home, at least so long as it belongs to me. I understand my tailor has turned Liberal, and is going to stand for one of the metropolitan districts, a friend of Lord Durham; perhaps I shall find him in it when I return. I fear there are evil days for the NEW GENERATION.'[34]

Some of the changes to come were unchallengeably benign, as well as inevitable – improved diet and hygiene, better living conditions for the Collegers, with the abolition of Long Chamber in 1846 – and others were not imposed from above or from outside but evolved organically from the responses of the boys themselves to a new experience. Fighting, once the criterion of honour, went out of fashion. The protracted ordeals based on the practices of the prize ring, which had led to the tragic death of Anthony Ashley, ceased to be admired. Up to the 1840s boys had battled in bloody combat on any pretext, 'hardly a day passing', as Gladstone has told us, 'without one, two, three, or even four more or less mortal combats'.[35] Brinsley Richards records that by the late 1850s there was almost no fighting, and it was almost unheard of among senior boys.[36] Evidence before the Commission confirms his recollection.[37] 'The manners of the great public schools,' said a commentator with approval, 'have been greatly improved of late years by the softened tone of society at large.'[38]

But there were germs of another kind of change gathering strength, a kind having its origins not in the boys themselves, but in objections to their social independence, which struck at the centre of the schools' identity and tradition. In their official pronouncements on the schools, the Commissioners paid homage to the 'freedom' of public-school life, ascribing to this distinctive condition of select English boyhood the promotion of 'independence and manliness of character'. But they were careful to link this praise to an equal tribute to the balancing feature of 'order and discipline'. To the public-school partisan there was no contradiction in the union. 'The best way of enforcing discipline was by leaving the boys to themselves,' Fitzjames Stephen had said.[39] But the words 'freedom' and 'liberty' and 'order' and 'discipline' had in practice widely different meanings for several of the witnesses called, sometimes even when the witnesses came from the same school and when that school was Eton. To Goodford, former headmaster of Eton, and himself a product of the old system, the issue of 'freedom' was 'whether schoolboys are formless dough to be manufactured by a schoolmaster', a concept 'as revolting to their spirit as the tutelage in which a continental government loves to keep its subjects is to the spirit of a free community'.[40]*

But the old notions of the sacredness of boys' independence were under growing pressure by an authoritarian spirit imponent of uniformity in morals and manners, as far as was possible, throughout society. Freedom of choice and the right to variety for boys thus became a subversive threat to the principle of uniformity for *men*. Even the moderate John Coleridge had responded to the pressure by conceding a danger in 'liberty which trembled on the edge of licence'. Leslie Stephen's sarcasm has already been noted. 'Nobody could have guessed that an ideal education would be provided by bringing together a few hundred lads and requesting them to govern themselves.'[43] Already there were those in and around the schools who not only manipulated the term 'freedom' to reconstitute its meaning in effect; they were ready to go further and denounce the application of the word as a malign influence. The 'vaunted self reliance and premature manliness', said Higgins, 'could be equated to the morbid precocity which the children of the poor acquire in our populous cities by being allowed to grovel uncared for in the gutter'. If Eton resisted reform and persevered in its evil courses, he warned, the other schools would do likewise.[44] There were now men of Higgins' and Reeve's persuasion inside, as well as outside, the schools, who would not in the least have recoiled from the notion, so odious and ignoble to their predecessors, of treating a boy as 'raw material' to be moulded. The new concept of propriety in the exercise of moral interference surfaces ingenuously in the novel genre, 'tales of school life for boys'. Here two assistant masters, Singleton and Holford, discuss the pupils of one of them:

* Goodford was one of the last of the old order. Worthy in scholarship of the headmastership, he was a surprising choice, as he was modest and retiring and appeared entirely without ambition. He was preferred to the favourite, Keate's son-in-law Edward Coleridge (much to the chagrin of Miss Brown), because Coleridge's high-church sympathies militated against him at a time when any opinion which might be construed as leaning towards Rome provoked alarm in the Church of England. William Johnson's estimate of his election is worth hearing. 'Goodford is honest, righteous, methodical, learned, brave, laconic, prudent. unmeddlesome. He is also weak in health, uninfluential, obscure, unpolished. No one admires him – everyone respects him. We shall probably be happier under him than under Coleridge.'[41] Brinsley Richards, who was sparing in his praise of pedagogues, called Goodford 'an excellent headmaster, not a genius, not a fussy autocrat setting down his foot where a little finger would do, not a stern man delighting in punishment, but equal in his rule and perfectly firm'.[42] A little anecdote imparts the impression he left behind him. One night when, candle in hand, he was making his round of the college dormitory, a bold little urchin in a night shirt stalked at his heels pulling faces and making traditional gestures of derision with fingers extended from nose at the august back. Goodford stopped at the end of the room and without turning round said, 'You forgot the shadow on the wall.' Then he went out.

'Well, your two protégés are coming now directly under your own management,' said Mr Singleton, in a conversation which he held with his brother tutor on the second day of the winter half year. 'They will be *wholly in your hands now*. *Quid vis argilla faceris uda* and I must allow it will not be your fault if the pottery does not turn out a very superior article under your workmanship. . . .' 'I wish the clay were moist,' said Mr Holford, shaking his head.[45]*

The concept of human putty for manipulation, repugnant to the old order as unworthy of free men, let alone English gentlemen, was already, when the Clarendon Commission was convened, regarded in some quarters as legitimate, desirable and benignly progressive. It might have brought Higgins and Reeve hope and encouragement to know that giving evidence at the same hearing as Goodford was a young assistant master at Eton called Edmund Warre who, far from rejecting the notion of manipulable human putty, cherished the ambition that all the pottery would be as nearly as possible identical. T. H. Green, when he was a busy political figure, looking back wistfully on the happier memories of his youth at Rugby, recalled with delight 'those most luxurious canoes in which one can paddle for hours without the least exertion and undisturbed by eights or such abomination'.[46] Warre would have winced with displeasure at such an image, especially when embarrassingly tendered by a man of exemplary moral energy. Himself a notable oar at Oxford, Warre was not content to row himself, and encourage others to row, competitively, after his fashion; he abhorred as moral evils, with the zeal of moral righteousness, diversity and freedom of choice, and he set himself the task, partly by design, partly in response to his own nature, in the favourable social atmosphere of his day, to weaken, and then extinguish, the traditions of personal initiative and the independence of boys' personal lives. He went about this by ordaining the official worship of a few chosen deities – rowing, cricket, football, 'the all devouring gods'† – and officially exalting into a privileged high priesthood the exponents of their rites.

When Milnes Gaskell had complained of some of his contemporaries' preoccupation with pugilism, he did not appreciate that their freedom to take this interest was the expression of the same freedom

* Adams was not an outsider, ignorant of public-school real life, but a Wykehamist, author of *Wykehemica*; he is writing in conformity with a new fashion of assailing and undermining the old gods of 'honour among boys' and enjoining total submission to adult commands.

† 'The all devouring god', sometimes used specifically to describe cricket. See *The Harrovian*, no. 16 (Thursday, 1 July 1880), p. 184.

he enjoyed *not* to follow pugilism but to pursue his own preferences. In the boys' republic of the old order a minority of thoughtful spirits was strong enough to preserve its right to life and liberty against a barbaric majority and to develop such a famous forum of debate as the Literary Society.

Warre compounded and nourished the incipient intolerance and jealousy of the worshippers of the 'all devouring gods' by giving them his support and encouragement, from *above*, to denigrate and even persecute those who showed insufficient piety at the sacrificial celebrations, or worse, who stubbornly persisted in preferring suspect or disfavoured pastimes.

In the old order, headmasters had taken too little interest in games. To George Butler, headmaster of Harrow, football had been a game 'only fit for butcher boys';[47] and when Moberly alluded to 'idle boys' he meant boys absorbed in cricket. But when Warre alluded to 'idle boys' he meant boys who were not seen to play cricket, or one of the other approved games, with sufficient enthusiasm and zeal. The kind of boys he did not like were 'strange boys' who showed mysterious, and therefore suspect, interest in alternative activities. He disliked to find six or seven boys sitting together talking.[48] The Literary Society could never have come into existence after Warre's ascendancy. The long walks and private conferences between Gladstone and Hallam and his friends to plan its programmes would not have been tolerated. To Warre, privacy was suspect, and leisure, in the meaning of freedom of choice, abomination. Punting he had forbidden while still assistant, for 'idling on the river' (a pastime dear to the memory of Green and others, but now too private) was 'prejudicial to the school'. Asked by Lord Clarendon, 'Why is punting forbidden?' Warre replied, 'With special reference to drinking, idling and vice of all kinds.* Now we have sealed up the river to them in that kind of way.† Any boy who is seen in any backwater is severely punished.'[50]

At a later date, as headmaster, Warre, in a letter to assistant masters marked 'Private and Confidential', expressed concern lest masters should talk without discretion on subjects other than work, for boys were capable of expressing 'not always harmless criticisms of authority'.[51] Independence of mind had become an offence. In return for the glorification of certain approved sports Warre required even the chief beneficiaries to surrender their heritage of initiative

---

* 'He [Warre] told us to beware of filth. I was completely baffled.'[49]
† By posting watermen as sentinels.

and command. The most exalted boy in the school did not escape the effects of the new headmaster's engrossment. The Captain of Boats had always been the ruler of his own domain, but when Warre arrived he began to assume all the functions of that office 'and very little was done thereafter without his advice, nothing without his approval'.[52]

When Warre became headmaster in succession to Hornby whom, as his lieutenant, Warre had dominated, he tightened up the policing of games and the close surveillance of all social activities. 'Do we know what they are doing?' he asked his assistant masters of any boys ingenious enough to have evaded his autocratic clutch.*

Warre himself succeeded, or seemed to have succeeded, in doing what generations of sporting majorities had not done nor, to do them justice, aspired to do: he deprived the minorities of their right to independent life. The virtue of encouraging athleticism was converted into the vice of an exclusive monopoly of credit and privilege. Once an athlete could also be a poet and wit. When Gladstone was old and famous he came to Eton to give one of his lectures on Homer (whom he is said to have pronounced 'Oomy'). He asked to be shown the Pop room again, and was taken there by the president to whom he said, 'Do you have any athletes in Pop now? We used to have a few, to shew we were not down on athletics, if they were not too dull.'[53] The president may have deemed it more tactful not to tell his distinguished guest that Pop and its prestige had been seized as a useful asset and the tribe which had founded it driven out by the athletes,[54] of which he was himself, of course, one.

There was nothing original in what Warre did; it was in conformity with the trend of the times, otherwise he would not have succeeded as far as he did. In other, newer schools, headmasters like Thring and Temple were able to go much farther faster in constitutional reform. What made Warre's operations notable was that they could happen even at Eton, where the right of boys to social independence and autonomy had been held in peculiar veneration. The feelings of the assistant masters were sharply divided. One of those who viewed the changes with unqualified satisfaction was Edward Lyttelton, who was destined to succeed Warre as headmaster. During these years, 'Eton,' Lyttelton reported, 'moved from open barbarism to something like decorum.'[55]

---

* By a coincidence of sublime incongruity Warre, when himself a new boy at Eton, had been placed next to a small red-haired Oppidan called Charles Algernon Swinburne.

A conspicuous manifestation of this 'decorum' may be seen in the pictorial records of altered attitudes to games in photographs of public-schoolboy players between the fifties and the eighties. The earliest photographs show casual assemblies of friends who look as if they had said what in fact they had said – something like, 'Who wants to play a game today? What shall it be?' – and then changed into a miscellany of old clothes, torn shirts, ancient jerseys and battered caps, tucked their trouser ends in the tops of their socks and got on with it. When they are photographed they sit or stand around in a variety of postures, not taking themselves or their roles very seriously. Up to the mid-century the use of distinctively different clothes at games was viewed with suspicion and distaste as the likely vulgar affectation of a pretentious muff. 'Old Rugbaean' alludes with contempt in 1848 to 'the use of a peculiar dress consisting of velvet caps and jerseys' at football. 'The latter,' he says, 'are of various colours and patterns and wrought with very curious devices. *Cave Adsum* worn by a boy who was generally found lurking outside the scrimmage . . . [and] during the whole of a game did not once kick the ball.'⁵⁶ In each succeeding decade the impression of ever-increasing self-importance and solemnity is conveyed, sometimes by the demeanour of the subjects, always by the growing splendour and religious regularity of their style. The uniformity of a military unit has prevailed. The boys are no longer a number of recognizably distinctive individuals who have come together to play a game as a team, but a uniformed and cultivated team, whose members may or may not be more of individuals than they look.

The sacrifices offered and the incense burned at the altars of the ascendant deities did not go entirely without criticism by sturdier individuals. Among the boys themselves there was some mild satire on the blossoming of colourful uniforms sacred respectively to the rites of particular deities. A boy at Eton in 1861 gives a quizzical report of looking out of his window and seeing his 'good friend from over the way issue out of his tutor's house, attired, not as I should have expected in the usual black coat and white neck-tie which authority has been good enough to assign for our wearing but in a marvellous conglomeration of coloured flannel, and looking much more like a holiday butterfly than (shall I say) a school grub', his festive garments indicating that he was on his way to play football. The same observer says that he has a 'distinct recollection of seeing somebody rush past for the fields attired in a loose and elegant suit of *mauve*, whereas all those who took part in the match seemed to have put on door mats and ancient blankets. Doormats and mauve!'[57]

A decade later badges and 'colours' and distinctive uniforms for the river and the cricket pitch and the playing fields, which had begun as voluntary novelties, had hardened into a solemn and strictly enforced code, which forbade any player to dress above his attainment in any game. A public school was divided, classified and clothed according to the proficiency of boys at games. At Harrow in the seventies and eighties it was condemned as 'swagger' to wear a cricket shirt until a certain social or cricketing position had been attained;[58] a coloured cap was worth ten times more than any prize. In 1861 William Johnson remarked that cricket at school had become a kind of profession.[59] Not long afterwards it had become a kind of religion. The fortunes of the country, it seemed, rested on an unfailing supply of schoolboy games heroes. The participants in inter-schools games were gravely assured that the eyes of England were upon them, and a popular periodical paid pious tribute to 'our glorious sporting products, honouring church and state'.[60] 'The Eton and Harrow match at Lord's,' said Edward Lyttelton, 'seemed to us to be the annual climax of the history of mankind.'[61] An affable Old Etonian at an Eton and Harrow cricket match, on inquiring playfully of a little Harrovian whether a bowler called F. C. Cobden was any relation to 'the great Cobden', was informed in reverent tones, 'He *is* the great Cobden.'[62] Hawtrey, the assistant master at Eton, who taught mathematics, stopped Maude, the Etonian bowler, in the street, and asked 'to be allowed to shake that noble hand'.[63] 'The best boys,' said an educationalist seriously, addressing adult readers, 'are the best players of games.'[64] When F. D. How declared that 'there was no spark of public school feeling' at Marlborough at its inception, he meant that there were no organized, compulsory team games;[65] and Sir John Kaye, the biographer of Lord Metcalfe, was sufficiently embarrassed by his subject's lack of interest in conventional sport to protest, by way of dissociation, that he would himself have preferred to write about someone with a healthy love of games, but he pleaded in mitigation that 'great men are not to be treated by ordinary rules; they make rules for themselves'.[66]

The claims of athleticism as an *official* policy permeated the public-school system so rapidly that it was difficult for many of those affected to understand the neologism of moral passion it had been, or that all the statesmen, divines, educationalists, soldiers and gentry of every preceding age would, as Canon Firth remarked, have treated such language of adulation as 'inconceivably childish', and 'the boys who had earlier founded their matches as a merry lark, and thought themselves lucky not to get flogged for it, would have been amazed to find themselves exalted thus'.[67]

Some headmasters, Montagu Butler and Cotton among them, viewed the momentum of professionalized games with misgivings, but they were helpless to resist the new worship without injuring the public status of their schools.* Other headmasters, like G. G. Bradley, Frederick Temple and Edward Wickham,† although themselves unathletic and without distinction at games, went with the tide and enlisted blues on to their school staff to prepare their boys for inter-schools competition on the playing fields. At Eton there was in the nature of the place more resistance to zeal for compulsory organiza-tion than elsewhere, and in 1857 the *Chronicle* lamented, 'At Harrow pleasure is subordinated to the science of cricket to an extent which would not be tolerated by Etonians, imbued with such notions of liberty and equality.' At Eton also, much wider diversity was found in standards and practice between houses. A little boy fagged to take a note to Drury's was startled to see the notice: *Any lower boy in this house who does not play football once a day and twice on half holidays will be fined half a crown and kicked.*[69] Another house could be almost another world.

At every school there were, among the crusaders, sceptics and heretics, adherents to the ancient and, by the sixties, fugitive spirit of independent pursuits, who discerned the new régime of 'decorum' not as a movement *away* from barbarism, but rather as the exaltation, as never before, of well-drilled, narrow and rigid barbarism to the status of monolithic orthodoxy. At Harrow, there being no tradition of rowing, the choice was even narrower than at Eton and the priests of the two prevailing games defended their monopolies with fierce intolerance against any suggestion of widening the choice. But nothing could silence the impious voices of the ungodly. Harrovians, having taken to publishing later than Rugbeians and much later than Etonians, were notably assertive when they did launch a magazine. Compulsory football was categorized in *The Harrovian* as 'a system . . . regarded . . . at present by upper as well as lower boys, as an

---

* Cotton tried to link and subordinate games to religion without success. 'Of one thing there is no doubt: that both intellectual and bodily excellence are only really blessed when they are a reflection of the moral and religious goodness. . . .'[68]
† Bradley, headmaster of Marlborough, 1858–70; Temple, headmaster of Rugby, 1857–69; Wickham, headmaster of Wellington, 1873–93.

invention to prevent their life here becoming too pleasant'.[70] In the summer term a bold objector ventured to denounce in most disrespectful terms 'the tyranny of cricket', what he called the 'bat and ball fever', enforced on those who would prefer to do something else. Victory at Lord's, he conjectured, might be some small recompense to fellows who had wasted eight or nine years. . . . He denied the charge of disparaging cricket. It was a good game, and a means of healthy exercise; those who liked it should be encouraged to play it; but it was not superior to other games which it displaced, and to convert a means of amusement into a duty was a 'manifest infringement of liberty'. Where, he asked, were the tennis courts which had been in use the previous year? Few as they were they had been abolished by the priests of the 'all devouring God' because they took fellows away from cricket.[71] It was a reasoning, atavistic voice, but it was out of joint with the times. The best the heretics could do was to make their protests heard, and this they did with notable tenacity. A decade later the voice of the next generation was again raised in *The Harrovian*, in the cause of 'a wider variety of games', but, said the writer with resignation, 'I have not the least hope of seeing any change made.'[72]

Those at Eton who viewed the advancing process of regimentation with uneasiness and distaste included athletes who were more than athletes, such as Gilbert Bourne, one of the best oars of his day and future zoologist, who felt with the erosion of the old spirit of independence, the approach of 'something Prussian, a savour of the Almanach de Goethe'[73] which he lived to see reach its apotheosis in the 1930s. Boys might now have fewer and less savage fights than of old, but when they did fight it certainly would not be over the disputed quality of an edition of Aeschylus! In the days which Lyttelton described as 'barbarism' everybody was free to pursue whatever pastime he preferred, without interference, official or otherwise, other than fagging. He could, like Gladstone, Doyle, Hallam and Colville, when they planned the programmes of the Literary Society, go for long walks with his own friends. As well as playing the games of his choice, or going swimming to Dorney or further afield, he could roam the countryside on botanical expeditions, collecting specimens, wild flowers or fossils, or studying antiquities.

The variety of choice which had formerly characterized life was now resented as deviation from the norm. Walks were looked upon with ominous suspicion. Warre deeply disliked seeing boys walking and talking together. 'No, gentlemen,' said George Fletcher to the medical officers of the Schools Association, 'I cannot believe in a walker as a walker pure and simple.'[74] Botany was likely to be taboo, at least in the more modern, and therefore more susceptible, schools under a code of militant pseudo-masculinity. A boy at Wellington interested in gardening decorated his room with rare and beautiful flowers until the captain of dormitary XI swept them on to the floor and trampled them underfoot saying, 'There is no room for this rotten effeminate stuff here.'[75]

Joined to the coarse and neurotic philistinism, posing as 'manliness', was a censorious and intolerant prudery, posing as purity. The examples of Bowdler and his pioneering literary mutilators were competitively advanced; and eager moral improvers meddled complacently with the work of their betters. Even Horace was not safe from admirers who wished to censor him, for his own good.* At the other end of the social scale, Billy Warner, the Harrow oyster-seller and poacher who, devoted to the school, had taught generations of Harrovians to fish and trap game by night, was at last excluded from the annual Eton and Harrow cricket match after years of staunch attendance, because his language was found unacceptable.[76] His language had not changed but susceptibilities had. When Cotton preached his sermon 'Christian Death', he offered as consolation that the dying boy had said 'not one word in his delirium that his parents did not wish to hear'.[77] The edict of Percival at Clifton (and of other headmasters) that boys' knees should be kept covered at football is now notorious, and often quoted as if it were a freakish aberration, but it can be paralleled by many curiosities of what might be called counter-codpiece fantasies. William Sewell solemnly warned his congregation against the sin of reading an illustrated manual of anatomy with an 'impure mind'.[78] As the century advanced schoolmasters and preachers became 'obsessed with impurity'.[79] Even Montagu Butler, who should have known better, issued an order, soon after becoming headmaster of Harrow, that all boys' pockets must be sewn up. It had to be rescinded owing to the indignation and ridicule it aroused, especially after the howls of mirth and derision from Etonians at an Eton and Harrow match whenever a Harrovian was seen absentmindedly trying to put his hands in his pockets.[80]

---

* Edward Yardley in his translation of *The Four Books of Horace's Odes* (1869) says in his preface that he had 'purposely deviated from Horace's meaning when by so doing indelicacy is avoided'. Four odes were falsified (twenty-five of the First Book, twenty of the Third Book and ten and thirteen of the Fourth Book); two because they were 'irremediably offensive', the other two because 'they give a disagreeable impression of Horace'.

Despite the assiduous, sometimes fanatical, campaigns waged against Eros by school authorities from the 1870s, at the end of the century official pursuivants of sensuality were still complaining of 'the tone of tolerance with which by boys among themselves such offences are too often viewed'.[81]

In the end the 'immorality' drives affected and disturbed the masters more than the boys; for once an inquisition becomes obsessional its fever tends to infect the inquisitors. The cycles of suspicion were to reach a point of farcical hysteria when, early in the following century, at a staff meeting at Rossall, it was resolved that no master was to have a boy alone in his room for more than ten minutes, and no master should ever allow a boy to be alone in a room with him with the door shut.[82] Unfortunately the first victims of moral purges are too often the nobler and more candid spirits: at Eton William Johnson's departure in 1872 was almost certainly managed by Warre, whose influence upon Hornby was already dominant. The cause was not necessarily a single dramatic revelation, but his aura belonged to an older and freer society in which no proposition was treated as unquestionable.

One sees the requirement of 'earnestness' as an indispensable mark of seriousness even in schoolboys' orthodox disapproval of the style and manners of their grandfathers' *beau ideal*. Lord Melbourne's 'air of indolence' gave offence to a young Harrovian critic. When he was 'addressed with gravity by a deputation', Lord Melbourne would occupy himself by 'blowing about a feather, or nursing a soft cushion'. It might have been an 'aid to concentration', our instructor concedes, but it must have 'offended many'. He dismisses the old world with stern finality. 'We certainly can hardly imagine Mr Gladstone doing it.'[83]

In the older schools innovations did not come in all at once, but like Warre's 'evil elephant',* bit by bit, but they amounted to an increase in direct surveillance by the headmaster and assistant masters over the boys' recreational activities and pastimes, and a decrease, therefore, in real leisure and in freedom of choice exercised by the boys themselves. It was part of the new educational doctrine of total control, according to which real leisure and liberty, that is to say, freedom of choice, were malign and undesirable. The aim of

---

* Warre spoke with ambiguous consonants and without pronouncing a terminal *g* when it followed an *n*. When he harangued Etonians one day what they heard was something like this: 'Dere's an evil elephant come into the school. Nobody saw it come in. It came in bit by bit. But we must stamp on it and destroy it. It's the elephant of bettin and gamblin.'[84]

the system which produced the general process understood today as a public-school education was to make all the boys as far as possible alike, playing the same games at the same time, wearing the same kind of clothes (subject to distinctions of rank and honour), thinking the same thoughts, living by the same code. Independence of spirit and individuality of thought were discouraged as inimical to the object of the system. The schools were, in fact, responding to the pressures and demands of an external world for a supply of the type of human produce required – forceful, but obedient and well-indoctrinated officers and apostles of imperial orthodoxy trained and 'prepared to be citizens' and, more, governors and developers 'of the greatest empire under the sun'; or, as J. S. Mill put it with less reverence, of 'a vast system of outdoor relief for the upper classes'. In this system of training 'games were the supreme test of moral excellence',[85] and they were the road to preferment and promotion. Said a hopeful candidate for the Sudan Political Service as late as the 1930s, 'I shall row myself into the Sudan, a country of Blacks ruled by Blues.'[86]

Salt was a tutor at Eton during the period of mutation; he saw what was happening, and when Warre was chosen to succeed Hornby, he left. Hornby had been a man of the old order, forced into a role he had not sought and could not, in good conscience, perform. He never found it possible to decide for senior boys in authority, although formally invited to do so, how they were to reconcile their newly conceived duties of allying themselves with the masters, with the traditional code of honour between boys which forbids spying or talebearing.[87] The *enfant terrible* of the tutorial staff had been preaching reform for years. Warre meant reform, but not the kind of reform Salt had envisaged. This was a remedy worse than the disease it purported to cure, and he bade a sad farewell to the Eton which, reformer though he was, he loved as deeply as the most pious Old Etonian. 'It must be the vegetarianism,'[88] Warre murmured, on receiving his resignation with regret, probably not unmixed with relief.

As the seventies were entered the boys themselves became conscious of changes which assailed what they regarded as their inheritance. The abolition of shirking and phasing out of Dames' houses were resented; but the force of the reaction was not for the institutions themselves but because their demise was the visible sign of a change in the quality of life which was felt by some boys as an outrage, wresting from them, under the pretence of material benefaction, their birthright, the 'liberties' which they had heard celebrated at their fathers' and grandfathers' knees. In 1871 there were outbreaks of violence and an unpopular master, Stiggins, was narrowly prevented from being thrown into Barnes Pool. In 1875 there was what would have been, if it had ever developed so far, another 'rebellion'. It might have been partially provoked by the kind of Old Etonian parents who had been writing abusive personal letters to Warre and who stoked the fires of their sons' disaffection by saying, as some of them had long done, 'There used to be rebellions, and the school was full of fun.'[89]

It was a forlorn hope and miscarried even as a juvenile *Götterdämmerung*. The spirit of confident defiance which had animated the youth of the public schools earlier in the century had no stronghold in a mid Victorian mixed upper class, concerned to preserve an image of decorum. In 1875 Etonians did not rise; a few conspirators were penalized. When the principal condemned departed under sentence of banishment in a black coach drawn by black horses and accompanied by an escort of solemn mourners, the whole of the front of his house was draped in black with huge streamers of black crepe and a pole bearing an enormous black flag.[90] The boys who followed the carriage were more than doing honour to a martyred hero, they were mourning the passing of the old order.

According to Edward Lyttelton[91] the initials of the grand offender were W. H. Thanks to investigations by Patrick Strong, Eton College archivist, we are now able to identify him as George Eden Hunt. The son of the Rt Hon. G. W. H. Hunt of Hadenhoe House, Oundle (briefly Chancellor of the Exchequer), Hunt devoted his life at Eton to the chase, alternating the role of hunter, in pursuit of game, with that of hunted, pursued by gamekeepers. He was celebrated as a marksman, and not merely with firearms. It was said he could throw stones by hand with the force and accuracy of a catapult. On being asked by an assistant master how he had killed a crow which he had brought into school and laid on his desk, he raised his arm and said, 'With this, sir.'

Hunt and his gang devised a secret means of egress and entry to their house, Rouse's, and used to go out on nocturnal sporting expeditions. On one occasion Hunt was in Ditton Park in the early hours of the morning in search of ducks or ducks' eggs, and had stripped, leaving his clothes in a ditch, to swim to an island which was his objective. While he was occupied there, he was seen by an approaching keeper and had not time to recover his clothes in making his escape. He ran naked, pursued by the keeper, through the park, on to the public road and streaked through Eton until he reached the refuge of the yielding window at Rouse's.

The window of Hunt's own room, known as Hunt's larder, was always decorated with the spoils of the chase, suspended from a string stretched across it. Far into the night the sounds of revelry and corks popping disturbed the peace of occupants of more orderly houses, and songs were sung which shocked the ears of respectable boys' maids. The most surprising part of the story is that Dionysian riot should have gone as long as it did; for 'mad 'Unt' and his followers were an anachronism, relics of a wilder earlier age before that change had come over the 'upper class' of society for which Edward Lyttelton, a scandalized observer of Rouse's revellers, gave devout thanks, and said, 'A plain demand was made by the public that these and other wild doings should be checked.'

Matters came to a head when Rouse's house suffered an explosion which wrecked a room and blew a hole in the ceiling. Mr 'Pecker' Rouse himself was fearful that this had merely been a rehearsal in miniature of the main event, which was to be the treatment of his house as Guy Fawkes had designed to treat the Houses of Parliament, but probably more effective in execution. Drastic measures were taken. No one is certain how many conspirators were banished; not as many as Lyttelton's 'fourteen', but undoubtedly more than Hunt alone. Hunt who, says Lyttelton, 'according to local gossips must have been stark mad', thereafter concealed that condition, if such it was, sufficiently to marry a baronet's daughter and become a Justice of the Peace, presiding in that capacity at the trial of many a poacher. According to Eton College Register he died in 1892.

It is unlikely that many boys at Eton, and at the other ancient public schools, could have defined what it was in these uneasy seventies that disturbed them with a feeling of dissolution and loss. The 'evil elephant' did his work softly, almost by stealth. But boys did feel that they were living through a process of simultaneous demolition and regimentation. Some welcomed the modernity, the specialization in games, and did not notice the reins growing tighter. But others apprehended that something precious and, in the foreseeable future, irrecoverable, was being taken from them 'when a big fellow cannot even come across a little fellow in the most casual way without its being remarked and . . . the most hideous construction being put on it'.[92] We, with the advantage of historical selection, can illustrate the change which they could only feel by gradual drift. We shall compare three scenes which, in actuality, were separated by time and space.

The date of the first is around 1855, the place Eton. Jickling, the delinquent junior of *Collegers v Oppidans* who was always in trouble, is complaining indignantly of the ill-bred conduct of an assistant master, when out of school. Jickling was returning to Eton by train from his holidays and was using a peashooter from the carriage window when this beak saw him and complained of him to the headmaster for an act which, being committed out of school, should have been no business of his. 'I call that snobbish,'* said Jickling with contempt. The fact that a beak had in fact behaved in a fashion questionable by the old standards was itself significant, and there were members of the staff who at that time would certainly have sided with Jickling.

The next scene is in Radley, one of the major new boarding schools, which came into existence in 1849. The headmaster, William Sewell, is reminding boys with keen satisfaction that they are under perpetual scrutiny. 'Constantly we shall be visiting the dormitory, coming upon you suddenly – (until we feel you have strength enough to resist the temptation of being left alone) coming among you at all hours, myself, the Fellows, the Prefects, and if we should find it necessary even our confidential servants.'[93] Sewell was a very ambitious, rather hysterical man, and pitched his claims for Radley high, presenting the foundation as in every sense a 'public school' on equal terms with Eton and Harrow; but between his righteous affirmation of the duty to spy on his charges, and the old public-school ways, to which Jickling still felt able to appeal, there could be neither mutual respect nor accommodation. It was Sewell's example which indicated the shape of things to come; by the seventies it had become an offence at Eton for lower boys to visit boys in other houses,[94] and a whole complex of restrictive regulations, any one of which would have provoked an uprising before 1850, encircled the lives of the boys in closer conformity with moral patterns elsewhere.

Our third scene takes us to the end of the century and shows a master, Grimstone, at an unspecified public school in a moment of what passed for relaxed social informality with some of the boys. Behind a bland, cordial exterior he nourished detective fever of a virulent type, and one sees him 'with one arm or two round the necks

---

* Jickling is using 'snobbish' not in its modern popular sense of tuft-hunting, but merely meaning 'vulgar, and ignorant of good manners'.

or waists of boys; the ostensible object being to express his affection for them, the real to see if they had pipes, catapults or other contraband matter about their persons'.[95] These are attitudes and methods wholly alien to the character of the 'old public schools', which would have been as repugnant to the masters as to the boys.

The schools, in fact, while retaining the name and appearance of continuity, had been transmogrified to correspond with the needs and standards of a much-changed outer society. There were gains and there were losses, and perhaps some of the gains could have been obtained without the loss of so much of what was good as well as of what was bad. One of the losses was a plunging decline from the 1840s onwards in the literary and intellectual quality of the writing by boys, and not only of the *boys*.* It reached its nadir in the seventies and eighties under Warre when, said Wingfield Stratford, the cult of the body was 'not exclusive of but actively hostile to that of the intellect'.[97] In such writing as there was, boys echoed the alternating tones of tremulous sentimentality and bellicose patriotism which came to be known as 'jingoism'. *The Capture of Lucknow* is an exhortation to British soldiers in India to visit fitting vengeance upon the defeated for the recent massacre in Cawnpore:

> No quarter required and no quarter bestowed
> Demand from the city the blood that is owed;
> Let death be your watchword and vengeance your cry
> As onward you hurry to conquer or die.

In the last verse the writer is more specific in his requirements, and admonishes the troops not to waste time in looting when they could be killing:

> On! cease not for plunder your conquering cheer
> But onward nor stay your wild bloody career
> Till the groans of the dying re-echo around
> And the weltering corpses lie thick on the ground

---

* The first headmaster of Eton to fall noticeably below the high standards set by his predecessors of the age of 'barbarism' was Edward Lyttelton, the apostle of improving decorum who, although held in affectionate esteem by many for his warm-hearted kindness and good intentions, was a scholastic embarrassment to the school. 'The dreadful tale of King Pheras,' said Geoffrey Madden, 'overflowed the banks of Eton and spread in widening circles' through the universities. A boy construed in school, without correction, '*Rex Pheras progressus est*' as 'King Pheras advanced'. Another boy, who knew that the Latin meant 'The King advanced to Pherae', asked, 'Sir, will you tell us about King Pheras?' The headmaster answered, 'One of those old Macedonian kings. Tell you about him another time.'[96]

344

Till the houses send forth their red rivers of gore
Oh! onward! cry, 'Vengeance, remember Cawnpore.'[98]

A second example blossoms from the very heart of the age of decorum, 1887, the year of Jubilee, and conveys a sense of uneasy defensiveness under a surface of a confidence which is grandiose yet querulous:

England, thine and ours! though foemen would confound her
Prophesying war and evil things to be
Hearing all her sons laugh loud and gather round her
Strong to stand by her as they have stood by thee
Thee, a rose among the roses that have bound her
Brows and made her the great glory of the sea.

Greece and Rome were twain but England joins their glory
Rome by might of battle, Greece by power of song
None shall weep the ruined world that now no more is
None bewail the fallen kingdoms that were strong
None shall dim her fame with triumphs told in stories
England shines and towers above the lesser throng.

Sea and cliff and wind, these stand for threefold token
Of the threefold love thy children bear to thee
Waves are not more boundless, rocks are sooner broken,
Nor the wind that wakes at sunrise is more free
England's life is theirs, her doom shall not be spoken
Till the last word sound of wind and cliff and sea.[99]

An earlier Harrovian verser treated the suggestion of England's 'doom' with playful ridicule, mocking the notion in a flight of whimsical fantasy. Its impact, a little more than a hundred years later, is startling, and not at all what the writer had purposed:

LONDON (as it is to be):

Some people have pleased to give out as their views –
(Belief pray accord if you like, or refuse)
That a horrible doom in future awaits
Poor England, which false (they say) power elates.

The 'doom' turns out to be:

When Kaffirs and Hottentots bask in the sun
On the semi-sunk turrets of lordly Bohun.[100]*

---

* The anonymous doggerelist appears to be ignorant of the correct pronunciation of the name he invokes, which corresponds with *boon*.

So, inconspicuously and pragmatically as ever, the public schools in the second half of the century adapted themselves to become the kind of places the name signified from soon after the Clarendon Commission until at least the end of the Second World War (and some critics would say, incorrectly, they still are), manufactories for the production of a serviceable élite, as stylized and readily identifiable as Samurai, resourceful, faithful, within limits versatile, and sustained by a morale grounded upon a virtually religious conviction of superiority. 'A man's a man for a' that, but,' Leslie Stephen observed in 1873, 'man includes public school men and other men – the minor classifications are of small importance.'[101]

What this 'reformation' effected has been familiar to all who have looked at the public schools, whether to applaud or censure, during the past century. The image is one of large, orderly and picturesque boarding schools, housing assemblies of clean, polite boys, uniformly dressed and, to the eye of an outsider at least, uniformly behaved, playing and worshipping at the altars of the same select games, their lives strictly regulated under the moral surveillance of a considerable body of professionally vigilant masters.

But even some of the most committed justifiers of reform had to confess that somewhere in the operation something had gone wrong. It was a perplexing suspicion, for they were committed to the prevailing principle of leisureless, controlled activity which left no time for natural development. 'A boy needs solitude to grow,' H. Lee Warner conceded, 'and it is just what his schoolmaster dare not allow him.' He did not deny that the effect of accounting for every hour of a boy's time under supervision was to stamp out originality, but he sought in vain for an alternative, for it was 'the only way a schoolmaster can meet the deadly danger of immorality'.[102]

Such was the priority, and the result found favour in the sight of the captains and the kings. Addressing an audience of Etonians in 1890, a politician, Mr Geoffrey Drage, remarked, 'I am afraid that compared to foreign boys the average Eton boy of my time at any rate could only be described as ignorant.' However, this judgement was not meant as a reproach or call for amendment, for he went on cheerfully to ask, 'What is it that sets the ignorant above the learned and gives them repose and dignity, which all the knowledge contained in the *Encyclopaedia Britannica* fails to do?' The answer turned out to be 'respect for women' and the performance of *unpaid* public service. Mr Drage spoke words of encouragement and congratulation. 'I assure you that at this moment an Englishman who deserves the name, stalks abroad through Europe like a Spartan through the fields of Greece in her degenerate days, or like Achilles through the meadows of asphodel and everyone says "Great Heavens, why are not our boys like that?" ' The purpose and vocation of this 'superiority' he was there to remind them, their one true and shared interest, was 'the conscientious administration and defence under the Queen and with God's help of the greatest empire the world has ever seen'.

Geoffrey Drage and many others like him expressed the character and purpose of the reformed, post-Clarendon Commission public schools as trainers and suppliers of successive generations of pro-consuls, consecrated to the service and perpetuation of an Empire worthily destined to immortality. 'For the last century in the great continent of Africa which we are gradually making our own,' said Mr Drage, 'England is the only country which has never failed to turn an attentive ear to the cries of the down trodden and oppressed, and for that purpose she has poured out not only treasure but the blood of the noblest of her sons like water. I *do* lay stress upon the fact that it is our rule in India and our rule alone which stands between countless millions and every kind of oppression, tyranny and wrong.'[103]

What men like Drage said was not without truth. The defect of their vision, and of the schools that bred them, was omission. Superficiality was enforced as virtue. There was always a tendency among a majority of boys to discourage the independent views of minorities; but under the old order the minorities had only their own kind as adversaries and were able to claim and enjoy a large measure of independence of thought and action. But in the reformed public schools the majority had the impress of magisterial approval, and a boy of independent and inquiring mind had to fight on two fronts for his cause. 'It is a great pity,' said a Harrovian, 'that independence of opinion, or word and deed, should be hopelessly confused with such a questionable quality as swagger,' the chief power of which to terrorize new boys lay in its vagueness. A decade later the next generation of stalwart protestors were still complaining of 'swagger', a charge originally invoked to keep down braggarts, having become 'a curse when it is used as a bogey to scare away individuality'.[104] A corresponding trend in adult life to standardization through the tyranny of an intolerant majority was the besetting fear of J. S. Mill,[105] and of certain men of quite different principles. 'The corporate life of England has in many principal things gone deplorably wrong,' said Archdeacon Denison in 1878, towards the end of a long life. 'The mass of men never go deep into things; and if we are to be governed, as we are now, by the masses, we must be content to be shallow people.'[106] His were neither popular nor welcome opinions, and he was never offered a bishopric, but some of his observations on education and politics remain relevant a hundred years later, when the judgements and expectations of the 'progressives' have become quaint relics of a calamitous naïvety.

In the years that lay ahead the public schools – the *reformed* public schools – were to play a role the importance of which it would be difficult to exaggerate both in maintaining and modifying the *status quo*. There were still the rebels and independents who denied and renounced all or part of the creed indoctrinated. But to prevail they needed guile and skill in dissimulation, vividly depicted in triumph and disaster by Rudyard Kipling in *Stalky & Co.*, and in one of the lesser known *Schoolboy Lyrics*. In 'The Dusky Crew' Kipling evokes the dangers and tribulations of individualists fighting on those two fronts in a society of severely exacted conformity:

> Our heads were rough and our hands were black
> With the ink stains midnight hue,
> We scouted all both great and small
> We were a dusky crew,
> And each boy's hand was against us raised
> 'Gainst me and the other two

But in addition to challenging the orthodoxy of their peers they had to outwit the surveillance of magisterial spies. Instead of worshipping the approved gods in due process, the conspirators set up their independent and exclusive social cell, a secret cave to which they retired for the enjoyment of privacy and the cultivation of a little vegetable garden:

> In secret caves in the cold dark earth
> The luscious lettuce grew.

Their sinful deviation was divined by a master who tracked down the three friends to their lair and surprised them:

> He found our cave in the cold dark earth
> He crept the branches through
> He caught us in our Council Hall
> Caught us, a dusky crew, –
> To punishment he led us all,
> Led me and the other two.

Our lettuces are dead and gone,
Our plans have fallen through
We wander free in misery,
We are a wretched crew
Will happiness no more return
To me and the other two?[107]

Kipling is never more clearly the product of a *reformed* mid Victorian public-school education than when he expresses sympathy with any kind of rebel. For even those men who have most resolutely abandoned the code and morality, or inhibitions, of a public-school education, retain distinct marks of its impress upon their personalities. The converse is equally true. However well-bred his speech and manners, a man who has not been to a public school may be distinguished from one who has, especially in his intercourse with other men.* George Moberly alluded to 'that peculiar character which is almost universally found in young men bred at public schools which all the world recognizes and which none appreciate so keenly as those who are devoid of it'.[108] He does not define this quality, but Leslie Stephen, who tries to do so, in making a comparison between the attributes of Pitt the Younger and his political rival Charles Fox, gives the advantage to the product of a private education, against the more sparkling and sociable but less profound and subtle, public-school playboy.[109]

The reformed public schools have aroused strong feelings and attracted praise and condemnation. Generous dispensations of both have come from the United States of America. Parents from Virginia and South Carolina had sent their sons to Eton and Westminster since the eighteenth century. An Etonian had signed the Declaration of Independence,† and amity was reciprocated in the sympathy shown by Etonians like Gladstone and Hallam for the United States' struggle for independence.‡

* The Earl Russell, better known for most of his life as Bertrand Russell, seemed on the surface a conventionally educated member of his class and times. His address was elegant but robust; there was nothing the least precious or affected about him; yet there was an elusive difference, which puzzled me, between him and other contemporaries of his with whom I was acquainted. At last I discerned what it was. Russell had not gone to a public school; indeed he had not gone to any school, but had been educated by tutors and his elder brother, until he went up to Cambridge. The absence of the obligation to adapt himself early in life in a community of boys was enduring in its consequences.
† Thomas Lynch of Prince George's Parish, Winyah, South Carolina. Eton, 1764–67.
‡ On 26 August 1826 Hallam wrote to Gaskell, 'To see America raised by his [Jefferson's] own hands from the abject situation in which she supplicated Lord North for Justice, but supplicated in vain, to an eminence as brilliant as secure, an eminence from which she looks proudly on admiring Europe and shows to that half enslaved continent the glorious and unprecedented spectacle of a vigorous, tranquil, civilised Democracy!'[110]

The public schools are probably the most famous system in the history of the education of male youth. On the whole, despite the charges of breeding 'snobbery', in the sense of class divisiveness, the schools' merits have been judged, by the test of *action*, to outweigh their defects. They have not been our concern, and have only been regarded at this late stage to take the measure of the differences which separate them from what went before. Our subject has been public schools on which much less has been written in modern times, different in almost all respects from the models on display for the past century. These also came under criticism and censure, though not for producing too near-identical products. Cowper had asked in exasperation:

> What causes move us, knowing as we must
> That these menageries all fail their trust,
> To send our sons to scout and scamper there
> While colts and puppies cost us so much care.[111]

The answer was that parents who advisedly chose to send their sons to those public schools believed that a period of having to 'scout and scamper',* and fend for themselves in a boys' world, was a desirable phase of male education for the adult world as it then was. It bequeathed to an age of decorum memories so exotic that they might have been the fables of legendary antiquity. But they were not fables, and the voice of one of the denizens reminds us in valediction of that pagan mixture of immense freedom within a framework of strong, sometimes brutal, controls, which gave its life a Homeric mixture of independence and danger, civilization and savagery:

> The same things do not all delight;
> These chose the black, and those the white;
> These like to watch the Thames Stream;
> And these to see-saw on a beam.
> Whilst some will daringly pursue
> The roads to Maidenhead or Kew
> Others more innocent will sing
> The praises of Queen Anne's liquid spring,
> Or near south meadow go to trace
> For a cool arbour a fit place.
> These with agility and speed

---

* Morely Saunders wrote home from Eton, 6 December 1767, 'I assure you papa I will not keep company with bad Boys, but indeed there are very few good ones in this place.'[112]

Will hunt the hare on Chalvey mead;
While these with jumping poles in hand
Hare Stocker's ditches at command.
Some for steal-baggage, others cry
Unanimous for I-spy-I.[113]

The differences which divided the old world from the new, the unreformed from the reformed public schools, were not alteration in the
choice and range of studies merely, but change in the nature of the
experience conferred. The effect was acclaimed by predicants of the
new order, like Edward Lyttelton, as a moral victory and advance.
In fact it was an adaptation, and expansion,* enforced eagerly, regret-
fully, or with resignation, to supply the requirements of a changed
environment and its demands. Since then environment and demands
have been changing again, and with them the public schools,
maintaining with ancient craft, as they change, a venerable image,
reassuring to those who cherish it, of numinous unchangeability.

* Cheltenham, 1841; Marlborough, 1843; Rossel, 1844; Wellington, 1853; Clifton, 1862; Haile-
bury, 1862. Older grammar foundations like Repton, Sherborne, Uppingham and Oundle were
promoted and reconstituted by ambitious headmasters and boards of governors to manifest,
in response to demand, the amended character and style of a post-Clarendon Commission
public school.

APPENDIX

The Eton Wall Game

'The origin of the Wall Game is hidden in mystery,' said R. A. Austen Leigh. There are those who say that the game itself is 'hidden in mystery'. Many Etonians have taken part in the historic annual contest between Collegers and Oppidans on St Andrew's Day without acquiring any clear notion of what the proceedings were about, while most of the spectators understood even less.

The game cannot be older than the wall between Slough Road and the playing fields against which it has always been played. The wall was built in 1717. The ground is a narrow strip bounded on one side by the wall and on the other side by a white line; at one end by a garden wall and at the other end by another white line. At each end, demarcated by a white line, is an area called 'calx', the one at the Eton end being 'good calx', and the one at the other end 'bad calx'. The goals are the door of the lower master's garden wall at one end, and at the other end, there being no garden door, part of an ancient elm tree marked with white lines. The object of play is to get the ball into your opponents' calx by a series of bullies* with a team composed of eleven† men. There are three 'walls', who evolved a functional garb of wall sack and wall caps and trousers, and two seconds who wear wall caps and knickerbockers. These five make the bully and form down against the wall, one holding the next up in sequence. Next to them comes the third man, then fourth, then 'line', whose work it is, besides kicking it out, to follow the ball and stop it or protect it, according to which way it is rolling. The ball is put into bully by the third, who is playing towards bad calx, and it must touch the wall. Behind the bully stands 'flying man', or 'fly', then 'the long', who stands near him, and lastly 'goals'. When the ball comes out of bully, the players, the best placed being the outsides,

---

* Bully (Etonian): scrimmage.
† In the 1950s this number was reduced to ten.

try to kick it out as far as possible towards the opposite calx. The bully is then formed again opposite the spot where the ball stops. The ball may also be 'rushed' into calx, but kicking is the usual mode of advance. The most famous kick in the history of the game by F. E. Stacey,* when he kicked nearly the whole length of the wall (120 yards), the ball, kicked from bad calx, stopped two feet out of good calx.

Attackers attempt to score a shy by touching the ball with their hands when it is above the ground and touching the walls, and the object of the attacking team is to get the ball into this position, and of the other to get the ball out behind and kick it away into good calx. If a shy is scored, the player who touched it throws at goal. A goal equals ten shies. In earlier times, when only what is known as the 'instantaneous process' of throwing at goal was allowed, it was little short of impossible to score a goal, and to improve the chances of success an operation known as 'furking'† was permitted.‡ When the ball gets into calx, that is, within striking distance for one team or another, a new form of bully is constituted, composed of a getter, a second, and a getting furker on the offensive side, and a stopper, a second, and a stopping furker on the defensive side.

The game has had a turbulent history. In 1827 the annual match on St Andrew's Day was stopped by Keate as a result of a fight between an Oppidan and a Colleger on the field, later developing into an affray between the two rival bodies of the school. The rules permit players to push their opponents, but not to grip them by limb or garment, nor kick, strike or knuckle them. In a loose bully down in bad calx by the tree goal, Bob Latham,§ a Colleger in Liberty, had kicked Crawshay,** a sturdy lower boy. Crawshay promptly hit out and knocked the aggressor down, but was himself immediately felled by Sanders,†† the Captain of College. Order was temporarily restored; but the Oppidans vowed to be revenged and later,

---

* Francis Edmund, ᴋs. Barrister, Lincoln's Inn.

† Furk (Etonian): to expel (L. *furca*, a fork). In connection with the Wall Game, meaning to extract the ball out of a bully by a defined process. Alternative derivations of furk: Winchester furk, ferk, firk: to expel, to send (as on a message); Old English *fercian*. High German *ferken*. Middle English to lead or send away.[1]

‡ The benefit of furking seems to have been so far successful that a goal – the last to be recorded – was scored in 1911, when the Collegers team included a player called Harold Macmillan.

§ Robert Gordon. Became a well-known ethnologist and author of works on grammar.

** Francis. 'The Ironmaster, lives between Cardiff and Merthyr Tydvil.'[2]

†† Thomas, a barrister; died at Richmond in 1852.

Taunton,* the Captain of Boats, incited by his con, Chisholm,† and supported by a large following, confronted a party of Collegers and a public mêlée ensued. In consequence the match was suspended for a number of years, but it had been resumed by 1836, when Dod (later Wooley-Dod) came to Eton. Before 1848 little was recorded. The historic period began when the modern rules (under which the imaginary game Jickling watched would have been played) were drawn up in 1849, on the sole authority of Stacey, senior Keeper of the Wall. In 1851 it was again proposed to abolish the match on the ground that it promoted ill feeling between Collegers and Oppidans, but the Wall Game has survived all threats and it continues to be played.

* Thomas, wine merchant, of Bond Street. Ashley's second in the fatal fight. See above, p. 142.
† Duncan Macdonald. The Chisholm, of Erchless Castle, Inverness. Coldstream Guards. Succeeded, 1838; died 1858.

Abbreviations

These are used in both the source notes and bibliography.

BAE	British Annals of Education		NC	The Nineteenth Century
BL	British Library		NCA	The Nineteenth Century and After
BLAM	British Library Add. MS.			
BM	Blackwood's Magazine		NE	The New Englander
BMSP	Baily's Monthly Magazine of Sports and Pastimes		NH	Northampton Herald
			NMM	New Monthly Magazine
CM	Cornhill Magazine		NQ	Notes and Queries
CR	Contemporary Review		NatR	National Review
DNB	Dictionary of National Biography		NR	New Rugbeian
			PE	Porticus Etonensis
ECC	Eton College Chronicle		PR	Prospective Review
ECR	Eton College Register		QJE	Quarterly Journal of Education
ECM	Eton College Magazine		QR	Quarterly Review
EF	Eton Fortnightly		QRE	Quarterly Review of Education
ER	Edinburgh Review		RM	Rugby Magazine
ESM	Eton School Magazine		SM	The Sporting Magazine
ETA	Etoniana		SQR	Scholastic Quarterly Review
FM	Fraser's Magazine		SR	Saturday Review
GM	Gentleman's Magazine		TBL	Town Boy Ledger
HSVL	Harrow School Vaughan Library		TE	The Etonian
			TH	The Harrovian
JB	John Bull		TRR	Temple Reading Room
JE	Journal of Education		TT	The Tyro
LAL	Life and Letters		WCL	Winchester College Library
LMR	Law Magazine and Review			
MC	Morning Chronicle		WR	Westminster Review
MM	Macmillan's Magazine		WSA	Westminster School Archives

Source Notes

Preface

1. [Collins], *Public Schools*, p. 5.

ONE
The Birth of the Mystic

1. [Johnston], p. 2.
2. Skrine, p. 8.
3. *FM*, vol. 42, September 1850, p. 296
4. Old Rugbeian, p. 1.
5. *TH*, no. 10, 11 November 1879.
6. [George Lyttelton], *ECM* no. 7, p. 273.
7. *ETA*, no. 105, April 1948, p. 70.
8. [Essington], 'Old Long Chamber', p. 107.
9. *ETA*, no. 115, 31 December 1954, p. 232.
10. Cooke, p. 306.
11. Clavering letters, Letter 49, 18 September 1848, WSA.
12. Ascham, Preface.
13. Pace, Preface, cited in Furnivall, pp. xii–xiii.
14. Hexter, p. 50; W. Harrison, vol. 1, pp. 77–8.
15. L. Stone, p. 686.
16. *ER*, vol. 16, April 1810, p. 326.
17. *BM*, vol. 47, June 1840, p. 779.
18. Heywood and Wright, pp. 388–93; *ETA*, no. 117, 27 November 1965, p. 259.
19. Sterry, p. 322; *ETA*, no. 117, 1965, pp. 260, 261.
20. Willis and Clark, vol. 1, pp. 321–2, quoted by H. M. Colvin in *ETA*, no. 117, 1965, pp. 260–61; Sterry, p. xxiii.
21. John Stowe in H. Morley, p. 101.
22. Evelyn, 13 May 1661, vol. 3, p. 287.
23. Davies, pp. 91ff, 114ff.
24. Leinster, p. 376.
25. Woburn papers in Blakiston, pp. 75–6.
26. Moultrie, p. 67.
27. [Collins], *Etoniana*, p. 66.
28. Gray.
29. Toynbee, vol. 1, p. 51.
30. Arnold, vol. 2, p. 128.
31. Byron.
32. Bartle Frere in Frere, vol. 1, p. 16.
33. L. Stephen, *Life*, pp. 79–80.

TWO
'Nurseries of all Vice'

1. Fielding, Bk 3, ch. 3, p. 201; ch. 5, p. 320.
2. Hare, *Memorials*, vol. 1, p. 163.
3. Pierce, pp. 114, 115.
4. L. Stephen, 'Thoughts', p. 287.
5. Quoted by Patrick Scott, 'The school and the novel: *Tom Brown's Schooldays*', in Simon and Bradley, p. 49.
6. Adams, *Wykehamica*, p. 206 n.; Minchin, *Our Public*, p. 335.
7. Cornish, pp. 151–2.
8. M. L. Clarke, p. 83.
9. C. Merivale, pp. 28–9.
10. [Apperley], p. 10.
11. H. Walpole, *Reminiscences*, p. 14.
12. Rowcroft, *Confessions*, vol. 1, p. 28.
13. [Russell], p. 174.

14. Wade, *Extraordinary*, p. 78.
15. Bagehot, *Works*, vol. 3, p. 246.
16. T. A. Trollope, p. 131.
17. Communicated by Mr S. R. Allsop and reprinted by permission of the Hansard Society from *Parliamentary Affairs*; *ETA*, 1965, p. 270.
18. Herbert, *Pembroke Papers*, pp. 9, 10, 35, 57n.; *ETA*, no. 96, 4 June 1943, pp. 726–8; *ETA*, no. 115, 31 December 1954, p. 239.
19. Besant, p. 84.
20. Carroll, vol. 1, p. 4.
21. Lounger, p. 13.
22. Kinglake, *Eothen*, p. 169.
23. W. C. Green, p. 22.
24. William Vincent, p. 51.
25. Morrice, pp. 6, 8, 15, 16.
26. [Collins], *Public Schools*, p. 158.
27. Macaulay, vol. 4, p. 327.
28. Holland, vol. 1, pp. 17–18.
29. T. H. Green, vol. 2, pp. cx–cxi.
30. *Third Report*, p. 58.
31. *ETA*, no. 15, 22 July 1913, p. 232.
32. S. Butler (headmaster), *Letter to Brougham*, pp. 10, 16.
33. *QR*, vol. 19, 1818, pp. 495, 499.
34. Lloyd, pp. 6, 8, 99.
35. Laughton, vol. 2, pp. 66, 67.
36. Brougham, *Letter*, p. 48.
37. Wm Churton, 11 October 1816.
38. *ETA*, no. 122, 7 June 1969, p. 341.
39. C. A. E. Moberly, p. 9, 1 January 1848.
40. A Parent, *Remarks*, pp. 5, 6, 11, 13.
41. [Lewis], *ER*, April-July 1830, March 1831.
42. [Lewis], *Letters*, p. 1.
43. A Parent, *Remarks*, pp. 10, 24, 25; [Lewis], *ER*, no. 101, pp. 67, 68, 69.
44. [H. H. Milman], 'Eton School', p. 128.
45. [Lewis], *ER*, no. 105, pp. 77, 78.
46. *QJE*, vol. 8, no. 16, 1834, pp. 279, 286.
47. ibid., pp. 280, 292–3.
48. Brown, vol. 64, 27 January 1839.
49. Gladstone, *Papers*, p. 57.

50. W. M. Thackeray, 'De Juventute', *CM*, vol. 2, October 1860, p. 504.
51. [H. H. Milman], *Eton System*, pp. 63–7.
52. [H. H. Milman], 'Eton School', p. 284.
53. 'Our public schools – their discipline and instruction', *FM*, no. 289, October 1854, p. 406.
54. Etonensis, *Observations*, p. 32.
55. [H. H. Milman], 'Eton School', p. 137.
56. Rowcroft, *Confessions*, vol. 1, p. 42.
57. *Table Talk*, vol. 2, 8 July 1833.
58. Cowper, p. 217.
59. Bartle Frere in Frere, vol. 1, p. 16.
60. Old-Etonian, *Letter*, p. 10.
61. *QJE*, January 1835, p. 88.
62. Stephens, vol. 1, p. 106.
63. Gladstone, *Papers*, p. 12.
64. L. Stephen, *Life*, p. 81.
65. A. Trollope, *Autobiography*, p. 2.
66. [Collins], *Public Schools*, p. 320.
67. Kingsley, vol. 2, pp. 26–7.
68. W. M. Thackeray, *Pendennis*, vol. 1, p. 16.
69. Bagehot, *Literary*, vol. 2, pp. 187–8.
70. [Collins], *Public Schools*, Preface.

THREE
Preparation

1. Palmer, vol. 1, pp. 66–9.
2. T. Trollope, pp. 7–8.
3. Torr, p. 55.
4. Pell, p. 15.
5. Doyle, pp. 18–21.
6. Gibbon, p. 26.
7. Gaskell, September 1821, *Eton Boy*, pp. 3–4.
8. Monson, *ETA*, no. 40, 1926, p. 634; no. 39, 1925, p. 620; no. 41, 1927, p. 656.
9. T. Arnold letters, WCL.
10. Grant letters, TRR.
11. Denison, p. 5.
12. Cecil, vol. 1, p. 9.
13. Bourne, p. 13.
14. Melly, p. 51.

FOUR
Trial by Ordeal

1. Gaskell, May 1824, *Eton Boy*, pp. 17, 19, 22, 23, 25, 35. 5 June. 7, 8, 9, 10, 11, 13.
2. Brown, vol. 31, 27 February 1822; vol. 32, 10 June 1822; vol. 33, 15 January 1823; vol. 38, 7 June 1825; vol. 62, 8 June 1838; vol. 100, 9 January 1855.
3. J. L. Warner, copies of letters, *c.* 1849, TRR.
4. Keppel, p. 217.
5. Tuckwell, p. 54.
6. Lloyd Brereton MS., letters 5 and 6, TRR.
7. G. M. Berford of San Remo to W. Cotton Oswell, 1892, Oswell, vol. 2, pp. 223–4.
8. [Tucker], p. 143.
9. T. Arnold, 'Warminster', letter 19.
10. William Adams, MS. Letters, TRR.
11. Copies of three letters, probably written by William Congreve, letter 1, 17 November 1839, TRR.
12. [Blake], p. 123.
13. Etonensis, *Observations*, p. 26.
14. *QJE*, vol. 8, no. 16, April-October 1834, pp. 277ff.
15. W. C. Green, p. 49.
16. *WR*, 1861, p. 499.
17. T. A. Trollope, vol. 1, p. 77.
18. Pearson, p. 26.
19. C. Merivale, pp. 35–6; A. Trollope, *Autobiography*, p. 30.
20. A. Trollope, *Autobiography*, pp. 27–8.
21. Wilkinson, p. 135.
22. W. Rogers, p. 19.
23. [Westmacott], *English Spy*, vol. 1, p. 38.
24. G. G. A. Lawrence, p. 4.
25. W. M. Thackeray, *Works*, vol. 3, p. 299.
26. Old Westminster, pp. 4, 9, 10.
27. ibid., p. 7.
28. Trotter, p. 9.
29. Arbuthnot, pp. 276–8, 283.
30. Clavering MS., letter 71, March 1850, WSA.
31. Pearson, p. 26; cf. Hare, *Memorials*, vol. 1, p. 161.
32. Tuckwell, p. 23.
33. J. L. Warner, November 1849.
34. Pell, pp. 41, 42.
35. Wilkinson, pp. 323–4.
36. E. Williams, vol. 1, p. 6.
37. [Collins], *Public Schools*, p. 316.
38. A. Trollope, *Autobiography*, p. 3.
39. Rich, p. 49.
40. J. E. Austen Leigh, ch. 11.
41. WSA.
42. Hawtrey, p. 112.

FIVE
Fags and their Masters

1. *QR*, 1860, p. 392.
2. F. W. Farrar, *St Winifred's*, p. 314.
3. [Tucker], p. 145.
4. [Collins], *Public Schools*, p. 166.
5. Barrow, vol. 2, p. 164.
6. [A. D. Coleridge], p. 1.
7. [Collins], *Public Schools*, pp. 165, 166.
8. Tuckwell, p. 163.
9. I have also drawn on the accounts of Arthur Ainger, R. W. Essington and H. J. Crickitt Blake.
10. 'The Autobiography of an Etonian', *ECM*, nos 3 and 5, 23 July and 8 October 1832.
11. 'My first letter', *Eton Bureau*, 1 February 1843, pp. 162–3.
12. 'Everard Letters', 15 November 1831; *ETA*, no. 118, 4 June 1966, p. 280.
13. A. Trollope, *Autobiography*, pp. 5–6.
14. [Tucker], p. 41.
15. 'Everard Letters', 23 October 1831; *ETA*, op. cit., p. 278.
16. Gaskell, 15 September 1825; *ETA*, no. 64, 11 September 1936, p. 217.
17. 'Fortescue Letters', 28 September 1832; *ETA*, no. 120, 25 November 1967, p. 318.
18. ibid., 10 October 1833; *ETA*, no. 121, 30 November 1968, p. 323.

19. Brown, vol. 30, 27 June 1821.
20. ibid., vol. 30; 13, 21 February 1822.
21. Joseph Lloyd Brereton, letter, 11 December 1839, TRR.
22. Melly, pp. 246–7.
23. Mansfield, p. 42.
24. Tuckwell, p. 107.
25. W. A. Fearon, giving evidence before the Clarendon Commission. Report, vol. 21, Winchester, para. 1064.
26. Mansfield, pp. 55–7.
27. [G. Lyttelton], no. 6, pp. 161–5.
28. Gaskell, *Eton Boy*, p. 74; 5 June 1826.
29. Thomas Churton, letter 23.
30. ibid., 15 and 24 February 1817.
31. William Churton, 11 October 1816.
32. Palmer, vol. 1, p. 107.
33. W. Ward, p. 17.
34. Palmer, vol. 1, p. 109.
35. [Tucker], p. 40.
36. [Southey], 'Elementary Teaching', p. 142.
37. Rowcroft, *Confessions*, vol. 1, pp. 113, 114.
38. [Lewis], *ER*, p. 76.
39. *NMM*, 1827, p. 481.
40. *QJE*, vol. 9, no. 17, January–April 1835, pp. 86–7, 90.
41. S. Rogers, pp. 226–7.
42. *FM*, vol. 1, no. 298, October 1854, p. 405.
43. Mozley, vol. 1, pp. 389–93.
44. See for example Melly, pp. 19–58.
45. Nettleship, p. 448.
46. 'On the discipline of schools', *QJE*, 1835, p. 286.
47. W. E. Gladstone to W. W. Farr, Farr papers; *ETA*, no. 122, 7 June 1969, p. 339.
48. Ainger, p. 26.
49. W. Rogers, p. 18.
50. [H. H. Milman], *Eton System*, p. 70.
51. W. C. Green, p. 43.
52. *PR*, vol. 4, no. 15, pp. 349–50.
53. [Murray], *Collegers*, pp. 8, 9, 10, 11, 29, 41, 78, 79, 82, 83, 84.

SIX

The Liberties

1. Wm Vincent, p. 11.
2. Palmer, vol. 1, p. 76.
3. ibid., p. 91; Old Wykehamists, p. 100.
4. Palmer, vol. 1, p. 94; T. A. Trollope, p. 129; [Rich], p. 7; Old Wykehamists, p. 13.
5. Palmer, vol. 1, p. 94.
6. Bloxam, p. 91.
7. [Tucker], p. 56.
8. 'Fortescue Wells Letters', 12 May 1833; *ETA*, no. 121, 30 November 1968, p. 321.
9. J. L. Warner, letter 5, TRR.
10. A. P. Stanley, letter of 4 February 1829, quoted in Prothero and Bradley, vol. 1, p. 4.
11. Minet, 23 September 1819.
12. T. Arnold to Mrs Delafield, 'Warminster', 8 June 1809.
13. ibid., 30 September 1809.
14. Richards, 'Eton days', p. 84.
15. [Tucker], p. 32.
16. [Blake], p. 79.
17. [Collins], *Public*, p. 168.
18. [Tucker], p. 35.
19. Mack, *Public Schools and British Opinion 1780 to 1860*, p. 38.
20. Ainger, p. 20.
21. Gaskell, 3 June 1824, *Eton Boy*, p. 30.
22. Grant, letter 4, to his mother, 8 November 1793.
23. Ainger, p. 20.
24. T. Arnold, 'Warminster', 16 June 1808.
25. Gladstone to his father, 10 October 1822; *ETA*, 8 July 1970, p. 312.
26. 'Everard Letters', 17 September 1831; *ETA*, no. 117, 27 November 1965, p. 267.
27. Wilkinson, p. 257.
28. Gaskell, 14 May 1826, *Eton Boy*, p. 72.
29. Wilkinson, pp. 259–60.
30. Salt, *Memories*, p. 28.

31. [J. K. Stephen], p. 127.
32. 'Members of Harrow School', *TT*, vol. 1, October 1863.
33. [Blake], pp. 76, 78.
34. 'Fortescue Letters', 15 June 1834; *ETA*, no. 122, 7 June 1969, p. 341.
35. Wilkinson, pp. 308–15.
36. ibid., pp. 318–21.

SEVEN
Liquor and Violence

1. Letter, 18 May 1813 (copy), TRR.
2. Information from Mr Alan Fisher.
3. Nettleship, p. 9.
4. [Johnston], p. 75.
5. Brown, vol. 48, 11 June 1829.
6. Brown, vol. 57, 7 June 1835.
7. 'Fortescue Letters', 26 February 1832.
8. *ETA*, vol. 120, 25 November 1967, p. 316.
9. John Morley, vol. 1, p. 32n.
10. [Richards], 'Mr Gladstone', p. 196.
11. [W. M. Praed], *TE*, vol. 1, no. 2, 1824, p. 2.
12. Gaskell, *Eton Boy*, pp. 24, 25; 11, 13 May 1824.
13. HSVL, unclassified MS..
14. [Murray], *Collegers*, p. 10.
15. (H. H. Milman], *Eton System*, p. 75.
16. *GM*, 1731, pp. 128, 351; *ECR 1698–1752*, p. 96.
17. Brown, vol. 12, 22 October 1809.
18. John Morley, vol. 1, p. 27.
19. [Rimmer and Adnitt], p. 137.
20. [Hemyng], p. 84.
21. In 'Slaughterhouse' Thackeray described a contest lasting 102 rounds: *Works*, vol. 2, pp. 317–22.
22. Barker and Stenning, vol. 1, p. 958.
23. Forshall, p. 26.
24. Harris, vol. 1, pp. 15–16.
25. Kinglake, *War*, vol. 2, pp. 552–7.
26. Gladstone, letter to 'My Dearest Aunt Johanna', 13 November 1821; *ETA*, no. 70, 8 July 1938, p. 311.
27. W. M. Thackeray, *Works*, vol. 2, p. 65.

28. [Blake], p. 46.
29. Brown, 8 March 1825, vol. 38.
30. Brown, 9 and 3 March 1825, vol. 38.
31. Doyle, p. 49.
32. Besant, pp. 84ff.
33. How, p. 260.
34. 'Reminiscences', *NR*, vol. 3, no. 1, 1 October 1860, pp. 80–81.
35. Tuckwell, p. 53.
36. Bloxam, p. 109.
37. Burns, unpublished, TRR.
38. Norwood, pp. 63–4.
39. Minet, loose pages supplementing bound diary.
40. Very Rev. Dr G. Gretton to Rev. Dr Butler, 24 November 1818, BLAM 34584, fo. 258.
41. Copy ('original destroyed by me. S. B. Feb. 7 1891') of letter, Rev. Dr Butler to Rev. Francis Holyoake, 8 October 1817, BLAM 34584, fo. 272.
42. Burns, ch. 7.
43. Minet, 1818.

EIGHT
A Little Learning

1. Cory, *On the Education*, p. 20.
2. Report, vol. 21, p. 148; vol. 20, 'Winchester', p. 361, para. 836.
3. Letter from Mrs Haslam to her son Arthur (copy), TRR.
4. Lang, p. 15.
5. Cecil, vol. 1, pp. 113–14.
6. Mozley, vol. 1, p. 441.
7. Wilkinson, p. 109.
8. [Apperley], p. 151.
9. D. W. Thompson, *Daydreams*, p. 25.
10. Darwin, pp. 9, 11.
11. [Russell], p. 155.
12. Report, vol. 20, General Report, p. 25.
13. Rowcroft, *Confessions*, vol. 1, p. 89.
14. [Hughes], *Tom Brown*, p. 35.
15. A Parent, *Thoughts*, p. 4.
16. A. Amos, *Four Letters on the Advantages of a Classical Education*, quoted in M. L. Clarke, p. 170.

17. [Clough], p. 301.
18. Wilkinson, p. 3.
19. [Kaye], 'Success', p. 729.
20. [Tucker], p. 216.
21. Wilkinson, pp. 66–9.
22. H. Paul, pp. 255–9.
23. A. D. Coleridge, *Reminiscences*, p. 56.
24. Salt, *Memories*, pp. 117–18.
25. Cory, *On the Education*, p. 321.
26. ibid., p. 357.

NINE
The Habit of Rebellion

1. Brown, vol. 58, 10 November 1835.
2. *GM*, 2 May 1799, pp. 375–6.
3. Monson, p. 453.
4. ibid., p. 450.
5. C. K. Paul, p. 91.
6. C. A. E. Moberly, *Dulce Domum*, p. 24.
7. Kaye, *Life*, vol. 1, p. 8.
8. J. Lawrence, vol. 1, p. 8.
9. [Johnston], pp. 87–8.
10. *LMR*, no. 3, pp. 62–4, quoting Lord Justice James.
11. 'Everard Letters', 7 October 1832; *ETA*, no. 119, 26 November 1966, p. 299.
12. H. V. Macnaghten, p. 141.
13. Philip Norman to the editor of *Etoniana*, 3 December 1924; *ETA*, vol. 116, 30 December 1955, p. 244.
14. [Tucker], p. 10.
15. 'Eton Diary of Sir Hubert Parry', *ETA*, no. 103, 1946, p. 34.
16. Mozley, vol. 1, p. 416.
17. *QJE*, vol. 10, 1835, pp. 102–3.
18. Palmer, vol. 1, p. 109.
19. ibid.
20. Tuckwell, p. 107.
21. TBL, entries 408, 420 (1851), J. M. Murray.
22. ibid., entries 482 (1854), 449 (1853).
23. Forshall, p. 113.
24. Clavering MS., letter 30, 28 July 1847, WSA.
25. Rowcroft, *Confessions*, vol. 1, p. 87.
26. *QJE*, vol. 8, no. 16, April-October 1834, p. 285.
27. [R. Durnford], *TE*, vol. 1, no. 1, 1824, p. 52.
28. Rowcroft, *Confessions*, vol. 1, p. 75.
29. Ainger, p. 214.
30. A. Milman, p. 14.
31. Letter from the Rev. T. B. Johnstone of Clutton Rectory, Bristol, to Lord Monson, 20 May 1861; *ETA*, no. 33, 4 June 1933, p. 519.
32. Monson, pp. 453–4.
33. A. Milman, p. 15.
34. S. Butler (novelist), *Life*, vol. 1, p. 4.
35. Brown, vol. 25, 31 October 1818.
36. Pierce, p. 114.
37. [Collins], *Public Schools*, p. 130.
38. Minet, fos 325–7.
39. Moberly, *Dulce Domum*, p. 21.
40. Brown, vol. 20, 16 October 1817.
41. [Tucker], p. 204.
42. Brown, vol. 25, 31 October and 1, 2, 3 November 1818.
43. [Tucker], p. 205.
44. Denison, p. 9.
45. S. Butler (novelist), *Life*, vol. 1, p. 158.
46. BLAM 34584, fo. 57, 19 August 1814.
47. BLAM 34583, fos 166, 169, 171, 179; Gretton, p. 12.
48. S. Butler (novelist), *Life*, vol. 1, p. 51.
49. [Collins], *Public Schools*, p. 241; [Rimmer and Adnitt], p. 142; Hartland.
50. BLAM 34584, fos 41, 43: Dickinson to Dr Butler, 18 June 1814; Francis Holyoake to Dr Butler, 26 June 1814.
51. ibid., fo. 202: Mr Murray to Dr Butler, 4 January 1817.
52. ibid., fo. 209: draft 28 January 1817.
53. Mrs Butler, December 1818. Copy 'Discarded and Duplicate Letters' (unpublished), BL LR.33b.19.
54. TBL, entry 34.

55. BLAM 34584, fo. 350: 'First Circular to Parents', 21 November 1818.

56. ibid., fo. 397: 'Second Circular to Parents', 10 December 1818.

57. S. Butler (novelist), *Life*, vol. 1, pp. 18, 33.

58. [Rimmer and Adnitt], pp. 139–40.

59. BLAM 34584, fos 350, 351: 'First Circular to Parents', 21 November 1818.

60. ibid., fo. 352.

61. ibid., fo. 350.

62. ibid., fo. 392, draft.

63. ibid., fo. 399: Thomas Coltman to Samuel Butler, 11 December 1818.

64. ibid., fo. 371.

65. ibid., fo. 350, 21 November 1818.

66. ibid., fo. 397, 10 December 1818.

67. BLAM 34593, fos 62, 63: Dr Butler to the Rev. James Price, draft.

68. ibid., fos 61, 62; 20 June 1820, 'First Register of Letters'; fo. 60.

69. Dr Butler to George Gaisford, 2 June 1810, Discarded and Duplicate Letters (unpublished), BL LR.33b.19.

70. BLAM 34593, fos 69, 70; 20 September 1820, 'First Register of Letters'.

71. [Gover], vol. 6, p. 643.

72. D. S. Colman, pp. 4–5; G. M. L. Clarke, pp. 77–8; J. Morley, vol. 1, p. 62.

73. S. Butler (novelist), *Life*, vol. 1, p. 163.

74. BLAM 34593, fo. 26: draft, 9 December 1818, 'First Register of Letters'.

75. BLAM 34584, fo. 354, 24 November 1818.

76. BLAM 34585, fos 273, 274.

77. BLAM 34594, fo. 9: draft, 2 November 1832.

78. BLAM 34585, fo. 289: copy ('original mislaid'), 21 October 1823.

79. S. Butler (novelist), *Life*, vol. 1, pp. 2–3.

80. BLAM 34593, fo. 101, Dr Butler to E. Pearson, 8 March 1822, 'First Register of Letters'.

81. BLAM 34587, fo. 143, Dr Butler to 'a parent', 7 or 9 April 1829, copy ('original destroyed by me').

82. BLAM 34584, fo. 390, S. Tillbrook to Dr Butler, 7 December 1818.

83. ibid., fo. 351, 21 November 1818, 'First Circular to Parents'.

84. BLAM 34587, fo. 142, transcribed from an original draft ('destroyed by me') of a letter to 'a parent' (Mr Brandreth), 7 or 9 April 1829.

85. S. Butler (novelist), *Life*, vol. 1, pp. 108–9.

TEN

The World of Dr Keate

1. 'Everard Letters', 23 October 1831; *ETA*, no. 118, 4 June 1966, p. 278.

2. Kinglake, *Eothen*, p. 183.

3. Blair, vol. 4, p. 371.

4. 'My First Week at Eton', *Kaleidoscope*, no. 5, 25 March 1833, p. 177.

5. Wilkinson, p. 108.

6. W. Rogers, p. 12.

7. Kinglake, *Eothen*, p. 183.

8. J. Lawrence, 'Ode to an Eton Friend', vol. 1, p. 5.

9. Wilkinson, pp. 138–9.

10. W. Rogers, p. 13.

11. Wilkinson, p. 245.

12. 'Everard Letters', 7 November 1831; *ETA*, no. 118, 4 June 1966, p. 280; 17 September 1831; *ETA*, no. 117, 27 November 1965, p. 268.

13. [Essington], pp. 108–9.

14. 'Everard Letters', 22 May 1832; *ETA*, no. 119, 26 November 1966, p. 296.

15. Richards, 'Gladstone', p. 199.

16. Doyle, p. 49.

17. Wilkinson, pp. 17, 38.

18. Gaskell, *Eton Boy*, p. 38; letter dated 11 June 1824.

19. Gladstone, *Diaries*, vol. 1, p. 17.
20. Doyle, p. 50.
21. Richards, 'Gladstone', pp. 201, 203.
22. [Tucker], p. 183.
23. Wilkinson, pp. 15, 16.
24. Lyte, p. 391.
25. By Dr Heath. MS. 'Sports File', letter of B. H. Drury, HSVL.
26. *ETA*, no. 112, 11 March 1953, p. 181.
27. Chandos, pp. 39–52.
28. ibid., pp. 43–5.
29. Gladstone, *Diaries*, vol. 1, p. 48.
30. Arnould, vol. 1, p. 223.
31. Richards, 'Northcote', p. 91.
32. Gray.
33. [Collins], *Public Schools*, pp. 46, 174.
34. *ECC*, 29 September 1932.
35. M. Williams, vol. 1, p. 28.
36. Denison, p. 10.
37. Richards, *Seven Years*, p. 75.
38. 'Everard Letters', 16 June 1832; *ETA*, no. 119, 26 November 1966, p. 298.
39. *SM*, September 1829, p. 650.
40. Brown, vol. 46, 31 March and 1, 2, 4 April 1829.
41. W. Rogers, p. 12.
42. Gladstone, *Diaries*, vol. 1, pp. xlviii–xlix, 101–2.
43. Richards, 'Gladstone', p. 212.
44. *ETA*, no. 55, 4 June 1934, p. 67.
45. J. Morley, vol. 1, pp. 44–5.
46. Gronow, second series, pp. 44-6.
47. J. Morley, vol. 1, pp. 45–6.
48. C. K. Paul, p. 206.

ELEVEN
The Unspared Rod

1. [Collins], *Public Schools*, p. 358.
2. Report, vol. 20, p. 153.
3. Adams, *Wykehamica*, p. 267.
4. Quoted, *LAL*, November 1934, p. 188.
5. Gaskell, *Eton Boy*, 14 May 1824, p. 27.
6. Gaskell, *ETA*, vol. 62, 17 March 1936, p. 186.
7. *ETA*, no. 117, 27 November 1965, p. 265.
8. Brown, vol. 56, 30 September 1834.
9. Wilkinson, p. 38.
10. [Collins], *Etoniana*, p. 82.
11. 'Everard Letters', 23 October 1831; *ETA*, no. 118, 4 June 1966, p. 279.
12. Brown, vol. 40, 9 May 1826.
13. [Tucker], p. 81.
14. Ascham, Prologue.
15. Tusser.
16. White, p. xix fn.; Carlisle, vol. 2, p. 419.
17. Whittinton's *Vulgaria*, fo. xxxii, in White, p. 102.
18. Evelyn, vol. 2, p. 11.
19. Cox, 'Education and Learning', vol. 1, p. 48.
20. Cust, *History*, p. 45.
21. Stowe, pp. 96n, 141.
22. Barrow, vol. 2, p. 156.
23. Keppel, p. 218.
24. *Victorian*, vol. 2, p. 196.
25. Sherwood, p. 267.
26. Barrow, vol. 2, p. 109.
27. *Children's*, p. 15.
28. Pierce, p. 21.
29. Palmer, vol. 1, p. 76.
30. Marryat, *Keene*, pp. 29, 37.
31. I.E.M., p. 43; cf. Wilkinson, p. 20.
32. 6 June 1831; *ETA*, no. 117, 27 November 1965, p. 266.
33. 'Everard Letters', 23 October 1831; *ETA*, no. 118, 4 June 1966, p. 279.
34. Wilkinson, p. 28.
35. Richards, 'Northcote', pp. 91, 96.
36. [Tucker], pp. 182–4, Wilkinson, pp. 39–40.
37. [Hemyng], pp. 159–60.
38. 'List of Precedents compiled by Dr Okes 1837–1841', *ETA*, no. 13, 1 March 1912, p. 202.
39. There are several versions of this story, one being in A. C. Benson, *Fasti Etonensis*, p. 394.
40. Brown, vol. 47, 29 May 1829.
41. 'The Block', *Guide*, p. 8.
42. Cowper, p. 196.

43. [Lewis], no. 101, p. 77.

44. 'On the discipline of a public school', *QJE*, vol. 10, no. 19, 1835, p. 110.

45. Esher, vol. 2, 5–7 July 1839, pp. 56, 57.

46. ibid., p. 57.

47. *Children's*, pp. 7, 11, 23, 24, 34.

48. Barker, pp. 67–9.

49. *Rodiad*.

50. [Collins], *Public Schools*, p. 161; G. Colman, vol. 1, pp. 220–22.

51. 'The Confessions of a Schoolmaster', *BAE for 1844* (*SQR*), vol. 1, p. 369.

52. [Collins], *Etoniana*, p. 108; 'The Adventure of Philip', *CM*, vol. 3, January 1861, p. 10.

53. Murray, *People*, p. 35.

54. *BM*, vol. 47, June 1840, p. 784.

55. *FM*, vol. 42, July–December 1850, p. 298.

56. [Ashbee], pp. xlii–xliv.

57. Nevill, p. 77.

58. Salt, *Memories*, p. 69.

59. [Apperley], p. 150.

60. Stratford, p. 123.

61. ibid., pp. 128, 129.

62. *ECM*, no. 3, 23 July 1832, p. 133.

63. [Johnston], pp. 135–7.

64. [Ashbee], p. xl.

65. *Punch*, 29 November 1856.

66. L. Stephen, 'Thoughts', March 1873, p. 284.

67. [Collins), *Public Schools*, p. 161.

68. [H. H. Milman], *Eton System*, pp. 72, 73.

69. *Plain*, pp. 11–16, 46–7.

70. [Ashbee], p. xliii.

71. *Plain*, p. 63.

72. [Ashbee], p. xl.

73. Ziegler, p. 107.

74. Esher, vol. 2, 14 October 1838, p. 56.

75. Gladstone, *Diaries*, vol. 3, p. xlvii, fn. 4; Newman, pp. iii, 376; Trevor, pp. 332–3, 376–7.

76. Salt, *Memories*, p. 70.

77. Bernard Shaw in Preface, Winsten, p. 10.

78. Salt, *Memories*, pp. 180, 220.

79. T. Arnold, *Miscellaneous*, p. 365.

80. Vaughan, *Letter*, pp. 5–12.

81. One who . . . Monitor, pp. 4–6.

82. Letter from G. H. Rendell in Verney and Thompson.

83. *The Globe*, 20 November 1872.

84. Hemyng, *Butler Burke*, p. 175.

85. *ESM*, no. 1, 1847, p. 26.

86. Hill, pp. 38–9.

87. L. Stephen, 'Thoughts', March 1873, pp. 282–4.

88. Swinburn, *The Flogging Block* 5256, *Frank Fane* 5751, *Eton: Another Ode* 5276.

89. 'From the Eton Diaries of J. M. Keynes', *ETA*, no. 127, 1973, p. 418.

TWELVE

Higher Thoughts and Thomas Arnold

1. Stanley, *Life*, p. 49.

2. ibid., pp. 118, 119.

3. T. Arnold, *Miscellaneous*, pp. 232, 423.

4. Bamford, *Arnold*, pp. 117–20.

5. Stanley, *Life*, ccxxxvii, 8 May 1840, p. 556.

6. Findlay, p. 106.

7. T. Arnold, *Miscellaneous*; letter 6, pp. 196–7; letter 2, p. 176; letter 10, p. 206.

8. Stanley, *Life*, ccxxxv, 12 April 1840, p. 554.

9. *JB*, 2 February 1835.

10. T. Arnold, *Miscellaneous*, letter 2, p. 176.

11. ibid., p. 213.

12. ibid., p. 128.

13. ibid., pp. 213–14.

14. Edward Churton to W. A. Greenhill, 18 September 1837 in Brotherton Collection, University of Leeds; in Stanley, *Life*, clxii, the phrase 'moral nastiness', etc., is suppressed. The complete version is printed in Bamford, *Education*, p. 149.

15. E. Churton, vol. 2, p. 221.

16. Stanley, *Life*, xcv, 4 March 1835, p. 353.
17. ibid., xvi, 28 June 1830, pp. 234–5.
18. ibid., p. 116.
19. ibid., pp. 116, 117n.
20. ibid., cxxviii, 9 May 1836, p. 406.
21. *QRE*, vol. 8, no. 16, April–October 1834, pp. 277, 278, 289, 292.
22. Stanley, *Life*, p. 110.
23. ibid., xx, 21 October 1827, p. 73.
24. Findlay, pp. 13–14.
25. *Report of the Proceedings Respecting Rugby School before the Rt Hon. Lord Langdale, Master of the Rolls, with his Lordship's Judgement Thereon* (1839); summarized in Bamford, *Arnold*, pp. 132–41.
26. T. Arnold, *Sermons*, vol. 2, p. 41.
27. Stanley, *Life*, ccxiii, 29 December 1839, p. 489.
28. T. Arnold, 'I Put Away Childish Things', *Sermons*, vol. 4, pp. 20–21.
29. Stanley, *Life*, clxxxvii, to the Rev. J. Hearn, 23 November 1838, p. 495.
30. ibid., p. 108.
31. Bowdler, *Remains*, vol. 2, p. 153.
32. T. Arnold, *Sermons*, vol. 2, p. 80.
33. ibid., vol. 2, p. 34.
34. Stanley, *Life*, pp. 155–6.
35. ibid., xviii, 15 April 1835, p. 358.
36. T. Arnold to the Rev. H. Hill, 5 September 1838, TRR.
37. Stanley, *Life*, xxxvi, 8 November 1831, p. 268.
38. T. Arnold, *Sermons*, vol. 2, p. 83.
39. ibid., vol. 4, p. 21.
40. ibid., vol. 4, p. 13.
41. ibid., vol. 2, p. 84.
42. Doyle, p. 48.
43. Lake, *Memorials*, p. 17.
44. Bloxam, pp. 71–2.
45. Trotter, p. 5.
46. Stanley, *Life*, p. 104.
47. E. L. Woodward, p. 486.
48. J. L. Warner to his mother, letter 5.
49. Booth, p. 24.
50. [Apperley], p. 14.
51. T. Arnold, *Sermons*, vol. 1, p. 36.
52. [Apperley], p. 14.
53. [Gover], 'Memories, pp. 833–4.
54. Report, vol. 21, p. 371, para. 1153.
55. Bamford, *Arnold*, p. 88.
56. *NH*, 14 December 1835, quoted in Bamford, *Arnold*, pp. 83–4.
57. *NH*, 23 November 1832, quoted in Bamford, *Arnold*, p. 125.
58. Stanley, *Life*, p. 101; cf. T. Arnold, *Sermons*, vol. 4, p. 73.
59. T. Arnold to F. C. Blackstone, 28 September 1828; Stanley, *Life*, p. 217.
60. For the March case, see *NH*, 19 January, 2, 23 February, 9 March 1833; summarized in Bamford, *Arnold*, pp. 49–52.
61. Stanley, *Brief*, p. 7; cf. *ER*, vol. 81, 1845, p. 202.
62. T. Arnold, *Sermons*, vol. 4, pp. 262–4.
63. T. Arnold, *Miscellaneous*, letter 7, p. 197.
64. Stanley, *Life*, cxxxvi, 20 July 1836, pp. 415–16.
65. T. Arnold, *Miscellaneous*, letters 7, 9, 11, pp. 196, 206, 214.
66. M. Arnold, *Culture*, p. 203.
67. Vaughan, *Funeral Sermon*, p. 5.
68. Bradley, p. 26.
69. Letter to Mary, 24 November 1833, TRR, quoted in F. J. Woodward, p. 25.
70. Prothero and Bradley, vol. 1, p. 102.
71. [Gover], vol. 7, p. 127.
72. ibid., p. 133.
73. [J. F. Stephen], *ER*, p. 186.
74. T. Arnold, 'The Law our Schoolmaster', *Sermons*, vol. 4, Sermon 10.
75. [Gover], vol. 7, pp. 233–6.
76. Stanley, *Life*, xix, 1 November 1830, p. 248.
77. Bagehot, 'Mr Clough', p. 316.
78. Pearson, p. 17.
79. [J. F. Stephen), *ER*, no. 217, vol. 107, January-April 1858, p. 186.
80. Doyle, p. 48.
81. Pearson, p. 17.
82. Freemantle, p. 16.

83. Pearson, p. 17.
84. Bradley, p. 11.
85. *NC*, vol. 43, 1898, p. 106.
86. Lowry *et al.*, p. 296.
87. *MC*, 3 June 1844.
88. Forster, vol. 2, p. 125.
89. *Letters . . . Wordsworth*, vol. 3, p. 1120.
90. Cust, *History*, p. 196.
91. Pearson, pp. 17, 18.
92. Lake, *QR*, p. 490.
93. T. Arnold, *Sermons*, vol. 4, pp. 13–15, 16–22.
94. Lake, *QR*, p. 470.
95. T. Arnold, *Miscellaneous*, p. 423.
96. ibid., pp. 395–6.
97. Pearson, p. 20.

THIRTEEN
Nearer to God

1. Stanley, *Life. . . Thomas Arnold*, p. 164.
2. G. Moberly, *Letters*, letter 3, p. 82.
3. [Cory], *Hints*, p. 15.
4. Minchin, *Schools*, p. 334.
5. T. Churton, letters, TRR.
6. Etonian, *Thoughts*, p. 6.
7. Richards, 'Northcote', p. 85 fn.
8. Salt, *Memories*, p. 135.
9. [Tucker], p. 129.
10. Richards, *Seven Years*, p. 243.
11. C. A. E. Moberly, *Dulce Domum*, p. 22.
12. 'Old Harrow Days', *NCA*, vol. 109, no. 647, p. 91.
13. Wilkinson, p. 118.
14. Gaskell, 8 May 1824, *Eton Boy*, p. 18.
15. *ETA*, no. 105, 1 April 1948, p. 80.
16. Wilkinson, p. 124.
17. Salt, *Memories*, p. 57.
18. ibid., p. 52.
19. [A. D. Coleridge], p. 94.
20. ibid., p. 95.
21. Wilkinson, p. 115.
22. W. C. Green, p. 14.
23. Salt, *Memories*, p. 68.
24. *Education*, p. 10.
25. Etonian, *A Few Words*, pp. 13–14.

26. Cornish, p. 11.
27. F. W. Farrar, *St Winifred's*, pp. 225, 515.
28. Lowry *et al.*, p. 296.
29. Moberly, *Letters*, letter 3, p. 82.
30. Duckworth, p. 126.
31. [Hemyng], *Eton*, p. 3.

FOURTEEN
A Demon Hovering

1. Martineau, p. 20.
2. T. Arnold, *Sermons*, vol. 5, p. 66.
3. ibid., vol. 5, p. 66.
4. Wymer, pp. 12, 19.
5. 13 May 1824; *ETA*, no. 60, 18 September 1935, p. 153.
6. Brown, vol. 32, 5 July 1822; vol. 20, 29 October 1815.
7. 'Everard Letters', 22 June 1834; *ETA*, no. 120, 25 November 1967, p. 314.
8. BLAM 34586, Letters Price to Butler, 21 and 27 June 1827; 'Discarded and Duplicate Letters', vol. 1, letter [October 1827].
9. Rev. C. W. Penny, MS. Journal, quoted in Newsome, *History*, p. 168.
10. Newsome, *History*, p. 169.
11. E. B. Pusey in Preface, Gaume, quoted in Honey, p. 169.
12. Simpson, p. 168.
13. 'The Recent Troubles at Eton', *NE*, vol. 35, 1876, p. 318.
14. Wilson, p. 253.
15. C. A. E. Moberly, p. 89.
16. Wilson, p. 254.
17. *JE*, 1 January 1882, p. 16.
18. Acton, p. 14.
19. Wilson, pp. 254, 255.
20. Acton, p. 31.
21. [Hughes], *Tom Brown*, p. 257.
22. [Hughes], *Notes*, pp. 64–5.
23. Acton, p. 31; Edward Lyttelton, *Training the Young*, p. 10; Honey, p. 170n.
24. Acton, p. 14; Thring, *Sermons*, vol. 2, p. 15.
25. Thring, *Sermons*, vol. 2, p. 15.

26. Armstrong, p. 8.
27. Edward Lyttelton, *Causes*, p. 17.
28. Acton, p. 14.
29. *JE* (supplement), 1 November 1883, p. 255.
30. Corbin, pp. 208–9.
31. G. G. T. Heywood, p. 296.
32. TRR. For reference to bed-sharing at Westminster into the nineteenth century, see Markham, p. 39; *Directions*, p. 9.
33. Leinster, vol. 1, p. 172, 28 July 1758.
34. [Blake], p. 125.
35. Brown, vol. 40, 9 May 1826.
36. *ETA*, no. 34, 31 July 1923, p. 536.
37. *FM*, April 1861, p. 436.
38. E. W. Benson, p. 365.
39. Coulton, p. 30.
40. Wortham, *Victorian*, p. 100.
41. Richards, *Seven Years*, p. 33.
42. [Nugent-Bankes], *Letters*, pp. 179–80.
43. Brown, vol. 67, 12 March 1840.
44. *JE*, no. 152, pp. 85–6.
45. [Hughes], *Tom Brown*, pp. 328–9.
46. T. Arnold, letters to Mrs Delafield, 20 September, 21 November 1809, WCA.
47. F. W. Farrar, *Eric*, pp. 49, 84, 85, 94, 102.
48. R. Farrar, p. 128.
49. F. W. Farrar, *St Winifred's*, p. 370.
50. TBL, 1859, entry 557, WSA.
51. 22 November 1818; *NQ*, 18 June 1920.
52. [A. C. Benson], *Memoirs*, pp. 24, 23.
53. Howson, 'Dr George Butler' in Howson and Warner, p. 67.
54. How, pp. 140, 143, 144.
55. R. R. Williams, p. 4; Charles S. Roundell, 'Dr Christopher Wordsworth – Harrow in the Forties' in Howson and Warner, p. 100.
56. Oswell, vol. 1, p. 49.
57. Lake, *Memorials*, p. vi.
58. Galloway, p. 51.
59. Tollemache, pp. 120–21.
60. Sir Charles Dalrymple, 'Dr Vaughan', in Howson and Warner, p. 106.
61. [Norman], p. 118.
62. Tollemache, p. 106.
63. Dalrymple, op. cit.
64. 'Old Harrow Days', *NCA*, no. 647, vol. 109, p. 95.
65. [Russell], p. 221.
66. Graham, p. 130.
67. Vaughan, *Memorials*, p. 187.
68. Symonds, p. 139.
69. ibid., p. 140.
70. ibid., p. 141.
71. Prothero and Bradley, vol. 1, p. 41.
72. H. J. Torre, *Recollections of Schooldays at Harrow*, p. 9, quoted in Honey, p. 380n.
73. Dalrymple, op. cit., p. 110.
74. Symonds, p. 144.
75. Symonds, p. 136.
76. Grosskurth, p. 48.
77. Symonds, pp. 147–88.
78. Vaughan, *Memorials*, p. 186.
79. How, p. 173.
80. Vaughan, *Memorials*, p. 477.
81. Sir George Trevelyan in Graham, p. xix.
82. Lake, *Memorials*, pp. 204, 206.
83. How, p. 179.
84. Trevelyan, op. cit..
85. H. Merivale, *Bar*, p. 179.
86. R. R. Williams, p. 12.
87. Trevelyan, op. cit., p. xix.
88. How, p. 177.
89. R. R. Williams, op. cit., p. 5.
90. How, pp. 138–9.
91. Symonds, pp. 171, 178, 188.
92. ibid., pp. 171, 383, 410.
93. ibid., pp. 188–9.
94. Richard Garnett, 'J. A. Symonds', *DNB*.
95. Symonds, p. 184.
96. Yglesias, 3 July 1881.
97. Vaughan, *Funeral Sermon*, p. 13.
98. Dalrymple, op. cit., p. 119.
99. R. R. Williams, p. 5.
100. Lake, *Memorials*, p. 323.
101. How, p. 174.

FIFTEEN
The New Order

1. C. K. Paul, p. 86.
2. Ainger, p. 118.
3. [Higgins], Letter 1, March 1860, pp. 609, 613; Letter 2, December 1860 p. 643.
4. Report, vol. 21, para. 3278.
5. [Higgins], Letter 3, March 1861, p. 260.
6. ibid., Letter 1, March 1860, p. 614.
7. [Reeve], p. 419.
8. Henry Reeve to Lord Brougham, 1 March 1861, in Laughton, vol. 2, p. 66.
9. [Reeve], p. 403.
10. J. Coleridge, pp. 10, 11, 17, 25.
11. Maxwell, vol. 2, p. 295.
12. Cust, *History*, p. 199.
13. *FM*, June 1864, p. 658.
14. [Cheney], *QR*, vol. 116.
15. 'The Gentleman in Black', *BMSP*, no. 54, vol. 8, August 1864, pp. 221–2.
16. Markham, p. 5.
17. Forshall, pp. ix, 21.
18. Report, vol. 21, Minutes of Evidence, Westminster, para. 3517.
19. ibid., vol. 20, p. 173, para. 17.
20. ibid., vol. 21, Minutes of Evidence, Eton, paras. 94–107.
21. *FM*, 1864, p. 660.
22. Report, vol. 21, Minutes of Evidence, Eton, para. 1365.
23. ibid., vol. 21, Minutes of Evidence, Westminster, para. 2490; denied by C. B. Scott, para. 3382.
24. Lang, vol. 1, p. 15.
25. Report, vol. 21, Minutes of Evidence, Westminster, paras. 2511, 2485, 2660.
26. *WR*, 1861, p. 499.
27. Cory, *Eton*, vol. 2, p. 30.
28. J. F. Stephen, *ER*, p. 178.
29. ibid.
30. R. A. Butler.
31. *SR*, 8 December 1860.
32. Report, vol. 20, p. 56.
33. *FM*, 1864, p. 658.
34. Disraeli, p. 61.
35. J. Morley, vol. 1, p. 27.
36. Richards, *Seven Years*, p. 84.
37. Report, vol. 21, paras. 8604, 8608.
38. [Cheney], *QR*, p. 496.
39. J. F. Stephen, *ER*, p. 177.
40. Mack, *Public . . . since 1860*, p. 24n.
41. Cory, *Extracts*, 21 January 1853, pp. 59–60.
42. Richards, *Seven Years*, p. 127.
43. L. Stephen, 'Thoughts', p. 291.
44. [Higgins], Letter 2, December 1860, p. 648.
45. Adams, *Schoolboy*, p. 99.
46. Nettleship, p. 10.
47. [Collins], *Public Schools*, p. 248.
48. C. R. L. Fletcher, pp. 51, 65.
49. L. E. Jones, p. 152.
50. Report, Minutes of Evidence, Eton, paras. 3517, 5313.
51. C. R. L. Fletcher, p. 151.
52. Richards, *Seven Years*, p. 213.
53. Reminiscence of Mr T. Lyon, former Eton College Librarian; *ETA*, no. 122, 7 June 1969, p. 340.
54. Kendall, p. 41.
55. Edward Lyttelton, *Memories*, p. 29.
56. Old Rugbeian, p. 131.
57. Costans, p. 110.
58. *TH*, no. 1, 2 February 1888, p. 52.
59. Cory, *Eton Reform*, vol. 1, p. 28.
60. *FM*, 1861, pp. 436–44.
61. Edward Lyttelton, *Memories*, p. 29.
62. [Russell], p. 136.
63. Salt, *Memories*, p. 81.
64. *JE*, February 1884, pp. 68–71.
65. How, p. 231.
66. Kaye, *Life*, vol. 1, p. 13.
67. Firth, p. 137.
68. Cotton, p. 406.
69. *Change*, p. 17.
70. *TH*, no. 4, 6 March 1879.
71. *TH*, no. 14, 5 May 1880; no. 15, 5 June 1880; no. 16, 1 July 1880.
72. *TH*, vol. 2, no. 2, 7 March 1889, p. 155.
73. Bourne, p. 32.

74. G. Fletcher, p. 25.
75. Tallboys, p. 51.
76. *TH*, vol. 2, no. 6, 5 July 1899, p. 196.
77. Henry Palmer, MS. Diary, Marlborough College Archives, quoted in Honey, pp. 176, 409.
78. Sewell, vol. 1, p. 187.
79. L. E. Jones, p. 200.
80. 'Some Eton and Harrow Matches 1858–1864', *NR*, July 1895, p. 691.
81. 'An Eton Education', *NR*, May 1905, p. 455.
82. Mais, p. 56.
83. *TH*, no. 23, 9 April 1881, p. 263.
84. L. E. Jones, p. 177.
85. Berners, p. 23.
86. Cowburn, p. 237.
87. Edith Lyttelton, p. 44.
88. Salt, *Memories*, p. 226.
89. *ESM*, 1847–8, p. 29.
90. Bourne, p. 12.
91. Edward Lyttelton, *Memories*, p. 29.
92. Wortham, p. 100.
93. Sewell, vol. 1, p. 19.
94. Berners, p. 52.
95. Portman, p. 209.
96. *ETA*, no. 121, 30 November 1968, p. 331.
97. Stratford, p. 129.
98. *PE*, no. 2, May 1859, pp. 22, 23.
99. *EF*, 20 June 1887, pp. 57–8.
100. *TT*, no. 17, 1 May 1865.
101. L. Stephen, 'Thoughts', p. 284.
102. H. L. Warner, p. 365.
103. Drage, pp. 9, 10, 11, 17.
104. *TH*, no. 9, 9 October 1879, p. 95; no. 1, 2 February 1888, p. 53.
105. J. S. Mill, *WR*, 1859, xxxii.
106. Denison, p. 27.
107. Kipling, 'The Dusky Crew', pp. 2, 3, 4.
108. G. Moberly, *Records*, second series, p. v.
109. L. Stephen, 'Thoughts', p. 288.
110. Gaskell, *Eton Boy*, pp. 26–7.
111. *Tirocinium*, p. 199.
112. *ETA*, no. 123, 29 November 1969, p. 364.
113. J. Lawrence, 'Ode to an Eton Friend', vol. 1, p. 5.

APPENDIX
The Eton Wall Game

1. Farmer and Henly.
2. Stapylton, p. 131a.

Bibliography

This bibliography is divided into primary sources (indicated by an asterisk) and secondary sources. Primary sources comprise not only contemporary and earlier records and opinions but also publications which, although written after the times they describe, contain authentic reports of writers who had had direct, personal experience of the events they recount.

* MANUSCRIPTS

Eton College Library
The Journal of Miss Margaretta Brown, 100 vols., 1802–55
  Miscellaneous letters and documents

Westminster School Archives
The Letters of Col. Henry Clavering to Rev. John Benn
Town Boy Ledger, 1815–62
The Letters of Michael Yglesias, 1881, 1882
A Letter from the Rev. Allen Cooper to the headmaster (copy)

Winchester College Archives
School letters of Thomas Arnold, written from Warminster School, and later from Winchester, where he was a Commoner in 1807 and a Scholar 1808–10. Ref. WCL 23508–23529
The Journals of C. W. Minet for the years 1818–19. Ref. WCL 24149

Temple Reading Room, Rugby School
Miscellaneous letters and copies of letters
A Victorian Schoolboy. Tom Burns' Schooldays; from the school letters of Thomas Harris Burns 1841–52, ed. Andrew Robert Burns (unpublished)

Harrow School Vaughan Library
MS. 'Sports File'
Unclassified MSS.

British Library

Ashley Add. MSS. 5256, 5376, 5395, 5751

Correspondence and papers of Samuel Butler DD., MSS. 34583–34587, 34593, 34594

London Library

The Autobiography of John Addington Symonds

SOURCES

Unless otherwise stated the place of publication is London.

Acton, Henry, *The Functions and Disorders of the Reproductive Organs in Childhood, Youth, Adult Age and Advanced Life, Considered in their Physiological, Social and Moral Relations* (1857)

* Adams, H. C., *Wykehamica: A History of Winchester College and Commoners from the Foundation to the Present Day* (1878)

Adams, H. C., *Schoolboy Honour. A Tale of Halminster College* (1861)

Adamson, J. W., *English Education 1798–1902* (Cambridge, 1930)

* Ainger, Arthur Campbell, *Memories of Eton Sixty Years Ago* (1917)

Airey, Reginald, *Westminster* (1902)

* Albemarle, 6th Earl of, *see* Keppel

* Angelo, Henry, *Reminiscences*, 2 vols. (1828 edn)

Annan, Noel, *Leslie Stephen, His Thought and Character in Relation to His Times* (1951)

* [Apperley, Charles James], *My Life and Times* by Nimrod, ed. E. D. Cuming (Edinburgh and London, 1927)

Appleman, Philip, *et al.* (eds.), *1859. Entering an Age of Crisis* (Indiana University Press: Bloomington, 1959)

A.R. and H.W.A., *see* [Rimmer and Adnitt]

* Arbuthnot, Sir Alexander J., *Memories of Rugby and India* (1910)

Archer, R. L., *Secondary Education in the Nineteenth Century* (Cambridge, 1921)

Armstrong, Richard, *Our Duty in the Matter of Social Purity* (1889)

* Arnold, Matthew, *Culture and Anarchy* (1869. 1960 edn, Cambridge)

* Arnold, Matthew, *A French Eton: or, Middle Class Education and the State* (1864)

* Arnold, Thomas, 'Some Letters of Arnold', ed. E. G. Selwyn, *Theology*, vol. 25, no. 145, July 1932

* Arnold, Thomas, *On the Discipline of a Public School* (1835)

Miscellaneous Works (1845)

* Arnold, Thomas, *Sermons*, 6 vols. (1878)

* Arnold, Thomas, Life and Letters, *see* Stanley

* Arnold, Thomas, 'The Warminster and Winchester Letters of Thomas Arnold', WCL

Arnould, Sir Joseph, *Life of Thomas, First Lord Denman*, 2 vols. (1874)

Ascham, Roger, *The Scholemaster* (1507)

* [Ashbee, Henry Spencer], *Index Librorum Prohibitorum*, by Pisanus Fraxi (1962 edn, NY, published 1877)

Askwith, Betty, *The Lytteltons. A Family Chronicle of the Nineteenth Century* (1975)

Austen Leigh, R. A., 'The Public Schools Commission', *ETA*, no. 67, 3 January 1938

* Bagehot, Walter, *Literary Studies*, 2 vols. (1879)

* Bagehot, Walter, 'Mr Clough's Poems', *NatR*, vol. 30, October 1862

Bagehot, Walter, *Works*, ed. Forrest Morgan, 5 vols. (Hartford, Conn., 1891)

Bamford, T. W., *The Rise of the Public Schools* (1967)

Bamford, T. W., *Thomas Arnold* (1960)

Bamford, T. W., *Thomas Arnold on Education* (Cambridge, 1970)

Bamford, T. W., 'Public Schools and Social Class 1801–1850', *British Journal of Sociology*, no. 12, 1961

Barker, G. F. Russell, *Memoirs of Richard Busby D.D.* (1895)

Barker, G. F. Russell, and Stenning, A. H. (eds.), *The Record of Old Westminsters* (1928)

Barnes, Arthur Stapylton, *Eton in the Olden Days* (1898)

* Barrow, William, *An Essay on Education*, 2 vols. (1892)

* Benham, W. (ed.), *Catherine and Crawford Tait, a Memoir* (1879)

* Benson, Arthur C., *Fasti Etonensis. A Biographical Review of Eton* (1899)

Benson, Arthur C., *Hugh: Memoirs of a Brother* (1915)

* Benson, Arthur C., *The Schoolmaster* (1904)

* Benson, Arthur C., *Upton Letters* (1902)

* [Benson, Arthur C.], *Memoirs of Arthur Hamilton*, by Christopher Carr (New York, 1886)

* Benson, Edward White, 'The Treasure of Treasures' in *Boy Life, Its Trials, Its Strength, Its Fullness. Sundays at Wellington College 1859–1873* (1874)

Berners, Lord, *A Distant Prospect* (1964)

Besant, Walter, *Fifty Years Ago* (1888)

Blackmantle, Bernard, *see* [Westmacott]

Blair, Hugh, *Sermons*, 5 vols., (1777–1801)

* [Blake, H. J. Crickitt], *Reminiscences of Eton*, by an Etonian (Chichester, 1831)

Blakiston, Georgiana, *Lord William Russell and his Wife 1815–1846* (1972)

* Bloxam, Matthew Holbeche, *Rugby, the School and its Neighbourhood*, ed. G. W. P. Payne Smith (1889, 1923 edn)

Booth, J. B., *Bits of Character – a Life of H. H. Dixon* (1936)

* Bourne, Gilbert C., *Memoirs of an Eton Wet Bob of the Seventies* (1933)

* Bowdler, Thomas, *Memoir of the Late John Bowdler* (1825)

Bowen, Edward, *A Memoir of the Rev. the Hon. W. E. Bowen* (1902)

* Bowles, W. L., *Vindiciae Wykehamicae, or a Vindication of Winchester in a Letter to Henry Brougham* (1818)

* Box, E. G., *Commoners Sixty Years Ago* (1934)

Boyd, A. K., *The History of Radley College 1847–1947* (Oxford, 1948)

Bradby, Henry Christopher, *Rugby* (1906)

* Bradley, George Granville, *Recollections of Arthur Penrhyn Stanley* (1883)

Brief Observations on the Political and Religious Sentiments of the Late Dr Arnold as contained in his life by the Rev. Arthur Penrhyn Stanley (1845)

Briggs, Asa, 'Thomas Hughes and the Public Schools', in *Victorian People* (1956)

Briggs, Asa, 'The Language of Class in nineteenth century England' in *Essays in Labour History in memory of G. D. H. Cole*, ed. Asa Briggs and John Saville (1960)

Brock, W., *A Biographical Sketch of Sir Henry Havelock* (1859)

* Brooke, Henry, *The Fool of Quality*, with an Introduction by the Rev. W. P. Strickland, 2 vols. (New York, 1860)

* Brougham, Henry, *Appendix to Mr Brougham's Letter containing Minutes of Evidence taken before the Education Committee* (1818)

* Brougham, Henry (afterwards Lord Brougham), *A Letter to Sir Samuel Romilly M.P. . . . .* (1818)

Brougham, Henry, *Practical Observations upon the Education of the People, Addressed to the Working Classes and their Employers* (1825)

Brougham, Henry, *The Speech of Henry, Lord Brougham in the House of Lords on Thursday, May 21, 1835, on the Education of the People* (1835)

Brown, Margaretta, *see under* Manuscripts, Eton

* [Browne, Richard Lewis], *The Eton Question Reconsidered*, by an Etonian (1834)

* Browning, Oscar, *Memories of Sixty Years at Eton, Cambridge and Elsewhere* (1910)

Bulwer, Sir William Henry Lytton, *The Life of John Temple, Viscount Palmerston*, 3 vols. (1870)

* Burns, Andrew Robert (ed.), *A Victorian Schoolboy: Tom Burns' Schooldays, from the Letters of Thomas Harris Burns . . . 1841–1852* (unpublished, TRR)

* Butler, H. Montagu, *Public School Sermons* (1899)

Butler, R. A., *The Art of the Possible* (1971)

* Butler, Samuel (novelist), *Life and Letters of Dr Samuel Butler*, 2 vols. (1896)

* Butler, Samuel (novelist), *The Way of All Flesh* (1903)

* Butler, Samuel (headmaster, Shrewsbury), *A Letter to Henry Brougham Esq., M.P.* (1820)

* Butler, Samuel (headmaster, Shrewsbury), Discarded and Duplicate Letters (unpublished), British Library LR.33b.19

* Butler, Samuel (headmaster, Shrewsbury), *Life and Letters*, *see* S. Butler (novelist)

* Butler, Samuel (headmaster, Shrewsbury), *see under* Manuscripts, British Library

Byrne, Lionel S. and Churchill, Ernest L., *Changing Eton* (1937)

* Byron, Lord, *Hours of Idleness* (1807)

Carleton, J. D., *Westminster* (1938)

* Carlisle, Nicholas, *Concise Description of the Endowed Grammar Schools in England and Wales*, 2 vols. (1818)

Carr, Christopher, *see* [A. C. Benson]

* Carroll, Lewis (Charles Dodgson), *The Diaries of Lewis Carroll*, ed. John Lancelyn Green, 2 vols. (1953)

Cecil, Lady Gwendolin, *The Life of Robert, 3rd Marquis of Salisbury, by his daughter*, 2 vols. (1871), vol. 1, 1830–1868

Chadwick, Owen, *The Victorian Church*, 2 vols. (1976)

Chandos, John (ed.), *In God's Name* (1971)

* 'Characteristics', 'Characteristics of the Nineteenth Century', *FM*, no. 46, 1840

* [Cheney, Robert],. 'A Public School Education', *QR*, vol. 108, July–October 1860

* [Cheney, Robert], 'Public Schools. Report of Her Majesty's Commissioners appointed to enquire into the Management of Certain Colleges and Schools . . . 1864', *QR*, vol. 116, July–October 1864

* Chesterfield, Philip Dormer Stanhope, Earl of, *Letters to A. C. Stanhope*, ed. Earl of Carnarvon (Oxford, 1890)

Change, *A Review of Eton in the last hundred years* (1932)

Child, Harold, 'The Public School in Fiction' in *The Public Schools from Within* (ed. unacknowledged) (1906)

* *The Children's Petition, or, a Modest Remonstrance of that intolerable grievance our youth lie under in the accustomed severities of the school discipline of this nation* (1699)

Christie, O. F., *The Transition from Aristocracy 1832–1867* (1927)

Churton, E., *Memoir of Joshua Watson*, 2 vols. (1861)

* Churton, Thomas Townson, and Churton, William Ralph, MS. letters, TRR

Clarendon Commission, *see* Report

Clark, G. Kitson, *The Making of Victorian England* (1968 edn)

* Clarke, Rev. Liscombe, *A Letter to H. Brougham in Reply to the Strictures on Winchester College contained in his letter to Sir Samuel Romilly* (1818)

Clarke, M. L., *Classical Education in Britain 1500–1900* (Cambridge, 1959)

[Clough, A. H.] *RM*, vol. 1, 1836

Cobbe, Francis Power, 'The Nineteenth Century', *FM*, vol. 69 (1864)

Coleman, George (pseudonym), the *Rodiad* ('1810', in fact published by J. C. Hottens, *c.* 1870)

* [Coleridge, Arthur Duke], *Eton in the Forties*, by an Old Colleger (1896)

* Coleridge, Arthur Duke, *Reminiscences*, ed. J. A. Fuller-Maitland (1921)

* Coleridge, G., *Eton in the Seventies* (1912)

* Coleridge, Sir John, 'Public School Education'. A lecture delivered at the Athenaeum, Tiverton (1860)

Collingwood, S. D., *Life and Letters of Lewis Carroll* (1898)

* [Collins, William Lucas], *Etoniana Ancient and Modern*, by W.L.C. (1865)

* [Collins, William Lucas], *The Public Schools*, by the author of *Etoniana* (1867)

Colman, David S., 'Sabrinae Corolla: the classics at Shrewsbury School under Dr Butler and Dr Kennedy', a paper read to the Classical Association, 14 April 1950 (Shrewsbury, 1950)

Colman, George, *Random Records of my Life*, 2 vols. (1830)

* Colton, C. C., *Lacon*, 2 vols. (1820)

Cook, A. K., *About Winchester College* (1917)

Cooke, Desmond T. F., *The Bending of a Twig* (1906)

* Cookesley, Henry Slingsby, *Brief Memoir of an Eton Boy* (1851)

Corbin, John, *Schoolboy Life in England, An American View* (New York, 1898)

* Cornish, Francis Ware (ed.), *Extracts from the Letters and Journal of William Cory* (Oxford, 1897)

* Cory, William [Johnson], 'On the Education of the Reasoning Faculties', in *Essays on a Liberal Education*, ed. Frederick Farrar (1867)

* Cory, William [Johnson], *Eton Reform* (1861)

* Cory, William [Johnson], *Extracts from Letters and Journal*, *see* Cornish

* Cory, William [Johnson], *Hints for Eton Masters*, by G. W. J. (1862)

* Cory, William [Johnson], *Ionica*, poems by William Johnson, with Biographical Introduction and Notes by Arthur C. Benson, Fellow of Magdalene College, Cambridge (1905)

Costans, 'Sketches of Eton', no. 4, 'Football!', *The Phoenix*, no. 5, March 1861

Cotton, G. E. L., *Sermons and Addresses, 1852–58* (Cambridge, 1858)

Coubertin, Pierre de, *L'Education en Angleterre* (Paris, 1888)

Coulton, G. G., *A Victorian Schoolmaster: Henry Hart of Sedbergh* (1923)

Cowburn, P., *Salopian Anthology* (1964)

* Cowper, William, *Tirocinium, or a Review of Schools* (first published, bound with *The Task*, 1785; 1817 edn)

* Cox, Thomas, *Endowed Schools: their Connections with the Universities and the Church. Two Lectures on the State of Education in the Sixteenth Century* (1869)

* Creasy, Sir Edward, *Memories of Eminent Etonians* (1850)

* Creasy, Sir Edward, *Some Account of the Foundation of Eton College and of the Past and Present Condition of the School* (1848)

* Croker, John, *Correspondence and Diaries of the late Honourable John Croker*, ed. Louis Jenning (1884)

* Cumberland, Richard, *Memoirs* (1806)

Cust, Lionel, *A History of Eton College* (1899)

Cust, Lionel, *Eton College Portraits* (1907)

* Darton, F. J. H. (ed.), *Life and Times of Mrs Sherwood* (1910)

* Darwin, Charles, *Autobiography and Selected Letters*, ed. Francis Darwin (New York, 1958 edn)

Davidson, R. T., *Life of Archbishop Campbell Tait*, 2 vols. (1891)

Davies, Gerald S., *Charterhouse in London* (1921)

* Denison, George Anthony, *Notes on My Life 1805–1878* (Oxford, 1878)

De Quincy, Thomas, 'Education of Boys in Large Numbers' in *Collected Writings of Thomas De Quincy*, 14 vols. (1897), vol. 14

Dibelius, Wilhelm, *Englische Romankunst*, 2 vols. (Berlin, 1910)

* *Directions to Academy Keepers* (1770)

* Disraeli, Benjamin, *Coningsby* (1844; 1961 edn)

* Dixon, Henry Hall ('The Druid'), *Saddle and Sirloin* (1870; 1895 edn)

* Doyle, Sir Francis Hastings, *Reminiscences and Opinions* (1886)

* Drage, Geoffrey, *Eton and the Empire* (Eton, 1890)

Dressler, Bruno, *Geschichte der englischen Erzichung* (Leipzig, 1928)

'The Druid', *see* Dixon

Duckworth, Russell, *A Memoir of James Lonsdale* (1893)

* Edgeworth, Maria, *The Barring Out* (1796)

* Edgeworth, Maria, *The Parent's Assistant* (1897 edn)

* Edgworth, Richard Lovell, *Memoirs*, 2 vols. (1820)

* *The Education of the Higher Classes Considered with Regard to its Objects, Its Organization, Its Moral Instruments* (1854)

Elyot, Sir Thomas, *The Book Named the Gouernor*, ed. H. S. Croft (1883)

* E.P.C., *Schoolboy Morality* (Social Purity Alliance, 1884)

* Esher, Reginald Baliol Brett, Viscount (ed.), *The Girlhood of Queen Victoria*. A selection from Her Majesty's diaries between the years 1832 and 1840, 2 vols. (1912; 1938 edn)

* [Essington, R. W.], 'Old Long Chamber', in *The Legacy of an Etonian*, ed. Robert Nolands, sole executor (Cambridge, 1846)

Eton, 'Eton', *WR*, April 1861, pp. 477–503

Eton Abuses Considered in a letter to the author of Some Remarks on the Present Studies and Management of Eton School (1834)

Eton Boy, *see* [Nugent-Bankes]

* Eton Boys, publications by: *Eton Bureau*, 1842, 1843; *Eton College Magazine*, ed. John Wickens, 1832; *Eton Miscellany*, vol. 1, June–July 1827; *Eton School Magazine*, 1847; *Etonian*, vol. 1, 1824; *Kaleidoscope, a Periodical by Eton Boys*, January–June 1833; *Phoenix*, conducted 1860 by Present Etonians; *Porticus Etonensis*, no. 1, April 1859; *Saltbearer* (1821)

* Etonensis, *A Few Words in Reply to Some Remarks upon the Present System and Management of Eton School*, by Etonensis (1834)

* Etonensis, *Observations on an Article in the Last Number of the* Edinburgh Review *Entitled Public Schools of England: Eton* (1830)

* Etonensis, *see Journal of Education*

* Etonian, *Thoughts on Eton Suggested by Sir John Coleridge's speech at Tiverton*, by an Etonian (1861)

* Etonian, *A Few Words to the Provost of Eton upon Certain Late Proceedings of his Religious Government of Eton College*, by an Etonian (1843)

* Etonian, *see also* [Blake], [Browne], I.E.M. [Johnston]

* *Etoniana*, the author of, *see* [Collins]
* *Etoniana*, nos 1–116, 1904–55; nos 117–31, 1965–75
Eton Master, *see* [Salt]
Evelyn, John, *Diary*, ed. E. S. de Beer, 6 vols. (Oxford, 1955)
Farmer, J. S., and Henly, W. E., *Slang and its Analogues* (New York, 1965)
* Farrar, Frederick W., *Eric, or Little by Little* (1858)
* Farrar, Frederick W., *St Winifred's, or the World of School* (1862)
* Farrar, Frederick W., *Some Defects of Public School Education* (1857)
* Farrar, Reginald, *The Life of Frederick William Farrar* (New York, 1904)
Fasti Etonensis, *see* [A. C. Benson]
Fearon, William Andrewes, *The Passing of Old Winchester* (1924)
* Field, William (ed.), *Memoirs of the Life, Writings and Opinions of the Rev. Samuel Parr L.L.D.*, 2 vols. (1828)
Fielding, Henry, *The Adventures of Joseph Andrews*, Book 3 (Oxford, 1967 edn)
Findlay, J. J., *Arnold of Rugby* (Cambridge, 1897)
Firth, J. D'E., *Winchester College* (1936, 1949 edn)
Fisher, G. W., *Annals of Shrewsbury School* (1899)
Fitch, J. G., *Thomas and Matthew Arnold* (1897)
* Fitzgerald, Brian (ed.), *see* Leinster
Fletcher, C. R. L., *Edmund Warre* (1922)
* Fletcher, George, MD, *Management of Athletics in Public Schools. A Paper Read before the Medical Officers of Schools Association on January 12, 1886* (1886)
Forshall, Frederick H., *Westminster School Past and Present* (1884)
Forster, John, *Life of Charles Dickens*, 3 vols. (1872–3)
* Fox, Charles James, *Memorials and Correspondence*, ed. Lord John Russell (1853)
* Fremantle, Rev. W. R., *Memoir of the Rev. Spencer Thornton* (1850)
Frere, John Hookham, *Works*, 2 vols. (1872)
* [Froude, James Anthony], *Shadows of the Clouds*, by Zeta (1874, suppressed)
Furley, John Sampson, *Winchester in 1867* (1936)
Furnivall, F. J. (ed.), *Early English Meals and Manners*, Early English Text Society, original series no. 32 (1868)
* [Gale, Frederick], 'Wrongs of my Boyhood', *CM*, vol. 3, 1861
* [Gale, Frederick], *Ups and Downs of a Public School*, by a Wykehamist (1856)
* Galloway, Earl of, *Observations on the Abuse and Reform of the Monitorial System of Harrow, with Letters and Remarks of the Earl of Galloway* (1854)
* Gaskell, James Milnes, *An Eton Boy. Being the Letters of James Milnes Gaskell from Eton and Oxford 1820–1830*, ed. Charles Milnes Gaskell (1939)
* Gaskell, James Milnes, 'Letters taken from a typescript copy of the originals, by kind permission of Lady Constance Gaskell', *ETA*, nos. 59–62, 30 July 1935–17 March 1936
* Gaskell, James Milnes, *Records of an Eton Schoolboy* (privately printed, 1883)
Gaume, Jean Joseph, *Advice to those who exercise the ministry of reconciliation*

through confession and absolution, being Abbé Gaume's Manual for Confession, with a preface by G. B. Pusey (Oxford, 1878)

Gibbon, Edward, *Autobiography* (1923 edn)

* Gladstone, William Ewart, *Arthur Henry Hallam* (Boston, 1898)

* Gladstone, William Ewart, *Gladstone Diaries*, vols. 1 and 2, ed. M. R. D. Foot (Oxford, 1968)

* Gladstone, William Ewart, *Gladstone Papers* (1930)

* Goulburn, E. M., *The Book of Rugby School*, chs 1–3 by E. W. B[enson] (privately printed, 1856)

* [Gover, William], 'Memories of Arnold and Rugby Sixty Years Ago', by a Member of the School in 1835, '36 and '37, *The Parents' Review*, vols. 6 and 7 (1895–6)

* Graham, Edward, *The Harrow Life of Montagu Butler*, with an Introductory Chapter by the Rt Hon. Sir George Trevelyan Bart (1920)

* Grant, William, MS. letters from Rugby, 1791–6, TRR

Graves, Frank Pierrepoint, *Great Educators of Three Centuries* (New York, 1912)

* Gray, Thomas, *Ode on a Distant Prospect of Eton College* (written 1742, published 1747)

* Green, W. C., *Memories of Eton and Kings* (Eton, 1905)

* Greg, William Rathbone, 'England as It Is', *ER*, vol. 93 (1851)

* Gregory, Sir William, *Autobiography*, ed. Lady Gregory (1894)

Green, T. H., *Works*, ed. R. L. Nettleship, 3 vols (1885–8)

Grenville Murray, *see* Murray

* Gretton, F. E., *Memory's Harkback through Half a Century 1808–1858* (1889)

* Greville, Charles Cavendish Fulke, *Memoirs*, ed. Henry Reeve (1887)

* Grier, R. M., *John Allen, a Memoir* (1889)

* Griffith, George, *The Life and Adventures of George Wilson, a Foundation Scholar* (1854)

* Gronow, Rees Howell, *Recollections and Anecdotes*, 2nd series (1863), fourth and final series (1866)

Grosskurth, Phyllis, *John Addington Symonds* (1964)

A Guide to Eton (1860)

* Gun, W. T. J. (compiler), *Harrow School Register 1800–1900* (1901)

* Gurney, Gilbert, *Theodore Hook* (1836)

* Guziot, F., *An Embassy to the Court of King James in 1840* (1863)

G.W.J., *see* Cory

* Hake, T. G., *Memories of Eighty Years* (1892)

* Hallam, Arthur Henry, 'Unpublished Letters', ed. Morris Zamick in *Bulletin of the John Rylands Library*, vol. 18 (1934)

Harcourt, L. V., *An Eton Bibliography* (1902)

* Hare, Augustus J. C., *Biographical Sketches* (1895)

* Hare, Augustus J. C., *Memorials of a Quiet Life*, 2 vols. (1872)

Harris, James Howard, *see* Malmesbury, Earl of

* Harrison, Frederick, *Autobiographical Memoirs*, 2 vols. (1911)

Harrison, J. F. C., *The Early Victorians* (1971)

* Harrison, William, *Description of England*, ed. F. J. Furnivall, New Shakespeare Society, publications nos 1, 5 and 8 (1877–81)

* Harrison, William, *Life at Westminster, Occasional Papers during three years, 1845, 1846, 1847*, no. 6, Saturday, 18 October 1845

* Harrow publications: *Harrow Almanack* (1865); *Harrovian*, 1870–2, 1878–81, 1888; *Souvenirs* (1903); *The Tyro*, 1864–7; *The Unicorn*, 1895, 1897

Hartland, W. E., 'Dr Butler of Shrewsbury School', *The Eagle*, vol. 19, March 1897, p. 429

* [Hathaway, C. L.], *Memorials of a Harrow Schoolboy by the late C.L.H.* (1849)

* Hawtrey, Edward Craven, *Sermons and Lectures Delivered in Eton College Chapel in the Years 1848–1849*. 'Not Published [*sic*]. Printed at Eton (1849)'

* Hazlitt, William, *Schools, School Books and Schoolmasters* (1888)

H.C.L., *Harrow School Memorials* (1873)

* Hemyng, Bracebridge, *Butler Burke at Eton* (1865)

* [Hemyng, Bracebridge], *Eton Schooldays*, by an Old Etonian (1864)

Herbert, Lord (ed.), *Pembroke Papers, 1780–1794* (1950)

Hexter, J. H., 'The Education of the Aristocracy in the Renaissance' in *Reappraisals in History* (1961)

Heywood, Rev. G. G. T., 'Boys at Public Schools', in *Unwritten Laws*, ed. E. H. Pitcairn (1899)

Heywood, J., and Wright, J., *The Ancient Laws of the Fifteenth Century for King's College, Cambridge and for the Public School of Eton College* (1850)

* [Higgins, Matthew James] (pseudonyms Jacob Omnium, Paterfamilias), *CM*, March and December 1860, March 1861

* Hill, M. D., *Eton and Elsewhere* (1928)

* *History of the Colleges Winchester, Eton and Westminster* (1816)

Hodder, Edwin, *The Life and Works of the Seventh Earl of Shaftesbury K.G.* (1887)

Hodgson, James T., *Memoirs of the Rev. Francis Hodgson*, 2 vols. (1878)

* Holland, Lady Saba, *A Memoir of the Reverend Sydney Smith*, 2 vols. (1855)

Honey, J. R. de S., *Tom Brown's Universe: the Development of the Victorian Public School* (1977). A richly documented and important work: Author.

* Hook, Theodore, *Passion and Principle* (1825)

* Hoole, Charles, *A New Discovery of the Old Art of Teaching School* (1660)

Houghton, W. E., *The Victorian Frame of Mind 1830–1870* (New Haven, 1957)

How, F. D., *Six Great Schoolmasters* (1904)

* Howson, E. H., and Warner, G. T. (eds.), *Harrow School* (1898)

Hudson, D., *A Poet in Parliament* (1939)

Hudson, Derek, *Lewis Carroll* (1954)

* Hughes, Thomas, *The Manliness of Christ* (New York, 1903)

* Hughes, Thomas, *Memoir of a Brother* (1873)

* [Hughes, Thomas], *Tom Brown's Schooldays*, by an Old Boy (1857, 1871 edn)

[Hughes, Thomas), *Notes for Boys*, by an Old Boy (1890)

* Hunt, Leigh, *Autobiography* (1850)

* Hutton, William, *Autobiography* (1890)

* I.E.M., *The Confessions of an Etonian* (1846)

Jacob Omnium, *see* [Higgins]

Jameson, Edward Mellor, *Charterhouse* (1937)

* [Jesse, Edward], 'A Day at Eton', *Bentley's Miscellany*, vol. 7, 1846

* Jesse, John Heenage, *George Selwyn and his Contemporaries*, 4 vols. (1843–4)

* Jesse, John Heenage, *Memoirs of Celebrated Etonians*, 2 vols. (1875)

* Johnson, William, *see* Cory

* [Johnston, C. F.], *Recollections of Eton*, by an Etonian (1870)

* Jones, L. E., *A Victorian Boyhood* (1955)

* *Journal of Education*, Supplement, 1 November 1881; no. 150 (no. 47 New Series) 1 January 1882; no. 152 (no. 49 New Series) 1 March 1882. J. M. Wilson, 'Morality in Public Schools' and subsequent correspondence (Olim Etonensis)

Kaleidoscope, *see* Eton Boys

* Kames, Lord, *Loose Hints . . . on Education* (1781)

* Kaye, Sir John William, *The Life and Correspondence of Charles, Lord Metcalfe*, 2 vols. (1858)

[Kaye, Sir John William], 'Success', *CM*, vol. 2, July–December 1860, pp. 729–41

Kendall, Guy, *A Headmaster Remembers* (1933)

* Kennedy, B. H. *et al.*, *Sabrinae Corolla* (1850)

* Keppel, George, Earl of Albemarle, *Fifty Years of My Life* (1876)

* Kilner, Dorothy, *The Holiday Present* (1803)

* Kinglake, Alexander William, *Eothen* (1844; 1935 edn)

* Kinglake, Alexander William, *War in the Crimea*, 8 vols. (1863–87)

* Kingsley, Charles, *His Letters and Memories of his Life*, ed. his wife, 2 vols. (1877)

* Kipling, Rudyard, *Schoolboy Lyrics* (Lahore, 1881, printed for private circulation only)

* Lake, W. C., *Memorials*, ed. Katherine Lake (1901)

* Lake, W. C., 'Stanley's Life of Dr Arnold', *QR*, vol. 84, no. 148, October 1844

Lamb, G. F., *Happiest Days* (1959)

* Lang, Andrew, *Life, Letters and Diaries of Sir Stafford Northcote, first Earl of Idesleigh* (Edinburgh, 1891)

* Laughton, John Knox, *Memoirs of the Life and Correspondence of Henry Reeve*, 2 vols. (1898)

Lawley, Francis, *Life and Times of the Druid (Henry Hall Dixon)* (1895)

* Lawrence, George G. A., *Guy Livingstone* (1857)

* Lawrence, Sir James, *The Etonian out of Bounds*, 3 vols. (1878)

Leach, A. F., *A History of Winchester College* (1899)

* Leinster, Duchess of, *Correspondence of Emily, Duchess of Leinster 1731–1814*, 3 vols., ed. Brian Fitzgerald (Dublin, 1949)

* *Letters from a nobleman to his Son during the Period of his Education at Eton and Oxford*, 2 vols. (1810)

Letters of William and Dorothy Wordsworth: The Later Years, 3 vols. (Oxford, 1939)

* Lewis, George Cornewall, *The Letters of George Cornewall Lewis Bart.*, ed. Rev. Sir Gilbert Frankland Lewis Bart., Canon of Worcester (1879)

* [Lewis, George Cornewall], 'The Public Schools of England: Eton', *ER*, no. 101, April–July 1830, pp. 65–80

* [Lewis, George Cornewall], 'The Public Schools of England: Westminster and Eton', *ER*, no. 105, March 1831, pp. 64–82

* Lloyd, Richard, *A Letter to a Member of Parliament showing . . . the serious and dangerous defects . . . of Mr Brougham's Bill* (1828)

* Locke, John, 'Some Thoughts Concerning Education' in *Educational Writings of John Locke*, ed. J. W. Adamson (1922)

Lockwood, Edward, *Early Days at Marlborough College* (1893)

A Lounger at the Clubs, *The Gentleman's Art of Dressing with Economy* (1870)

Lowry, H. F. *et al.* (eds.), *The Poems of Arthur Hugh Clough* (Oxford, 1951)

* Lubbock, Alfred, *Memories of Eton and Etonians* (1899)

* Lunn, Arnold, *The Harrovian* (1913)

* Luxmoore, H. E., 'Public School Education', *QR*, October 1860

* Lyte, H. C. Maxwell, *History of Eton* (4th edn, 1911)

Lyttelton, Edith, *Alfred Lyttelton. An Account of his Life* (1917)

* Lyttelton, Edward, *The Causes and Prevention of Immorality in Schools*, Social Purity Alliance (1887)

* Lyttelton, Edward, *Training the Young in the Laws of Sex* (1900)

* Lyttelton, Edward, *Memories and Hopes* (1925)

* Lyttelton, Edward, *Mothers and Sons; or problems in the home training* (1892)

* [Lyttelton, George], 'The autobiography of an Etonian', *ECM*, no. 6, 22 October 1832; no. 7, 5 November 1832

Lyttelton, Colonel the Hon. N. G., 'Some Eton and Harrow Matches', *NatR*, no. 149, July 1895

* Macaulay, Thomas Babington, *Letters*, ed. Thomas Pinney, vol. 4 (Cambridge, 1977)

McIntosh, P. C., *Physical Education in England since 1800* (1958)

Mack, Edward C., *Public Schools and British Opinion 1780–1860. An examination of the relationship between contemporary ideas and the evolution of an English institution* (1938)

Mack, Edward C., *Public Schools and British Opinion since 1860. The relationship between contemporary ideas and the evolution of an English institution* (New York, 1941)

Mack, Edward C., and Armytage, W. H. G., *Thomas Hughes: The Life of the Author of* Tom Brown's Schooldays (1952)

* Macnaghten, Hugh Vibart, *Fifty Years of Eton in Prose and Verse* (1924)
* Macnaghten, Melville, *Sketchy Memories of Eton* (1885)
* Macready, W. C., *Reminiscences* (1875)
Mais, S. P. B., *All the Days of My Life* (1937)
Maison, Margaret M., 'Tom Brown and Company. Scholastic Novels of the 1850s', *English*, vol. 12, autumn 1958
* Malet, Sir Alexander, *Some Account of the System of Fagging at Winchester School with remarks and a correspondence with Dr Williams, Headmaster of that school, on the late expulsions thence for resisting the authority of the prefects* (1828)
* Malmesbury, James Howard Harris, Earl of, *Memoirs of an Ex-Minister* (1884)
* Mansfield, Robert Blachford, *School Life at Winchester College 1834–40* (1866)
* Markham, Captain F., *Recollections of a Town Boy at Westminster 1849–1855* (1903)
* Marryat, Frederick, *Masterman Ready* (1841)
* Marryat, Frederick, *Perceval Keene* (1856 edn)
Martello Tower, *see* [Norman]
Martineau, Harriet, *Health, Husbandry and Handicraft* (1861)
Mathison, W. C., *England in Transition 1789–1832* (1920)
* Maude, John, *Memories of Eton and Oxford* (1936)
* Maxwell, Rt Hon. Sir Herbert, *The Life and Letters of George William Frederick, Fourth Earl of Clarendon*, 2 vols. (1913)
Meissner, Paul, *Die Reform der engleschen hoheren Schulwesens in 19 Jahrandert* (Leipzig, 1929)
* Melly, George, *The Experiences of a Fag* (1854)
* Merivale, Charles, *Autobiography*, ed. his daughter, Juliette Anne Merivale (1899)
* Merivale, Herman, *Bar, Stage and Platform* (1902)
Mill, J. S., 'Reorganization of the Reform Party', *WR*, vol. 32, 1859
* Milman, Arthur, *Henry Hart Milman . . . a biographical Sketch* (1900)
* [Milman, Henry Hart], ' "Eton School" – Education in England', *QR*, vol. 52, August 1834
* [Milman, Henry Hart], *Eton System of Education Vindicated . . .* (1834)
* Minchin, J. G. Cotton, *Old Harrow Days* (1898); *Our Public Schools, Their Influence on English History* (1901)
* Minet, Charles, Minet Diary, MS., WCL
* Moberly, C. A. E., *Dulce Domum, George Moberly, his Family and Friends, by his Daughter* (1911)
* Moberly, George, *Five Short Letters to Sir William Heathcote on the Studies and Discipline of Public Schools* (1861)
* Moberly, George, *Sermons Preached at Winchester College* (second series) (1848)
* Moncrieff, A. R. Hope, *A Book about Schools* (1925)
* Moncrieff, Robert H., *A Book about Dominies* (Edinburgh, 1871)

* Monson, William John, sixth Lord, 'Reminiscences of Eton', *ETA*, no. 29, 30 November 1921

* Monson, William John, 'A Private School in 1804', *ETA*, no. 40, 1926; no. 41, 1927

Morley, Henry (ed.), *A Survey of London* (1908)

Morley, John, *Life of William Ewart Gladstone*, 3 vols. (1903)

* Morrice, David, *An Attempted Reply to the Master of Westminster School* (1802)

* Moultrie, John, 'The Dream of Life' in *Lays of the English Church* (1843)

* Mozley, T., *Reminiscences, Chiefly of Towns, Villages and Schools*, 2 vols. (1885)

Mure, James, *Some Account of Westminster School* (1860)

* [Murray, Grenville], *Collegers v. Oppidans* by an Old Etonian (1884). First published in *CM*, 1871

* Murray, Grenville, *People I Have Met* (1883)

* Murray, Grenville, *see also* Richards

National Review, no. 149, July 1895

Nevill, Henry Ralph, *Floreat Etona. Anecdotes and Memoirs of Eton College* (1911)

New Monthly Magazine and Literary Journal, 1827

Newman, J. H., *Loss and Gain* (1848)

Newsome, David, *Godliness and Good Learning* (1961)

Newsome, David, *A History of Wellington College 1859–1959* (1959)

Nimrod, *see* [Apperley]

Nolands, Robert, *see* [Essington]

* [Norman, Francis Martin], *At School and at Sea: or, Life and Character at Harrow, in the Royal Navy, and at the Trenches before Sebastopol*, by Martello Tower (1899)

* Northcote, Sir Stafford, first Earl of Idesleigh, *Life, Letters and Diaries of Sir Stafford Northcote, first Earl of Idesleigh, see* Lang (Edinburgh, 1891)

Norwood, Cyril, *The English Tradition of Education* (1929)

* [Nugent-Bankes, G. H.] *About Some Fellows, or Odds and Ends from my Notebook*, by an Eton Boy (1878)

* [Nugent-Bankes, G. H.], *Letters of an Eton Boy* (1910)

O.E., *see* [Salt]

Ogilvie, Vivian, *The English Public Schools* (1967)

Old Boy, *see* [Hughes]

Old Colleger, *see* [Coleridge, A. D.], [Tucker]

* Old Etonian, *A Letter to Sir Alexander Malet . . . with a word in passing to the editor of the Literary Gazette* (1829)

* Old Etonian, *Public School Life* (1910)

* Old Etonian, *Eton Memories*, edited with a preface by P.B. (1909)

* Old Etonian, *see* [Hemyng], [Murray]

* Old K.S., *Eton: Things Old and New* (1868)

* Old Rugbaean, *Recollections of Rugby* (1848)

* Old Westminster, *A Very Short Letter from one Old Westminster to Another touching some matters connected with their school* (1829)

Old Wykehamist, *see* [Rich]

* Old Wykehamists, *Winchester College 1339–1893* (1893)

Oldham, J. Basil, *Headmasters of Shrewsbury School 1552–1952* (Oxford, 1952)

Olim Etonensis, *see Journal of Education*

One who has kept a Diary, *see* [Russell]

* One who was once a Monitor, *A Few Words on the Monitorial System at Harrow from one who was once a Monitor* (1854); *see also Reply*

* Osbaldeston, George, *Squire Osbaldeston – His Autobiography*, ed. E. D. Cumming (1926)

Oswell, G. W. E., *William Cotton Oswell, Hunter and Explorer*, 2 vols. (1900)

Pace, Richard, *De Fructu* (Basel, 1517)

* Palmer, Roundell, Earl of Selborne, *Memorials*, 2 parts, 4 vols. (1896), part 1, vol. 1

* A Parent, *Some Remarks on the Present Studies and Management of Eton School* (1834); *see also* Etonensis

* A Parent, *Thoughts of a Parent on Education* (1823)

* Parkin, Sir G. R., *Edward Thring, Life, Diary and Letters* (1898)

* Parry, Sir Hubert, 'Eton Diaries', *ETA*, no. 103, 1946; no. 104, 1947; no. 105, 1948

* Paston, J. Lewis, *The English Public Schools* (1805)

Paterfamilias, *see* [Higgins]

* Pattison, Mark, *Memoirs* (1899)

* Paul, C. Kegan, *Memoirs* (1899)

* Paul, Herbert, *Stray Leaves* (1906)

* Pearson, Charles Henry, *Memorials*, ed. William Stebbing (New York, 1900)

* Peel, Sir Robert, *Sir Robert Peel in early life . . . from his Private Papers*, ed. Charles Stuart Parker, 3 vols. (1891)

* Pell, Albert, *Reminiscences of Albert Pell, sometime M.P. for South Leicestershire*, ed. with an Introduction by Thomas Mackay (1908)

Perkin, Harold J., *The Origin of Modern English Society 1780–1880* (1969)

Peterson, A. D. C., *A Hundred Years of Education* (1952)

* Pierce, Elizabeth, *The Letters of Elizabeth Pierce 1751–1775, with letters from her son, Pierce Joseph Taylor, a schoolboy at Eton*, ed. Violet M. MacDonald (1927)

Pisanus Fraxi, *see* [Ashbee]

* Pitcairn, E. H. (ed.), *Unwritten Laws and Ideals of Active Careers* (1899)

* *A Plain Statement of Fact relative to Sir Eyre Coote* (1816)[W. Bagwell?]

* Platt, H. E., *A Letter to the Right Hon. Earl of Galloway* (1854)

* Portman, Lionel, *Hugh Rendell* (1906)

* Powell, Rev. H. Townsend, *Liberalism Unveiled, or Strictures on Dr Arnold's Sermons* (1830)

* Praed, Winthrop Mackworth, *Poems, with a memoir by the Rev. Derwent Coleridge* (1864)

[Praed, W. M.], *The Etonian*, vol. 1, no. 2, 1824, p. 2

* Prothero, Rowland E. and Bradley, G., *The Life and Correspondence of Arthur Penrhyn Stanley D.D.*, 2 vols. (1893)

* *Quarterly Journal of Education*, vol. 5, January–April 1833; vol. 7, January–April 1834; vol. 8, April–October 1834; vol. 9, January–April 1835

Quick, Robert Henry, *Essays on Educational Reformers* (1868)

Quick, Robert Henry, *The Schoolmaster, Past and Future*, Cambridge Introductory Lecture, 18 October 1879

Radclyffe, C. W., *Memorials of Rugby* (1843)

Rawnsley, H. D., *Edward Thring, Teacher and Poet* (1889)

Ray, Gordon N., *Thackeray, a Biography*: vol. 1, *The Uses of Adversity 1811–1845* (1955); vol. 2, *The Age of Reason 1847–1863* (1958)

[Reeve, Henry], *ER*, April 1861

Reid, Stuart J., *Lord John Russell* (1893)

Reid, Stuart J. (ed.), *Memoirs of Sir Wemyss Reid 1842–1885* (1905)

Reid, T. Wemyss, *The Life, Letters and Friendships of Richard Monckton Milnes, first Lord Houghton*, 2 vols (1890)

Remarks on the Actual State of the University of Cambridge (1830)

* *Remarks on the Rev. Dr Vincent's Defence of Public Education* (1802)

Remarks on the System of Education in Public Schools (1809). (For a review of this book *see* Smith)

* *A Reply to 'One who was once a Monitor'* (1854)

* Report of Her Majesty's Commissioners, *Parliamentary Papers 1864*, vol 20, 21

* [Rich, F. J. G. H.], *Recollections of the Two St Mary Winton Colleges*, by an Old Wykehamist (1883)

Richards, James Brinsley, the name adopted by Reginald Grenville Murray, see p. 105n. *See also* Murray

Richards, James Brinsley, 'Mr Gladstone's Schooldays', *Temple Bar*, vols 67, 68, 1883

[Richards, James Brinsley?], 'Eton Days of Sir Stafford Northcote', *Temple Bar*, no. 278, vol. 70, 1884

* Richards, James Brinsley, *Seven Years at Eton 1857–1864*, ed. (or rather, written by) Richards (1883). *N.B.*: this book is indispensable reading to anyone who wishes to receive an honest and relatively uninhibited account of what life was like at Eton in the mid-nineteenth century: Author.

Ridding, Laura, *George Ridding, Schoolmaster and Bishop* (1908)

* [Rimmer, Alfred and Adnitt, Henry William], *A History of Shrewsbury School* (1889)

Rodgers, John, *The Old Public Schools* (1938)

* The *Rodiad*, The ascription to 'George Coleman' [*sic*] is spurious (*c.* 1870)

* Rogers, Samuel, *Table Talk of Samuel Rogers*, ed. Morchard Bishop (1952)

* Rogers, William, *Reminiscences*, ed. R. H. Haddon (1888)

Rouse, W. H. D., *A History of Rugby School* (1898)

* Rowcróft, Charles, *Confessions of an Etonian*, 3 vols. (1852)

Rugby Magazine, vol. 2, 1836

Rugby Miscellany, March 1845

Rugbaean, no. 1, March 1840

* [Russell, G. W. E.], *Collections and Recollections*, by one who has kept a Diary (1898)

* Ryder, D., *Diary*, ed. W. Matthews (1939)

Salmon, E., *Juvenile Literature as it is* (1888)

* Salt, Henry, *Memories of Bygone Eton* (1928)

* [Salt, Henry], *Eton under Hornby*, by O.E. (1910)

* [Salt, Henry], 'Confessions of an Eton Master', *NC*, January 1885

Sandford, E. G. (ed.), *Memoirs of Archbishop Temple* by Seven Friends (1906)

Sandys, J. E., *Classical Scholarship* (1901)

* Sargeaunt, John, *Annals of Westminster School* (1898)

Selfe, Lt Col. Sydney, *Chapters from the History of Rugby School* (1910)

* Sewell, William, *A Year's Sermons to Boys, Preached in the Chapel of St Peter's College, Radley*, 2 vols. (Oxford, vol. 1, 1864; vol. 2, 1869)

* Sherwood, Mary Martha, *The History of the Fairchild Family* (1818–1847)

* Shrewsbury School, *see* [Rimmer and Adnitt]

Simon, Brian, and Bradley, Ian (eds.), *The Victorian Public School* (Dublin, 1975)

Simpson, J. Hope, *Rugby Since Arnold* (1967)

* Skrine, J. H., *A Memory of Edward Thring* (1889)

* Smedley, Frank, *Frank Fairclough, or scenes from the life of a Private Pupil* (1850)

* Smith, Sydney, Review of *Remarks on the System of Education in Public Schools*, *ER*, vol. 16, 1810

* Smith, Sydney, *Works*, 3 vols. (1848)

Solly, Godfrey E., *Rugby School Register*, vol. 1, *April 1675 to October 1857. Revised and Annotated for the Old Rugbeian Society by Godfrey Solly* (Rugby, 1933)

* Southey, Robert, *Life and Correspondence*, 6 vols. (1849, 1850)

* [Southey, Robert], 'Elementary Teaching', *QR*, vol. 39, January–April 1829

* *Souvenirs*, a Harrow publication (1903)

* Spencer, Herbert, *Education, Intellectual, Moral and Physical* (1861)

Sporting Magazine, September 1829

* Stanley, Arthur Penrhyn, 'Arnold and Rugby', *MM*, July 1874

* Stanley, Arthur Penrhyn, *The Life and Correspondence of Thomas Arnold* (1901 edn)

* Stapylton, H. E. C., *Eton School Lists 1791–1850* (1864)

* Stapylton, H. E. C., *Eton School Lists 1853–1892* (1900)

* Staunton, Howard, *The Great Schools of England* (1865)

* Stephen, James Fitzjames, 'Eton Reform', *NatR*, January 1864
* Stephen, James Fitzjames, 'Report of the Public Schools Commission', *NatR*, November 1864
* Stephen, James Fitzjames, 'Tom Brown's Schooldays' (review), *ER*, no. 217, vol. 107, January–April 1858
[Stephen, J. K.], *Lapsus Calumni*, by J.K.S. (1891)
* Stephen, Leslie, 'Thoughts of an Outsider: Public Schools', *CM*, March, November 1873
* Stephen, Leslie, *The Life of Sir James Fitzjames Stephen Bart* (1895)
* Stephens, W. R. W., *A Memoir of the Rt Hon. William Page Wood, Baron Hatherly*, 2 vols. (1883)
Sterry, Sir Wasey, *Eton College Register 1441–1698* (1943)
Stone, C. R., *Eton Glossary* (Eton, 1902)
Stone, Lawrence, 'Education and Culture', *The Crisis of the Aristocracy* (Oxford, 1965)
Stowe, A. Monroe, *English Grammar Schools in the Reign of Queen Elizabeth* (New York, 1908)
* Stowell, Hugh, *The Age We Live In* (1850–51)
* Stoy, K. V., *Zwei Tage in englischen Gymnasien* (Leipzig, 1860)
* Stratford, Esmé Wingfield, *Before the Lights Went Out* (1945)
Swinburne, Algernon, Ashley MSS., fos 5256, 5751, 5276
* Symonds, John Addington, Autobiography, unpublished MS., London Library
* Taine, H., *Notes on England* (1872)
Talboys, R. St C., *A Victorian School* (Oxford, 1943)
Tanner, Lawrence F., *Westminster School. A History* (1934)
* Teignmouth, Lord, *Memoirs of . . . Sir William Jones*, 2 vols. (1835)
* Temple, Frederick, *Sermons preached at Rugby School in 1858, 1859, 1860* (1861)
* Thackeray, Francis St John, *Memoir of Edward Craven Hawtrey* (1896)
* Thackeray, W. M., *The Book of Snobs* (1852)
* Thackeray, W. M., *The Irish Sketch Book* (1842)
* Thackeray, W. M., *Letters and Private Papers*, ed. Gordon N. Ray, 4 vols. (Cambridge, 1945–46)
* Thackeray, W. M., *The Newcomes* (1853–55)
* Thackeray, W. M., *Pendennis*, 2 vols. (1849)
* Thackeray, W. M., *Works*, 17 vols., ed. George Saintsbury (1908)
Third Report of the Select Committee on the Education of the Lower Orders (1818)
* Thompson, D'Arcy Wentworth, *Daydreams of a Schoolmaster* (Edinburgh, 1864)
Thompson, D'Arcy Wentworth, *Wayside Thoughts* (Edinburgh, 1868)
Thompson, F. M. L., *English Landed Gentry in the Nineteenth Century* (1963)
* Thornton, P. M., *Harrow School and Its Surroundings* (1885)
* *Thoughts on Education* (1820)
* Thring, Edward, *Theory and Practice of Teaching* (Cambridge, 1885)

* Thring, Edward, *Sermons Preached at Uppingham School*, 2 vols. (1858)
* Tod, Alexander Hay, *Charterhouse* (1900)
* Tollemache, Lionel A., *Old and Odd Memories* (1908)
Torr, Cecil, *Small Talk at Wreyland* (Bath, 1970)
Toynbee, Paget (ed.), *Correspondence of Gray, Walpole and Ashton*, 2 vols. (1915)
* Trench, Rev. Francis, *A Few Notes from Past Life 1818–1832* (Oxford, 1862)
Trevor, M., *Newman: The Pillar and the Cloud* (1962)
* Trollope, Anthony, *Dr Wortle's School*, 2 vols. (1881)
* Trollope, Anthony, *Autobiography* (1947 edn)
* Trollope, Thomas A., *What I Remember*, 3 vols. (1887)
Trotter, Lionel James, *A Leader of Light Horse. Life of Hodson of Hodson's Horse* (1901)
* [Tucker, William Hill], *Eton of Old; or Eighty Years Since 1811–1822*, by an old Colleger (1892)
* Tuckwell, Rev. W., *The Ancient Way* (1893)
Tuer, Andrew White, *Pages and Pictures from Forgotten Children's Books* (1898)
Tusser, Thomas, *Five Hundred Points of Good Husbandrie United to As Many of Good Housewifrie* (1573)
* *The Tyro*, a Harrow School publication (1864–67)
* *The Unicorn*, a Harrow School publication (1895, 1897)
* Vaughan, Charles J., *A Letter to Viscount Palmerston . . . on the Monitorial System of Harrow School* (1853)
Vaughan, Charles J., *Counsels for Young Students* (1870)
* Vaughan, Charles J., *Funeral Sermon on Arthur Penrhyn Stanley preached in Westminster Abbey July 24, 1881* (1881)
* Vaughan, Charles J., *Memorials of Harrow Sundays* (1859)
* Vaughan, Charles J., *Two Aspects of the Tempter* (1851)
* Vaughan, Charles J., *The Vocation of a Public School: an address* (1857)
* Verney, L. J., and Thompson, W. D. J. Cargill (eds.), *Harrow Memorabilia* (1949, unpublished)
Victorian History of the Counties of England: Buckinghamshire Schools, vol. 2 (1908)
Vincent, W. A. L., *The State and School Education 1640–1800* (1950)
* Vincent, William, *A Defence of Public Education* (1802)
* Wade, John, *History of the Middle and Working Classes* (1833)
* Wade, John, *Extraordinary Black Book* (1831)
* Walpole, Horace, *The Letters of Horace Walpole fourth Earl of Orford*, ed. Mrs Paget Toynbee, 16 vols. (Oxford, 1903); *see also* Gray
* Walpole, Horace, *Reminiscences written by Mr Horace Walpole in 1788 . . . Now first presented in full from the original MSS. with Notes and Index by Paget Toynbee* (Oxford, 1924)
Walpole, Sir Spencer, *The Life of Lord John Russell*, 2 vols. (1889)
* Warboise, Emma, *The Life of Thomas Arnold D.D.* (Hamilton, 1859)
* [Ward, E.], *Boys and Their Rulers*, by E.W. (1853)
Ward, Wilfred, *William George Ward and the Oxford Movement* (1889)

* Warner, H. Lee, 'House Boarders and Day Boys', *CR*, vol. 46, July–December 1884

Warner, James Lee, Letters, TRR

* Warwick and Brooke, Earl of, *Memories of Sixty Years* (1917)

West, J. M., and Pendlebury, William J. von M., *Shrewsbury School . . .* (1932)

* [Westmacott, Charles Molloy], *The London Spy*, by Bernard Blackmantle, 2 vols. (1825, 1826)

[Westmacott, Charles Molloy], *WR*, April 1861, p. 477

White, Beatrice (ed.), *The Vulgaria of John Stanbridge and the Vulgaria of Robert Whittinton* (1932)

Whitehouse, J. H. (ed.), *The English Public Schools: a symposium* (1919)

* Wickens, John, *see ECM*

* Wiese, Leopold, *Deutsche Briefe über englische Erziehung* (Leipzig, 1852)

Willey, Basil, *The English Moralists* (1964)

Willey, Basil, *More Nineteenth Century Studies* (1956)

Willey, Basil, *Nineteenth Century Studies* (1964 edn)

* Wilkinson, Charles Allix, *Reminiscences of Eton (in Keate's Time)* (1888)

* Williams, Ellen, *Life and Letters of Rowland Williams D.D.*, 2 vols. (1874)

* Williams, Montagu, *Leaves of a Life*, 2 vols. (1890)

Williams, R. R., *The Educational Work of C. J. Vaughan*, First Vaughan Memorial Lecture, 18 May 1953

Willis, R. and Clark, J. W., *The Architectural History of the University of Cambridge*, 4 vols. (1886)

* Wilmot, Edward Parry Eardley, *Charterhouse Old and New* (1895)

Wilmot, Sir John Eardley Eardley, *Reminiscences of the Late Thomas Assheton Smith or the pursuits of an English Country Gentleman* (1860)

* Wilson, J. M., *see JE*

Winstanley, D. A., *Early Victorian Cambridge* (1955 edn)

Winsten, Stephen, *Salt and his Circle*, with a Preface by Bernard Shaw (1951)

W.L.C., *see* [Collins]

* Wood, William Page, *Memoirs of Baron Hatherly* (1883)

Woodward, Ernest L., *The Age of Reform 1815–1870* (Oxford, 1938)

Woodward, Francis J., *The Doctor's Disciples* (1954)

* Wordsworth, Charles, *Christian Boyhood at a public school; a collection of sermons and lectures at Winchester College*, 2 vols. (1846)

* Wordsworth, Charles, *Annals of My Early Life 1806–1846* (1891)

Wortham, H. E., *Oscar Browning* (1927)

Wortham, H. E., *Victorian Eton and Cambridge* (1956 edn)

Wykehamist, *see* [Gale]

Wykehamists, *A Roll of Old Wykehamists* (1956)

Wymer, Norman, *Dr Arnold of Rugby* (1953)

Yglesias, *see under* Manuscripts

Young, George Malcolm (ed.), *Early Victorian England 1830–1865*, 2 vols (Oxford, 1934)

Zeta, *see* [Froude]

Ziegler, Philip, *Melbourne: A Biography of William Lamb, second Viscount Melbourne* (1976)

Index

Abercrombie, Sir Alexander, *Rugby and India*, 46

Abingdon, Lord, flagellation parties, 223

Acton, Dr, anti-sex apostle, 'total ignorance rule', 288; role of wives and mothers, 289; school fantasies, 291 and n., 292; and illicit sexuality in infancy, 292

Adams, Mrs Frances, 239

Adams, H. C., 231 and n.; *Schoolboy Honour* (quoted), 330–31; *Wykehemica*, 331n.

Adams, William, happiness at Rugby, 72, 95

Ainslie, Aymer (Bum Bathsheba), 309; and Dering, 309 and n.

Alford, Lord, 228

Angelo, Florella, Eton Dame, 123; on loss of adolescent favourites, 302 and n.

Apperley, Thomas, and classical authors, 32

Arbuthnot, Sir Alexander, and physical endurance in games, 76–7; reminiscences of school life, 77–9

Armstrong, Rev. Richard, and masturbation, 292

army, influence of its demands on admission standards, 320–21

Arnold, Frances, sister of Thomas, 60

Arnold, Matthew, on Vaughan, 306; *Culture and Anarchy*, 259n.

Arnold, Dr Thomas, headmaster of Rugby, 70, 218n., 282; and fagging, 26n., 101, 104, 266; letters home from Warminster prep school, 58, 59, 60, 72; character as a boy, 59, 60, 253,

266; at Winchester, 60, 72, 117–19, 266, 298 and n.; and sixth form, 76; obsession with 'sin' and 'wickedness of boys', 118, 258, 264, 265, 284; denounces drunkenness, 133, 284; and poaching, 149; influence on moral reformers, 174, 249; and corporal punishment, 242, 256–7; and a classical education, 247; character formation at schoolmasters objective, 248; and needs of middle classes and their future, 248; character and temperament, 248–9, 257–8; changes face of Rugby, 249; and social equality, 249; irresponsible English gentlemen, 249; ambivalent rhetorical utterances, 249–50, 251, 258; and the aristocracy, 249–50, 259; and academic ability, 251, 252; variation in saying and doing, 251; attitude to local children, 252; boy/God relationship, 252 and n., 256 and n.; dislike of boyhood as a genus, 252–3, 254, 266; irreconcilable attitudes to public schools, 253–4; and boy/governor relationship, 254; appeals from the pulpit, 255–6, 262, 277–8; Old Boy and parental hostility, 256–7; dealings with miscreants, 256–7; flogging of March, 257–8; 'idealist, moralist, Christian' myth, 258, 264–5; theological utterances, 258 and n.; and Australian colonizing convicts, 258–9; and rioting working classes, 259; his sixth-form élite, 259–60, 262, 263; encounter with Gover, 261–2; moral influences on his pupils, 262–3;

OXFORD

MORE OXFORD PAPERBACKS

Details of a selection of other books follow. A complete list of Oxford Paperbacks, including The World's Classics, Twentieth-Century Classics, OPUS, Past Masters, Oxford Authors, Oxford Shakespeare, and Oxford Paperback Reference, is available in the UK from the General Publicity Department, Oxford University Press, Walton Street, Oxford, OX2 6DP.

In the USA, complete lists are available from the Paperbacks Marketing Manager, Oxford University Press, 200 Madison Avenue, New York, NY 10016.

THE OLD SCHOOL

Edited by Graham Greene

An entertaining and often very funny collection of essays about the school-days of some of the best writers of our time.

Includes: Anthony Powell on Eton, W. H. Auden on Gresham's School, Holt, H. E. Bates on Kettering Grammar School, Elizabeth Bowen on Downe House, L. P. Hartley on Harrow, William Plomer on Rugby, Stephen Spender on University College School, Harold Nicolson on Wellington, Arthur Calder-Marshall on St. Paul's, and many others.

'A classic collection.' *Sunday Times*

THE HEIRS OF TOM BROWN
The English School Story
Isabel Quigly

The Heirs of Tom Brown is an entertaining and original investigation into the literary, social, and cultural history of the school story in the heyday of the English Public School. Isabel Quigly discusses her chosen stories in relation to the themes which recur most frequently throughout the genre—the cult of games, the love story, the boarding school as a training ground for the Empire, schoolboy heroics, and an extraordinary preoccupation with death. Her selection ranges from such masterpieces as *Stalky & Co.* and Wodehouse's cricketing stories, to the schoolgirl tales of Angela Brazil, and the scandalously subversive *The Loom of Youth*.

'an excellent guide to this curious but interesting chapter in social and literary history' *Listener*

'it's hard to recall a more telling analysis' *Sunday Times*

'clear-sighted and enjoyable' *Financial Times*

FIRST CHILDHOOD and
FAR FROM THE MADDING WAR

Lord Berners

'Aesthete, artist and wit, Lord Berners grew up among fox-hunting philistines and attended a prep-school where excellence at games, to which he did not aspire, provided the only refuge from a sadistic headmaster. *First Childhood* is a wry record of his early kicks against the pricks, while *Far From the Madding War* is a delightful novella set in wartime Oxford with a thinly disguised self-portrait which anticipates Nancy Mitford's Lord Merlin.' *Books and Bookmen*

'Lord Berners spices his very funny account of a rather isolated and unhappy childhood, *First Childhood*, with a wicked wit.' *British Book News*

'It is a bargain and a delight—particularly the autobiography . . . by any standards an absorbing book.' *Times Literary Supplement*